Culture and Management in A

Local culture has long been recognized as a critically important factor in shaping management styles in different Asian countries. This book provides a comprehensive overview of culture and management in major East and South-East Asian economies. It covers the following countries: China, Hong Kong, India, Indonesia, Japan, Malaysia, Pakistan, Philippines, South Korea, Taiwan, Thailand, Singapore, and Vietnam. Each chapter provides a survey of the country's history, culture and economy, going on to examine management in the country, together with management education and how management is currently changing. The book is an invaluable introduction for students of international management, for those studying management within East and South-East Asia and for business people trading with the region.

Malcolm Warner is Professor and Fellow at Wolfson College, Cambridge and is a member of the Faculty of the Judge Institute of Management, University of Cambridge. He has written or edited over twenty-five management books, and is the Editor-in-Chief of the *International Encyclopedia of Business and Management*, as well as Co-Editor of the *Asia-Pacific Business Review*.

Culture and Management in Asia

Edited by Malcolm Warner

RoutledgeCurzon
Taylor & Francis Group

LONDON AND NEW YORK

First published 2003
by RoutledgeCurzon
11 New Fetter Lane, London EC4P 4EE

Simultaneously published in the USA and Canada
by RoutledgeCurzon
29 West 35th Street, New York, NY 10001

RoutledgeCurzon is an imprint of the Taylor & Francis Group

Typeset in Times by Taylor & Francis Ltd
Printed and bound in Great Britain by The Cromwell Press,
Trowbridge, Wiltshire

British Library Cataloguing in Publication Data
A catalogue record for this book is available from the British Library

Library of Congress Cataloging-in-Publication Data
Culture and Management in Asia/Malcolm Warner, editor.

  Includes bibliographical references.
  1. Management–Asia–Case studies. I. Warner, Malcolm.

  HD70.A78C85 2003
  658'.0095–dc21   2002044733

ISBN 0–415–29727–3 (hbk)
ISBN 0–415–29728–1 (pbk)

Contents

Tables

Contributors

Vinita Atmiyanandana, Researcher, Urbana (Illinois) School District, Urbana, Illinois, USA.

Johngseok Bae, Assistant Professor of Management, Business School, Korea University, Seoul, South Korea

Pawan S. Budhwar, Senior Lecturer in Human Resource Management, Cardiff Business School, Cardiff University, Cardiff, Wales, UK.

John Child, Professor and Chair of Commerce, Birmingham Business School, University of Birmingham, Birmingham, UK, and Distinguished Visiting Professor, China Management Centre, School of Business, University of Hong, Hong Kong SAR.

Wen-Chi Grace Chou, Assistant Professor, National Chung-Cheng University, Department of Labour Relations and the Institute of Labour Studies, Chia-Yi, Taiwan.

Philippe Debroux, Professor of International Management, Faculty of Business Administration, Soka University, Tokyo, Japan.

Charles M. Hampden-Turner, Senior Research Associate, Judge Institute of Management, University of Cambridge, Cambridge, UK.

Shaista E. Khilji, Assistant Professor in Management and Strategy, Eric Sprott Business School, Carleton University, Ottawa, Canada.

John J. Lawler, Professor, Institute of Labor and Industrial Relations, University of Illinois at Urbana–Champaign, Illinois, USA.

Corinna de Leon, Management Consultant, Hong Kong SAR.

Ashar Sunyoto Munandar, Emeritus Professor in Industrial and Organizational Psychology at the faculty of Psychology, University of Indonesia, Indonesia.

Chris Rowley, Reader in Human Resource Management, Cass Business School, City University, London, UK.

Jan Selmer, Professor of Management, Department of Management, School of Business, Hong Kong Baptist University, Kowloon Tong, Kowloon, Hong Kong SAR.

Wendy A. Smith, Director, Centre for Malaysian Studies, Monash Asia Institute, and Senior Lecturer, Department of Management, Monash University, Melbourne, Australia.

Malcolm Warner, Professor and Fellow, Wolfson College, and Judge Institute of Management, University of Cambridge, Cambridge, UK.

Ying Zhu, Senior Lecturer, Department of Management, University of Melbourne, Melbourne, Australia.

Preface

How managers cope with managing across cultures has fascinated me for some years now. Doing business in one country differs very much from conducting it in another. Setting up a firm in an unfamiliar economic environment is a real challenge. In today's globalized business world, managers have to learn to cope with many new challenges. Yet both undergraduate and MBA students are taught what are claimed as generalizable business concepts and practices but find that these are often hard to apply 'on the ground'. This book attempts to show in appropriate detail how management is anchored at 'ground level' in specific cultural contexts across Asia.

Although it explores the role of culture in shaping management in general, it closely focuses on management in Asia in particular. It is hoped that this will help both academics and practitioners better understand how business works in this increasingly important region of the world and its links with the international economy, as the World Trade Organization (WTO) extends its membership in the new millennium.

The book may be used as text for either undergraduate or postgraduate courses, or as an academic resource for more specialized programmes, such as MBA electives or doctoral options.

It goes without saying that I should like to thank the willing band of collaborators who have helped me put this work together. They come from a wide array of academic backgrounds, nationalities and universities. Some are based in the West; others in the East. A number are Westerners who work in Asia. A few are 'Asians' in terms of their own cultural origins. Each author read the drafts of the others' chapters and not only commented on them in terms of comparisons but also used their colleagues' work to enrich their own contributions. We have also tried to extensively cross-reference the work as a whole, by referring to other country chapters as often as possible. Thus, we have a culturally mixed team who have worked hard to produce chapters of both detail and distinction.

I also should particularly like to thank Peter Sowden, who initially commissioned this project, for all his support and the many members of the editorial staff of RoutledgeCurzon who have shown both care and skill in the editing of this book and who have assisted its progress through the various stages of the production process.

Malcolm Warner
University of Cambridge
September 2002

Abbreviations

ACFTU	All-China Federation of Trade Unions
AIDS	Acquired Immune Deficiency Syndrome
ANOVA	Analysis of Variance
APEC	Asia Pacific Economic Consortium
APROC	Asia Pacific Regional Operation Centre
ASEAN	Association of South-East Asian Nations
CEO	Chief Executive Officer
CEPD	Council for Economic Planning and Development
COE	Collectively Owned Enterprise
DPE	Domestic Private Enterprise
EA	Employment Act
EJV	Equity Joint Venture
EOI	Export-Oriented Industrialization
EPZ	Export Processing Zone
EU	European Union
FDI	Foreign Direct Investment
FIE	Foreign-Invested Enterprise
FOE	Foreign-Owned Enterprise
GDP	Gross Domestic Product
GNP	Gross National Product
HIV	Human Immunodeficiency Virus
HKSAR	Hong Kong Special Administrative Region
HPWS	High-Performance Work Systems
HR	Human Resources
HRM	Human Resource Management
HSBC	Hong Kong and Shanghai Bank
IBM	International Business Machines
ICA	Industrial Coordination Act
ICT	Information and Communication Technology
IDA	Industrial Disputes Act
IFC	International Finance Corporation
ILM	Internal Labour Market
ILO	International Labour Organization

IMF	International Monetary Fund
IRA	Industrial Relations Act
IRS	Industrial Relations System
IT	Information Technology
ISI	Import-Substitution Strategy
JMC	Joint Management Council
JSC	Joint Stock Company
JV	Joint Venture
LEP	'Look East' Policy
LMC	Labour–Management Council
MBA	Master of Business Administration
MCA	Malaysian Chinese Association
MIT	Massachusetts Institute of Technology
MNC	Multinational Corporation
NDP	National Development Plan
NEP	New Economic Policy
NIC	Newly Industrializing Country
NP	National Development Plan
OD	Organization Development
OECD	Organization for Economic Cooperation and Development
PAP	People's Action Party
PERT	Programme and Evaluation and Review Technique
PLFS	Philippine Labour Flexibility Survey
PRC	People's Republic of China
PSE	Public Sector Enterprise
SAR	Special Administrative Region
SEZ	Special Economic Zone
SME	Small and Medium Size Enterprise
SOE	State Owned Enterprise
TCC	Quality Control Circles
TNC	Transnational Corporation
TQC	Total Quality Control
TQM	Total Quality Management
TUA	Trade Union Act
TUC	Trades Union Congress
TVE	Town and Village Enterprise
UMNO	United Malays National Organization
VW	Volkswagen
WOFE	Wholly Owned Foreign Enterprise
WSO	Wholly Owned Subsidiary
WTO	World Trade Organization

1 Introduction

Culture and management in *Asia*

Malcolm Warner

Introduction

More and more goods and services are traded globally these days; more and more managers operate across both borders and cultures. 'Globalization', on the one hand, coexists with 'localization' on the other. Understanding the balance between these two ends of the spectrum has become increasingly important.

This book asks the question how far culture shapes business, economic and management behaviour and values, in general, and in Asia, in particular. It is hoped that this edited work will help both academics – researchers, teachers and students – and practitioners to understand better how business works in this increasingly important region of the world and the international economy. We hope it will, for instance, also assist management in multinationals in deciding to set up plants in this region or already invested there, as well as expatriate executives and their spouses intending to work there or already settled in.

Observing that regions – and the countries and cultures within them – are different is one thing, but explaining differences, particularly between and within such entities, is another. Bold, sweeping theories of human or social behaviour are often attractive, but equally it is often said that the 'devil is in the details'. Instead of invoking a crude economic or technological determinism, it may be suggested that there is a subtle link between the cultural distinctiveness of nation states and their business and economic performance. The role of values on economic behaviour is not a new perspective; Weber (1947) for instance, at the beginning of the last century, had evoked the concept of the 'Protestant Ethic', namely a set of beliefs and values, to help explain how capitalism evolved before and during the Industrial Revolution. Others later have generalized this from a European setting to one that was more global. More recently, Child (2002) has attempted to synthesize the 'low-context' approach (based on material resources, such as the economic or technological) with the 'high-context' one (based on ideational and institutional components) in order to explain cross-national and cross-cultural organizational differences.

Why 'culture'? The role 'culture' plays in economic development has long fascinated scholars. In using this term, we mean a pattern of taken-for-granted assumptions about how a given collection of people think, act and feel that affects how they produce goods and services. But there are many competing definitions of culture and the term has been used in a number of ways, some more precise then others, others less so.

Culture as a term has long-standing linguistic origins: – it was probably adapted from the Latin *cultura*, which was related to 'cult' or 'worship'. Over centuries, it was associated with elite refinement, such as the cultivation of the arts, as in the French language. In German, *Kultur* implied the intellectual dimension of civilization. Anthropologists have used the term extensively; some have defined it as 'ideas, beliefs and values' that form a 'conceptual framework' (Gertz and Geertz 1975: 2–3) for instance. In recent years, many have spoken of cultures as associated with nations, such as with American, Japanese or Russian cultures. Others have invoked the 'societal effect' (Maurice *et al.* 1980). We may also now speak of corporate cultures, such as IBM, Nestlé or VW 'in-house' cultures.

There are two interesting and possibly useful perspectives that have emerged in recent years in the academic literature dealing with organizations. The first may be called the 'culturalist' school (for example, Hofstede 1980; Hampden-Turner and Trompenaars 1997; 2000) and focuses on variances in values across cultures (see Chapter 10 in this volume); the second may be called the 'institutionalist' school (for example, Wilkinson 1996) stressing the historical and political structures influencing economic and organizational activity. A view that uses 'culture' in the widest sense of the term might be seen as more encompassing, in that it might include both values as well as institutions. It is clear that we must be careful how we use the term and which definition we use.

Why 'management'? Management may seen as a major link (or intervening variable) between the cultural environment of a given economy and the resultant level of business performance (see Warner and Joynt 2002). If the 'cross-cultural' view holds water, then it would follow that there would be differences in management and organization between different cultural and national systems and these would be important vis-à-vis their resultant outputs. If the 'institutionalist' view is stressed, then paying greater attention to attention to historical and political factors – as well as values – may be *de rigueur*. We should add here that we do not advocate a simplistic one-to-one approach. It is clear that there are complex causal relationships between 'culture' and the economic and management variables it may shape. There are also feedback loops and 'culture' itself may be in turn reshaped by major economic and management innovations.

Why 'Asia'? This problem takes a particular form in its geographical context. Although a continent in itself, Asia covers a wide range of geographical, economic and cultural spheres. We concern ourselves here mainly with East and South-East Asia, as well as most of South Asia. The rationale for doing this relates to the concentration of economic and population resources to be found there. In this book we deal with over a dozen countries in the continent broadly defined, namely China, Hong Kong, India, Indonesia, Japan, Malaysia, Pakistan, the Philippines, Singapore, South Korea, Taiwan, Thailand and Vietnam. These nations not only contain over half of humankind but in many cases are on the road to becoming the economies of tomorrow. In the case of China – the People's Republic of China (see Chapter 2) – the World Bank sees an economic superpower in the making; Japan (see Chapter 6) is already second to the dominant US economy in its ranking.

Taking Asia as a whole, it had an average GDP per capita that was less than that of Africa in the 1960s; now it has double that average level of income per head, although this glosses over its dispersion. With 3.3 billion people, Asia still has three-quarters of the world's poor, due to its income inequalities, both between states and within them. But the poverty rate, again on average, has gone down from 65 per cent in 1960 to 17 per cent in 2000, at least as claimed by UN statisticians. Infant mortality fell from 141 of live births then, to 48 now, according to such sources. And the 'typical' Asian can expect to live longer, on average, up from 41 to 67 years. The standard of life in terms of human development has thus improved for a good number of the 'many', although most of the 'few' still retain their privileged lifestyle, if the 'Gini coefficients' that measure income inequality are to be believed (see Human Development Report 2002). .

'Asia', it is evident, comprises a wide range of countries, economies and national systems. Geographical factors do feature very strongly, with the PRC pre-eminent so clearly in terms of its vast land mass and huge population. The countries of the region range from those with such relatively huge populations like the PRC with around 1.3 billion inhabitants (see Chapter 2), to relatively small city-states like Singapore (see Chapter 10) with only a few million citizens. The population variable helps to shape the level of economic development, amongst other factors. However, this variable may be seen as relatively invariant only in the short term (see Warner 2002).

An attempt to evaluate the direction of Asian economies and their managements in terms of the 'late-development effect' has recently been proposed (see Ng and Warner 1999). It breaks down the whole set of countries into two main sets, namely the advanced economies and sectors on the one hand and the less developed countries on the other. Yet there remain analytical problems with compressing so much into such a basic dichotomy. The economies of the region have on the other hand often been economically and industrially dominated by a powerful neighbour, namely Japan. The 'little Dragon' economies in turn also stand apart from many others in their set, particularly in terms of the level of economic development they have achieved.[1] Most of the regions' economies had a rapid rate of growth over the last two decades, although it might have been uneven from one year to the next. Whether the Asian so-called 'miracle' will be sustainable into the twenty-first century is of course moot. Even if Asian economies continue to grow at more or less respectable rates of growth, they may not pick up the pace of the 1990s again or at least for some time. For instance, China has had a fluctuating growth rate for the last ten years and it has fallen below the trend rate in the last few years, if official statistics are to be believed.[2] But even this level has been credibly above the average of, say, EU economies.

As Rowley (1997: 1) has put it: 'Asia provides a paragon of practices around which companies searching for "success" and the "one best way" can converge'. The Asian way, many believed, was identifiable and then trans-plantable. It was perceived as a formula for fast economic growth and social development. There are a number of common features present in many Asian Pacific Rim economies in these respects and in others, although the specific institutional forms may have varied from one country to another (see Hamilton 1995). But we can say with hindsight that the 'Asian model' has been 'stretched thin' (Godement 1999: 15). It was probably too simple an explanation, in retrospect, to have imagined a truly homogeneous set of countries, institutions and practices in a given region, or indeed a given, single 'Asian model' as such. There are too many subtle, and sometimes less subtle, variations. It was perhaps due to the blatant 'self-confidence' of the times, namely the late 1980s and early 1990s, that such an idea could be promulgated. 'Japan' as a major player was riding high as an economic success and the 'flying ducks' notion was, for many, *de rigueur*. Furthermore, the Asia-Pacific model had been presented as an 'alternative' to the Western standard industrial relations and HRM 'templates' that had emerged in the post-war years, although we would have to argue here that across Asia or even in the West, these systems and subsystems have only a limited 'family resemblance'. By this, we mean they have some prima facie common charac-teristics but these remain of a 'rather bounded' kind. The region, of course, is as a whole a large and varied one, economically, politically and socially, and hence it would not be that surprising if it proved difficult to cast it into a single mould.

As can be seen from the above, Asia is a complex region with many varia-tions, not only in terms of its societal factors and values (see Chapter 10 for comparative data across the region vis-à-vis the nation in question) but also in terms of its economies and management. It has indeed prospered in recent years and after some setbacks will no doubt bounce back but prob-ably not evenly. While the Asian crisis of 1997 undermined confidence in the region's prospects, it did not deal a 'knock-out blow'. Many economies recovered relatively quickly; some were less affected by the downturn such as the PRC. Nonetheless, it dented the 'myth' of the Asian economic miracle.

As *The Economist* news analysts had put it at the time: 'Changing global winds will blow differently through the region's individual economies' (21 October 2000: 128). The grouping suggested they picked the 'big bets' economies, Japan as well as the PRC; then listed the 'best bets' like Hong

Kong and Singapore; after them, the 'middling' ones like Malaysia, South Korea and Taiwan; then the weakest 'bad bets', namely Indonesia, the Philippines and Thailand. India is probably a 'middling' bet and Pakistan a 'bad' one. Of course, only time will tell if these odds ring true!

Globalization expands via markets but there are important intervening variables, such as export-dependency, developmental state strength, intermediate institutions and so on. While it may not be possible to put forward neat econometric models to delineate these links precisely, it is apparent that the external economic environment is closely connected to the internal, national one by a number of gears. In quantitative terms, these may be expressed as 'coefficients', such as that of export-dependency, but this may only convey half the story. In Asia, the institutional 'filters' such as 'cronyism', 'transparency' and the like may well count for as much as corporate and government debt levels, foreign exchange reserves and so on.

The 'convergence' debate

Some North American scholars in the post-war period (see Kerr *et al* 1960) argued that given the industrialization process sweeping the world, societies and systems adopting modern technology and management would become more similar than dissimilar. They used the term 'convergence' in emphasizing how economies and the organizations within them have become more alike as development has progressed in the modern world.

Contemporary writers have tended to refer to 'globalization' as the latest version of the 'convergence' scenario. Globalization, as a term, was the by-word of the late 1990s; it was to herald the creation of both worldwide markets and transnational enterprises. Smith's classic, eighteenth-century generalization that 'the division of labour depended on the extent of the market' seems to be as valid today as it was in 1776. Marx, too, had envisioned globalization as an eventual outcome of capitalism. Economies of 'scale and scope' were to depend on a growing internationalization of markets – hence large business corporations striving to buy and sell as far and wide as they could. The WTO was to seek to shape the 'rules of the game' to make this easier. The intention has been to extend the global markets beyond goods to services and to parts of the world where they did not reach because of the 'Developmental State'. Critics believed this to be a form of 'neo-imperialism'. But not all economists saw globalization as a wholly deterministic phenomenon; some pinpointed it as both an endogenous as well as an exogenous factor 'determined in its pace by governments, firms and other social actors, but influencing in its turn the behaviour of these same actors' (Kogut and Gittelman 1997: 220).

Others have stressed 'divergence' as their main point of interest (see Joynt and Warner 1996; Warner and Joynt 2002). Not total divergence but enough to make sense. There have been many debates between these two apparently conflicting perspectives. Many theories of organizations do not take localized factors like culture into account; they stress other variables like technology, size and on. However, others have more in their turn posited culture as playing an important role. This disagreement has led to the so-called 'culture-free' and 'culture-led' debate.

As Braun and Warner put it:

> The scholarly debate on organizational convergence has been ongoing for some years now. A main prop of this discussion has been the arguments about the 'industrialization' thesis so-called (Kerr et al. 1960) which got under way in the post-war period. It was an intellectually bold idea in its day, if somewhat deterministic in its thrust. It had many supporters but also its critics. In any event, it led to a serious debate that has had very useful consequences for the field... The debate itself grew out of a fertile period as far as the emergent sub-disciplines of industrial sociology and organizational behaviour were concerned ... [vis-à-vis] the forces influencing organizations in perhaps often contradictory directions, generally with respect to cross-cultural management and particularly with respect to Human Resource Management (HRM). Such influences are divided into two groups: one, 'culture-free' and the other 'culture-specific'.
>
> (2002: 13)

It is possible that there is a more useful way of dealing with this issue.

Convergence has featured as a common thread in the literature on this theme for some time now, stretching over many decades, from Kerr *et al.* (1960) to Bamber *et al.* (2000). The discussion presented here follows earlier work by the present writer that looked at 'convergence' and 'divergence' in management practices in this part of the world, namely in Asia (see Warner 2000). The analysis there distinguished between different types of 'convergence' and 'divergence', permutated as between 'hard' and 'soft' versions. One may also even speak of 'Cross - Vergence', in some contexts.

There have recently been some theoretical or conceptual refinements made concerning this dichotomy and the setting out of logical possibilities with respect to what has been dubbed, respectively, the 'soft' – or relative (on the one hand) – and 'hard' – or absolute (on the other) – types of convergence and divergence (see Warner 2002). This view has argued that 'soft' – that is, relative convergence (see position 2 below) – is a more likely concept, since an absolute, distinct version of 'hard' convergence (position 1) is probably unlikely where all systems become alike, given the specific historical traditions out of which each national cultural system has grown and where only a 'family resemblance' is the most likely outcome. It is also more likely that the 'soft' or relative divergence (position 3) is also possibly more realistic than absolute 'hard' divergence (position 4), a case where cultural systems become totally different from each other.[3]

We do not wish to pursue the details of the debate further here and readers can refer to the earlier source for the background to this discussion (Warner 2002: 13–25). We would, however, now like to analyse the implications of culture as a factor shaping management in its specific Asian context.

Convergence/divergence: a four-fold analytical framework		
	Convergence	divergence
Hard	1	4
Soft	2	3

Levels of culture

Culture may be interpreted as acting at three distinct levels, as follows:

1 *Primary level*: by this we mean where culture as a variable affects the whole of the society. An example of a primary cultural level might refer to the dominance of the Han culture in China. Here, we would look at the 'hegemonic' culture dominating others in the same spatial environment. The presence of a primary culture would not preclude minority ones playing a role there but it would be a subordinate one. In some countries, like China and Japan (see Chapters 2 and 6 in this volume), the dominant culture does often appear almost to swamp the lesser ones even if there is a degree of official tolerance. The issue of hegemonic culture also arises in the case of India (see Chapter 4). But in other states there is a more or less subtle balance, as in Malaysia (see Chapter 7).

2 *Secondary level:* this pertains to parts of the wider culture. Here, robust minority cultures may coexist with the dominant culture, or in some cases may have been perceived as a threat because of their economic power. In some cases, there may be tensions between a number of minority ethnic groups as in the case of Indonesia (see Chapter 5). A further illustration here might be an ethnic group such as those of Chinese origin in the Philippines (see Chapter 9). The overseas Chinese (*Nanyang*) community as a minority has often times experienced varying degrees of resentment from the local majority, as in the cases of Thailand (Chapter 13) and Vietnam (Chapter 14).

3 *Tertiary level:* by this we mean a level where we are speaking of an effect that relates to a clearly *derivative* culture, possibly non-indigenous, within a given national system. An illustration here may be that of a 'foreign' corporate culture, within a subsidiary of an MNC. Or there may be a *residual* culture where there was an observable influence, whether local or foreign, long ago, that may have weakened over time.

What is culturally specific to Asia? There is no one consistently uniform culture that binds the regions found in that continent together; however, there are 'family resemblances', both in historical legacies and common traits and in terms of values that social scientists have measured, as elsewhere in the world. The term 'late development' implies a time dimension and that other parts of the world went through defined stages of economic and social evolution earlier, involving the process of modernization. We therefore posit the dichotomy between forms of emergent Western-style modernization and lagging forms of non-Western pre-modernization; that is, varying kinds of traditionalism.

One reason for choosing to look at Asia has been the apparent link between defined cultural traits and the rapid economic growth of this continent and its subregions in the post-war period. As Tung (1996: 233) points out, there has been a cluster of countries with apparently similar characteristics that have performed very well for a sustained period of time and these have shared Confucianism as a common feature.[4] Although here we must point to the many variations of the belief-system, over both space and time, even within a given country, as can be seen in the respective country chapters of many East Asian countries in this edited work.

Its distinctiveness vis-à-vis 'Western' characteristics has long been seen as a factor influencing its image and perhaps suggesting clues as to its economic success. Yet its very defining characteristics were in past years sometimes associated with backwardness. Confucianism was even regarded as an obstacle to growth, for example in the period following the Second World War, and it has largely only been in recent times the case that countries influenced by it have been linked to positive economic results.[5] Could we then be seeing a case of *post hoc, non propter hoc*?

'East is East and West is West' is a phrase often used but rather too vague to be of analytical importance. The Weberian 'Protestant Ethic', we well know, arose in the specific case of Europe, but the Confucian ethic – with several comparable characteristics, of achievement, hard work and so on – was clearly Asian. Indeed, Hofstede's (1980) research has shown that European values have not been that distinctive and are found in varying degrees elsewhere. Another expert argues that neither 'Asian', nor for that matter 'Western', culture (if such single entities exist at all, other than caricatures) is unitary and internally consistent (see Friedman 2000). There is something in this view and it is clear from reading the country chapters in this edited book that each culture analysed is so distinct that to deduce a single 'Asian' cultural model would be no simple matter.

We can see from the respective chapters in this edited book that there is much *couleur locale* and that what makes each country 'tick' is its distinctive mix of characteristics. While there are common strands that may be found across Asian states, we firmly believe there are culturally counter-balancing, culturally specific, ones. We believe that these are still critically important, even though they may be weakening at the margin since, as we pointed out earlier, a degree of convergence, albeit relative, may be observed.

Such changes may operate in at least three ways:

1 *Meta-convergence*: this phenomenon may be found where paradigms such as 'Scientific Management' are said to occur *across* a wide range of national systems (see Kerr *et al.* 1960) although even then there may be adaptations to local norms and values, as for example in the case of Japan (see Warner 1994). Here we may find 'Americanization' so called, or indeed even 'Japanization' in varying degrees. Some now even use the broader phrase 'globalization'. Such changes are seen as occurring such that, regardless of where you are, management system characteristics begin to look alike. For instance, a big bank in Hong Kong or Seoul appears to operate more or less like one in Jakarta or Manila. These changes may be mitigated or at least mediated by culture acting as an intervening variable. Across-the-board change may include those that are believed to occur as a result of economic, psychological or technological universalisms that are said to apply regardless of local contexts. We would still argue that this 'meta-convergence' was relative.

2 *Macro-convergence*: this phenomenon may be seen where society- or economy-wide characteristics may appear to be relatively converging in a particular direction *within* a given cultural setting and/or *within* a national context, such as in the case of a state-led 'privatization' programme.[6] To some degree, we have seen China becoming more like its neighbours, in terms of having adopted market reforms (see Child 1994; Warner 1995). Again, in turn, culture may shape the way such changes are implemented. Such macro-convergence may be largely seen as relative.

3 *Micro-convergence*: this tendency may be found where industry- or organizational-level change occurs – but which is not at a higher macro-level – *within* part of a national entity; for example, in a given MNC operating in a particular country. Here, again, cultural constraints may limit the extent of the changes that take place. Thus, we should bear in mind the 'relative' nature of such possible convergence.

We now turn to the plan of the book, how it is divided into specific subsections and the rationale for such a division.

Plan of the book

Each chapter of this book follows a common pattern, with albeit minor variation in some cases. The authors, all of whom are experts on the respective countries they have covered in this volume, were asked to build their chapters around the following ten main headings. These were selected after careful consideration, after an extensive reading of the literature on the broad links between culture and economic development in general, as well as the interaction between these and management across the region in particular.

They were, respectively:

1   Introduction
2   Historical setting
3   Economic background
4   Societal culture
5   Corporate culture
6   Management behaviour
7   Managerial values
8   Labour–management conflict resolution
9   Implications for managers
10 Conclusions

We chose the above subsections – that feature in all the country chapters – because they provide coverage (in terms of description, as well as analysis) of what shapes a cultural environment in a given country, such as its historical development and in turn how its economy and management are affected by it. We then look at its implications for managers and, last, draw a number of conclusions from it.

In this section, we turn to the specific country chapters where we have asked expert contributors to build their discussion around the schema referred to above.

China

In Chapter 2, John Child and Malcolm Warner, both British but with long field experience of China and Hong Kong, look in detail at the PRC. It is clear that this ancient nation has been shaped by its history and that in turn its modern management practices have sprung from its cultural roots, whether in the context of the economic and institutional changes of the last half-century, or even earlier. The authors here note that the late Deng Xiaoping's reforms of the last two decades have changed the management system from one based on a command economy to one more market driven and with increased private ownership. However, Chinese people are quick to maintain that the changes have been given 'Chinese characteristics', implying that whatever the immediate institutional and organizational details, the underlying norms and values may reflect continuity as much as change. In a rapidly changing and varied context such as contemporary China, it is thus very difficult to assess the degree to which traditional culture continues to exert an influence on management values and behaviour. Rather than attempt any definitive conclusions, it is more helpful to reiterate the issues and questions that readers need to bear in mind when addressing this subject. First, it is always necessary to recognize China's great diversity and start by asking 'to which China are we referring and which sector, which region, which generation?' Second, what is taking place in China, keen to learn from the outside world yet also conscious of its history, may force us to abandon the notion that people necessarily conform to a simple notion of 'culture'. In these circumstances, they may not necessarily fit neatly at a single point along the cultural dimensions beloved of cross-cultural psychologists, but instead display an apparent paradox. The authors have noted, for example, how studies of the values held by PRC managers suggest that those who have internalized certain 'Western' values such as *individualism* may at the same time continue to value traditional Confucian precepts such as *collective* loyalty and responsibility. The social identity of modern Chinese managers may be more complex than has generally been appreciated, requiring a cultural theory that is more complex and subtle than present formulations. A third possibility, Child and Warner argue, that is deserving of further investigation, is that Chinese managers, and perhaps people in general, are more flexible in their cultural referents than theorists such as Hofstede (1980; 1991) assume is normal for adults. Those Chinese who are exposed to 'Western' values, according to the authors, through their roles at work, or equally through their roles as consumers, may retain the option to segment their cultural mind-sets and switch between them. For instance, if conforming to certain Western norms and practices offers material attractions, such as higher pay in return for accepting individual responsibility for performance, then Chinese staff may decide to go along with them within the confines of their workplace roles. They may also be encouraged to accept practices imported from another culture if these are perceived to be part of a more comprehensive policy, justified as 'best international practice', offering other benefits such as equitable treatment, comprehensive training and good prospects for advancement. This is why employment with an MNC's joint venture or subsidiary is usually highly prized by Chinese managers. At the same time, as they switch social identity in 'converting' to their non-work roles in the family and community, they could, the authors conclude, well revert to a more traditional Chinese cultural mind-set.

Hong Kong

In Chapter 3, Jan Selmer – a Swedish national teaching at a business school in Hong Kong – and Corinna de Leon – a psychologist and consultant born in the Philippines, also working in Hong Kong – look at its culture and its management. Having set out the historical and economic background, with the former colony having lived in the shadow of both Mainland China and the British regimes for so long, the authors note that since the 1997 handover, the Special Administrative Region (SAR) is now at a 'crossroads' and its internationally impressive economic record may be under threat, not least of all from neighbouring financial centres, like Shanghai. Circumstances that had previously induced rapid growth in the SAR may now inhibit further economic development, in spite of its cultural legacy of entrepreneurship. Alternative means of achieving competitive advantages must be developed. As telecommunications and infrastructures for transportation swiftly modernize in China, the competitiveness of the former colony cannot simply rely on its geographical proximity to the mainland. Hong Kong needs new ideas for tackling unforeseen challenges and a knowledge-based economy would be critical. Comprehensive and drastic development of human resources building on its cultural affinity with its giant neighbour, the authors argue, may initiate and maintain structural changes required for Hong Kong's survival and future prosperity. The traditionally laissez-faire government has a distinctive role to play here. Larger investments in and less restrictive policies on education in general are obviously the most facile action that can be taken by the government. In particular, improving the scope and quality of business and management education may be helpful. However, the driving force for a knowledge economy has to be the numerous small business firms and their owner–managers that comprise the backbone of Hong Kong business with their cultural antecedents, who should bridge the human resources gap by extensive programmes on skills upgrading, empowerment and technology development.

India

In Chapter 4, Pawan Budwar, an academic of Indian cultural background, now teaching in the UK, reviews an economy with a vast population but one with a very different cultural and institutional inheritance from that of China. India, he notes, is the birthplace of three of the world's main religions, namely Hinduism (about 7000 BC), Buddhism (487 BC) and Sikhism (AD1699). These three religions have had a significant impact on the social, political and economic landscape of the country. No less complex a society than China (see Chapter 2), it has a legacy of first Moghul and then British imperial rule to confront. Independence from the latter came in 1947. Over the last fifty years or so, India, having split off from Pakistan (see Chapter 8), has gone through an economic cycle of dominance, decline and turnaround of industrial development within Asia. To a great extent this can be attributed to the adoption of different economic development approaches. India has now tasted the pros and cons of both the state-regulated and free-market economic systems. During the decades of the 1950s and 1980s, India adopted a mixed approach to its economic development. However, in the early 1990s, it was forced to introduce major institutional change and switch over to a market-based approach and liberalize its economic policies. Such a macro-level shift seems to have paid rich dividends to the Indian economy. As a result, it is forecasted by the World Bank that, by 2020, India could become the world's fourth-largest economy. However, to achieve this, the author argues, India has to make significant progress in economic development. It has to exploit optimally its human and natural resources and build a modern management system, given its cultural pluses and minuses, and overcome some of its long-existing problems (such as poverty, population explosion, corruption in the workplace), responsible for creating hindrances to a steady and regular national economic growth. In this regard, a number of steps such as economic liberalization and structural reforms have been initiated. This seems to have taken care of the economic issues impacting national development. However, the socio-cultural and political aspects, which also play a crucial role in the economic development of India, also need updating. The traditional mind-set of Indian entrepreneurs, managers, workers, unions and policy makers towards managing human resources has to be changed to suit the globalized work-place. The author argues that there are indications that this is already taking root, though on a very slow, small scale. Overseas businesses, to operate successfully in India, he concludes, need to have sufficient information regarding the management and cultural aspects of doing business in India.

Indonesia

In Chapter 5, Ashar Munandar, an indigenous expert with a lifetime of teaching psychology in his country, analyses the culture and management of Indonesia, a highly complex multi-ethnic and a multicultural society at the far south-eastern extremity of the region. The Indonesian national culture, he argues, is enhanced by the intensive use of the Indonesian language, the national curriculum executed in all primary and secondary schools and the core values of various religions (Islam especially; see Chapter 8 on Pakistan for its nearest counterpart here). The intensive interactions between Indonesia and other states, European, American, Asian and Australia, have had a significant impact on the national culture and on the economy of Indonesia. The monetary crisis followed by the economic crisis starting in 1997, he points out, also created a political and morality crisis. The govern-ment has not yet succeeded in overcoming these multiple crises. The remaining small-, medium- and large-sized business organizations and their managers have to struggle, not only to sustain their existence, but also to be able to grow significantly to support the government in overcoming the economic crisis. Managers in Indonesia, he concludes, should become 'perpetual learners', working together in each business organization, and assist their top bosses, their CEOs, to become absolute leaders able to recon-cile the dilemmas they face in their business organizations.

Japan

In Chapter 6, Philippe Debroux, a Belgian national living and teaching in Japan, as well as a native speaker for many years, turns his attention to culture and management in that land. From the Meiji era onwards, in the mid-nineteenth century, Japanese industrial leaders adopted capital, produc-tion systems and business management practices from Western countries, in fact much earlier than their Chinese counterparts did (see Chapter 2). But this occurred in a different institutional, social and economic context from where these innovations originated. The roots of modern Japan were very much anchored in its past. The incorporation of a Confucian-influenced concentric model gave significance to ranking, relatedness and tier on the insider–outsider gradation; the development of Japanese companies as members of industrial groups can be traced back to the household rules of Tokugawa family-owned trading houses in the seventeenth century. It allowed Japanese companies to confront the challenge of industrialization and make the transition to 'developed country' status before the Second World War and before its neighbour, Korea (see Chapter 11). Nevertheless, although seniority, lifetime employment and other attributes of Japanese modern corporate management can indeed also be traced back to the seventeenth-century system, and were in turn later utilized in the pre-war large industrial *zaibatsu* firms as management tools, it was only after the Second World War that they were given a socially normative connotation, to fit into a business system geared towards catching up with the advanced, Western countries. The 'catching-up' process is, however, now over and a new management system is now required, linked to the necessities of globalization and able to respond to the diversifying values of an affluent and open society.

Malaysia

In Chapter 7, Wendy A. Smith, currently teaching in an Australian university, examines the case of Malaysia, a plural society arising from British colonial rule, with immigration creating many different ethnic strands. This society represents an important case for the analysis of management and culture in Asia. The presence of three ethnically distinct communities, the Malays (60 per cent), the Malaysian Chinese (30 per cent) and the Malaysian Indians and others (10 per cent), means that managers and employees with different values and lifestyles must cooperate in modern organizations, without a clear hegemony by one group's culture based on sheer numbers (although there is a greater local Chinese influence in Singapore: see Chapter 10). The intercultural management dynamics of this are made more complex by other outside influences: British colonial management precedents, numerous national management systems from more recent direct foreign investors, following Malaysia's export-oriented, FDI industrialization development policy since 1971, and a state-directed 'Look East' policy which has imposed Japanese work ethics and management practices since 1981 (see Chapter 6 on Japan). Among Malaysian managers and employees themselves, values and managerial behaviour are influenced by the Confucian dynamism of the Chinese, the Islamic work ethic and patron–client orientation of the Malays, mainly first-generation urban professionals with roots in rural peasant society, and the pervading aspirations to globalized consumer lifestyles, which influence not only the managerial class but also the working class in their career strategies for self-advancement. Malaysia well deserves the title of 'second-tier NIC', with its sustained growth rate of over 8 per cent for a decade until the Asian currency crisis of 1997 and the ability to recover well. This achievement is based on its abundance of natural and human resources and also the ability of the government to plan economic development and manage the inherent tensions of ethnic diversity.

Pakistan

In Chapter 8, Shaisti E. Khilji, born in Pakistan and now teaching in a Canadian business school, explores the nature and complexities of issues in culture and management in modern-day Pakistan, a country whose history is inextricably linked to that of India (see Chapter 4), as dealt with earlier. Pakistan also obtained independence from the British in 1947. Many changes have taken place since then, she notes, both in its politics and economy. After many years of state direction, it changed direction in its business and economic strategy. Of particular interest, the author points out, is the deregulation of the economy, initiated in 1990, and the exposure to Western management thought-processes, in particular American ones, that have reshaped the organizational environment. A striking change has surfaced in the values espoused by a new generation of employees, reflecting a modern market economy. As such, organizations are caught between the preservation of their core cultural values and the need to modernize in an era of globalization. The findings of recent surveys reveal that the organizations that have departed from old centralized and bureaucratic management cultures and structures have been able to motivate employees. The chapter illustrates that Pakistan has much to offer to foreign investors in terms of its large consumer market and its educated elite workforce that proves to be quite at ease with Western values. However, the author concludes, consistent commitment and stability is required to bring Pakistani organizations, managers and employees to the forefront of world markets.

The Philippines

In Chapter 9, Jan Selmer and Corinna de Leon (herself born there) look at culture and management in the Philippines. A casual visitor to Manila for example, they note, may quickly conclude that the society is thoroughly Westernized. Nothing could be farther from the truth the authors continue, and anyone dealing with Filipinos needs to be familiar with the complex value system that intertwines the indigenous Filipino, Chinese, Spanish and American cultures. Looking beneath the veneer of societal openness and cultural flexibility, there is a uniquely 'Filipino' way of acting in most situations. As seemingly simple behaviours are essentially complicated in intent, an appreciation of the Filipino nature is basic to any understanding of management in the only Christian, English-speaking democracy in Asia, liberated from Spanish colonial rule in the late nineteenth century, in many ways strongly influenced by the USA. Its economic and social progress from that date has been uneven, blighted by the Japanese Occupation in the 1940s. Although it has had a free-market economy since 1945, the future development of Filipino management cannot be readily predicted. The wave of rapid globalization currently ongoing will probably not stop at the shores of the Philippines and the influx of worldwide changes will eventually influence the nature of Filipino management. There has been an increase in autonomous business enterprises that are patterned after Western corporate structures, with skilled professional managers. However, as indigenous values in the Philippines have proven to be resilient, the authors conclude, it is highly unlikely that comprehensive changes in corporate culture and management behaviour will occur in the near future.

Singapore

In Chapter 10, Charles Hampden-Turner – British by origin, now a truly multinational 'guru' – examines the case of Singapore, a relatively small multicultural city-state, formerly a British colony. Its development since independence, first from the UK and then from its present neighbour with the break with Malaysia (see Chapter 7), has not staunched its appetite for business and commerce, largely promoted by its dominant overseas Chinese or *Nanyang* community. But the observer may ask if it is surprising in view of the emphasis on meritocracy that Singaporean society has not produced as many entrepreneurs as in other overseas Chinese communities, with their specific cultural values encouraging enterprise, such as those in Hong Kong, Malaysia, Indonesia, Taiwan, the USA and Canada. Indeed, Singapore produces fewer entrepreneurs per head of population than almost all advanced economies. Only Belgium and Japan fare worse, he points out. A recent report from California traced one-third of Silicon Valley's wealth of US$58 billion to Chinese and Indian immigrants to the USA post-1970. If low levels of entrepreneurship cannot be traced to Chinese culture (see Chapter 2), there has to be something distinctive about Singapore that fails to encourage what overseas Chinese in, say, Hong Kong and Taiwan typically do well (see Chapters 3 and 12). The author's view is that meritocracy impedes entrepreneurship and is a distinctively *different* way of generating wealth – a very successful way, but still antithetical to entrepreneurship. Singapore has itself reached a watershed. Its policies thus far have been that of a 'catch-up economy', a 'late developer', using the coat tails of advanced economies and helping to refine, manufacture and distribute their inventions in Asia. The question must now be faced. 'What does a catch-up economy *do* now that it has caught up?' One option is to start to innovate and create new products and new managers able to deal with these, like other advanced economies. Yet this will require a major 'culture change' in Singapore, where nearly all work and study is 'applied' to economic development. Creativity and innovation requires some slack, some disorder, some ferment and casting around before the best solution is discovered. Does Singapore have a culture that encourages entrepreneurship? The present evidence says not. Can it change and adapt as it has so often before? Perhaps; the jury is out. The problem ironically is *just how successful* the 'catch-up' system has been. Nothing so spectacularly effective is easily put aside. Cultures, he concludes, tend to overplay their winning combinations with diminishing returns; Singapore now has to confront some fateful decisions about its future.

South Korea

In Chapter 11, Chris Rowley – a British-based academic – and Johngseok Bae – a Korean-born one – examine the important topic of culture and management in South Korea (to be subsequently referred to as Korea). On China's periphery, Korea experienced a strong Confucian influence from that source over the centuries, as did Japan (see Chapter 6). But Korea's culture developed in its own distinct and complex way. Under Japanese domination for many decades, Korea emerged in the post-1945 period but also underwent a Cold War division into North and South, with even more turmoil in 1950–1 with the Korean War and UN intervention. The new nation was faced with heavy destruction and a hostile, Marxist neighbour to the north. The post-1960s rapid development of the southern part of country from a poor agricultural society into a rich, industrialized, Asian 'little Tiger' or 'little Dragon' economy was known as 'the miracle on the Han River'. The country prospered and living standards rose dramatically. However, the authors continue, this seemed to be more of a 'mirage' following the 1997 Asian crisis. With this event, the role of management and culture changed from being eulogized as a 'saint' to castigated as a 'sinner'. Both these labels may be too deterministic, stark and naive. The authors note that we need a greater balance as the power of particular management and culture is pertinent and persists. Furthermore, culture, they conclude, may produce paradoxical outcomes and is often seen and portrayed as ingrained, deep and slow moving, while management and its practice may well need to be less so. These differentials may produce incongruence between cultural norms and management practice.

Taiwan

In Chapter 12, Wen-chi Grace Chou, born in Taiwan and trained as a researcher in the UK – considers the case of culture and management of her native land. Living in the shadow of its mainland kin (see Chapter 2) since it was founded in 1948, the Republic of China, set up by the Nationalists, known as the *Kuomintang* (or *Kuomindang*), has many distinct features. Like Hong Kong, Singapore (see Chapters 3 and 10) and the like, Taiwan is part of the *Nanyang* overseas Chinese community. Besides the 'blurring' of the term, the effects of Confucianism have been prominent in that latter country's development. In this analysis of culture and management, alongside the current massive economic restructuring that has taken place in recent years, we will closely take note of its pervasive influence; conversely, we must also note how changes in economic structures and management methods have in turn impacted on culture. Here, the author sets out to emphasize that the formation of culture has a long and specific history and has influenced Taiwanese institutions, from the distant historical past to the present time. Having been occupied by different nations, such as Japan, and with different ethnic groups, Taiwan has, however, gradually developed its own culture. Like other countries experiencing global competition, Taiwan is now finding its way out. We can see that 'globalization' has had its impact on Taiwan's current culture but it has also pushed Taiwan to pursue or rediscover its own values. We further can see that in recent years 'globalization' and 'localization' have respectively penetrated each other and that this will result in a synthesis. Therefore, owing to different historical contingencies, changes in different countries may not be necessarily homogeneous. Culture and management in Taiwan, we therefore may say, are not constantly unchanged and only Confucianism based. More importantly, the chapter will discuss how this relation has been affected and changed by the new economy, without, however, the analysis falling into uncritical economic determinism.

Thailand

In Chapter 13, Vinita Atmiyanandana – Thai by origin – and John J. Lawler – an American academic – look at contemporary Thailand. The authors have explored significant aspects of management there, observing the many ways in which it is rooted in Thai culture and religious practice. Although these forces are often similar to those in other parts of Asia, there are clearly unique features that serve to differentiate Thailand from its neighbours. Thais share in common with most other East and South-East Asian societies strong collectivist and hierarchical tendencies. However, the Thai focus has most often been on the family or community, not the business organization. Thus, Thais are not likely to exhibit the sort of commitment to their employers traditionally seen in Japan or Korea and are more like the Chinese in this respect (see Chapter 2). But in contrast to East Asian cultures, Thais often note that there is a 'soft' side to their culture that mandates benevolence and caring on the part of employers towards their subordinates. Thus, the 'harsh' side of management that can be observed in an Asian company is much less apt to be seen in Thailand. Effective management in Thailand must also recognize a more relaxed attitude towards work, and perhaps life in general, that is a part of Thai culture (that is, what is called *sanuk*). Thailand shares much in common with other more traditional societies, including those of South-East Asia and many outside Asia. The important question here is how increasing modernity will impact Thailand and the manner in which its organizations are managed. As with many developing countries, there is a major split between urban and rural areas, with urban dwellers, particularly in Bangkok, exhibiting values and work orientations more like those found in highly advanced economies. However, at least from anecdotal evidence, the degree of urban cultural transition is much less than in places such as Hong Kong, Singapore and Taiwan (see Chapters 3, 10 and 12) as well as the most rapidly growing parts of China (see Chapter 2). As with other parts of South-East Asia, there is a concern with preserving traditional values in the face of immense economic and social change. We should not, then, expect Thais to be rapid adopters of the core values that drive Western culture and business. This may be good for the Thai psyche, but could have important and possibly deleterious consequences in the case of Thai management. The issue of corporate governance comes most immediately to mind, particularly in light of the 1997 Asian financial crisis. The heavy use of personal connections, the prevalence of 'particularism' and lack of transparency in business transactions have meant that Thai organizations are likely to have continuing difficulty in functioning well in the global economy. Despite the adoption on the surface of many Western business practices, the authors conclude, Thai managers are likely to place greater weight on the implications of business decisions for the maintenance of social relationships rather than on economic efficiency.

Vietnam

In Chapter 14, Ying Zhu – originally from the PRC, now teaching in Australia – examines the case of Vietnam, a country with a long and complex history. The cultural foundation of that society, he notes, has undoubtedly played a significant role in the process of formation of a distinct management approach. In Vietnam, there is a 'core' value system based on the combining characteristics of Confucianism, Western (largely French) colonization and communism that have a strong hold on the 'mind-set' of its people. Like Korea (see Chapter 11), it was divided into a communist north and a capitalist south. In the 1960s, both it and its neighbours experienced the tragic turmoil of the Vietnam War and its destabilization and devastation. With peace came national reunification. In common with the PRC (see Chapter 2), Vietnam had been subjected to a command economy for a long period in the post-war world and is only now undergoing a more market-driven experiment, albeit with modest political and social liberalization. The chapter's author illustrates the relationships between culture and management in Vietnam by using case studies, predominantly of state-owned enterprises. In today's Vietnam, there is a greater degree of market flexibility than in the pre-reform system, although he concludes that we cannot posit a full degree of convergence of Vietnamese management towards the Western business paradigm. However, the author concludes, we may see the current Vietnam management as moving towards a distinctive 'hybrid' if 'transitional' outcome.

Discussion

We can note a number of major themes, at this juncture, that relate to the country experiences noted above.

First, the idiosyncratic nature of each country's history is almost self-evident, as most of the contributing authors have made clear. While nearly all of them have shared the turbulence of recent centuries, namely the legacy of colonialism and imperialism, the implantation of nascent capitalism and so on, they all have in turn evolved and nurtured a relatively differentiated blend of values and institutions (see Orru *et al.* 1997). Many were 'capitalist' only partially, as they mostly engendered 'dual economies', with for the most part a 'modern' urban sector and a 'traditional' rural one.

Second, the resilience of each national culture in spite of invasions and foreign influences is noteworthy. Although some have experienced an amalgam of religious and later ideological influences, they have all evolved a distinct cultural framework and in many cases a form of management with local characteristics (see Warner 2002). Some traditional influences and practices have weakened considerably, but what is remarkable is what has survived. Even where there were 'revolutionary' upheavals, as in China under Mao Zedong, we find that when the market was reintroduced, there was a reversion to older patterns of behaviour, such in the upsurge of private entrepreneurship over the last decade or so (see Chapter 2).

Third, often country-specific cultures and/or economic structures in many cases have resulted in an observable set of highly identifiable institutions (see Whitley 1992). No two economies are wholly alike, whether capitalist or communist. Even one Confucian 'little Dragon' differs from another in its business and management. Hong Kong (see Chapter 3) remains identifiably distinct from, say, Taiwan (see Chapter 12).

Fourth, the distinctiveness of each national managerial style has come about as a result of cultural adaptation to wider influences. Managers in one Asian country tend to manage somewhat differently from their counterparts in another, as some of the scores reported in Chapter 10 clearly show. Even in the economic 'big league', Chinese managers have their distinct traits, if compared with their Japanese counterparts.

Even so, we find that there are overarching phenomena that cross the national boundaries and still dominate the shape of economies and societies.

We can now enumerate a number of *common strands* that can be found in most if not all of the countries noted above and considered in greater depth in the respective chapters to come.

To start with, we can observe the recurrent incidence of the Asian 'traditional', capitalist family firm that is found in most of South-East and East Asia (often Chinese-owned and run) and/or its indigenous equivalent (see Redding 1990). It still appears to dominate the SME sector that remains the bedrock of many a local economy. It has even come back to life in the PRC (see Chapter 2) and Vietnam (see Chapter 14) in recent times.

Next, the state-owned enterprise (SOE) that once was very prevalent in many Asian economies is now decidedly on the wane, although many examples are still to be found around the countries in the region (see Warner 2002). The shrinking of the state sector, often as a result of 'privatization' policies associated with structural reform programmes encouraged by the IMF and World Bank, has been *de rigueur*.

Last, the multinational corporation, though not as ubiquitous as some imagine, has now become more prevalent, whether North American, West European or Japanese owned. As the agent of 'globalization', the MNC is now both more pervasive and influential in the sophisticated part of the 'dual economy' that characterizes many Asian countries (see Kogut and Gittelman 1997).

Conclusions

This edited book has tried to present an overview of the role culture plays vis-à-vis economies and managements in a number of countries. In this introduction, we set out some of the contemporary debates about culture and management, both in general and with specific reference to Asia. We then went on to present the main headings under which the contributing authors have presented up-to-date material on the specific countries they have tackled. We can see from the short summaries of these above that there is a wide range of outcomes, ranging from those that have achieved near-Western levels of GDP per capita to those with improving but more modest achievements. Although many economies and their managements have moved towards 'relative convergence'and maybe even 'Cross - Vergence', they have all retained many distinctive features. It is therefore very important for those studying or doing business in those parts to understand fully the idiosyncratic complexities of each national system, particularly what distinguishes them one from the other, as much as understanding their common experiences in terms of globalization.

Notes

1 The 'little Dragon' economies were originally Hong Kong, Korea, Singapore and Taiwan (see Chapters 3, 10, 11 and 12 in this volume).
2 The official economic growth rate was estimated to be around 7.5 per cent by 2003.
3 We dismissed this outcome as extremely unlikely since there was no evidence to substantiate it as a possibility.

4   It is clear from reading the contributions to this edited book that Confucianism is not a homogeneous phenomenon; so, we are talking about a number of variations in its development over time and space.
5   We are referring here to both the 'big' and 'little Dragon' economies of East Asia.
6   By 'privatization', we mean the transfer of ownership of the means of production out of state to private hands.

References

Bamber, G., Park, F., Lee, C., Ross, P.K. and Broadbent, K. (2000) *Employment Relations in the Asia-Pacific: Changing Approaches*, London: International Thomson Business Press.

Braun, W. and Warner, M. (2002) 'The "culture-free" versus the "culture-specific" management debate', in M. Warner and P. Joynt (eds), *Managing Across Cultures: Issues and Perspectives*, 2nd edition, London: Thomson Learning, pp. 13–25.

Child, J. (1994). *Management in China During the Age of Reform*, Cambridge: Cambridge University Press.

Child, J. (2002) 'Theorizing about organizations cross-nationally', in M. Warner and P. Joynt (eds), *Managing Across Cultures: Issues and Perspectives*, 2nd edition, London: Thomson Learning, pp. 26–39.

The Economist (2001) various issues.

Friedman, E. (2000) 'Since there is no East and there is no West, how could either be best?', in M. Jacobsen and O. Bruun (eds), *Human Rights and Asian Values: Contesting National Identities and Cultural Representations in Asia*, Richmond, Surrey: Curzon.

Geertz, H. and Geertz, C. (1975) *Kinship in Bali*, Chicago and London: University of Chicago Press.

Godement, F. (1999) *The Downsizing of Asia*, London: Routledge.

Hamilton, G. C. (1995) 'Overseas Chinese Capitalism', in W. Tu (ed.), *The Confucian Dimensions of Industrial East Asia*, Cambridge, MA: Harvard University Press.

Hampden-Turner, C. M. and Trompenaars, F. (1997) *Mastering the Infinite Game*, Oxford: Capstone.

Hampden-Turner, C. M. and Trompenaars, F., (2000) *Building Cross-Cultural Competence*, Chichester: John Wiley.

Hofstede, G. (1980) *Culture's Consequences: International Differences in Work-Related Values*, Beverly Hills, CA, and London: Sage.

Hofstede, G. (1980) *Cultures and Organizations: Software of the Mind*, New York: McGraw-Hill.

Human Development Report (2002) *Human Development Report*, New York: United Nations.

Joynt, P. and Warner, M. (1996) 'Introduction: cross-cultural perspectives', in M. Warner and P. Joynt (eds), *Managing Across Cultures: Issues and Perspectives*, 1st edition, London: International Thomson Business Press, pp. 3–6.

Kerr, C., Dunlop, J. T., Harbison, F. H. and Myers, C. A. (1960) *Industrialism and Industrial Man*, Harmondsworth, Middlesex: Penguin.

Kogut, B. and Gittelman, M. (1997) 'Globalization', in M. Warner (ed.), *Concise Encyclopedia of Business and Management*, London: International Thomson Business Press, pp. 219–33.

Maurice, M., Sorge, A. and Warner, M. (1980) 'Societal differences in organizing manufacturing units: a comparison of France, West Germany and Great Britain', *Organization Studies* 1(1): 58–86.

Ng, S.-H. and Warner, M. (1999) 'Human resource management in Asia', in B. Morton and P. Joynt (eds), *The Global HR Manager*, London: IPD.

Orru, M., Biggart, N. W. and Hamilton, G. C. (eds) (1997) *The Economic Organization of East Asia*, Thousand Oaks, CA: Sage.

Redding, G. (1990) *The Spirit of Chinese Capitalism*, Berlin: de Gruyter.

Rowley, C. (1997) 'Introduction: comparisons and perspectives on HRM in the Asia Pacific', Special Issue: Human Resource Management in the Asia Pacific Region Questioned, *Asia-Pacific Business Review* 3(4): 1–18.

Tung, R. L. (1996) 'Managing in Asia: the cross-cultural dimension', in M. Warner and P. Joynt (eds), *Managing Across Cultures: Issues and Perspectives*, 1st edition, London: Thomson Learning, pp. 233–45.

Warner, M. (1994) 'Japanese culture, Western management: Taylorism and human resources in Japan', *Organization Studies* 15(4): 509–33.

Warner, M (1995) *The Management of Human Resources in Chinese Industry*, London: Macmillan.

Warner, M. (2000) 'Introduction: the Asia-Pacific HRM model revisited', *International Journal of Human Resource Management* 11(2): 171–82.

Warner, M. (2002) 'Globalization, labour markets and human resources in Asia-Pacific economies: an overview', *International Journal of Human Resource Management* 13(3): 384–98.

Warner, M. and Joynt, P. (2002) *Managing Across Cultures: Issues and Perspectives*, 2nd edition, London: Thomson Learning.

Weber, M. (1964) *The Theory of Social and Economic Organization*, trans. A. M. Henderson and T. Parsons, New York: Free Press.

Whitley, R. D. (1992) *Business Systems in East Asia*, London: Sage.

Wilkinson, B. (1996) 'Culture, institutions and business in East Asia', *Organization Studies* 17(4): 421–47.

2 Culture and management in China

John Child and Malcolm Warner

Introduction

This chapter examines the relationship between culture and management in the People's Republic of China (PRC). Culture will be treated as one of the main variables accounting for the specific management scenarios that have evolved in China over the last few decades (Warner and Joynt 2002).[1]

While China is home to the world's oldest and most continuous culture, it has also been subject to massive institutional changes since the nation-wide establishment of the communist regime in 1949. Comparison with other parts of China, namely Hong Kong and Taiwan, which have not experienced the same socio-economic regime, raises the question as to how much that is distinctive about management in China can be attributed to Chinese culture as opposed to the prevailing institutional system. Certainly, the chapters in this book on Hong Kong (Chapter 4) and Taiwan (as well as on Singapore) indicate that there are substantial differences in corporate and managerial behaviour between Mainland China and these other territories. The substantial divergence between East and West German management practice and performance, which created a massive challenge after reunification in 1990, is a comparable example, as is also the two Koreas today. In these cases, differences in behaviour cannot readily be accounted for by culture alone, and this warrants a brief consideration of what culture and national institutions can respectively be expected to explain.

As the introduction to this book notes, the cultural perspective has for some time provided the dominant paradigm in comparative studies of management and organization. It is indicative that Hickson and Pugh (1995) chose to subtitle their review of the field 'The Impact of Societal Culture on Organizations around the Globe'. Even before Hofstede's seminal work (1980), international studies of organization generally regarded culture as the key explanatory factor for cross-national differences, as reviews such as Roberts (1970) make clear. Attention to culture also has intuitive appeal to practising international managers, for whom it serves as a convenient reference for the many frustrating difficulties they can experience when working with people from other countries, the source of which they do not always comprehend.

A contrasting perspective emphasizes that management and business have different institutional foundations in different societies. Key institutions are the state, the legal system, the financial system and the family. Taken together, such institutions constitute the distinctive social organization of a country and its economy. The forms these institutions take and their economic role are seen to shape different 'national business systems' or varieties of capitalism (Whitley 1992a; 1992b; Orru *et al.* 1997). In turn the norms and rules of such systems impact importantly on corporate and managerial behaviour. It has to be admitted that although the institutional perspective draws on a long sociological tradition, there is still not much agreement about, or understanding of, the processes whereby institutions are formed and in turn impact on organizations (Tolbert and Zucker 1996). There is, however, more consensus about the potential analytical power that the perspective offers.

Institutional theorists stress the historical embeddedness of social structures and processes. This implies that nations have their own logic of social and economic organization, and that this is difficult to distinguish from their cultural heritage. In China, for example, the foundation of Chinese respect for hierarchy and the family social collective is based upon the relational norms expounded by Confucius and legal codes such as those developed during the Tang Dynasty[2] (Gernet 1982). This institutionalized relational logic has shaped a society whose transactional order rests on social obligation to higher authority and to the family rather than on rules oriented to protecting the individual. Chinese capitalism is seen to be intrinsically different from Western capitalism because of this contrast in institutional framing over a long period of time (Gerth and Mills 1946; Weber 1964). The hierarchical and collective orientation it has produced has become today commonly regarded as an inherent characteristic of Chinese culture.

In other words, over historical time, the distinction between cultural and institutional causation becomes blurred by the interrelationship between the two. While many institutions are initially shaped by political and legislative actions, those that survive do so because they express and support enduring cultural values. Nevertheless, in the shorter term, institutional regimes condition the attitudes and behaviour to be found in organizations, and they can modify cultural effects. As 'same culture, different system' examples like Mainland China and Hong Kong illustrate, the impact of institutional differences is sufficient for Hong Kong managers to regard managing operations in the Mainland as problematic (Child *et al.* 2000).

At any given time, culture and institutions tend to influence different aspects of management and organization. Culture impacts primarily on individual attitudes and behaviour, including interpersonal behaviour. Its influence in organizations is therefore likely to be pervasive, extending to matters such as the motivational consequences of managerial practices and styles, norms of communication, the willingness to take individual responsibility, the conduct of meetings, and modes of conflict resolution. Institutions, by contrast, impact directly on features that are shaped or constrained by formal norms and rules. These include systems of corporate ownership, accountability and governance, conditions of employment and collective bargaining, and the reliance on formal contracts for intra- and inter-organizational transactions (Child 1981).

There are further qualifications we need to bear in mind in the case of a huge and highly complex country like China. First, China embraces many regions with their own subcultures[3] (Cannon and Jenkins 1990). Fairbank was of the view that, in China, 'regional differences are too great to be homogenized under a unitary state' (1987: 363). Second, over the past twenty years or so it has experienced the world's largest social experiment in the shape of its economic reform, which has led to rapid industrialization and significant generational differences. These changes have been most evident in coastal regions, and they have added to regional differentiation. Third, China's business system now includes a variety of enterprise forms, ranging from state-owned enterprises, former state enterprises converted into joint stock companies, collectively owned companies, a rapidly developing privately owned sector, and enterprises with foreign investment either in joint venture or wholly owned subsidiary form (Child and Tse 2001). This changing and extremely varied scene raises questions about whether or not one can detect a single characteristic and culturally determined model of Chinese management.

Historical background

China's long history has until very recently been marked by two overriding social imperatives. The first imperative concerned the preservation of its integrity in terms of protecting its immensely long borders and maintaining internal unity. This justified and reinforced the hierarchical status and centralized powers of the emperor and imperial officials. While they normally treated imperial authority with great deference, the peasantry occasionally revolted against the abuse of this authority, especially when driven to desperation by famine. The second imperative in fact concerned the need for communal self-help in the face of recurrent natural disasters, particularly famine and flood. The precariousness imposed by a combination of threats from natural causes and arbitrary imperial rule led to a reliance on mutual support within extended family units and the local community. This historical legacy helps to account for the paradox characterizing China today: that high trust is accorded to group members or those with whom there are special relationships, while others are actively mistrusted.

Chinese culture and tradition is therefore deep rooted and before the nineteenth century was largely undisturbed by foreign influence. The majority Han people had managed to absorb foreign invaders, such as the Mongols and the Manchu, into that culture. Their culture is a strong attribute of Chinese society and its members remain very self-conscious of it. As Fairbank noted (1987: 367), 'the influence of China's long past is ever-present in the environment, the language, the folklore, and the practices of government, business and interpersonal relations'. Many writers have stressed the influence of China's culture on the way that its organizations are managed (e.g. Pye 1985; Lockett 1988; Redding 1990; 2002).

Economic background

The PRC has been one of the fastest growing economies in the world in recent times. China's achievement has been a dazzling success and quite unanticipated in many respects, particularly after the debacle of the Great Leap Forward and the woes of the Cultural Revolution under Mao Zedong. Since Deng Xiaoping initiated the 'Open Door' reforms in 1978, however, it has expanded by leaps and bounds. By the start of the new millennium, China was hailed as a coming economic superpower. Living standards have risen greatly but the distribution of benefits has been uneven. By 2000, nominal GDP growth was over 8 per cent per annum. Industrial production grew even faster than this. Per capita GDP was just over US$800, a modest level by international standards, but purchasing power parity was much higher, around US$4,500 for that year, according to World Bank estimates. The last few years have seen more deflation than price rises. Those living in towns have done better than those inland over the decade; urban workers have benefited more than peasants but living standards of both have risen absolutely even if there have been differences in their relative degrees of prosperity. A new middle class has also emerged, and a consumer revolution has been unfolding, if unevenly.

Labour resources, a main feature of China's comparative advantage, have been increasingly more effectively channelled into productive uses than under the command economy system. As of April 2001, the latest available official census statistics indicate that over 705.75 million people were 'employed' in the Chinese economy at the end of 1999, out of the 'economically active' population aged 16 and over of around 720 million. The employed represented 56.1 per cent of the total number of Chinese people working. Women comprised 46.5 per cent of total employment, which is on the high side by international standards, though one should bear in mind that the Chinese Population Census of 2000 suggested that there were 117 females for every 100 males in the PRC.

The PRC has to date avoided the worst of the Asian economic crisis in the late 1990s, but it may not be wholly invulnerable vis-à-vis the possible next one (*The Economist* 2002a). GDP growth is still buoyant, but bad debts continue to be an albatross around the neck of the financial system. Asian devaluations risk undercutting its strong exports. In addition, the downturn in the US economy in 2002 augurs poorly for future export expansion. Recent US tariffs against imported low-cost steel from the PRC and elsewhere may signal stormy times ahead (*The Economist* 2002b). No doubt, there are further threats (as well as opportunities) just around the corner.

Societal culture

There have been many different strands in the cultural evolution of China over the centuries. Historians like Fairbank and Goldman (1998) ably bring out both the cultural homogeneity and diversity of China over its long chain of evolution. We have already signalled the presence of considerable regional and generational differences.

The core Han culture is probably the most important factor in understanding how China developed. It is almost impossible to discuss any aspect of Chinese life without referring to it. It dominates both the map and the mind-set of modern China. Despite the strong influence of institutional features, informed by communist ideology and a totalitarian state, as in other countries cultural variables have also help to mould the institutional ones. They permeate social relations in everyday life, both inside and outside the basic work unit (*danwei*). China is widely assumed to be 'different' from the West. Both outsiders and locals tend to emphasize its cultural distinctiveness or even uniqueness, although perhaps not to the same degree as the Japanese (Dale 1986). Today, the qualifier 'with Chinese characteristics' is still often heard.

One of the most important influences on Chinese everyday life was Confucianism in its many varieties, and it remains so. Three bonds of loyalty bound the society (loyalty to the ruler, filial obedience and fidelity of wife to husband). Two of these were set within the family and all represented relationships 'between superior and subordinate' (Fairbank and Goldman 1998: 19). Confucius (Kongzi, 551–479 BC), writing around the time of Socrates but a while before Jesus Christ, based his ideas on absolute respect for tradition, on a strict hierarchy of primary relationships between family members, and then again between the people and their rulers. His was a philosophy intended to guide people's daily life and it established a mode of thought and habit that has persisted and that blended well with other belief-systems that many of its adherents often held at the same time, such as Buddhism and Daoism. The major ideas of this Confucian system of beliefs were three basic guides (ruler guides subject, father guides son, and husband guides wife), five constant virtues (benevolence, righteousness, propriety, wisdom and fidelity) and the doctrine of the mean (harmony). Confucius laid down that *Ren* or benevolence was the supreme virtue the follower can attain. As a strictly natural and humanistic love, it was based upon spontaneous feelings cultivated through education. To attain *Ren*, you have to practise *Li*, which represents social norms. The latter can be interpreted as rituals, rites or proprieties and includes all moral codes and social institutions.

As *Li* is a term for moral codes and social institutions, many assume that the practice of *Li* is to enforce social conformity at the cost of the individual. However, an individual personality is not an entity cut off from the group. Confucius said: 'In order to establish oneself, one has to establish others. This is the way of a person of *Ren*' (McGreal 1995: 5).

According to Confucius, the optimal way to govern is not by legislation but by way of moral education and by example. The ideal government is thus a government of *wuwei* (non-action) through a rock-solid groundwork of moral education. Confucius notes that:

> If you lead the people with political force and restrict them with law and punishment, they can just avoid law violation, but will have no sense of honour and shame. If you lead them with morality and guide them with *Li*, they will develop a sense of honour and shame, and will do good of their own accord.
>
> (McGreal 1995: 7)

This message is an appeal to the human heart: self-realisation towards world peace (harmony), to a peaceful world and to an orderly society as the ultimate goal of this belief-system. The strong Chinese cultural preference for basing business transactions upon the quality of interpersonal relationships and for settling disputes through mediation rather than relying upon contracts and legal process can be seen to stem from this philosophy.

By and large, Confucianism occupied the mainstream of Chinese philosophy for many centuries. The neo-Confucian project under the Southern Song, Yuan and Ming Dynasties formalized Confucianism into a set of rituals that then had a tremendous impact on thinking and behaviour throughout Chinese society (Faure 2001). Even so, other branches of philosophy before and after the Master's contribution were also influential, if with different focuses. Daoism, for instance, may be cited as another significant school of thought. The founding father of Daoism was Lao Zi (sixth century BC) who introduced the idea of yielding to the deep-rooted 'flow' of the universe. This part of the belief-system remains deeply embedded in the Chinese psyche. Buddhism, Confucianism, Daoism, legalism, Christianity and the rest, indeed communism in its turn, all came and were integrated into contemporary mind-sets.

Chinese society today is the result of a long process of adaptation to changes in this cultural environment. Core cultural influences appear to have persisted as the bedrock of the Chinese system on the Mainland, but they were arguably submerged for the best part of half a century by newer layers of institutional change in the social archaeology of people's mind-sets. The roots of this institutional change indeed go further back to the revolution of 1911. Cultural characteristics were suppressed for what turned out to be a historically brief period under Mao's rule but were, we would argue, so strong they prevailed and have reappeared in recent decades as the system became more 'open' under the post-1978 reforms.

Various authorities have identified the values underpinning Chinese culture that are relevant to management and organizational behaviour (e.g. Shenkar and Ronen 1987; Lockett 1988; Redding 1990; 2002; Bond 1996). It is widely accepted that Confucianism has been the most important historical foundation for many of these values. Redding's (2002 :234-5) list is one of the more comprehensive and is quoted:

1. *Societal order*. This reflects the sense of Chinese civilization as based on the learning and practice by individuals of clearly defined roles, all within a dominating state structure with a remit to preserve order, and all socialized into a belief in the need for appropriate conduct in the interests of harmony.
2. *Hierarchy*. Stemming largely from Confucian ethics, these values legitimate paternalism at the levels of family and organization, and patrimonialism at the state level, and provide a moral justification for hierarchy by stressing reciprocal vertical obligations.
3. *Reciprocity and personalism*. This is the currency of horizontal exchange, and the guarantor of the limited but adequate trust that maintains the particular structure of transactions.
4. *Control*. In a society of competing families, under conditions of scarce resources, and in an interventionist state, control of one's fate becomes a core ideal for many, particularly business owners, and sensitivities to control become highly tuned.
5. *Insecurity*. This is endemic in an essentially totalitarian state, with weak property rights, and it is associated with competitiveness and a work ethic. Building defences and reserves becomes a moral duty towards dependents, as well as a practical necessity.
6. *Family based collectivism*. The architecture of horizontal order in Chinese society is based on identity with family as the core social unit.
7. *Knowledge*. The Chinese respect for learning appears to have survived the ravages of the Cultural Revolution and the related persecution of intellectuals, although its support in the institutional fabric is less strong than in the Imperial period. The value of learning, however, remains high, and there is doubtless some connection made with social mobility in its retention as a core ideal.

These values are commonly expressed in a number of forms that are of particular relevance to management in China. Respect for hierarchy and learning means that long-serving senior figures in organizations are readily accorded leadership status. Family-based collectivism manifests itself in the survival, and today the resurgence, of family business, as well as in personnel practices such as recruitment of family members. Collectivism manifests itself in an orientation towards groups so that, for example, there is often resistance to the introduction of individually based performance-related pay. Insecurity and personalism combine to accord significance to the preservation of 'face', and non-Chinese people therefore need to be very careful when negotiating with older senior managers or officials who are lacking in modern technical knowledge not to cause them to lose face.

The perceived need to guarantee trust and maintain harmony leads to special importance being placed upon personal relationships. An example is 'relational networking' based on interpersonal connections (known in Chinese as *guanxi*).[4] It works extensively as a coordination mechanism, as we find in both socialist and capitalist Chinese organizations. But there are also those who doubt if it is still important in today's more market-oriented economy in the PRC. This behavioural pattern is arguably basically East Asian and very much ascriptive, communitarian and particularistic, and thus quite distinct from the *Gesellschaft* type of social integration often associated with Western ways of doing things and with 'modernization' (on China's search for 'modernity', see He 2002). It may even illustrate the persistence of Chinese societal patterns, in spite of changes from imperial rule to republican, and from revolutionary to reformist. Indeed, such is the *continuity* in the culture that the phrase 'Confucian–Leninism' has been used by Pye to link the past and the near present (cited in Warner 1995: 147).

Guanxi, for example, has been deep rooted in China since Confucius codified the societal rules over 2,000 years ago. These welded the hierarchies holding national Chinese (and overseas Chinese) social structures together, such that fief-like loyalties and clan-like networks have long been the main links in the societal chain (Boisot and Child 1996). Together with *guanxi* (relationships), *li* (rite), *mianzi* (face) and *renqing* (obligations) reinforce the social bonds that make the Chinese system function smoothly. In terms of organization theory, this represents the elements of a reciprocal informal system that acts as neither market nor hierarchy; it acts reciprocally with whatever institutionalized bureaucratic structures exist at the time and may help to make them work more smoothly. As Chen (1995: 144) puts it, 'a Chinese should first and foremost know his place in society and how to interact with others in a proper manner. *Guanxi*, face and *renqing* are important components in regulating interpersonal relationships'.

The dismantling of the socialist order laid down during the Mao period might be expected to release the expression of traditional Chinese culture from the bounds, even rejection, that were imposed on it. Wang (2002), however, concludes that this has not happened to an extent sufficient to fill the gap left by the demise of the old order. Instead, she maintains that a serious contradiction between official ideology and China's socio-economic reality has given rise to a disorganized hedonism and 'above all, a devastating poverty of moral and cultural resources for self-critique and self-betterment' (p. 17). The huge scale of corruption in contemporary China appears to bear this claim out. In Wang's view, there is an 'almost total lack of a new type of person whose values and motivations can help sustain China's emerging capitalist society as the Maoist type of person did the old "communist" order' (p. 1).

Corporate culture

It is impossible to characterize a corporate culture that typifies China for two reasons. First, the context for Chinese business is changing rapidly, under the impetus of the economic reform. Second, as a result of the reform, Chinese enterprises vary extensively, ranging from state-owned enterprises (SOEs), some of which are still protected from market forces, through former SOEs which have converted to joint stock companies, to collectively owned enterprises and private firms. In addition, companies with foreign ownership now make up a sizeable part of the non-agricultural economy.

The most recent landmark changes in corporate culture were initiated in late 1978. The 'new' Chinese managerial model may be seen as a pragmatic experiment that was first piloted in Sichuan Province in 1979 under the leadership of the then Party Secretary, Zhao Ziyang. In the early 1980s, those changes seen to be effective were then applied, with varying degrees of intensity, across the whole of the PRC, but it was not until the mid-1980s that management reforms began to take root. As mentioned earlier, SOEs had once dominated industrial production, and their work units (*danwei*) embodied the so-called 'iron rice-bowl' (*tie fan wan*) which ensured 'jobs for life' and 'cradle to grave' welfare for mostly urban industrial SOE employees (Lu and Perry 1997). The system was partly derived from earlier Chinese communist experience in the liberated zones, and Soviet practice, but in addition may have had roots in Japanese precedents in Occupied Manchuria.

Under the reform since 1979, there have been major shifts in enterprise ownership and growing exposure to market forces. Before the reform, China's SOEs dominated its national economy, producing three-quarters of its industrial output value. They operated according to bureaucratically mandated plans, including input and output quotas. By 2002, SOEs accounted for just under 25 per cent of industrial output. There is today a wide range of firms with contrasting ownership and governance structures. Urban and rural collective enterprises account for around 40 per cent of industrial output, firms with foreign investment over 15 per cent, and private firms over 20 per cent. Except for a few SOEs, all these firms secure resources and dispose of outputs through markets.[5]

China's industrial structure has become complex and differentiated owing to moves towards exposing firms both to markets and to private ownership. Government policy is to retain SOEs in key industries, which are strategic in nature and/or where considerable economies of scale are anticipated, while others are to have their ownership restructured or to be sold outright. The government has also encouraged SOEs to merge into business groups, ostensibly to achieve scale economies, but often in reality to bail out weaker enterprises and avoid the social costs of closure (Keister 2000). A significant development in the 1990s has been the conversion of SOEs to joint stock companies, of which there were 13,103 by the end of 1997. Analysis of 40,238 SOEs surveyed in 1998 by the State Statistical Bureau indicated that 17 per cent of them had completed restructuring (Lin and Zhu 2001). Of the restructured SOEs, 55 per cent had become limited liability companies, 16 per cent had transformed into employee shareholding cooperatives and 7 per cent had become private enterprises. Restructured enterprises generally had a significant private stake, though conversely some of the newly formed private enterprises still had a majority of their shares held by the state. The SOEs that had converted into fully private firms were generally small and in most the top manager was the main owner and likely to hold tight control.

Collective enterprises, especially so-called township and village enter-prises (TVEs), owned and operated by village and municipal governments, have become a unique and significant force in China's economy. Many of them are low tech, wasteful and poorly managed (*The Economist* 2002b: 10–11). Nonetheless, with the collapse of many SOEs, and the increasing authority delegated by the state to local governments in China, TVEs are likely to remain significant players in China.

In addition to the reconstitution of some SOEs as private firms, the core private sector has been the fastest growing in China and now employs over 13 million people. In the past, private firms have experienced a harsh institu-tional environment (IFC 2000). In 2000, however, they were granted full legal rights, and the establishment of a venture capital market in Shenzhen may provide needed financial capital to the promising few. Not many private firms have so far become joint venture partners or acquisition targets for foreign firms, but some of them will become more attractive especially in areas such as software and Internet development (Becker 1999). Another privately owned part of the economy comprises foreign subsidiaries. Beginning in 1986, foreign direct investors were permitted to establish their own wholly owned subsidiaries (WOSs), and in 1997 the number of newly established WOSs exceeded that of equity joint ventures (EJVs) with Chinese partners for the first time.

These developments mean that there are today many and varying Chinese corporate cultures. In many SOEs, the residual of the iron rice-bowl model continues to persist, though under increasing threat from restructuring. There are, however, an increasing number of reformed SOE cultures, even very 'state-of-the-art' entrepreneurial ones, especially in those SOEs which have converted to joint stock companies. Collective enterprises, including the TVEs, vary greatly between conservative unsophisticated cultures to some modern entrepreneurial ones. Different corporate cultures also arise through links with foreign firms and their different national ownerships. The greatest impact on Chinese enterprise cultures and practices appears to come when the foreign partner or owner is a multinational enterprise (Child and Yan 2001).

Through inheriting a culture with strong feudalistic origins, China provides a favourable context for paternalistic corporate cultures (Farh and Cheng 2000). Enterprises at both extremes of the range, traditional SOEs and private firms, both exhibit corporate cultures that reflect paternalistic cultural values. In traditional SOEs, the culture has been one of top-down leadership and authority, collectivism and mutual dependence, with an emphasis on conformity and attachment to the organization based on moral rather than material incentives (Child 1994). A kind of *noblesse oblige* has prevailed. Loyalty to superiors and to the work unit has been complemented by employment protection and the provision of welfare benefits. This moral contract is now fast breaking down, as SOEs either reform or go bankrupt. There is little evidence as yet of what the corporate culture of reformed SOEs may turn out to be, though case studies suggest that it will combine an emphasis on personal achievement with a strong collective spirit (e.g. Xu Jian 1997; Nolan 2001).

In the private sector, most firms are still small and their culture is very centred on the owner. In a questionnaire survey of 628 private firms in China, supplemented by interviews with 338 private company chief executives, the IFC (2000) found that the most usual forms of ownership were sole ownership (40 per cent of the firms) and partnership (30 per cent). In such firms the proprietor or a small group of close associates, which often included spouses and relatives, made most decisions personally and informally. Only among some larger and longer-established private firms was there evidence of decisions being made by more formal bodies such as a board of directors or a management meeting. A small-scale, but more ethnographic, study of rural private firms conducted by Pleister (1998) found that the direction of these firms was almost exclusively in the hands of their owner–managers.

Within private firms, be they urban or rural, workers do not normally participate in decision making, even on questions concerning benefits. In the typical urban private firm, employees can be divided into two groups. The first comprises local people and externally recruited university graduates. These employees generally hold better positions in the firms, enjoy superior wages and benefits, and stay with the firm longer. They are regarded as long-term primary members of the corporate collectivity and are likely to identify with its culture. The second group consists of migrants from rural areas, who occupy a much more marginal position.

Managerial behaviour

Managerial behaviour in modern China has been greatly influenced by political circumstances and the institutional regime that government decreed. Initially, the PRC managed its labour force using a 'top-down' model that endured for half a century. Studies of Chinese economic management in the critical years after 1949 (such as Schurmann 1966) show the links between Chinese communist practices before 1949 as well as Soviet influence after that date. In addition, established Chinese capitalist and foreign-owned businesses before these were 'nationalized' in the 1950s left a legacy of personnel procedures. Other influences came from the Japanese public and private enterprises set up in Manchuria from the turn of the century (Warner 1995).

What we call contemporary Chinese management dates from the period after 1978. Even here, which model of management predominates depends on the period chosen, as well as which sector and region of the economy it is located in. At the time of writing, in 2002, it is hard to identify one single stereotypical model as such. The most useful way of approaching the subject is to focus on the two contrasting types of firm that are likely to have long-term prominence within the system. These are SOEs, which it is official policy to maintain at least within strategic sectors of the economy, and private firms.

SOEs tend to be larger enterprises than those in the non-state categories. A conjunction of size and the legacy of government administration means that such enterprises tend towards bureaucratic behaviour. The behaviour of SOEs also exhibits some influences from Chinese culture that reinforce this tendency. A large 'power distance' tends to be maintained between top managers and other members of the organization, with relatively little delegation of authority and a strong emphasis on vertical links within hierarchies. The structures of SOEs are often quite elaborate, with many specialized departments, which tend to experience or face major problems of communication and collaboration of a horizontal kind between themselves. Identities and loyalties are primarily vertical in nature, and reflect the traditional respect among Chinese people for loyalty to the 'ruler'. The problem is accentuated by group orientation. This tends to be most strongly directed towards the immediate working group and its leadership, which is the workplace equivalent of the family, the focal social unit in Chinese culture (Child 1994). The combination of a strong group orientation with a penchant towards egalitarianism generates reluctance among many Chinese to accept responsibility and systems that reward performance on an individual basis. These attitudes and behaviours are now showing signs of weakening among members of the urban younger generation. In addition, modern management methods are being introduced into SOEs at an accelerating rate often spurred on by their conversion into joint stock companies enjoying both greater autonomy and responsibility for their economic survival (Tse and Chung 1999).

Private Chinese firms tend to operate in a highly centralized manner, in which the entrepreneur–owners tend to maintain their authoritative position through keeping tight control of information and decision making. They do not bear the socialist legacy of SOEs nor suffer from the same bureaucratic rigidities. This means that private firms more clearly exhibit the application of Chinese cultural values to managerial behaviour. While conflict can arise between members of the owning family, a high value is attached to preserving loyalty to the 'boss' and overt harmony within the general body of the firm. As Chen (1995) notes, the owners of private Chinese firms tend to attach greater significance to the loyalty of their subordinates even than to their performance. They develop special ties with those upon whom they can rely and give special ad hoc rewards to them rather than adopting a standardized reward system. The Chinese cultural preference for an implicit and moral basis for business dealing rather than a more formal footing is very characteristic of private firms. The viability of their business dealings rests heavily upon trust between the transacting parties.

Both SOEs and private firms depend on *guanxi* to develop their external networks and to acquire business opportunities. This is especially true for private firms. They lack the institutional supports offered by government agencies, and good *guanxi* connections therefore provide an important substitute for gaining access to scarce raw materials and other resources (Luo 2000). Similarly, it has been the tradition in China to rely more on the mutual obligations expressed by a relationship rather than on legal contracts. In fact, resort to a contract was taken as a sign of bad faith, a feature that many Western firms investing in China found it hard to understand. Yet again, however, the scene is changing with more positive attitudes growing towards commercial law in general and the use of contracts in particular (Guthrie 1998; Luo 2002). Luo (2002) suggests from the results of his research that, while business transactions between local Chinese companies may still often be conducted on the basis of personal relationships rather than by arm's-length contractual principles, the latter become significant in joint ventures with foreign firms and in such cases are accepted, even welcomed, by Chinese partners.

In addition to the acceptance of legal contracts, the influx of foreign investment into China since 1978 is having an impact on Chinese managerial behaviour in other ways, and in so doing is distancing it from its traditional cultural roots. Child and Yan (2001) concluded from a study of sixty-seven Sino-foreign joint ventures that transnational companies – those with production facilities in two or more continents and with worldwide sourcing and/or distribution – are particularly influential agents for the inward transfer of management practices, especially the use of formal provisions for governing joint venture behaviour and the adoption of foreign company cultural norms. Three distinctive characteristics of transnational partners that supported the transfer of practices into China were their appointment of expatriates to key joint venture positions, the heavy emphasis they placed on training local personnel, and their tendency to supply a higher percentage of the venture's inputs. Even Hong Kong companies, few of which are transnational, have an impact on managerial behaviour within their Mainland China operations through the transfer of practices, which on the whole appears to have a positive impact on the performance of the

Mainland units (Child *et al.* 2000). In these ways, companies investing into China are playing a part in developing managerial behaviour beyond its traditional cultural forms. However, as we note in the following section, the cultural impact of China's opening to the outside world appears to be extending beyond in-company behaviour. It appears to be changing cultural values themselves.

A concomitant of the drive by transnational corporations to import their management practices into China is that they experience greater conflict with local managers (Child and Yan 2001). Wang (1998) notes that managing conflict can be particularly difficult, yet important, within settings where two cultures – Chinese and foreign – are involved. He reports several studies of conflict management covering both conflict between Chinese managers themselves (intracultural conflict) and conflict between Chinese and foreign managers (intercultural conflict). When presented with cases of intracultural conflict, Chinese managers showed a concern to restore harmony and always responded to the situation. They might act indirectly and behind the scenes by approaching the colleagues with whom they disagreed in an attempt to resolve the conflict, or alternatively regard it as their duty to take the issue to their boss or raise it in a formal meeting. In cases of intercultural conflict, however, Chinese managers were reluctant to contemplate dealing directly with the foreign colleague. Wang suggests that problems could arise since foreign managers may be offended if their Chinese colleagues fail to approach them directly to discuss a problem and instead make the conflict public through raising the issue in a formal meeting or telling their friends.

Managerial values

We noted earlier that regional and generational differences were to be expected in Chinese managerial values. People in the coastal regions, especially the cities, and who belong to the younger generation have been more exposed to new economic and social forces such as consumerism, the Internet and contact with foreign firms. Such exposure might be expected to encourage them to deviate from traditional Chinese cultural norms and possibly to question some of that culture's underlying values as well.

Ralston *et al.* (1996) surveyed the values held by 704 managers located in six cities in China. They found that 'individualistic' attitudes (individualism, openness to change and self-enhancement) were more prevalent among the 'cosmopolitan Chinese' – those located in regions exposed to foreign influence – than in 'local' Chinese. On the other hand, managers in all six regions maintained the same strong commitment to 'Confucianism' (societal harmony, virtuous interpersonal behaviour, and personal and interpersonal harmony). The differences in adherence to the components of individualism tended to be greatest between coastal and inland areas. A further comparison of Chinese managers from the relatively cosmopolitan city of

Guangzhou with those from the more traditional city of Chengdu (Ralston *et al.* 1999a) confirmed this conclusion. The Guangzhou managers attached greater importance to individualism, openness to change and self-enhancement. They also attached significantly less importance to collectivism than did managers from the more traditional location, though Ralston and his colleagues again suggest that Chinese managers (and those in other countries with a Confucian heritage) may be reluctant to forsake long-held Confucian values such as collectivism. They concluded that these value differences are primarily due to (1) the historic impact of the geographic location, (2) its level of industrialization and (3) its level of educational development.

Ralston *et al.* (1999b) also compared the work values of 869 Chinese managers and professionals employed in SOEs. These differed systematically between three generational groups: the 'New Generation' of managers who were 40 years old or younger, the 'Current Generation' aged between 41 and 51 years, and the 'Older Generation' of managers aged 52 years or more. Even when controlling for other demographic factors such as region, gender and position held in companies, generational factors emerged as significant predictors of value differences. The 'New Generation' managers scored higher on individualism and lower on collectivism and Confucianism. The decline in adherence to the latter two values was monotonic from older, through 'Current' to 'New Generation' managers. Ralston and his colleagues conclude that

> the emergent profile of the New Generation of Chinese managers and professionals who will be leading China into the 21st century is one of a generation whose values are clearly more individualistic, less collectivistic and less committed to Confucian philosophy than their previous generation counterparts ... [they are] more similar to Western managers than are the previous generation, especially in respect to individualistic behavior.
>
> (1999b: 425)

This conclusion has, however, been challenged by a survey of 210 PRC managers (Heffernan and Crawford 2001) which employed a more comprehensive assessment of Confucian values. This study suggested that among the new generation of Chinese managers some elements of Confucianism are weakening while others are maintained.[6] Exposure to, or even adoption of, a Western lifestyle did not reduce their adherence to three fundamental Confucian values, namely benevolence, temperance (including harmony) and persistence (which included perseverance, patience and adaptation).

Taken together, these studies and others (e.g. Chiu *et al.* 1998) of Mainland Chinese managerial values suggest that younger managers in urban coastal locations are adopting new values. This points to the impact that modernization and increased contact with the rest of the world may be having on Chinese managerial values. However, the extent to which traditional Confucian values are being diluted or forsaken remains open to question. Whether the 'new' Chinese managers hold a combination of new and traditional values deserves further investigation, as does the possibility that such managers maintain a distinction between the values they apply to the workplace and those they regard as appropriate to private and community life. The apparently changing nature of Chinese managerial values reflects, at the individual level, China's paradoxical struggle to compete and succeed in the modern world economy while at the same time maintaining the social traditions (the unique 'Chinese characteristics') that have preserved the unity of the country for over 2,000 years (Boisot and Child 1996).

Labour–management conflict resolution

The Chinese model of labour–management conflict resolution since 1949 has been based on a 'top-down' structure that was imported from the Soviet Union. Workers were enrolled in the only trade union that was permitted, namely the All-China Federation of Trade Unions (ACFTU) (Chan 1995). Most of its members were to be found in SOEs until recently. There was often no alternative to being a union member and there was widespread passivity rather than activism amongst workers.

Trade unions in the PRC have been for a long time, on paper at least, the largest in the world in terms of the numbers they recruit. These unions are mass organizations in Chinese communist parlance. They have currently over 103 million members in all, with their component parts belonging to the official state-sponsored union federation, in more than 586,000 primary trade union organizations.

No worker organization is allowed to organize outside its ranks. Independent unions may not freely organize; if they do, they are most likely to be suppressed. There is also no 'right to strike' and the hypothetical 'right' to do so was deleted from the Chinese Constitution in 1982; however, we find a complex arbitration and conciliation system for dealing with whatever disputes occur.

Since the rate of unionization varies between one SOE and another, one may rightly conclude that membership whilst socially encouraged is not mandatory. Indeed the trade union legislation of 1993 gives the worker scope to opt out. But, many of the state-owned plants have official union membership of as much as 100 per cent, with an average of 92 per cent found on many sites (Ding *et al.* 2002). It is also worth noting that only full-time urban industrial workers have normally been permitted to join unions over the last fifty years, as opposed to temporary workers or peasants.

The rate of unionization is very much lower in firms outside the state sector. It is higher in larger joint ventures but very limited in smaller foreign-invested enterprises (FIEs), as well as collective and private firms. Among rural private firms, trade unions are almost completely absent (IFC 2000). By contrast, urban private firms quite frequently choose to have a union within the company represent the interests of the workers when disputes arise, rather than allow the matter to be handled externally by a court or government agency. For the alternative runs the risk of inviting external interference. Some private firms, especially in Beijing, also consciously use labour unions and Communist Party organs to strengthen their management and to secure legitimacy for party members to work for a private capitalist.

The ACFTU members proclaim their ambitions to recruit the Chinese 'masses'. It is formally stipulated in the Constitution of the ACFTU, for example,

> that membership in trade unions is open to all manual and mental workers in enterprises, undertakings and offices inside China whose wages constitute their principal means of livelihood and who accept the Constitution of the Chinese Trade Unions irrespective of their nationality, race, sex, occupation, religious belief or educational background.
> (ACFTU Constitution 1993, Ng and Warner 1998)

The ACFTU was set up in 1925, organizing workers on industrial lines, although also with occupational groupings. After 1949, this set-up prevailed and was perpetuated in the Trade Union Law of 1950, the first in the Chinese communist state, which systematized the trade union structure, with the ACFTU designated as its highest body. It was designed on Leninist lines, as a 'transmission belt' between the Party and the 'masses', when it was set up after the Liberation. Trade union organizations, at least prima facie, may be said to have institutionalized the power of the workers as 'masters' (*zhuren*). They had the role of implementing labour–management relations in enterprises to boost production output; this was a persistent theme through most of the unions' existence in the PRC, including the present. They had an administrative as well as a representative function (Child *et al.* 1973). But they also provided adequate collective welfare services, and organized workers and staff in spare-time cultural and technical studies, vocational training and recreational activities. To this end, they had – and still retain – considerable funds to finance their activities, since enterprises deduct 2 per cent of payroll for ACFTU welfare and associated purposes. However, the unions were formally dismantled during the Cultural Revolution in 1966.

With the onset of the economic reforms at the end of the 1970s, the ACFTU was encouraged to promote economic development and maintain social stability (White 1996; Ng and Warner 1998). The trade unions were formally reintroduced in 1978, through the influence of Deng Xiaoping. They gradually built up their influence over the 1980s, helping to support the economic reforms. Today, their goals remain consistent with those laid down in 1950, at least on paper. It is worth noting that the 'right to work' is still included (unlike the 'right to strike') in its goals, although many Chinese workers are being 'downsized', particularly in the SOEs (Lee *et al.* 1999).

Worker representation, such as it was, was integrally linked with the above institutional framework of the 'iron rice-bowl', the 'jobs for life' and the 'cradle to the grave' welfare system found mainly in Chinese SOEs and urban collectives. Wages were centrally laid down under this pre-reform system; the pace of work was steady; dismissals were rare (Takahara 1992). Everyone there, it was said, ate 'out of one big pot' (*daguo fan*); incentives were minimal in many plants. But only about one in seven Chinese workers out of the huge workforce, whether urban or rural, enjoyed this protected status, some with greater protection than others.

Whether most Chinese workers were content with the labour status quo is hard to say. Social critics (Chan 2001) point to 'black holes' in labour standards, especially in FIEs in the coastal areas, such as those near Hong Kong. For many years, independent studies of living and working conditions were not possible. Those workers in the cities, particularly in public employment, appeared at least to have a relatively protected existence, with virtually lifetime employment in the system referred to above until recently. But life has changed in the last decade or so and the social costs of economic restructuring, as in other parts of Asia, are now being increasingly felt in the PRC (Warner 2002). Overstaffing is now being confronted by both government as well as corporate policy; downsizing and unemployment are now increasingly *de rigueur*.

Implications for managers

The implications of the shift from a centrally planned economy to market socialism so called and from the iron rice-bowl model to a more market-oriented one have been considerable for managers. Translating high-level macro-economic policy into micro-economic detail is no mean task but many key shifts have taken place. Before the early 1980s for instance, managers had very limited autonomy and managers and they could neither hire nor fire their workers. Like their employees, their performance was not linked to their effort; motivation was low; mobility was very restricted and, in many cases, non-existent. Today, all that has changed and managers have significantly expanded powers, but it did not occur at once. Over the 1980s and 1990s, China underwent a 'managerial revolution' (Warner 2000).

The enterprise and management reforms of 1984, the labour reforms of 1986, the personnel reforms of 1992 and so on were to prove to be major landmarks on the 'long march' to market-driven management. After these reforms of the 1980s and 1990s promoted by Deng Xiaoping, managers found their roles were made much more market driven. But more than strategy and structure changed: mind-sets also were radically transformed. Chinese managers became responsible for financial performance targets and could be more significantly rewarded if they did well. Some larger, formerly state-owned firms have been floated on the internal and external stock exchanges. Recently, there have even been a significant number of 'management buy-outs'.

The strong element of particularism in Chinese culture (Trompenaars 1993) has a practical significance for business transactions there in terms of who you know and the basis on which the relationship is understood to rest. This accounts for the considerable attention given to the notion of *guanxi* that captures this characteristic. It contrasts with universalism, which denotes that it is culturally appropriate to apply the same rules and standards whoever the person may be. Given the latitude that local officials generally enjoy in dealing with the foreign firms located within their purview, particularism adds considerably to the uncertainty that China presents as an environment for international business.

Now that China has committed itself to full engagement in international trade and investment through membership of the WTO, the question of how it will adjust to the competitive requirements for modern effective management has become even more pressing. While Chinese management values and behaviour have been importantly conditioned by the country's political and economic system, Chinese culture has also had an enduring influence and is today free of the active hostility it experienced under Maoism. The big issue has become the extent to which management in China will be fashioned according to international 'best practice' as opposed to following its own principles and practices.

Given the external competitive pressures to adopt new forms of organization such as teamwork (Child and McGrath 2001), it will be instructive to see whether Chinese cultural attributes help or hinder this process. As Chen *et al.* (2000) note, the collectivist orientation, importance of relationships and concern for harmony in Chinese culture might assist crucial aspects of teamwork such as a common purpose, task interdependence and a group orientation. On the other hand, the Confucian emphasis on rigid hierarchies and upward deference to leaders could maintain top-down control in a way that contravenes the essence and distinctive contribution of teamwork to processes such as innovation and learning.

Conclusions

It is clear that China has been shaped by its history and that in turn modern Chinese management has sprung from deep cultural roots, whatever the economic and institutional changes of the last half-century. We have seen in the above account that the Dengist reforms of the last two decades have changed the management system from one based on a command economy to one more market driven and with increased private ownership. However, Chinese people are quick to maintain that these changes have been given 'Chinese characteristics', implying that whatever the immediate institutional and organizational details, the underlying norms and values may reflect continuity as much as change.

In a rapidly changing and varied context such as contemporary China, it is very difficult to assess the degree to which traditional culture continues to exert an influence on management values and behaviour. Rather than attempt any definitive conclusions, it is more helpful to reiterate the issues and questions that we need to bear in mind when addressing this subject. First, we always have to recognize China's great diversity and start by asking 'to which China are we referring? Which sector, which region, which generation?' Second, what is taking place in China, keen to learn from the outside world yet also conscious of its history, may force us to abandon the notion that people necessarily conform to a simple notion of 'culture'. In these circumstances, they may not necessarily fit neatly at a single point along the cultural dimensions beloved of cross-cultural psychologists, but instead display an apparent paradox. We noted, for example, how studies of the values held by PRC managers suggest that those who have internalized certain 'Western' values such as *individualism* may at the same time continue to value traditional Confucian precepts such as *collective* loyalty and responsibility. The social identity of modern Chinese managers may be more complex than has generally been appreciated, requiring a cultural theory that is more complex and subtle than present formulations.

A third possibility deserving of further investigation is that Chinese managers, and perhaps people in general, are more flexible in their cultural referents than theorists such as Hofstede (1980; 1991) assume is normal for adults. Chinese people who are exposed to 'Western' values through their roles at work, or equally through their roles as consumers, may retain the option to segment their cultural mind-sets and switch between them. For instance, if conforming to certain Western norms and practices offers material attractions, such as higher pay in return for accepting individual responsibility for performance, then Chinese staff may decide to go along with them within the confines of their workplace roles. They may also be encouraged to accept practices imported from another culture if these are perceived to be part of a more comprehensive policy, justified as 'best international practice', offering other benefits such as equitable treatment, comprehensive training and good prospects for advancement. This is why employment with a multinational corporation's joint venture or subsidiary is usually highly prized by Chinese managers. At the same time, as they switch social identity in 'converting' to their non-work roles in the family and community, they could well revert to a more traditional Chinese cultural mind-set.

In short, China offers a challenging and fascinating arena for further exploration of the theoretical and practical issues associated with culture and management. Whether the future will lead to a degree of convergence is not the question; it is what will be the pace and ultimate limit of such change.

Notes

1   For definitions of 'culture', see Warner and Joynt (2002).
2   Confucian influences are interpreted here relatively broadly.
3   Subcultures include, for instance, regional, ethnic, as well as religious ones.
4   The role of *guanxi* has been given great prominence by most writers on contemporary Chinese culture but may be diminishing as market forces become more predominant.
5   The non-state sector has expanded relentlessly each year and will no doubt do so further with WTO entry.
6   This occurrence is also happening in the overseas Chinese communities; see the chapter on Hong Kong or Taiwan, for instance.

References

Becker, J. (1999) 'Fortune at China's fingertips', *South China Morning Post Saturday Review* 28 August: 1.

Boisot, M. and Child, J. (1996) 'From fiefs to clans and network capitalism: explaining China's emerging economic order', *Administrative Science Quarterly* 41(4): 600–28.

Bond, M. H. (ed.) (1996) *The Handbook of Chinese Psychology*, Hong Kong: Oxford University Press.

Cannon, T. and Jenkins, A. (eds) (1990) *The Geography of Contemporary China*, London: Routledge.

Chan, A. (1995) 'The emerging patterns of industrial relations in China and the rise of the two new labour movements', *China Information: A Quarterly Journal* 9(4): 36–59.

Chan, A. (2001) *China's Workers Under Assault*, Armonk, NY: M.E. Sharpe.

Chen, M (1995) *Asian Management Systems*, London: Routledge.

Chen, X., Bishop, J. W. and Dow, S. K. (2000) 'Teamwork in China: where reality challenges theory and practice', in J. T. Li, A. S. Tsui and E. Weldon (eds), *Management and Organizations in the Chinese Context*, Basingstoke: Macmillan, pp. 269–82.

Child, J. (1981) 'Culture, contingency and capitalism in the cross-national study of organizations', in L. L. Cummings and B. M. Staw (eds), *Research in Organizational Behavior*, 3: 303–56, Greenwich, CT: JAI Press.

Child, J. (1994) *Management in China During the Age of Reform*, Cambridge: Cambridge University Press.

Child, J. and McGrath, R. G. (2001) 'Organizations unfettered: organizational form in an information-intensive economy', *Academy of Management Journal* 44 (6): 1135–48.

Child, J. and Tse, D. K. (2001) 'China's transition and its implications for international business', *Journal of International Business Studies* 32(1): 5–21.

Child, J. and Yan, Y. (2001) 'National and transnational effects in international business', *Management International Review* 41(1): 53–75.

Child, J., Loveridge, R. and Warner, M. (1973) 'Towards an organizational study of trade unions', *Sociology* 7 (1): 71–91.

Child, J., Chung, L., Davies, H. and Ng, S.-H. (2000) *Managing Business in China*, Hong Kong: Hong Kong General Chamber of Commerce.

Chiu, C. H., Ting, K., Tso, G. F. K. and He, C. (1998) 'A comparison of occupational values between capitalist Hong Kong and socialist Guangzhou', *Economic Development and Cultural Change* 46(3): 144–51.

Dale, P. N. (1986) *The Myth of Japanese Uniqueness*, London: Croom Helm.

Ding, D. Z., Goodall, K. and Warner, M. (2002) 'The impact of economic reform on the role of trade unions in China', *International Journal of Human Resource Management* 13(3): 431–49.

Fairbank, J. K. (1987) *The Great Chinese Revolution, 1800–1985*, London: Chatto and Windus.

Fairbank, J. K. and Goldman, M. (1998) *China: A New History*, Cambridge, MA: Harvard University Press.

Farh, J.-L. and Cheng, B.-S. (2000) 'A cultural analysis of paternalistic leadership in Chinese organizations', in J. T. Li, A. S. Tsui and E. Weldon (eds), *Management and Organizations in the Chinese Context*, Basingstoke: Macmillan, pp. 84–127.

Faure, D. (2001) 'Beyond networking: an institutional view of Chinese business', Unpublished paper, Oriental Institute, University of Oxford.

Gernet, J. (1982) *A History of Chinese Civilization*, Cambridge: Cambridge University Press.

Gerth, H. H. and Mills, C. W. (eds) (1946) *From Max Weber: Essays in Sociology*, New York: Oxford University Press.

Guthrie, D. (1998) 'The declining significance of *Guanxi* in China's economic transition', *The China Quarterly* No. 154: 254–82.

He, P. (2002) *China's Search for Modernity: Cultural Discourse in the Late 20th Century*, Basingstoke: Palgrave.

Heffernan, K. and Crawford, J. (2001) 'The relationship between managerial values and the adoption of Western lifestyle practices in the People's Republic of China', Paper presented to the Australia and New Zealand Academy of Management (ANZAM) Conference, Auckland, December.

Hickson, D. J. and Pugh, D. S. (1995) *Management Worldwide: The Impact of Social Culture on Organizations Around the Globe*, London: Penguin.

Hofstede, G. (1980) *Culture's Consequences: International Differences in Work-Related Values*, London: Sage.

Hofstede, G. (1991) *Cultures and Organizations: Software of the Mind*, Maidenhead: McGraw-Hill.

IFC (International Finance Corporation) (2000) *China's Emerging Private Enterprises*, Washington, DC: IFC.

Keister, L. A. (2000) *Chinese Business Groups: The Structure and Impact of Interfirm Relations During Economic Development*, Hong Kong: Oxford University Press.

Lee, G. M., Wong, L. and Mok, K.-H. (1999) 'The decline of state-owned enterprises in China: extent and causes', Occasional Paper No. 2, City University of Hong Kong, December, 79pp.

Lin, Y.-M. and Zhu, T. (2001) 'Ownership restructuring in Chinese state industry: an analysis of evidence on initial organizational changes', *The China Quarterly*, No. 166 (June): 305–41.

Lockett, M. (1988) 'Culture and the problems of Chinese management', *Organization Studies* 9(4): 475–96.

Lu, X. and Perry, E. J. (eds) (1997) *Danwei: The Changing Chinese Workplace in Historical and Comparative Perspective*, Armonk, NY: M.E. Sharpe.

Luo, Y. (2000) *Guanxi and Business*, Singapore: World Scientific.

Luo, Y. (2002) 'Partnering with foreign firms: how do Chinese managers view the governance and importance of contracts? *Asia Pacific Journal of Management* 19(1): 127–51.

McGreal, I. (1995) *Great Thinkers of the Eastern World*, New York: HarperCollins.

Ng, S.-H. and Warner, M. (1998) *China's Trade Union and Management*, London: Macmillan.

Nolan, P. (2001) *China and the Global Business Revolution*, Basingstoke: Palgrave.

Orru, M., Biggart, N. W. and Hamilton, G. G. (eds) (1997) *The Economic Organization of East Asian Capitalism*, Thousand Oaks, CA: Sage.

Pleister, H. (1998) 'Organisational behaviour of township, village and private enterprises in China: a transactions approach', Unpublished PhD thesis, University of Hong Kong.

Pye, L. W. (1985) *Asian Power and Politics*, Cambridge, MA: Harvard University Press.

Ralston, D. A., Yu, K., Wang, X., Terpstra, R. H. and He, W. (1996) 'The cosmopolitan Chinese manager: findings of a study of managerial values across the six regions of China', *Journal of International Management* 2: 79–109.

Ralston, D. A., Van Thang, N. and Napier, N. K. (1999a) 'A comparative study of the work values of North and South Vietnamese managers', *Journal of International Business Studies* 30(4): 655–72.

Ralston, D. A., Egri, C. P., Stewart, S., Terpstra, R. H. and Yu Kaicheng (1999b) 'Doing business in the 21st century with the new generation of Chinese managers: a study of generational shifts in work values in China', *Journal of International Business Studies* 30(2): 415–28.

Redding, S. G. (1990) *The Spirit of Chinese Capitalism*, Berlin: de Gruyter.

Redding, S. G. (2002) 'The capitalist business system of China and its rationale', *Asia Pacific Journal of Management* 19(2/3): 221–249.

Roberts, K. H. (1970) 'On looking at an elephant: an evaluation of cross-cultural research related to organizations', *Psychological Bulletin* 74: 327–50.

Schurmann, F. (1966) *Ideology and Organization in Communist China*, Berkeley, CA: University of California Press.

Shenkar, O. and Ronen, S. (1987) 'The cultural context of negotiations: the implications of Chinese interpersonal norms', *Journal of Applied Behavioral Science* 23: 263–75.

Takahara, A. (1992) *The Politics of Wage Policy in Post-Revolutionary China*, London: Macmillan.

The Economist (2002a) 'George Bush, protectionist', 9 March: 13.

The Economist (2002b) 'Out of puff: a survey of China', 15 June: 1–16 (following p. 62).

Tolbert, P. S. and Zucker, L. G. (1996) 'The institutionalization of institutional theory', in S. R. Clegg, C. Hardy and W. R. Nord (eds), *Handbook of Organization Studies*, London: Sage, pp. 175–90.

Trompenaars, F. (1993) *Riding the Waves of Culture*, London: Economist Books.

Tse, D. K. and Chung, M.-L. (1999) 'New ownership forms in transitional economies: emergence, characteristics and performance of China's joint stock companies', Chinese Management Centre, University of Hong Kong Working Paper #1999–003–01, March.

Wang, X. (2002) 'The post-communist personality: the spectre of China's capitalist market reforms', *The China Journal* No. 47 (January): 1–17.

Wang, Z.-M. (1998) 'Team management conflict', in J. Selmer (ed.), *International Management in China: Cross-Cultural Issues*, London: Routledge, pp. 29–44.

Warner, M (1995) *The Management of Human Resources in Chinese Industry*, London: Macmillan.

Warner, M. (ed.) (2000) *Changing Workplace Relations in the Chinese Economy*, London: Macmillan.

Warner, M. (2002) 'Globalization, labour markets and human resources in Asia-Pacific economies: an overview', *International Journal of Human Resource Management* 13(3): 384–98.

Warner, M and Joynt, P. (eds) (2002) *Managing Across Cultures: Issues and Perspectives*, London: Thomson Learning.

Weber, M. (1964) *The Theory of Social and Economic Organization*, trans. A. M. Henderson and T. Parsons, New York: Free Press.

White, G. (1996) 'Chinese trade unions in the transition from socialism: towards corporatism or civil society?', *British Journal of Industrial Relations* 34(4): 433–57.

Whitley, R. D. (1992a) *Business Systems in East Asia*, London: Sage.

Whitley, R. D. (ed.) (1992b) *European Business Systems: Firms and Markets in their National Contexts*, London: Sage.

Xu, J. (1997) 'Managerial communication within a Chinese state-owned enterprise in a period of transition', Unpublished MPhil thesis, University of Hong Kong.

3 Culture and management in Hong Kong SAR

Jan Selmer and Corinna de Leon

Introduction

The Hong Kong Special Administrative Region (HKSAR) covers an area of 1,075 square kilometres south of the mainland of the People's Republic of China. Hong Kong is a modern, mostly urban metropolis that epitomizes a prosperous capitalist society. Currently, it has a population of 6.7 million, predominantly comprised of the Cantonese dialect group who originated from the adjacent province of Guangdong in Mainland China (Cheung and Chow 1999; Roberts 1992; Westlake 2001).

The industrialization of Hong Kong began in the late 1960s, as manufacturing concentrated first on textiles/clothing and later on electronics, watches, clocks and plastic goods. Beginning in the 1980s, many of these industries moved across the border at the New Territories of the SAR to take advantage of the lower costs on the mainland. Since the decline of manufacturing, the most important sectors of the Hong Kong economy have been financial services, regional trade services and tourism. Since 1983 to the present, the Hong Kong dollar has been linked to the US dollar at a fixed exchange rate of HK$7.80 (Westlake 2001).

The population has remained primarily focused on achieving and maintaining economic security within the family framework. Based on traditional Chinese values, the prosperity of the family remains the critical achievement not only for the present but also for future generations, obliging the individual's incessant economic contributions to the shared wealth (Lau 1982). Consequently, opportunistic entrepreneurialism has emerged as a distinct feature of the Hong Kong work culture.[1]

More than 150 years as a British colony exposed Hong Kong to the forces of Westernization. Hong Kong organizations have been subjected to increasing Western if not international influence, resulting in the adoption or adaptation of modern management techniques (Fosh *et al.* 1999). However, more indigenous approaches have not been replaced, as traditional cultural values have maintained the particularly Chinese business practices of Hong Kong (cf. Chen 1995; Redding 1990; Westwood 1992; Whitley 1992).

The historical setting and economic background form the framework for a description of the Hong Kong societal culture, from which the prevailing corporate culture is derived. Management behaviour and values are discussed, followed by an analysis of labour–management conflict resolution. Implications for practitioners are drawn and the main conclusions are presented, to conclude the chapter.

Historical setting

Hong Kong was first politically incorporated into China by the military conquests of the Qin (221–207 BC) and Han (206 BC to AD 220) Dynasties. During the crumbling Qing Dynasty, the UK forcibly seized Hong Kong as an imperial colony. The British accession of the territory proceeded in stages, such that the present-day HKSAR is comprised of three main geographical areas. In 1842, Victoria Island (Hong Kong) was acceded through the Treaty of Nanjing. The Kowloon peninsula was ceded by the Convention of Beijing in 1860. Comprising the area adjoining Kowloon and Mainland China as well as 235 outlying islands, the New Territories were leased to the UK for ninety-nine years by the Second Convention of Beijing in 1898. With the exception of the period of Japanese occupation from 1941 to 1945, Hong Kong was under British administration from 1842 to 1997 (Westlake 2001).

The population of the colony increased from about 33,000 in 1851 to 880,000 by 1931. The Civil War and communist victory in China in 1949 caused a further surge in the population of Hong Kong, which had increased to 2.2 million by 1955. However, the Japanese occupation wrought significant destruction in Hong Kong, as well as the flight or death of a large proportion of its population. Afterwards a desperate and chaotic situation was worsened as the population quadrupled through the influx of refugees from the Civil War in China (Westlake 2001).

As agreed in December 1984, the British government returned the whole territory of Hong Kong to Chinese sovereignty on 30 June 1997, at the end of the ninety-nine-year lease of the New Territories. Under the last British governor, Chris Patten, relations between China and the UK over Hong Kong seriously deteriorated with British attempts to institute democratic reforms. A shipping magnate whose family originated from Shanghai, Tung Chee-Hwa, became the first chief executive of the HKSAR in 1997 (Westlake 2001). In March 2002 Mr Tung was re-elected unopposed by the 800-member election committee appointed by the central Chinese government in Beijing, for his second five-year term which began in July 2002.

Traditionally, the government has sought to engage the local population in neither political process nor civic responsibilities. The government has consistently pursued a laissez-faire approach, adopting a stance of 'positive non-intervention'. Hong Kong is a prime example of free-market capitalism, with an extremely open economic system. The fiscal system may be described as minimalist, and most trade, financial and labour market activities are only weakly regulated.[2]

Economic background

During the first hundred years under British rule, Hong Kong replaced the nearby port–cities of Guangzhou and Shanghai as well as the Portuguese-administered Macau as the most important entrepôt that channelled trade between China and the West (Carney and Davies 2000; Westlake 2001). At this time, manufacturing was not a significant activity in Hong Kong. The initial phase of economic development came to an abrupt end with the Japanese occupation during 1941–5. Owing to the Korean War, a trade embargo on China was enforced by the USA and the UN, effectively preventing any resumption of the entrepôt function. By 1953, Hong Kong faced an apparently hopeless prospect with an impoverished population of 2.4 million of largely uneducated refugees from the Civil War in China, no natural resources apart from a harbour, and a very limited manufacturing base (Carney and Davies 2000).

The economy of Hong Kong was dominated by the hongs, large management service companies owned and managed by mainly British interests. These firms originally used Chinese or Eurasian compradors to manage transactions between themselves, and with Chinese businessmen and authorities. These non-Chinese organizations were relatively large, having substantial hierarchies staffed at senior levels by expatriates. The enterprises displayed significantly different organizational capabilities from the traditional Chinese trading businesses with which they dealt (Crisswell 1981).

The second phase of economic development was from 1953 to 1981, a period characterized by export-oriented manufacturing. Hong Kong's competitive advantage in exports was in providing low-cost labour-intensive products to foreign markets with low entry barriers. Employment in the manufacturing sector peaked from about 150,000 in 1953 to 1 million in 1981. The industrialization of Hong Kong was an extremely successful adaptation to the unstable environmental and social circumstances, and the flexibility and speed of market response was legendary (Carney and Davis 2000).

The manufacturing sector rapidly grew through the establishment of tens of thousands of new small firms rather than the expansion of existing organizations (Riedel 1974). These small firms were overwhelmingly Chinese family businesses, since large hongs had limited involvement with production operations and foreign direct investment in the manufacturing sector was negligible. The GDP during the initial period rose sharply from 1 per cent to 17 per cent and the average GDP between 1953 and 1981 was about 9.1 per cent per annum (Riedel 1988).

The third and current phase of economic development began in 1981. Some of the hongs have maintained their prominent participation in contemporary Hong Kong business: for example, Swire and Jardine's. Towards the end of the 1970s, there was widespread concern that Hong Kong's competitiveness in exports was being eroded by rising wages, lower costs in other Asian locations, and more protectionist policies in major markets. Senior government officials, academics and industry leaders advised Hong Kong manufacturers to move away from their traditional focus on cost leadership. It is widely believed that Hong Kong's future in export marketing lies in the manufacture of value-added products with enhancement of product design, the development of own brands, and improvement in marketing capabilities (Davies 1999). Considerable government resources have provided many incentives for the modernization of Hong Kong manufacturing, responding to the outcry from all business sectors. However, Hong Kong manufacturers in general have persisted in selling unsophisticated products at the lowest possible cost, with little marketing support (Carney and Davies 2000).

The opening of the Chinese economy in the late 1970s seriously hindered the upgrading of the manufacturing sector. Hong Kong firms found access to excessive supplies of inexpensive labour and land throughout China, at a time when these vital resources were increasingly unavailable in the small territory and population of Hong Kong. By transferring labour-intensive phases of the production to China, Hong Kong enterprises succeeded in maintaining their cost-leadership strategy in low-cost segments of foreign markets.

The success of Hong Kong's manufacturing sector lies in its legendary entrepreneurial adaptation, resulting from the autonomous responses of thousands of small firms to signals of pending market demands. Consequently, by largely avoiding the commercial pressure to develop new and different organizational capabilities, the rigidity of Hong Kong's production systems instead rapidly accelerated a major change in the economic structure (Lee and Davis 1995). The de-industrialization of Hong Kong began in the early 1980s, resulting in a fall in manufacturing employment from about 1 million workers to 400,000 in 1994 (Carney and Davies 2000).

Hong Kong business comprised mostly foreign-invested enterprises in the adjacent Guangdong Province, whose production output was destined almost entirely for export to third countries through Hong Kong. The large-scale transfer of the manufacturing base to Mainland China created new opportunities for other related activities in the Hong Kong service sector: for example, shipping, banking. In the present era, Hong Kong has returned to its historical role as an entrepôt, with manufacturing accounting for less than 13 per cent of GDP (Carney and Davies 2000).

At the beginning of 2002, the Hong Kong economy was in dire straits, largely due to the global business slowdown. The crash in the technology industry and the slow recovery of the US economy since September 2001 indicated that Hong Kong's slowdown was likely to continue, reversing its brief recovery from the Asian economic crisis of 1997–9. From a healthy 10.5 per cent in 2000, Hong Kong's economic growth has slowed to just 1.4 per cent in the first half of 2001 and the government lowered its full-year growth forecast to just 1 per cent (Westlake 2001). Unemployment has risen rapidly, reaching an all-time high of 7.0 per cent in the first quarter of 2002[3] (Cheung 2002).

Societal culture

As in other Chinese societies, Hong Kong has been deeply influenced by traditional Confucian values that emphasize family socialization, as noted in the chapter on China in this volume (Redding and Wong 1986). Chinese philosophy emphasises that one's conduct should always be within the norms of propriety (*Li*) and in conformity to a rigid hierarchy of social relations (*Wu-Lun*). Hong Kong has a collectivist culture that is characterized by a large power distance (Hofstede 1994) based on traditional patriarchal systems. The five cardinal virtues of Confucianism are loyalty, filial piety, faithfulness, caring and sincerity (Redding and Wong 1986).

As harmony is an essential element of Chinese culture, Hong Kong people consider the preservation of outward social unanimity to be their crucial obligation. In all relationships, there is the tendency to avoid extreme, disruptive behaviour. However, although there are elaborate mechanisms to prevent conflict, there are fewer social mechanisms for coping with and resolving conflict once it has emerged (Kirkbride and Westwood 1993).

Western cultures conceive of the individualistic self as associated with uniqueness, separateness, free will and self-determination. On the other hand, the Chinese notion of self connotes interconnections within the collective identity. Hong Kong people regard individuals as inseparable from membership of a distinct social group, and define themselves in direct reference to the communal situation in which they are entrenched (Kirkbride and Westwood 1993).

It is then not surprising that Hong Kong culture has been observed to be highly contextual, wherein events are interpreted with reference to the actual situation in which they occur (Hofstede 1994). Behaviours are evaluated as relative to the specific context and social relationship, not in view of abstract and universalistic principles. The high-context nature and the particularistic orientation have encouraged the strong sense of pragmatism that permeates contemporary Hong Kong culture (Trompenaars 1993).

The concept of 'face' is particularly significant in the ethnic Chinese societies in Asia. Hong Kong people are highly sensitive, in regard to their own and others' self-image, such that social conduct is directed towards gaining, protecting and giving face. Furthermore, Chinese culture can also be described as a 'shame' culture as opposed to the Western 'guilt' cultures. In Hong Kong, social behaviour is judged in terms of social approval or disapproval, whereby shame is experienced if one believes that others see one's behaviour as improper (Kirkbride and Westwood 1993; Snape *et al.* 1998).

The main characteristic of Hong Kong culture is a strong 'utilitarian' familism. The extended family unit or clan is still the most meaningful social structure, which also functions as the critical socio-economic unit. As the family is highly cohesive, in-group members are significantly differentiated from the out-group. As the individual identity is intertwined with kinship relations, a typical Hong Kong Chinese is family centred, materialistic, pragmatic, particularistic, adaptive and phlegmatic (Lau 1982).

As Hong Kong has a 'masculine' society (Hofstede 1994), economic security and material advancement are the prime motivators. Family members are obligated to contribute to the common good of the family by securing financial security and family wealth, both for current and future generations (Lau 1982). Even with the wide expansion of educational opportunities in recent years, tertiary education is given no more than instrumental value, merely the means to attain desired material ends. Wealth and financial independence are important status markers contributing to the prevalent culture of 'conspicuous consumption' in Hong Kong: for example, the obvious prevalence of luxury cars and status-laden goods.[4]

The concept of 'Chineseness' as a forceful determinant of behaviour persists in Hong Kong. Core assumptions and values rooted in the precepts of Taoism, Buddhism and especially Confucianism provide a distinctive cultural coherence. Priority is given to family/clan interests, authority is accepted without question, and a strong sense of obligation is followed in all relationships (Snape *et al.* 1998). Despite the global impact of modernization, the traditional values of the Hong Kong Chinese have shown remarkable persistence and continuity across time and place (cf. Bond 1986; Lim and Gosling 1983; Wang 1991).

Corporate culture

Hong Kong's corporate arena comprises three types of business organizations that are very different in nature. First, the locally based and mostly British-owned hongs are long-established, large trading and service conglomerates. Second, the multinational corporations and other businesses originating from the USA, Western Europe and Japan operate through local subsidiaries. Third, the typically small-scale family enterprise is the organizational structure that is widely prevalent in Hong Kong (Kirkbride and Westwood 1993).

Immigrant traders, merchants and entrepreneurs who escaped from the Civil War and communist takeover on the Chinese mainland in the late 1940s and early 1950s started most family-owned businesses in Hong Kong. The contemporary 'heroes' of Hong Kong society are the business tycoons who rose from impoverishment to acquire great fortunes through hard work and business acumen. In the fluid society, the greatest security rests in owning one's own business. Chinese-owned firms remain family dominated, including large and publicly traded organizations. Separation of ownership from control is not as frequent as in the Western corporate world.

The small-business sector in Hong Kong is characterized by an exceptionally large number of firms; for example, in 1992, Hong Kong had 618 firms per 10,000 people compared with 344 firms per 10,000 people in the USA (Cheah and Yu 1996). The start-up and failure rates are high, as it is common practice to close businesses which are no longer profitable, so as to establish immediately a new enterprise better able to meet a changing environment (Lau *et al.* 1999). The proliferation of small businesses in Hong Kong can partly be explained by the prevalent cultural values

The cultural imperatives in Hong Kong have several implications for the corporate culture. Social relationships are the crucial determinants of all forms of economic and organizational transactions. The family-owned business is the preferred mode for economic activity, as it facilitates the moral obligation to contribute to the financial stability and future prosperity of the family. The social ethic of harmony makes it imperative that family face is not damaged by overt conflict. Furthermore, family involvement and other social relationships facilitated the sharing and pooling of capital for diversification (Wang 1977). The ownership structure based on kinship eased the building up of business networks for securing supplies and increasing sales. The family provided a critical support that encouraged entrepreneurship, as collective responsibility decreased the fear of risk taking (Siu and Martin 1992).

The small, family-dominated business in Hong Kong has notable characteristics: simple corporate structure, short-term orientation, learning through imitation, extensive subcontracting system, and effective export orientation. Owing to the highly centralized organisation, decisions are made quickly and with much flexibility, enhancing the company's competitive advantage in fluid market conditions (Lau *et al.* 1999). However, it has been argued that family control provides an inherent limitation on the growth and size of organizations (Redding and Wong 1986). Also, it has been observed that family enterprises present several organizational problems: restricted management succession, inability to make long-term plans, lack of attention to human resource planning and development, and a dearth of loyalty from non-family members of the organization (Kirkbride and Westwood 1993).

The high level of pragmatism in Hong Kong has promoted the adoption of management and organizational practices from around the world as well as openness to new technologies, new work methods and new systems of trade. This has infused vibrancy to the economic system and lent considerable flexibility to organizational form and management systems. As pragmatism and materialism remain the major stimuli for entrepreneurial activity, a family-owned and family-managed business is the prime aspiration of many in Hong Kong (Westwood *et al.* 1999).

Managerial behaviour

Legitimized by traditional cultural values still prevalent in modern Hong Kong, the hierarchical and patriarchal relationships of the family are replicated in the organizational structures. Chinese family-owned enterprises are highly centralized organizations, wherein all subordinates are required to be deferential and obedient to their superiors. The leadership style is generally described as 'paternalistic headship' (Westwood 1997) or 'benevolently autocratic' (Redding 1990).

Chief executives of organizations have a status, role and function that are similar to those of a family head, resulting in high levels of authoritarian decision making and collective responsibility. Hong Kong bosses practise delegation infrequently, restricting staff autonomy and discretion. Superiors make an effort to be distant and aloof, but are person centred at the same time. Wielding considerable power and authority, senior managers are also expected to guarantee the welfare of all organizational members.

Chinese collectivism delineates an intense need to sustain harmonious relationships. In Hong Kong much effort is invested in establishing, maintaining and expanding social networks, both within and outside organizations. Business relationships are facilitated by and often dependent upon *guanxi*, a notion that pertains to the reciprocal trust that is developed over time. *Guanxi* relationships are diffuse rather than specific, emphasizing the social rules of favours and their return, reciprocity and mutual obligation over time (Trompenaars 1993). Such established relationships are not confined to a particular context, but persist across time and extend across situations. *Guanxi* is diffuse, indicating that work is not easily separable from the family or other social activity. Hong Kong people are apparently prepared to engage in work-related activities at any time and in any place, especially if such would secure the prosperity of the family business (Fosh *et al.* 1999).

The family control of businesses often results in the exclusion of professional managers and technical expert staff from top executive positions. Traditionally, small firms adopt a simple structure with no or few horizontal divisions, enhancing direct face-to-face supervision by the owner–manager (King and Leung 1975.) Chinese management practices involve low formalization, since family members exert personal control and are reluctant to place outsiders in key positions (Whitley 1992).

Hong Kong employers have been criticized as backward in human resource management techniques, mainly because of the little investment in training and staff development (Kirkbride and Tang 1990). It has been suggested that the lack of sustained and encompassing efforts at human resource development poses a serious threat to the long-term growth potential of Hong Kong (Rowley and Fitzgerald 2000b; Selmer 2001). As in the West, there is controversy as to whether the adaptation of Japanese-style management practices can be successfully implemented widely in the Hong Kong cultural context (Kirkbride and Tang 1994; Fukuda 1993). On the other hand, since the 1980s there has been increasing use of management innovations such as quality circles, total quality management and corporate culture change initiatives. Furthermore, despite the reluctance of employers to make substantial investments in human resource development, there is evidence that Hong Kong is developing better-educated and more professional managers, if only through the growing interest among Hong Kong executives for self-development (Fosh et.al., 1999).

Managerial values

Viewing the very modern, urban cityscape of Hong Kong in which global trade and services operate, one may easily conclude that its society has become largely Westernised. Evidently, the Hong Kong mentality is an amalgamation of traditional Chinese values with the modern cultural dynamics fostered by a colonial history and a capitalist economy (Bond 1986; Lau and Kuan 1988). However, the Hong Kong Chinese are able cognitively and emotionally to separate modernization from Westernization. Remaining Sino-centric, they regard themselves as contemporary citizens of the world, without compromising their ethnic roots (Bond and King 1985; Kirkbride and Westwood 1993). The cosmopolitan sophistication of HKSAR inhabitants is deceptive, because the Westernized demeanour is simply a pragmatic overlay on characteristically Chinese mentality and behaviour

Western cultures view time as linear and monochronic, whereas the Chinese notion of time is polychronic and cyclical. As there is little separation between past and present, some Hong Kong managers may rather stress the completion of transactions whenever convenient rather than at the deadline. Again, they are less likely to engage in formal planning and detailed scheduling than their Western counterparts (Kirkbride and Westwood 1993).

Western managers tend to view control and coordination abstractly and impersonally, guided by formal systems. In their high-context culture, Hong Kong managers may choose to regard control and coordination in terms of the specific situation, taking into consideration the particular circumstances and social relationships (Kirkbride and Westwood 1993). Hong Kong managers exercise control and coordination by emphasizing the obligations of the person and the importance of *guanxi*, as well as by utilizing implicit mechanisms of conformity. It has been argued that because of a lack of a structured time frame, there is a greater need for centralized control and increased reliance on particularistic/personalistic methods of coordination (Redding 1980).

Hong Kong culture abides by Chinese norms of propriety and emphasizes hierarchical relations and Confucian virtues. Managers who perform their roles in accordance with these precepts can expect to have their authority accepted and legitimized. Chinese organizations encompass an elaborate but informal system of behavioural norms, in which mutual expectations and obligations maintain order (Kirkbride and Westwood 1993). This reduces the need for more explicit, formal and impersonal control systems in Chinese organizations (Redding and Wong 1986).

The self that is defined always in relation to others presents implications for managerial values in Hong Kong. Since self-actualization and individual achievement may be less meaningful in a Chinese culture, such Westernized notions may have little impact on reward systems as well as training and development in Hong Kong (Kirkbride and Westwood 1993). 'Losing face' is a social sanction of the highest order, representing a major threat for regulating social behaviour.

As uncertainty avoidance among the Hong Kong Chinese is low, the transitory and fluid nature of the society evidently has predisposed Hong Kong people to have a high tolerance for ambiguity (Hofstede 1980, 1994). They easily accommodate work settings in which organizational flexibility is considered a premium and work formalization is minimal (Kirkbride and Westwood 1993). Such predispositions may explain the versatility of Hong Kong business as well as the pragmatic entrepreneurship that are the basis of its economy. Furthermore, as time orientation in the culture tends towards the long term, Hong Kong managers and workers are able to defer rewards and gratification, to persist in specific tasks, and to be thrifty in their economic activity (Hofstede 1994; Hofstede and Bond 1988). Evidently, the persistence of Chinese cultural imperatives provides the foundation for the legendary work ethic of the Hong Kong Chinese.

It is then understandable that a Hong Kong manager may seek to optimize harmony at the expense of organizational efficiency (Hofstede 1994; Hofstede and Bond 1988). Protecting one's face may cause conflict avoidance, an unwillingness to surface important issues, and a fear of criticism. Managers in Hong Kong must be mindful of the implications of face and shame in all interactions. For example, Hong Kong Chinese managers tend to avoid openly criticizing their subordinates as well as taking disciplinary action, because of the implications of face and shame (Kirkbride and Westwood 1993; Snape *et al.* 1998).

Pragmatism is a Chinese core value, and the tendency towards the particularistic (as opposed to the universalistic) is enhanced in Hong Kong managerial values. Such a pragmatic orientation may have serious implications for control systems, manager–employee relations, selection and performance evaluation (Kirkbride and Westwood 1993). Less likely than their Western counterparts to apply objective standardized systems, Hong Kong managers tend to regard events on 'a case-by-case basis', whereby the specific merits of the particular social relationship are considered first before any moralistic argument. The practice of nepotism is derived from Hong Kong managers' particularistic framework that justifies such actions as socially acceptable

The cultural value of collectivism, widely prevalent in Hong Kong society, may provide some limitations for the transferability of Western managerial practices. In a Western work context, the individual is the focus for the design of jobs, standard and target setting, performance evaluation, rewards allocation and motivational techniques. These may not be applicable even in the modernized society of Hong Kong where people subordinate their personal gain to the family's prosperity and persist in their loyalty to the collective in exchange for security and protection (Kirkbride and Westwood 1993).

The distinct hierarchical tenets of Chinese society have been directly transferred to the organizational context. Authority is accepted with little question, and the norm prohibits challenging one's superiors. The legitimate power of management is highly centralized among Hong Kong Chinese, even in large organizations. Consequently, lower ranking mangers are left with little discretion and initiative, and their contributions to organizational success is limited by their restricted participation in decision making. Furthermore, senior managers show little tendency to share information or objectives with subordinates, and show little enthusiasm for horizontal organizational structures (Redding and Casey 1976).

Labour–management conflict resolution

Owing to the low uncertainty avoidance of their culture, Hong Kong people adapt easily to rapid changes in the work environment (Fosh *et al.* 1999). Workers appreciate the free labour market in which they can trade their skills with relatively few inhibitions. Since performance is typically assessed subjectively, employees tend to pattern their work behaviour according to their surmise of their superior's implicit expectations. Traditionally, there is not much formal recognition of or even informal praise for good work (Westwood *et al.* 1999). The authoritarian management style in Hong Kong extends beyond the family business sector, such that most employers usually resist unionization and employee participation schemes (Fosh *et al.* 1999).

The colonial British government introduced a steady flow of regulations to improve industrial safety, as well as to provide a range of benefits for workers. In Hong Kong, laws promulgate severance pay, compulsory rest days and paid holidays, compensation for injured workers, and measures to protect women and young people (Turner *et al.* 1980). In contrast, the colonial administration took a non-interventionist approach to wage determination, following its laissez-faire policies for industrial development. As such, there is no legal framework for collective bargaining, no centralized wage structures, no legally binding collective agreements, no minimum wage and no unemployment insurance (Chow and Ng 1992; Ng *et al.* 1997). In the strongly capitalist economy, the high power distance of Hong Kong society leads to the widespread acceptance of large disparities in wealth and wage differentials (Fosh *et al.* 1999).

The right to seek redress for unfair dismissal was introduced only in 1997 during the last few days of British rule, since the colonial administration had earlier ignored union pleas for the employment protection of workers on strike. Without legal support for workers' demands and hindered by the prevalent hostility of employers towards trade unions, collective bargaining in Hong Kong is rare, occurring in less than 5 per cent of the private-sector workforce. Although public-sector employees and those in a few large private-sector companies are covered by joint consultation arrangements, most of the private sector has no formal mechanism for employee representation (Fosh *et al.* 1999).

The weakness of the trade unions and the predominance of unsympathetic employers have contributed to a low level of industrial conflict in Hong Kong. However, workers' dissatisfaction may simply be unexpressed and injustices may be largely ignored. The absence of effective workplace representation means that there are few opportunities for ordinary employees to make their opinions known to their superiors, short of voicing complaints on an individual basis in person. Owing to Chinese cultural imperatives, a Hong Kong employee may prefer to suffer in silence or perhaps just quit the job (Fosh *et al.* 1999).

Trade unions in Hong Kong have been fragmented throughout its history. The average union membership is about a thousand workers, and many unions are much smaller. The weakness of the trade unions has been attributed to the modest size of businesses in the private sector, to an alleged cultural resistance among Hong Kong workers to join trade unions, as well as to employer' general hostility towards union activities. Many of the unions are affiliated to three main federations: the pro-democracy Hong Kong Confederation of Trade Unions (CTU), the Beijing-oriented Federation of Trade Unions (FTU) and the Taiwan-oriented Trades Union Congress (TUC). In view of their limited effectiveness in employment terms and conditions, trade unions in Hong Kong have usually emphasized other advantages to potential members, such as the direct provision of welfare benefits and other services (Snape and Chan 1999).

Consequently, there is no apparent trade union presence in most workplaces in the private sector. The conventional view is that industrial relations are characteristically non-problematic, as overt conflict is minimized by the resolution of grievances on an individual, face-to-face basis. On the few occasions that industrial conflict does occur, the Hong Kong government provides a voluntary conciliation service for employees and employers. 'Disputes' refer to collective grievances that involve more than twenty employees. 'Claims' usually emanate from a breach of the employment contract or an alleged failure to follow the requirements of the Employment Ordinance that affects an individual or a small number of employees (Snape and Chan 1999).

As Hong Kong employees do not express their complaints, disputes and claims rarely become overt grievances that threaten the working relationship. Hence, industrial conflict usually occurs at the termination of employment due to cessation of business or insolvency, where the objective is to secure unpaid wages or other conditions mandated by the Employment Ordinance. The overwhelming majority of disputes occur in the manufacturing, construction and restaurant/hotel sectors as a result of business closures, relatively small workplaces and relatively low union density. The Labour Department conciliators often assist employees in these sectors who do not have effective representation and dispute-resolution procedures at their workplace (Snape and Chan 1999).

Hong Kong trade unions face an uncertain future, hindered by unfriendly employers who are reluctant to recognize them as negotiating partners. Furthermore, the HKSAR government has shown its commitment to policies and practices which are strongly pro-business. It should be noted that the constitutional tenets embodied in the SAR Basic Law provide for freedom of association, and the relative autonomy of Hong Kong from the rest of China provides some latitude for independent trade unions. However, it is clear that the development of industrial relations in Hong Kong will depend on the pattern of economic development and on the direction of government labour market policies that will evolve in the future. The trade unions themselves are in a position to chart their destiny, mainly through their commitment to pursuing job-based functions more vigorously than before and to demand effectively better employment conditions for their members (Snape and Chan 1999).

Implications for managers

Although the HKSAR is striving towards further economic development, it is difficult to foresee the outlook for business structures in general and management in particular. Although the characteristics of manufacturing firms remain the same as in the 1950s, the very attributes that make these organizations successful at present are inconsistent with innovation. The ability to shift rapidly from one supplier or customer to another can be regarded as a strength, but such a practice prevents the development of long-term relationships required for continuous innovation. Although close monitoring of cheap labour reduces production costs as well as increasing speed and flexibility of delivery, it also limits workers' opportunities for learning new skills. Furthermore, innovation needs 'patient money', and such a long-term view on the uncertain returns of large investments is not usually found in Hong Kong where quick turn-key operations are more common. Research and development requires investment in specialized assets, the placement of trust in technical experts and the development of close links with the most sophisticated customers, all of which are inconsistent with the objectives and actions of Hong Kong firms (Davies 1999).

Accordingly, Hong Kong businesses are not likely to shift towards high-technology manufacturing, making it improbable that the HKSAR will become a 'world class industrial power' (as recommended by Berger and Lester 1997: xiii). Since current trends most likely will persist, the characteristics of the traditional entrepôt system will remain as the most remarkable feature of the economy, increasingly reliant on a trade-related service sector which responds continually to changing market signals. There may be tens of thousands of tiny family enterprises that add volume to the manufacturing output of Mainland China, but such small businesses will become dysfunctional where there are economies of scale. Therefore, they may continue to operate in the transport infrastructure, communication networks and financing systems provided by the HKSAR government, MNCs, and the few large Hong Kong firms as well as Mainland China (Davies 1999).

What are the managerial implications of the peculiar circumstances that have emerged for Hong Kong? It is important to determine whether the low-skill, low-value manufacturing that migrated from Hong Kong to Mainland China has been replaced with more improved productive employment. A crucial area for human resources management in Hong Kong is the supply of necessary labour through training and education (Rowley and Fitzgerald 2000b). Although the demand for technicians and professionals is increasing, gaps between supply and demand in human resources are widening, especially in trade, retailing and services. Despite efforts to expand tertiary education, Hong Kong will most probably continue to suffer a shortfall in qualified personnel (Lee 2000).

Corporate strategies may need to take into serious consideration the varying attitudes to organizational commitment of Hong Kong employees, if the investment in human resource development is to be fully utilized. Whereas Westerners view their firms as a collection of people, systems and opportunities, the Chinese typically perceive organizational commitment through personal relationships and social networks. Large domestic or multinational enterprises have more opportunities for skills upgrading, empowerment and technology development (Wheaton 2000). Undeniably, business success is determined to a large extent by the policies and practices in human resource management, which foster the long-term loyalty and commitment of Hong Kong Chinese managers and workers (Wong and Hendry 2000).

Conclusions

More than ever before in its history, Hong Kong is at a crossroads. Its internationally impressive economic record is under threat. The factors and structures that had induced rapid growth in the past may now inhibit further economic development. It seems imperative that Hong Kong has to develop alternative means of achieving competitive advantage, including improvements in production and upgrading of human resources. Although innovation is a common theme in much of Asia, it can be argued that Hong Kong has to excel especially in product and service quality. As telecommunications and transportation swiftly modernize in China, the competitiveness of the HKSAR cannot simply rely on its geographical proximity to the mainland. It can be argued that the territory's success now lies in providing highly skilled human resources (Rowley and Fitzgerald 2000a).

The scenario for Hong Kong's prospective development includes its breaking away from influential traditions that have been the proven way to success. Resistance to fundamental changes in work and management is the straitjacket that binds Hong Kong to the fading glory of its past. Indeed, as Hong Kong needs new ideas for tackling unforeseen challenges, a knowledge-based economy would be critical. Advancements in knowledge would be essential if Hong Kong were to provide services that add value to the manufacturing output of the Chinese mainland.

Comprehensive and drastic development of human resources may initiate and maintain structural changes required for Hong Kong's survival and prosperity. Certainly, the traditionally laissez-faire government has a distinctive role to play here. Larger investment and less restrictive policies on education in general are obviously the most facile action that can be taken by the government. In particular, improving the scope and quality of business and management education may be helpful. However, the driving force for a knowledge economy has to be the numerous small firms that comprise the backbone of Hong Kong business, which should bridge the human resources gap with extensive programmes on skills upgrading, empowerment and technology development.

Notes

1 This phenomenon may also be shared with other Nanyang overseas Chinese enclaves; see Chapters 10 and 12, on Singapore and Taiwan, in this volume.
2 The nature of Hong Kong's special status has helped preserve its free-market status but by the fifth anniversary of the Handover in 2002 there were anxieties about growing mainland 'interference'.
3 The decline of exports to the weakening US market in 2002 raised further anxieties about a further rise in unemployment.
4 Hong Kong remains a sizeable market for French luxury brands, for example, well beyond its relatively small population base.

References

Berger, S. and Lester, R. K. (eds) (1997) *Made by Hong Kong*, Hong Kong: Oxford University Press.

Bond, M. H. (1986) *The Psychology of the Chinese People*, Hong Kong: Oxford University Press.

Bond, M. H. and King, A. Y. C. (1985) 'Coping with the threat of Westernization in Hong Kong', *International Journal of Intercultural Relations* 9: 351–64.

Carney, M. and Davies, H. (2000) 'From entrepot to entrepot via merchant manufacturing: adaptive mechanisms, organizational capabilities and the structure of the Hong Kong economy', in C. Rowley and R. Fitzgerald (eds), *Managed in Hong Kong: Adaptive Systems, Entrepreneurship and Human Resources*, London: Frank Cass, pp. 13–32.

Cheah, H. B. and Yu, T. F. L. (1996) 'Adaptive response: entrepreneurship and competitiveness in the economic development of Hong Kong', *Journal of Enterprising Culture* 4(3): 241–66.

Chen, M. (1995) *Asian Management Systems*, London: Routledge.

Cheung, C.-F. (2002) 'Jobless rate at record high of 7pc.', *South China Morning Post* 19 April: 1.

Cheung, G. W. and Chow, I. H.-s. (1999) 'Subcultures in Greater China: a comparison of managerial values in the People's Republic of China, Hong Kong, and Taiwan', *Asia Pacific Journal of Management* 16: 369–87.

Chow, K. K. and Ng, S. H. (1992) 'Trade unions, collective bargaining and associated rights: the case of Hong Kong', *Hong Kong Law Journal* 22(3): 293–318.

Crisswell, C. (1981) *The Taipans: Hong Kong's Merchant Princes*, Hong Kong: Oxford University Press.

Davies, H. (1999) 'The future shape of hong kong's economy: why high-technology manufacturing will prove to be a myth', in P. Fosh, A. W. Chan, W. W. S. Chow, E. Snape and R. Westwood (eds), *Hong Kong Management and Labour: Change and Continuity*, London: Routledge, pp. 43–58.

Fosh, P., Ng, C., Snape, E. and Westwood, R. (1999) 'Hong Kong At the end of the twentieth century: management and labour trends', in P. Fosh, A. W. Chan, W. W. S. Chow, E. Snape and R. Westwood (eds), *Hong Kong Management and Labour: Change and Continuity*, London: Routledge, pp. 3–24.

Fukuda, K. J. (1993) *Japanese Management in East Asia and Beyond*, Hong Kong: Chinese University Press.

Hofstede, G. (1980) *Culture's Consequences: International Differences in Work-Related Values*, Beverly Hills, CA: Sage.

Hofstede, G. (1994) *Cultures and Organisations: Intercultural Cooperation and its Importance for Survival*, London: HarperCollins.

Hofstede, G. and Bond, M. H. (1988) 'The Confucius connection: from cultural roots to economic growth', *Organizational Dynamics* 17: 4–21.

King, A. Y. C. and Leung, D. H. K. (1975) 'The Chinese touch in small industrial organisations', Social Research Centre, the Chinese University of Hong Kong.

Kirkbride, P. S. and Tang, S. F. Y. (1990) 'Personnel management: challenges and prospects for the 1990s', *The Hong Kong Manager* March/April: 3–11.

Kirkbride, P. S. and Tang, S. F. Y. (1994) 'From Kyoto to Kowloon: cultural barriers to the transference of quality circles from Japan to Hong Kong', *Asia Pacific Journal of Human Resources* 32(2): 100–11.

Kirkbride, P. S. and Westwood, R. I. (1993) 'Hong Kong', in R. B. Peterson (ed.), *Managers and National Culture: A Global Perspective*, Westport, CT: Quorum Books.

Lau, S.-K. (1982) *Society and Politics in Hong Kong*, Hong Kong: Chinese University Press.

Lau, S.-K. and Kuan, H.-c. (1988) *The Ethos of the Hong Kong Chinese*, Hong Kong: Chinese University Press.

Lau, T., Chan, K. F. and Man, T. W. Y. (1999) 'Entrepreneurial and managerial competencies: small business owner/managers in Hong Kong', in P. Fosh, A. W. Chan, W. W. S. Chow, E. Snape and R. Westwood (eds), *Hong Kong Management and Labour: Change and Continuity*, London: Routledge, pp. 220–36.

Lee, J. and Davies, H. (1995) 'Transforming Hong Kong: from manufacturing to service', in H. Davies (ed.), *China Business: Context and Issues*, Hong Kong: Longman Hong Kong, pp. 22–36.

Lee, S. K. V. (2000) 'The demand for business and management education in Hong Kong beyond 1997', in C. Rowley and R. Fitzgerald (eds), *Managed in Hong Kong: Adaptive Systems, Entrepreneurship and Human Resources*, London: Frank Cass, pp. 56–72.

Lim, L. and Gosling, P. (1983) *The Chinese in Southeast Asia*, Vols 1 and 2, Singapore: Maruzen Asia.

Ng, S. H., Stewart, S. and Chan, F. T. (1997) *Current Issues of Workplace Relations and Management in Hong Kong*, Hong Kong: Hong Kong Centre of Asian Studies, University of Hong Kong.

Redding, S. G. (1980) 'Cognition as an aspect of culture and its relation to management processes: an exploratory view of the Chinese case', *Journal of Management Studies* 17: 127–48.

Redding, S. G. (1990) *The Spirit of Chinese Capitalism*, Berlin: Walter de Gruyter.

Redding, S. G. and Casey, T. W. (1976) 'Managerial beliefs among Asian managers', in R. L. Taylor, M. J. O'Connell, R. A. Zawacki and D. D. Warwick (eds), *Proceedings of the Academy of Management 36th Annual Meeting*, Kansas City: Academy of Management, p. 355.

Redding, S. G. and Wong, G. (1986) 'The psychology of Chinese organisational behaviour', in M. H. Bond (ed.), *The Psychology of the Chinese People*, Hong Kong: Oxford University Press.

Riedel, J. (1974) *The Industrialization of Hong Kong*, Tubingen: J.C.B. Mohr.

Riedel, J. (1988) 'Economic development in East Asia: doing what comes naturally?', in H. Hughes (ed.), *Achieving Industrialization in East Asia*, Cambridge: Cambridge University Press, pp. 1–38.

Roberts, D. (ed.) (1992) *Hong Kong 1992: A Review of 1991*, Hong Kong: Government Information Services.

Rowley, C. and Fitzgerald, R. (2000a) 'Hong Kong's development: prospects and possibilities', in C. Rowley and R. Fitzgerald (eds), *Managed in Hong Kong: Adaptive Systems, Entrepreneurship and Human Resources*, London: Frank Cass, pp. 123–31.

Rowley, C. and Fitzgerald, R. (2000b) 'Managed in Hong Kong: economic development, competitiveness and deindustrialization', in C. Rowley and R. Fitzgerald (eds), *Managed in Hong Kong: Adaptive Systems, Entrepreneurship and Human Resources*, London: Frank Cass, pp. 1–12.

Selmer, J. (2001) 'Review of *Managed in Hong Kong: Adaptive Systems, Entrepreneurship and Human Resources*, Rowley, C. and Fitzgerald, R. (eds.), London: Frank Cass Publishers, 2000', *ASEAN Economic Bulletin* 18(2): 247–9.

Siu, W. S. and Martin, R. G. (1992) 'Successful entrepreneurship in Hong Kong', *Long Range Planning* 25(6): 87–93.

Snape, E. and Chan, A. (1999) 'Hong Kong trade unions: in search of a role', in P. Fosh, A. W. Chan, W. W. S. Chow, E. Snape and R. Westwood (eds), *Hong Kong Management and Labour: Change and Continuity*, London: Routledge, pp. 255–70.

Snape, E., Thompson, D., Yan, F. K.-C. and Redman, T. (1998) 'Performance appraisal and culture: practice and attitudes in Hong Kong and Great Britain', *International Journal of Human Resource Management* 9(5): 841–61.

Trompenaars, F. (1993) *Riding the Waves of Culture: Understanding Cultural Diversity in Business*, London: Nicholas Brealy.

Turner, H. A., Fosh, P., Gardner, M., Hart, K., Morris, R., Ng, S. H., Quinlan, P. and Yerbury, D. (1980) *The Last Colony: But Whose? A Study of the Labour Movement, Labour Market and Labour Relations in Hong Kong*, Cambridge: Cambridge University Press.

Wang, G. (1991) *China and the Overseas Chinese*, Singapore: Times Academic Press.

Wang, S. H. (1977) 'Family structure and economic development', *Bulletin of the Institute of Ethnology* 44: 1–11.

Westlake, M. (2001) *Asia 2002 Yearbook*, Hong Kong: Far Eastern Economic Review.

Westwood, R. I. (1992) *Organisational Behaviour: Southeast Asian Perspectives*, Hong Kong: Longman.

Westwood, R. I. (1997) 'Harmony and patriarchy: the cultural basis for 'paternalistic headship' among the overseas Chinese', *Organization Studies* 18(3): 445–80.

Westwood, R., Leung, A. S. M. and Chiu, R. K. (1999) 'The meaning of work: the reconfiguration of work and working in Hong Kong and Beijing', in P. Fosh, A. W. Chan, W. W. S. Chow, E. Snape and R. Westwood (eds), *Hong Kong Management and Labour: Change and Continuity*, London: Routledge, pp. 127–50.

Wheaton, A. (2000) 'The generation of organisational commitment in a cross-cultural context', in C. Rowley and R. Fitzgerald (eds), *Managed in Hong Kong: Adaptive Systems, Entrepreneurship and Human Resources*, London: Frank Cass, pp. 73–103.

Whitley, R. (1992) *Business Systems in East Asia: Firms, Markets and Societies*, London: Sage.

Wong, M. M. L. and Hendry, C. (2000) 'Comparing international human resource practices between Yaohan and Jusco in Hong Kong', in C. Rowley and R. Fitzgerald (eds), *Managed in Hong Kong: Adaptive Systems, Entrepreneurship and Human Resources*, London: Frank Cass, pp. 104–22.

4 Culture and management in India

Pawan S. Budhwar

Introduction

This chapter discusses India in terms of its historical development as well as its economy, societal and corporate culture, management behaviour and values and various conflict resolution techniques appropriate to the Indian context. Finally, key conclusions are drawn regarding the direction in which the Indian economy and firms operating in India are heading.

During its independence in 1947, India was among the two most industrialized nations in Asia (Venkata Ratnam 1992). There were no 'Tigers' or 'Dragons' at that time and even the quality of Japanese goods was of poor quality. At that time, India was a state-regulated economy and adopted a 'mixed economy' approach – emphasizing both private and public enterprise (Datt and Sundharam 2001). This step had the effect of reducing both entrepreneurship and global competitiveness – both necessary for national growth. It also hindered the optimum utilization of India's immense resources – both natural and human. Such an approach proved to be the main obstacle in India's economic development. This was further supplemented by the existence of strong internal labour markets (ILMs) based more on social relationships then rationalized and formal human resource management (HRM) systems (see Budhwar and Khatri 2001a). In order to re-establish itself as an economic force in the region, India was forced to liberalize its economic policies in 1991 (see Venkata Ratnam 1995). It initiated a move towards the adoption of the 'free-market economy' model from the established 'state-regulated model'. This shift created not only great opportunities for foreign businesses but also serious challenges for local businesses to survive and flourish. In such competitive conditions, Indian firms were forced to adopt a more professional approach to the management of their human resources (HRs).[1] Evidence in this regard is now emerging from various sources such as research, company and government reports and from various professional bodies (see for example Ghoshal *et al.* 2001). Still it is too early to generalize such a trend. The next section discusses the historical setting of India.

Historical setting

Perhaps one of the most ancient nations, India has a continuous and documented history from about 2000 BC (see Husain 1992). The name India is derived from *Sindhu* (Indus), the great river of the north-west. Since ancient times India has been invaded by foreigners, starting from 1500–1200 BC by the Aryans from Central Asia and later on by Alexander the Great in 325 BC, Genghis Khan, the Mongol, in AD 1221, the Moguls in the fifteenth century and the British in the eighteenth century. India is the birthplace of three of the world's main religions, namely Hinduism (about 7000 years BC), Buddhism (487 BC) and Sikhism (AD 1699). These three religions have significantly impacted the social, political and economic landscape of the country. Despite such a long history, India was only first reached by a Westerner by sea in 1498, namely the Portuguese explorer Vasco Da Gama (Thomas and Philip 1994).

The British entered India in 1603 with the establishment of the East India Company. The Company established its rule in the states of Bengal and Bihar in 1757 after the Battle of Plassey. After successfully putting down the famous revolt of 1857 by Indian nationalists, the East India Company was replaced by the British Crown (see Budhwar 2001). India obtained independence from the British in 1947. In the same year Pakistan was formed and Jawahr Lal Nehru was elected as the first Prime Minister of India. About 1 million lives were lost in communal violence during the partition. Mahatma Gandhi (the father of the nation) was assassinated in 1948. On 26 January 1950, India formed her new constitution and became a republic. In 1961, Goa was liberated from Portuguese rule and became an integral part of India, and 1966 witnessed the coming to power of Mrs Indira Gandhi and the first devaluation of the Indian Rupee after independence (from 4.76 rupees to the US dollar to 7.5). In 1969 fourteen banks were nationalized.

In many administrative and constitutional affairs, India still follows British traditions (see Basu 1998; Jones 1989). The Constitution of India states that it as a sovereign, socialist, secular and democratic republic (Basu 1998). It comprises twenty-nine states and seven union territories. India has emerged as the largest democracy in the world. Its total population is over 1 billion (as per the 2001 Census), making it the second most populous country in the world. The percentage share of the six main religious groups is: Hindus (83.2 per cent), Muslims (11 per cent), Sikhs (2 per cent), Christians (2 per cent), Jains and Buddhists (less than 1 per cent). There are over 3,000 castes. India has seventeen major languages and 844 different dialects. The Constitution recognises 'Hindi' and English as the two official languages. India has one of the largest English-speaking populations in the Asia-Pacific region (see Budhwar 2001; Nabhi 1998).

India follows the Westminster model. Parliament is the supreme body consisting of two houses of Rajya Sabha (the Upper House) and Lok Sabha (the Lower House), the government being formed by any political party or coalition of parties securing a majority in the Lok Sabha in national elections. The president is the constitutional head, while the prime minister is the executive head of the government. Both are elected for a period of five years.

The legal system is based on the 1950 Constitution and, reflecting India's colonial inheritance, English common law. Further, India has a three-tier legal system. The Supreme Court is the apex body, followed by the state High Courts and Subordinate (or District) Courts. For special events different commissions and tribunals are set up. The Constitution of India officially grants its citizens the fundamental right to equality, freedom against exploitation, freedom of religion and freedom of speech, along with the right to property and cultural and educational rights (Basu 1998). The judicial and legal systems are very strong and are capable of bringing even top officials to justice. However, owing to the misuse of power by ruling political parties it is difficult for common citizens (who do not have close links with politicians or civil servants) to get their work done. There are also serious problems related to child labour, human rights, working conditions and minimum wages. The next section talks about the economic background of India.

Economic background

In the pre-British period, agriculture, muslin, calicos, cotton fabrics, textile handicrafts, silk, marble-work, stone carving, jewellery, brass, copper, bell-metal wares, woodcarving, spices, indigo and opium dominated the India economy. During the British era, manufactured goods, textiles, spices, jute, cotton, coal, iron and steel, paper and pulp, sugar and safety matches became the dominant industries. Just after independence, the government set up the Planning Commission in 1950 to formulate national plans. Economic planning is mainly carried out through the five-year plans and industrial policies. Presently, the ninth five-year plan and the industrial policy of 1991 are in progress (see Datt and Sundharam 2001).

Despite the formalities of planning, the Indian economy reached its worst point in 1991. It witnessed a double-digit rate of inflation, decelerated industrial production, fiscal indiscipline, a very high ratio of borrowing to GNP (both internal and external) and a dismally low level of foreign exchange reserves. Foreign reserves had become so low that they were barely sufficient to meet the cost of three weeks' imports. The Indian government was forced to pledge gold to the Bank of England to meet the country's foreign exchange requirements. The World Bank and the IMF agreed to bail out India on the condition that it changed to a 'free-market economy' from a regulated regime. To meet the challenges, the government announced a series of economic policies beginning with devaluation of the rupee, followed by a new industrial policy and new fiscal and trade policies. A number of reforms were made in the public sector, trade and exchange policy, and the banking sector, and foreign investment was liberalized (see the special issue of *The Columbia Journal of World Business* 1994).

Since these reforms, the economy has responded positively and India is now considered as one of the largest emerging nations, having avoided the Asian economic crisis. The World Bank forecasts that, by 2020, India could become the world's fourth-largest economy. In the last few years state control and ownership in the economy have been reduced, and bold steps have been taken to correct the fiscal imbalance, to bring about structural adjustments and to attract foreign direct investment. However, India still has a long way to go before it can compete fully with some of the more economically advanced Asian nations.

The USA, Japan, Germany, the UK, the UAE, Singapore and Russia are India's major economic partners. Around 20 per cent of India's exports go to the USA alone. The USA is also the main exporter to India. Other significant exporters to India include the UK, Japan and Germany. India has the largest pool of scientific and technical personnel in the world. The technical education system of India produces over 200,000 engineering/technical graduates annually (all trained in English, providing one of India's real strengths).

Considering the present political, social and economic set-up in India, it can be deduced that, although an important emerging market, India currently faces a number of problems. These include political and religious instability; ever-increasing levels of population; unemployment and poverty; corruption in government offices; a low per capita income; instability of output in agriculture and related sectors; slow privatization of the bloated public sector; lack of adequate intellectual property protection; excessive bureaucracy (red tape); and an increasing gap between rich and poor (Budhwar 2001; Venkata Ratnam 1995). The societal culture of India is discussed next.

Societal culture

Husain (1992) presents one of the most comprehensive reviews of Indian society and Indian national culture. According to Husain, the analysis of the national culture of India started about 5,000–6,000 years ago. It was during this period that holy books of 'Vedas' were written and the Indian culture was referred to as 'Vedic culture'. After that Lord Buddha started 'Buddhism' and the national culture inherited a strong influence of the doctrine of Buddhism. The impact of Buddhism stayed for a short period and was replaced by 'Hindu culture'. In comparison with the 'Vedic culture', it can be called the 'Puranic culture'. This cultural life was disturbed before the establishment of the Delhi Sultanate (around the tenth century AD) after which the Hindu–Muslim culture developed, known as 'Hindustani culture'. This culture was not based on any religion but on some sort of vague national feelings in the political sense. The British left a strong impact of their culture (primarily in the form of an excessively bureaucratic system and a large amount of legislation) that is still very prominent in India, and again affected the Hindustani culture. Hence, over a period of time, the national culture of India has transformed from one type to another (for details see Husain 1992; Thomas and Philip 1994).

Indian society is a mixture of various ethnic, religious, linguistic, caste and regional collectivities, which further differ in historical and socio-cultural specificity. It is a panorama which has absorbed diverse languages, cultures, religions and people of different social origins at different points of time in the past. These diversities are reflected in the patterns of life, styles of living, land tenure systems, occupational pursuits, inheritance and succession rules (Sharma 1984). Indeed, a number of commentators have presented interesting views on conceptualizing Indian culture. For example, Sinha and Kanungo (1997) refer to India as a soft state where people are so dependent on the state that they cease to tackle their own problems with local initiatives. Kennedy (1993) emphasizes the 'tender mindedness' of Indians, which prevents taking bold decisions. Research by Sinha (1990) also confirms such a 'soft work culture' (marked by continued dependence of one set or group of people on another for regular guidance, for example, of subordinates on superiors) characteristics of Indian organizations.

On the basis of Hofstede's (1991) four initial dimensions of power – distance, uncertainty avoidance, individualism and masculinity – Kanungo and Mendonca (1994) have shown significant cultural differences between India and Western countries. India stands relatively high on uncertainty avoidance and power distance and relatively low on individualism and masculinity dimensions. Relatively high uncertainty avoidance implies an unwillingness to take risks and accept organizational change. The relative low individualism implies that family and group attainments take precedence over work outcomes (Sharma 1984). The relative high power distance implies that managers and subordinates accept their relative positions in the organizational hierarchy and operate from these fixed positions. Obedience is due to the holder of a position not on a rational basis, but simply by virtue of the authority inherent in that position. The relative low masculinity implies that employees' orientation is towards personalized relationships rather than towards performance[2] (Kanungo and Mendonca 1994: 450).

Along the same lines, other researchers (see for example Sharma 1984; Sinha and Kanungo 1997; Tayeb 1987) report that on average Indians resist change, hesitate to delegate, or even accept authority, are fearful of taking an independent decision, are possessive towards their inferiors and frequently surrender to their superiors. A possible explanation for such behaviour can be traced to the long imperialist history of India. From the tenth century till 1947, foreigners (Thomas and Philip 1994) ruled India. Similarly, the traditional hierarchical social structure of India has always emphasized respect for superiors, be they elders, teachers or superiors at work, i.e. the nature of Hinduism evidenced by the caste and social system (Budhwar *et al.* 2000; Sahay and Walsham 1997).

To summarize, Indians are known for their obedience to seniors, dependence on others, a strong belief in fate, a low ability to cope with uncertainties, a reluctance to accept responsibilities, and are less disciplined, more modest and reserved than most nationalities (see Tayeb 1987). There is also a great deal of collectivism, caste consciousness, friendliness and more clan orientation. Females are highly respected in Indian society, but respect does not always translate into equality in the workplace, in earnings or in society in general (see Devi 1991). Women are still expected to be more submissive and obedient, though these attitudes are changing, the more so in urban areas. At the negotiating table, Indians are slow starters (like other Asians, Indians grow up bargaining for everything; this brings patience and the ability to hold out for better terms) in comparison with Westerners. Social relations are very important in business management. In general, Indians are very hospitable and are highly tolerant of the foreign population (see Budhwar 2001).

From the above discussion, it can be deduced that the Indian societal culture has a lasting impact on most management functions such as staffing, communication, leadership, motivation and control. Staffing for top managerial positions among Indian organizations (especially in the private sector) is generally restricted by familial, communal and political considerations. Authority in Indian organizations is likely to remain one sided, with subordinates leaning heavily on their superiors for advice and direction. Motivational tools in Indian organizations are more likely to be social, interpersonal and even spiritual (see Sparrow and Budhwar 1997). What is the situation regarding the corporate culture and the basis of management behaviour in India? This is discussed in the next two sections.

Corporate culture and management behaviour

As stated above, a power-based hierarchy exits in most Indian organizations. As a result, Indians are disposed to hierarchical relationships, and for this reason they usually work well individually rather than in groups (Sinha and Sinha 1990). Furthermore, management in India is often autocratic, based on formal authority and charisma (Budhwar and Khatri 2001b). Family norms emphasizing loyalty to the family authority figure or superior in an organization underlie the limited decision-making experience and unfamiliarity with responsibility found in most employees (Kakar 1971). Consequently, decision making is very centralized, with much emphasis on rules and a low propensity for risk (Hofstede 1991; Tayeb 1987). In addition, complicated family ties and strong authority figures are responsible for a paternalistic managerial style in India.

It has been argued that since the original source of power in India is family and friends, nepotism is common at both the lowest and highest levels (see Sinha 1990). Furthermore, it is asserted that within Indian organizations, expert power is frequently relegated in favour of position power (see Bass and Burger 1979). Consequently, it is difficult for non-family members to advance into upper management positions particularly in private businesses. Managerial thinking in India is also influenced by a conflict of cultures, arising because the managers have often been trained in the West or in Indian colleges that have adopted Western educational models (Garg and Parikh 1986; Neelankavil *et al.* 2000). Thus, Indian managers frequently internalize two sets of values: those drawn from the traditional moorings of the family and community, and those drawn from modern education, professional training and the imperatives of modern technology (Budhwar 2001). These two sets of values coexist and are drawn upon as frames of reference depending on the nature of problems that people face.

In the context of culture and organizational functioning, many suggestions have been put forward to help managers move towards more effective leadership. Tripathi (1990) suggests 'indigenous values, such as familism, need to be synthesised with the values of industrial democracy'. Similarly, as mentioned above, Sinha (1990) proposes that, while a leader in India has to be a 'nurturant type', taking a personal interest in the well-being of each subordinate, he or she can use that nurturance to encourage increasing levels of participation. Sinha and Kanungo (1997) observe that the manager may achieve this by directing subordinates to work hard and maintain an excessive level of productivity, reinforcing each stage with increased nurturance. According to Sinha and Sinha (1990), a prerequisite to effective cross-cultural leadership in India is to establish work as the 'master value'. Once this is done, 'other social values will reorganise themselves to help realise the master value'.

Managerial values

As indicated above, Indian society is a mixture of various ethnic, religious, linguistic, caste and regional collectivities, which further differ owing to historical and socio-cultural specificities. It is a panorama which has absorbed diverse languages, cultures, religions and people of different social origins at different points of time in the past. These diversities are reflected in patterns of life, styles of living, land tenure systems, occupational pursuits, inheritance and succession rules. The idea of unity is inherent today in India's Constitution, which pronounces values of secularism, socialism and democracy as its main ideals. The British rule in India accentuated some of these socio-cultural and economic differences (Sharma 1984).

Hierarchy and inequality are deeply rooted in India's tradition and are also found in practice in the form of unequally placed caste and class groups. These have become persistent and resulted in equilibrium because of the organic linkages and interdependence of the different socio-economic groups (Jain and Venkata Ratnam 1994). However, as discussed above, Indian society has witnessed change due to foreign invasions, migration, natural calamities, struggles for power and the policies of the Mughal and the British Empires. Changes in the post-independence era have occurred mainly because of economic planning (spearheaded by the five-year plans) and development schemes in the fields of industry and agriculture (Datt and Sundharam 2001). The post-independence era has witnessed the emergence of new forms of social and economic disparities. Most of the development programmes have helped the traditionally better-off more than those who were down-trodden and who genuinely needed social and economic better-ment. However, the reserved class peoples (scheduled castes (SCs), scheduled tribes (STs) and weaker sections of society) benefited in the fields of educa-tion and employment. But the more needy and deserving have not benefited as much as they were entitled to (Jain and Venkata Ratnam 1994).

Over the years, both academics and practitioners have shown an interest in exploring the impact of Indian national culture on management policies and practices (see for example Daftur 1993; Mankidy 1993; Sharma 1984; Sparrow and Budhwar 1997). These writers have examined the impact of Anglo-Saxon and Japanese models of management on Indian HRM prac-tices and policies. They say that despite the heterogeneity of languages, dialects and customs in India, there exist common attitudinal and behavioural patterns that knit most of the people together to give a sense of uniformity. Sharma (1984), while comparing Indian and American manage-rial styles, found a number of differences. These differences have a strong theoretical and historical base and have empirical support.

The average American is achievement oriented and is consequently geared to work at a level of maximum efficiency. In comparison, the average Indian is essentially 'fatalistic' and believes in the theory of 'predeter-minism'. As a result, the average Indian has an infinite capacity to suffer and a tough resilience in the face of all the hazards which a scarce economy and an indifferent society present daily and persistently. It is not surprising then that, as inheritors of such a legacy, Indian managers often vacillate and dither when crucial decisions are to be made (Sharma 1984: 73). Nevertheless, in the present competitive context, such findings can be seri-ously challenged. However, there is a scarcity of research in this regard.

Compared with that in the USA, the gap between ownership and management is less in India. Apart from merit, relations matter a lot and change is not accepted so easily, as a result of which the optimum level is achieved very rarely. Today's proprietor–manager has still to shake off his trading and speculative background. Along these lines, Silveria (1988) has shown the strong impact of the East India Company on Indian managers and government. Present public servants reflect a similar 'mistrust' towards the general public as shown by the Company towards Indian natives. The Company also left India with a legacy of red tape that it inherited from the Moghuls. Silveria further blames the British for leaving India without an industrial culture, as a result of which, after independence, Indian businessmen thought and behaved like traders and commission agents rather that entrepreneurs and industrialists (Silveria 1988: 8–9).

Kanungo and Mendonca (1994) have also shown the effect of societal norms (through the socialization process) on work behaviour and job performance of individuals and groups in organizations. Individuals enter an organization with certain beliefs, expectations, attitudes and values regarding work that are based on their socio-economic background and influence their work behaviour in either a positive or negative direction.

Since Indians are socialized in an environment that values strong family ties and extended family relationships, they are more likely to develop stronger affiliative tendencies or greater dependence on others. So in the work context, interpersonal relations will likely be more salient to them and, as a result, their job-related decisions might be influenced more by interpersonal considerations than by task demands[3] (Kanungo and Mendonca 1994: 448).

It can be concluded, then, that cultural influences shape the employees' needs and expectations, their hopes and aspirations, and their perceptions of what constitutes desirable forms of conduct. Managers' beliefs, values and assumptions about the job and employees are also a product of cultural influence (Hofstede 1991). The HRM policies and practices are an outcome of such managerial beliefs, values and assumptions. In India, until recently, HRs were seen as relatively fixed with limited potential and organizations were encouraged to take a passive/reactive stance to task performance, success was judged on moralism derived from tradition and religion, people orientation was paternalistic and consideration of the context overrode principles and rules (Kanungo and Jaeger 1990).

There could not be a more plausible explanation (than the one given above) for the average Indian's resistance to change, his willingness to delegate, or even to accept authority, his fear of taking an independent decision, his possessive attitude towards his inferiors and his abject surrender to his superiors, his strict observance of rituals and his disregard of them in practice, his preaching of high morals against his personal immorality, and his near-desperate efforts at maintaining the status quo while talking of change (Daftur 1993; Sharma 1984).

Apart from this, the Indian management culture is characterized by the principle of 'particularism' and 'stability' as compared with the West, where 'individualism' and 'mobility' are the prominent ways of organizations (Sharma 1984). Researchers (see Mankidy 1993; Krishna and Monappa 1994) have also shown the influence of the Japanese models of management in Indian organizations. The main Japanese concepts adopted in Indian organizations are the 'quality circles', 'lifelong employment', Kaizen, just-in-time, total quality management, and a seniority-based wage system. Though these concepts are adopted in Indian organizations, they are not as successful as they are in Japan. The main reason behind this failure is the cultural differences between the two countries. Indian organizations lack commitment towards individual goals and their integration with the organizational objectives. Chatterjee (1992) very correctly comments in this regard. He says:

> A nation's management system is not just a set of tools and techniques that can be applied without regard to the socio-cultural context. The effectiveness of any management style can be understood only within the cultural, socio-political and economic framework of the people who are doing the managing and being managed.

Understandably, the success or failure of Japanese management systems elsewhere would depend to a large extent not only on the inherent characteristics of those practices themselves, but also on the extent to which Japanese techniques can be adapted to the peculiar conditions of alien environments (Hofstede 1991).

Jain (1991) made an attempt to check if there is a coherent HRM system in India. He concluded that there is no coherent or unified management system which can be called 'Indian Management'. This was mainly due to the existence of inconsistencies and contradictions which abound within the Indian management system. The main reason for such inconsistencies is the unsuccessful attempt to implement Western management theories and concepts in the Indian socio-economic and cultural environment. India has two management systems operating side by side: the philosophy is paternalistic but the organizational structure is bureaucratic and hierarchical in nature. Indian decision making is a process of consultative activity but the final decision is always made at the top.

Labour–management conflict resolution

The Industrial Disputes Act (IDA) of 1947 provides the main machinery for the settlement of workers' grievances and conflict between management and labour (see Kothari 2000). Broadly speaking, these consist of four levels (see Venkata Ratnam 1995): bipartite negotiations, conciliation, arbitration and adjudication.

Section 3 of the IDA recommends the creation of 'works committees' in industrial establishments employing over 100 or more workers. A works committee should consist of an equal number of representatives of both the employers and employees. There can be many works committees in one organization, such as the canteen or the safety committee. These committees meet at regular time intervals and try to resolve any management–labour disputes. In 1958, under the Industrial Policy Resolution (1956), 'joint management councils' (JMCs) were initiated. These emphasized joint consultations between workers and technicians and management related to welfare, safety, vocational training, changes in work practices, productivity and preparation of holiday schedules (Venkata Ratnam 1996). The JMCs are also used to resolve conflict between management and labour.

The second mechanism to resolve labour–management conflicts in India is through conciliation. As per the IDA, the government has discretion to appoint a conciliation officer for a specific area or a specified industry either permanently or for a limited period to mediate and promote the settlement of industrial disputes (Kothari 2000). The conciliation officer acts as an administrator rather than as a judicial head. This officer is required to interview representatives of both parties (management and labour) and generally completes a case within a period of two months.

The third mechanism to resolve labour–management conflicts is through arbitration (see the IDA). Any registered union which is a representative of employees, and which is also an approved union, may refer any industrial conflict for arbitration to the Industrial Court under Section 73A of the IDA. The arbitrator can be a court judge or someone who has occupied a high position in public office. Once the case is referred to the arbitrator, both management and labour are bound to abide by the final decision of the arbitrator. The arbitration mechanism has not been popular in India owing to adverse labour–management relations (see Venkata Ratnam 1995).

Lastly, adjudication is by far the most used mechanism to resolve industrial conflicts in India. This can be in the form of labour courts, industrial tribunals and national tribunals depending on the nature, scope and magnitude of the conflict. For details of these see the IDA (Kothari 2000).

Generally, labour–management conflicts have implications for the three key actors (management, unions and the state) of an industrial relations system (IRS). Of the three key actors in the Indian IRS, a change is being noticed in the behaviour of trade unions. This has implications for the functioning of the machinery dealing with conflict resolution discussed above. The union's attitude is now becoming more cooperative. The strong position of the trade unions (which existed till the late 1970s) suddenly began to weaken at the start of the 1980s. A number of reasons were identified in this regard, starting with the failure of a number of strikes such as those in Bombay (textile mills, 1982; Hindustan Lever), West Bengal (Dunlop Rubber and Bata India Ltd) and Pune (TELCO). As a result of the failure of these strikes workers started losing faith and confidence in militant trade unionism (Sodhi 1999). In comparison with the 1960s and 1970s, the trade unions started to become weak, signalling that trade union militancy was on the wane. Such a trend is further evident by a decrease in the number of lockouts, duration of strikes and industrial disputes (for more details, see Venkata Ratnam 1996).

Another significant development on the Indian industrial relations front has taken place over the last few years. This is the emergence of 'Managerial Unionism' (Sharma 1992). Such a development is mainly due to the feeling of alienation by managers in industry. Similarly, there has also been a change in the stance of government towards the labour. Prior to the new economic policies the stance of the government was pro-labour; it encouraged trade unions and discouraged retrenchment and closures. In such situations the labour laws proved counter-productive (as the employees were/are overprotective), the adjudication process was time consuming and a multiplicity of unions existed which was highly political in nature. Most of these problems still exist. However, a number of changes are presently being pursued in the existing labour legislation to safeguard management also and resolve any organizational conflict at the earliest opportunity (see Budhwar 2001; Sodhi 1999).

Implications for managers

Indian managers see a strong impact of power distance on their functioning. This element operates through the misuse of power due to different pressures (such as political, caste, group and bureaucratic ones) and within a logic of 'power myopia' which influences their thinking about most management functions. As a result, Indian managers tend to rely on the use of power in superior–subordinate relationships in their organizations and are not actively inclined towards consultative or participative styles.[4] However, in the present competitive context, Indian managers are required to change their traditional style (discussed above) in order to create a more participative environment, flexible working patterns and a more open approach to information sharing amongst their subordinates. Many Indian companies may have already initiated this (see Ghoshal *et al.* 2001). Still it is too early to generalize this trend.

A recent analysis (see Budhwar 2000) shows that political influence, an uncertain future, a dynamic business environment, a fatalistic attitude and the risk-averse nature of Indian managers are the main factors which contribute to a high level of uncertainty avoidance. This creates a climate of calculative risk taking and this dimension has a negative influence on policies related to selection, training and development, pay and benefits, and separation. The recommendation here for Indian managers is to adopt a more professional and practical approach to their working to survive and flourish in the present-day dynamic business environment.

A combination of the Indian national culture, stereotypes developed for females and the nature of the job decides the emphasis on masculinity or femininity in Indian organizations. This also influences managerial thinking regarding recruitment, transfers and appraisals. However, such a glass ceiling is being broken as more and more females enter the workforce and move to higher levels of Indian management hierarchies. In such conditions it is important for both the Indian management and Indian legislation to ensure continuous support in this regard. Traditionally, India is known as a long-term oriented nation (see Hofstede 1991; Tripathi 1990). However, Budhwar's (2000) analysis suggests that, because of the severe pressure created by the recent liberalization of economic policies and foreign operators on Indian organizations, the question of immediate survival has become important, and hence Indian managers now put more emphasis on short-termism. Nevertheless, once the Indian national companies get used to and start flourishing in the competitive environment, the focus should be on both long- and short-term orientations.

Moreover, traditionally, Indian organizations have utilized ILMs based on social contacts and relationships. However, in the present context, Indian organizations need to build strong ILMs which should focus solely on performance and should be less influenced by social, economic, religious and political factors. There are some indications that such developments are taking place in the form of an increased emphasis on training and development, a preference for talent in recruitment and performance-based compensation (see Budhwar and Khatri 2001b). However, it is too early to generalize such trends.

Conclusions

The 'first generation' of Indian economic reforms initiated in 1991 ran out of steam after four or five years. The national growth rate, which reached 7 per cent in the mid-1990s, slipped to 5 per cent in 1998. Owing to political uncertainty, most of the 1991 reforms were put in jeopardy. However, over the last three years or so things have started to look positive, as India was not greatly affected by the Asian economic turmoil in 1997. After a gap of three or four years, the Indian economy is showing clear signs of recovery. This has been triggered by rising demand and orders for different goods and services, higher national output, comfortable forex reserves, a steadily depreciating nominal exchange rate, a current account deficit likely to be well within 2 per cent of GDP and the prospect of political stability. Industrial output has been steadily rising over the past twelve months. With an anticipated GDP growth rate of 6 per cent, India is now projected as one of the fastest growing economies in Asia.

With a parliamentary majority it is likely that the present government will complete its five years' tenure, hence providing the needed political stability at the national level. The present government has been quick to initiate the much-needed 'second generation' of reforms. If successful, these significant changes could push the growth rate to 9 or 10 per cent. A number of steps have already been taken in the form of privatization programmes; introduction of a national competition policy; opening up of the insurance sector to private and foreign investors; and changes to securities legislation to allow trading in derivatives on the gilt markets.

Similarly, some steps have been taken to attract more FDI. The Department of Industrial Policy and Promotion has proposed to shift more from a case-by-case regime to an automatic system of approvals for FDI proposals. The new proposed system aims to reduce red tape and hasten the pace of clearances. The government is also planning to liberalize FDI norms for e-commerce activities, giving foreign investors control over their operations in India.

With full ownership allowed, MNCs no longer need to put up with the constraints of struggling joint ventures, or share the fruits of success with other Indian companies. The success of the Indian software and hardware sectors is now well acknowledged worldwide. Along with cheap labour, Indian 'brain power' is now contributing to real cost advantage.

Notes

1 The ability of a large number of Indian managers to speak English has no doubt helped this process.
2 This phenomenon may be seen as an 'Asian' phenomenon; for example, see the chapter on China in this volume.
3 Whether this trait is more characteristic of India vis-à-vis other Asian countries is, of course, moot.
4 This would be consistent with Hofstede's rating of India as high on 'power distance'.

References

Bass, B. and Burger, C. (1979) *Assessment of Managers: An International Comparison*, New York: Free Press.

Basu, D. D. (1998) *Constitutional Law of India*, New Delhi: Prentice Hall of India.

Budhwar, P. (2000) 'Indian and British personnel specialists' understanding of the dynamics of their function: an empirical study', *International Business Review* 9(6): 727–53.

Budhwar, P. (2001) 'Doing business in India', *Thunderbird International Business Review* 43 (4): 549–68.

Budhwar, P. and Khatri, N. (2001a) 'Comparative human resource management in Britain and India: an empirical study', *International Journal of Human Resource Management* 13(5): 800–26.

Budhwar, P. and Khatri, P. (2001b) 'HRM in context: the applicability of HRM models in India', *International Journal of Cross Cultural Management* 1(3): 333–56.

Budhwar, L., Reeves, D. and Farrell, P. (2000) 'Life goals as a function of social class and child rearing practices: a study of India', *International Journal of Intercultural Relations* 24: 227–45.

Chatterjee, B. (1992) *Japanese Management and the Indian Experience*, New Delhi: Sterling.

The Columbia Journal of World Business (1994) Spring.

Daftur, C. N. (1993) Should we apply foreign management theories to Indian system. *Industrial Relations News and Views,* 5 (3), 8–12.

Datt, R. and Sundharam, K. P. H. (2001) *Indian Economy*, New Delhi: S. Chand.

Devi, R. D. (1991) 'Women in modern sector employment in India', *Economic Bulletin for Asia and the Pacific* June–December: 53–65.

Garg, P. and Parikh, I. (1986) 'Managers and corporate cultures: the case of Indian organizations', *Management International Review* 26: 50–62.

Ghoshal, S., Piramal, G. and Budhiraja, S. (2001) *World Class in India*, New Delhi: Penguin.

Hofstede, G. (1991) *Culture and Organisations: Software of the Mind*, London: McGraw-Hill.

Husain, A. S. (1992) *The National Culture of India*, New Delhi: National Book Trust.

Jain, H. C. (1991) 'Is there a coherent human resource management system in India?', *International Journal of Manpower* 12 (1): 10–17.

Jain, H. C. and Venkata Ratnam, C. S. (1994) 'Affirmative action in employment for the scheduled castes and the scheduled tribes in India', *International Journal of Manpower* 15(7): 6–25.

Jones, S. (1989) 'Merchants of the Raj', *Management Accounting* September: 32–5.

Kakar, S. (1971) 'Authority pattern and subordinate behaviours in Indian organisation', *Administrative Science Quarterly* 16: 298–307.

Kanungo, R. N. and Jaeger, A. M. (1990) 'Introduction: the need for indigenous management in developing countries', in A. M. Jaeger and R. N. Kanungo (eds), *Management in Developing Countries*, London: Routledge, pp. 1–19.

Kanungo, R. N. and Mendonca, M. (1994) 'Culture and performance improvement', *Productivity* 35(3): 447–53.

Kennedy, P. (1993) *Preparing for the 21st Century*, London: Fortune Press.

Kothari, G. M. (2000) *A Study of Industrial Law*, New Delhi: Wadhwa.

Krishna, A. and Monappa, A. (1994) 'Economic restructuring and human resource management', *Indian Journal of Industrial Relations* 29(3): 490–501.

Mankidy, J. (1993) 'Emerging patterns of industrial relations in India', *Management and Labour Studies* 18(4): 199–206.

Nabhi (1998) *Manual for Foreign Collaboration & Investment in India*, New Delhi: Nabhi Publication.

Neelankavil, J. P., Mathur, A. and Zang, Y. (2000) 'Determinants of managerial performance: a cross-cultural comparison of the perceptions of middle-level managers in four countries', *Journal of International Business Studies* 31(1): 121–40.

Sahay, S. and Walsham, G. (1997) 'Social structure and managerial agency in India', *Oganisation Studies* 18: 415–44.

Sharma, B. R. (1992) 'Managerial unionism: implications for industrial relations', in J. S. Sodhi and S. P. S. Ahluwalia (eds), *Industrial Relations in India*, New Delhi: Shri Ram Centre for Industrial Relations and Human Resources, pp. 148–167.

Sharma, I. J. (1984) 'The culture context of Indian managers', *Management and Labour Studies* 9(2): 72–80.

Silveria, D. M. (1988) *Human Resource Development: The Indian Experience*, New Delhi: New India Publications.

Sinha, J. B. P. (1990) *Work Culture in Indian Context*, New Delhi: Sage.

Sinha, J. B. P. and Kanungo, R. (1997) 'Context sensitivity and balancing in Indian organization behavior', *International Journal of Psychology* 32: 93–105.

Sinha, J. B. P. and Sinha, D. (1990) 'Role of social values in Indian organizations', *International Journal of Psychology* 25: 705–15.

Sodhi, J. S. (1999) *Industrial Relations and Human Resource Management*, New Delhi: Shri Ram Centre for Industrial Relations and Human Resources.

Sparrow, P. R. and Budhwar, P. (1997) 'Competition and change: mapping the Indian HRM recipe against world wide patterns', *Journal of World Business* 32(3): 224–42.

Tayeb, M. (1987) 'Contingency theory and culture: a study of matched English and the Indian manufacturing firms', *Organisation Studies* 8: 241–61.

Thomas, A. S. and Philip, A. (1994) 'India: management in an ancient and modern civilisation', *International Studies of Management and Organisation* 24(1–2): 91–115.

Tripathi, R. C. (1990) 'Interplay of values in the functioning of Indian organizations', *International Journal of Psychology* 25: 715–34.

Venkata Ratnam, C. S. (1992) *Managing People: Strategies for Success*, New Delhi: Global Business.

Venkata Ratnam, C. S. (1995) 'Economic liberalization and the transformation of industrial relations policies in India', in A. Verma, T. A. Kochan and R. D. Lansbury (eds), *Employment Relations in the Growing Asian Economies*, London: Routledge.

Venkata Ratnam, C. S. (1996) *Industrial Relations in Indian States*, New Delhi: Global Business Press.

5 Culture and management in Indonesia

Ashar Sunyoto Munandar

Introduction

Indonesia is a multi-ethnic and multicultural society consisting of over 200 ethnic groups, each with its own distinct culture. The 'Indonesian' culture is also strongly influenced by various religions (Islam, Christianity, Buddhism, and Hinduism), by the Dutch culture (during the colonization period), and the Japanese culture (during the occupation in the Second World War). After the proclamation of the Republic of Indonesia in 1945 until today, Western culture, in particular the culture of the USA, has had a great impact on the life of the Indonesian people, especially on the life of the city population.

No specific management science or style has developed in Indonesia. As a Dutch colony, the management of various enterprises lay in Dutch hands. After independence, however, the Indonesians took over, forced to learn through direct experience. Growth in industry has resulted in a demand for managers, with a parallel interest in management education (US oriented), which has become increasingly popular. Although greatly influenced by Western, especially US, management concepts and approaches, Indonesian CEOs and managers have, in general, a pragmatic attitude. They act and react based on their personal values and situational conditions.

The economic and management developments in Indonesia started with independence in August 1945, and can be divided into three periods: the 'Orde Lama' (Old Order) period, the 'Orde Baru' (New Order) period, and the 'Orde Reformasi' (Reformation Order) period. The characteristics of the societal culture, the economic developments, the corporate culture, the managerial values and management behavior, labour–management conflict resolution, and the implications for managers will be treated in turn.

Historical setting

Once known as the East Indies, Indonesia consists of about 13,600 islands covering 1.9 million square kilometres of land area. The islands are spread in an arc south-east of the Asia mainland, north-west of Australia and straddling the equator for a distance equal to that between Philadelphia and Los Angeles. Only about 6,000 islands are inhabited. The largest islands are Sumatra (473,606 square kilometres), Java together with Madura (133,035 square kilometres), Kalimantan (539,460 square kilometres), Sulawesi (189,035 square kilometres), and Irian Jaya (421,952 square kilometres). Indonesia has a population of about 210 million people, consisting of about 200 ethnic groups, each with its own specific cultural characteristics and language. The official language is Indonesian.

Indonesia has been moulded by the cultures of different people who have lived there throughout the ages. The Malays, the Proto-Malays (3000 BC), and the Deutero-Malays (3 BC) have absorbed the original inhabitants. Later, Indians came to the Indonesian archipelago and influenced the cultural, political, and religious life of the people. Centuries after Hinduism, Buddhism was also introduced by the Indians. This situation stood until the fourteenth century, when Islam took over as the dominant religion.

In the sixteenth century the Dutch arrived, lured by the lucrative spice trade. The United Dutch East India Company was established and aimed at monopolizing this trade. After it went broke the Dutch government took over and the company's territories were named the Netherlands Indies. Rule by the Dutch was colonial and met fierce resistance throughout the nineteenth and into the early twentieth century. Together with the Dutch came the Christian religion, the Catholics, and the Protestants. The Dutch culture, and both Christian religions, had some impact on the Indonesians. Dutch values impacted only on a small 'educated' group of scholars and aristocrats, a group responsible for the conception and growth of the Indonesian national movement based on independence and unity for Indonesia.

Later, during the Second World War, the Japanese occupied Indonesia. Occupation resulted not only in a Japanese influence, but also in an active and intensive exchange of cultural influences between various resident ethnic groups. This had the effect of strengthening the national movement, and the use of Indonesian as a national language.

After Japan surrendered, Indonesia proclaimed its independence (17 August 1945). In the fifty-seven years since its independence the march towards industrialization reflects the increasing influence of the West, especially the USA, pervading all aspects of Indonesian life.

Since independence the Indonesian government has tried to set up a democratic government, implementing Western democratic values, but with no success. Apparently democratic values were still strange values not internalized by the Indonesian people. In 1959, with a presidential decree Indonesia became a state with a 'guided' democracy, which was in fact an autocratic paternalistic government, which lasted until October 1965.

Indonesia's political and economic fortunes shifted significantly in October 1965, following an attempted coup against the first president. In 1967, the legislative assembly removed the first president from power, and with military backing installed the second president of the Republic of Indonesia who proclaimed a 'New Order', calling the period from 1945 to 1965 the 'Old Order'. He concentrated on policies of economic rehabilitation and development. Indonesia grew steadily, transforming itself from an agricultural backwater to a highly diversified manufacturing and export-driven state. Per capita income levels rose from US$70 in 1966 to US$900 in 1996.

The monetary crisis in Asia starting with the devaluation of the baht in Thailand in July 1997 spread through all South-East Asian governments, included Indonesia. The monetary crisis became an economic crisis, followed by a political crisis. Riots erupted over rising food prices and the negative consequences of government policies. Students, through daily demonstrations and protests, demanded reformation of the government; the president bowed to pressure, and resigned in May 1998, which marked the end of the 'New Order' period and the beginning of the 'Reformation' period.

The third president, who was appointed by his predecessor to become his successor, was unable to quell the unrest. He succeeded, however, in holding a fair democratic general election for a new parliament (Dewan Perwakilan Rakyat, DPR) and a new people's general assembly (Majelis Permusyawaratan Rakyat, MPR), which elected the fourth president of Indonesia. He, however, could not maintain political stability and was not able to solve the social, economic, and moral problems satisfactorily. In July 2001 the MPR elected a new president, who became the fifth president of the Republic of Indonesia.

Even today, it is still hard to predict what the future will bring for Indonesia. The political situation is relatively stable. The government, however, has not yet succeeded in overcoming the huge economic problems it faces.

Economic background

The economy during the Dutch colonial period was completely in the hands of the Netherlands Indies government. The companies, Netherlands and Netherlands-Indies, were all owned and managed by the Dutch. Under Japanese occupation, many Indonesians replaced the Dutch in the various plantations, commercial, manufacturing, and other companies. Since independence, the number of Indonesians managing organizations has increased greatly.

During the 'Old Order' period, Indonesia followed an erratic path in its development but managed to establish its identity and integrity. In 1957, all Dutch commercial companies were nationalized as state enterprises or 'Badan Usaha Milik Negara' (BUMN). Corporate performance was far from satisfactory because of internal and external constraints (Anwar and Prakarsa 1992). External constraints included the existence of many decision centres, which issued conflicting regulations and decisions, some even interfering with details of corporations' daily operations. Internal constraints included lack of trained and experienced managers, overabundance of clerical personnel, heterogeneous groups of employees, and the imbalance in capital structure between a company's owned equity and debts from third parties (such as bank loans or suppliers' credits).

After 1965, during the 'New Order' period a more rational development plan saw the stabilization of the currency, the strengthening of the economy, and an improvement in living standards.

On its way to becoming an industrialized nation, Indonesia is a multicultural state in a 'mixed state' of development, containing characteristics of the three industrial society stages: pre-industrial, industrial, and post-industrial. Although the agricultural sector continues to survive, the industrial sector contributes more to Indonesia's GDP. Technology and information technology are increasingly being applied. Such a situation makes for many influences on the way management is practised in Indonesia.

In 1968, Indonesia developed its first long-term development plan (twenty-five years) which was to be implemented in five five-year development plans. Significant growth was achieved with the long-term development plan due among other reasons to the open-door policy of the government, inviting foreign investors to Indonesia.. Apart from government businesses, a large number of private companies supported by both foreign and domestic capital have also been established, while many small-scale industries (mainly family businesses) developed into conglomerates. Further economic reforms in the early 1980s liberalizing trade and finance and expanding foreign investment and deregulation meant a boom; Indonesia's economy grew more than 7 per cent annually from 1985 to 1996. Per capita income levels rose, as stated earlier, from US$70 in 1966 to US$900 in 1996. The inflation rate during the 'New Order' period was kept below 10 per cent. The manufacturing sector expanded at an annual rate of about 10 per cent a year (Azis *et al.* 2002)

The devaluation of the baht in Thailand in July 1997 caused the value of the Indonesian currency – the rupiah – to drop as much as 80 per cent at one point. Foreign investors fled and many companies adversely affected by the currency devaluation went bankrupt. Like other Asian countries, Indonesia's banks were hit especially hard by the Asian crisis of the late 1990s; by 16 January 1998, many banks had their operations suspended.

The financial crisis in 1997 followed by the economic and political crisis damaged the basic foundation of economic, political, and social institutions (Anwar 2002), which made it very difficult for the government to overcome the crisis. Economic growth in 2000 was 4.8 per cent, down from 7 per cent in 1999. In 2001, the economic growth rate went down again to 3.3 per cent. The growth rate in 2002 is estimated at 3–4 per cent, which still will not create enough jobs for the 2.5 million school leavers each year. Slow economic growth is also inadequate for servicing the high burden of domestic and external debt.

The high expectations of the Indonesian people towards the new government, at the beginning of the 'Reformation' period, resulted in a feeling of disappointment and dissatisfaction. Although politically relative stable, the government, however, is still facing huge economic problems like massive foreign debts by the government, conglomerates still in trouble with big foreign debts, some of its companies going bankrupt, low investment rate, not attractive for foreign investments, etc. Some positive developments, however, can be observed. The Indonesian currency rate, for example, which was about Rp.15,000 per US dollar, averaged Rp.10,200 per US dollar in 2001, and became stronger in the first quarter of 2002 with a rate of about Rp.8,500 per US dollar. However, other economic indicators showed a decrease in 2001. GDP, which grew by 4.8 per cent in 2000, became a less promising, but still not disastrous, 3.3 per cent in 2001. In 2000, the unemployment rate amounted to 6 per cent, compared with 4.9 per cent in 1996 (Anwar 2002) The population who live below the poverty line was 19.92 per cent in 1996, increasing to 26.03 per cent in 1999 (Statistical Year Book of Indonesia 2000).

The economic outlook, however, is still difficult to forecast. Sjahrir (2002), an economics expert, mentioned that a new economic science is needed to understand and explain the diverse and apparently controversial economic data in Indonesia. From the existing economic growth indicators, which can be interpreted as having different meanings, and the diverse, often-controversial opinions given by economists (Anwar 2002, Mubyarto 2002, Mari 2002), one can come to the conclusion that the government has not yet succeeded in finding the correct and effective way to overcome the economic crisis in Indonesia.

Societal culture

Indonesia's multi-ethnic and multicultural society consists of over 200 ethnic groups, each with its own language and distinct culture. The main large ethnic groups are the Acehnese, with a dominant Islam culture, in the northern part of Sumatra; the Batak, below the region of the Acehnese; and the Minangkabau, having a matrilineal system, in the central part of Sumatra. Then there are the Javanese, in the central and eastern part of Java, the Madurese on the Island of Madura (east of Java), the Malay, the Dayak in Kalimantan, the Bugis in Celebes, the Ambonese on the Island of Ambon, the Balinese on the Island of Bali, and about fifteen ethnic groups in Papua (Irian Jaya). Indonesia has the slogan 'Bhineka Tunggal Ika', meaning 'unity in diversity'. Although Indonesia consists of a few hundred ethnic groups with different languages and cultures, it remains a single state. There are several values which are common in the diverse ethnic culture.

Hofstede (1982) found in his research that Indonesians scored high on power distance: 'People in Large Power Distance societies accept a hierarchical order in which everybody has his/her place and which needs no further justification' (p. 10). Hofstede did not distinguish the ethnic groups in the Indonesian respondents His findings are valid for several ethnic groups, like the Javanese, the Sundanese, and the Balinese. The Javanese in Javanese society accept the power of someone with a higher status. They will obey their superiors and their parents, and they will not oppose or argue with them. When a superior communicates with a subordinate, in a Javanese society, he will use a 'low (rude) Javanese' language. The subordinate, on the other hand, has to use a 'high (sophisticated) Javanese' language in communicating with his superior. Other ethnic groups, however, like the Batak, would most probably score low on the power distance scale. Batak society is an egalitarian society. A Batak colleague informed the author that he and other Batak people have difficulties adjusting to and accepting the power and authority of their superiors. The same is true for the Minangkabau ethnic group. It is also an egalitarian society (Mursal 1993, Amir 2001).

The significant influences of the various religions on the culture of each ethnic group, Catholics on Catholic Javanese and Catholic Ambonese, Protestants on Protestants Bataks and Protestants Javanese, Hinduism on the Balinese, and Islam practically on all the main ethnic groups mentioned above, lead to a set of common values and norms. There are Javenese who are Muslims, Javanese who are Catholics, Javanese who are Protestants. There are also Ambonese who are Muslims. There are Bataks who are also Muslims. The Indonesian government is very supportive in permitting people to perform their obligatory religious services according to their own beliefs. All over Indonesia houses of prayer (for each religion) can be observed. For the Muslims, about 80 per cent of the Indonesian population, for example, each business organization, foreign as well as national domestic, provides in its office building a special space, a *Musholla*, for the Muslims to say their daily obligatory prayers (the noon and afternoon prayers). The intensive use of the Indonesian language in education and in daily interactions, and the basic national curriculum taught in the primary and secondary schools all over Indonesia, result in several changes in the culture of each ethnic group towards the development of a set of common values and norms which constitute the Indonesian national culture.

The different population densities in the different regions and the unequal number of skilled labour caused the government to move people from high population density regions to low ones. In an unpublished report of the Ministry of Information of the Republic of Indonesia (1985) it is stated that the high population density in Indonesia occurs on the islands of Java, including Madura (690 people per square kilometre), and Bali (444 people per square kilometre). In the document it is also stated that since the Dutch colonial period many Javanese, Madurese, and Balinese have been moved to the low population density parts of the islands of Sumatra (59 people per square kilometre), Kalimantan (12 per square kilometre), and Papua (3 people per square kilometre).

The transmigration areas on the diverse islands were developed as economic and industry centres. The migrants work as farmers, cultivating rice fields, developing plantation estates, and breeding cattle, as labourers in timber industries, and in mining. Most of them have no schooling at all; some have had primary education, some secondary education, but only a few have had several years of tertiary education.

Apart from the migrants, there are two kinds of foreigners: first, those who came as immigrants from China, settling in various regions of Indonesia; and second, those from the USA, Australia, Europe (Dutch, German, French), Japan, and Korea who came to work and to stay for a while in diverse regions spread over all of Indonesia, and bringing with them their culture, values, and habits, all strange to the local culture.

The Chinese who came in the last two centuries from various parts of China consist of several ethnic groups with different Chinese dialects. These ethnic groups tend to retain their Chinese citizenship. Nowadays many have applied for Indonesian citizenship and become Indonesian. Recently there has been a move to recognize as Indonesian citizens all Chinese who have lived in Indonesia for several decades. There are two groups of Chinese: one consists of big traders and industrialists (becoming big conglomerates) who have retained their Chinese culture and religion, and are industrious and frugal; and the second group consists of intellectuals, university graduates, and scientists with a dominant Western orientation.

Business organizations are spread all over the Indonesian archipelago. They are located in three different areas:

1   In less developed areas where several ethnic groups are dominant, having a culture very different from that of the newcomers, the migrants, and temporary residents (belonging to another ethnic group, mostly Javanese, or foreigners employed by the government as teachers, or working in a company). The cultural difference can be very big; there is also a big difference in the level of education and the daily interactions are low. For example, the culture of the US Freeport mining industry (PT Freeport Indonesia) in Papua is very different from the culture of the ethnic groups surrounding the plant. The Amungme, Kamoro, and Damal have in general a low educational level (no schooling or only a primary school education; some have a secondary school education, and very few have university degrees). The cultural difference between these ethnic groups and the corporate culture of PT Freeport Indonesia causes huge problems. In their efforts to overcome the cultural gap, PT Freeport Indonesia funded several development and social empowerment projects, such as building houses and infrastructure, giving scholarships for education, conducting training programmes, providing health services and clean water to the community, and other services (unpublished document of PT Freeport Indonesia 2002).

2   As industrial estates or single business organizations in more developed rural areas, where the culture of one ethnic group dominates, like the Acehnese, with their dominant Islamic culture in the northern part of Sumatra, the Batak in the area below the Acehnese, the Minangkabau with their matrilineal system in middle Sumatra, the Javanese on Java, the Madurese on Madura, the Dayak in Kalimantan, and in other areas. As mentioned above, except for Java, Madura, and Bali, all the other areas have a significant number of newcomer Chinese or migrants from Java, Madura, and Bali. They still maintain their own culture and generally tolerate each other's culture. However, some changes in their culture are unavoidable. They are also exposed to other values (Western, especially US, values) during their education at the primary, secondary, and tertiary levels, and in their daily lives through newspapers, magazines, television, and movies. The cultural gap between the industrial estate and the surrounding ethnic groups is in general small. The relations between the industrial estates and the surrounding community are in general good, not causing significant problems. It is the social responsibility of the industrial estates and business organization to take care of their waste, not to destroy the environment, and to participate in the development of the surrounding community (e.g. help in setting up schools and health care units, support religious events, etc.).

3   In cities, small, medium, and large ones, especially the capital city of the province, like Jakarta (the capital city of Indonesia), Medan (North Sumatra), Padang (West Sumatra), Makasar (South Celebes), Surabaya (East Java), Bandung (West Java), and other cities populated by many different ethnic groups. The different ethnic groups interact daily with each other at work and socially. They are all exposed and influenced by the national values, through all levels of education, with the use of the Indonesian language, which, as the official language, is spoken by all ethnic groups. They are also exposed and influenced by international (Western) values, customs, and habits at work and socially, and by various mass media, namely newspapers, radio, television, and movies. The impact of Western and US values can be observed also at universities and higher education institutions (the academies with a Diploma 1, 2, or 3 program for graduates of the senior high schools). Students of the universities and higher education institutions, all located in the cities, come from different ethnic groups. At these institutions the influence of Western, especially the US, culture can be experienced. Many British and American journals and books are available in university libraries, and are used as textbooks or references. In fact, children at kindergarten (only in the big cities like Jakarta) are already exposed to Western and American values. There are kindergartens where they teach the children English songs, and even talk to the children in English. In general, though, English is

taught neither at kindergarten nor at the primary or elementary school. It is taught at junior and senior high school. The higher the education, the more students are exposed to Western values. When in constant contact with foreigners through their work, members of this group could behave like them or accept their different behaviour as part of a different culture. They are educated to higher secondary or tertiary level; some of them are educated abroad (in the USA, Australia, the UK, Germany, France). They are employed in government offices, educational institutions, or business organizations. They can be found also as small entrepreneurs, or independent workers.

Nowadays most CEOs of medium-sized and large companies have experienced a Western (Dutch) senior high school education or university education, and many of them are university graduates. They can interact easily with their Western CEO counterparts. Nevertheless, they still have a national Indonesian identity.

Corporate culture

Owing to the 'open-door' policy of the government, during the 'New Order' period, many foreign business organizations (American, Australian, Dutch, German, French, Japanese, Korean, and other foreign countries) set up their subsidiaries in the cities and in industrial estates in the middle of rural areas. They usually bring with them their own (corporate) culture, Asian as well as Western.

There are three kinds of business organizations: (1) Subsidiaries of multinational business organizations, (2) national private business organizations, and (2) state-owned business organizations.

The corporate culture of the subsidiaries of multinational business organizations has the same essential values as its 'parent' business organization. A French business organization in Indonesia, for instance, has a corporate culture of its French parent organization. The same holds for each foreign multinational business organization. General Electric Indonesia, for example, has the value system as introduced by the founder, Jack Welch: simplicity, speed, and self-confidence are the three main values that should be internalized by each employee of all ranks. Apart from the three Ss, each employee should have a customer-centred orientation, regard change as an opportunity, and be free to express their opinion on the one hand; they should also listen and be open tor other opinions. Employee interrelations are free and on an equal basis, which in the beginning, for many new Indonesian employees, were very difficult to accept. One dominant habit for Indonesians is the use of a family term before a name, when calling a person. For example, 'bapak' for father, or 'ibu' for mother, or 'mas' for brother, or 'kak' for brother/sister, or 'dik' for little brother/sister. In daily life it is considered a bad habit if one just pronounces the name without using a family term. However, in a personal interview with the personnel director, Mr Effendi Ibnu stated that all the Indonesian employees working at GE Indonesia could adjust themselves quite easily to the corporate culture of GE. When asked which employees from what ethnic group had most difficulties in adjusting, the answer was employees from the Javanese ethnic group. The Bataks could adjust themselves relatively easily; they are more open, and express their feelings and opinions directly and bluntly. The Javanese, on the other hand, are more reserved; they will not disclose their feelings and opinions directly or spontaneously.

The main values of the fast food retailer McDonald's, 'the speed of service', 'the good quality of food', and 'the cleanliness of the place', are all being applied in all McDonald's outlets in Indonesia. Generally, Indonesian employees and managers working in foreign business organizations will try to adjust to the corporate culture of the business.

The employees of other foreign business organizations do not always share the main values of the corporate culture extensively. The main values of the Japanese corporate culture in their business organization, for example, experienced a change of meaning and applied behaviour, and were adapted to the Indonesian employers' value system. For example, Indonesian workers undertake the Total Quality Control (TQC) system and Quality Control Circles (QCC) because they are ordered to do so. In Japan TQC and QCC are undertaken by workers voluntarily. Japanese businesses accentuate the five Ss: *Shitsake* (industrious, diligent, active), *Seiketsu* (caring, nursing, looking after), *Seiso* (clean, tidy), *Seiton* (proper, orderly, accurate), *Seiri* (concise, brief, epitomize). The five main values, however, are not largely shared and internalized by the employees. A Japanese office design, one large room where, except the factory workers, all administrative employees from the lowest employee to the director work together, reflecting the values of openness and equality, can be observed in Indonesian–Japanese business organizations in Indonesia.

Management researchers Dwiatmadja *et al.* (1997) made a comparative study of Japanese and American joint ventures in Indonesia. They found among other things that Indonesian managers are more directive, Japanese more participative, American managers more democratic. They also found that Japanese managers are more able to motivate Indonesian employees than American managers. Another finding is that Indonesian employees managed by American managers have significant less stress than Indonesian employees managed by Japanese or Indonesian managers.

National private business organizations can be distinguished as conglomerates, large organizations, medium-sized business organizations, and small-sized businesses. The corporate culture of those business organizations is in general a family culture. It is

> a power-oriented corporate culture in which the leader is regarded as a caring parent who knows better than his subordinates what should be

done and what is good for them. Rather than being threatening, this type of power is essentially intimate and (hopefully) benign. The work of the corporation in this type of culture is usually carried forward in an atmosphere that in many respects mimics the home.

(Trompenaars 1994)

This specific, namely Trompenaar's, description of family culture is valid in state-owned business organizations, as well as in several private business organizations, and in large-, medium-, and small-sized business organizations. In several private business organizations the family culture is in fact a family business. The CEO or the business leader is the head of a family, and members of the family hold leading key positions in the organization. An outstanding pharmaceutical industry, founded by the Kouw brothers, has grown into a conglomerate of businesses. The sons and daughter of the Kouw brothers occupy leadership positions in the various businesses. They are of Chinese descent, but they are university graduates, mostly from US universities. Although they still have respect for their seniors, and still have the habit of addressing other persons using the specific titles, like 'bapak' (father) or 'ibu' (mother), or 'saudara' (brother/sister),

They are more individualistic than collectivistic. There are many other Chinese business organizations founded by the Chinese, with Chinese culture, that have grown into big businesses headed by scholarly Chinese with a strong Western orientation. There are other Chinese business organizations which still have a typical Chinese corporate culture based on Confucianism, which is pragmatic, materialistic, promoting honesty, goodness, devotion, consideration, and soberness (Dewi 2002). They also create effective networks with other Chinese businesses based on a trust called 'guanxi', which was also observed by Trompenaars and Hampden Turner in a large Chinese corporation in Taiwan (2001: 235).

Recently, Djokosantoso Moeljono (2002) has identified the corporate culture of a state-owned bank, Bank Rakyat Indonesia (Indonesian's People Bank), as expressed in the following core values: Integrity, Professionalism, and Respecting the human resources.

Managerial values and behaviour

A study by Dananjaya (1985), on the difference in personal and cultural value orientations among managers, found that most Indonesian managers have a pragmatic primary value orientation. A small number have moralistic primary value orientation. Dananjaya also found that the more successful managers possess operative values related to or necessary for the achievement of success.

Mann (1994), based on his experience working in Indonesia, described

several characteristics of the Indonesian way of doing business. He warned
foreign businessmen against showing certain behaviour:

> Indonesians, especially Javanese, do not like people to strike aggressive
> postures or to speak loudly bordering on shouting. Standing with arms
> folded or legs apart or crooking the finger should therefore be avoided.
> They especially dislike those who lose their temper, or come close to it.
>
> (Mann 1994: 116)

He also stated that many Indonesians, especially Javanese, 'do not like to be
the bearers of bad tidings and most do not like to say outright "no" in case
this gives offense' (Mann 1994: 116). There are several ways indeed to say
'no' in an indirect manner: for instance, when invited to an meeting, one can
say 'insya Allah' (if God permits), or 'I will try to come', 'I will look in my
appointment book, which I left in my office', etc. Another characteristic of
Indonesian managers is paternalism, or bapakism. Superiors and elders are
all called 'bapak' (father) or 'ibu' (mother), terms which embody the notion
of someone who will make decisions for you, will listen to you, protect you,
know your needs, and do the best for you. The terms represent a benevolent
authoritative person. These two values – 'conflict avoidance' and 'vertical
orientation' – feature in Hofstede's 1982 study. Indonesian managers scored
high on the dimensions 'collectivism', 'power distance', and 'femininity', and
low on 'uncertainty avoidance'. Indonesian managers thus tend to: protect
the interest of the members of their extended families, but in exchange
expect permanent loyalty (benevolent authoritative/collectivism); accept the
inequality between the 'strong' and the 'weak' (vertical orientation, power
distance); like to contemplate, are not aggressive, unemotional, and relatively tolerant (conflict avoidance); stress quality of life and welfare for the
weak – men need not be ambitious or competitive (femininity).

Again, Trompenaars (1994) found similar results in his research. About
half of Indonesian managers perceive the organization as a system rather
than a social group (66 per cent), half of them experience the organization
as a means to be able to work rationally, efficiently, and effectively. They also
tend to be more being 'particularists' than 'universalist'; relationships tend
to be more important to them than the application of rules without any
consideration of the existing specific conditions. Another research finding is
that only a small percentage of Indonesian managers are opting for individual responsibility (13 per cent). In other words, they tend to be more
collectivistic, which is in accordance with Hofstede's findings. This is
reflected in the group decision-making process. Indonesia uses the expression 'musyawarah untuk mufakat' (deliberations for the sake of getting a
common agreement, consensus). When agreement is not achieved then the
supervisor, someone with higher authority (the leader, 'bapak' or 'ibu'),
makes the decision. Voting is avoided in the group decision-making process.

Budihardjo (1991) found that most managers tend to use an authoritative style in solving individual as well as group problems.

On the affective versus the neutral cultures, Trompenaars found that 75 per cent of the Indonesian respondents would not express their feeling upset at work openly. This would be true if the majority of respondents were Javanese or Sundanese. People from the Batak and Minangkabau ethnic groups would most probably give an affirmative answer. They are more free and spontaneous in expressing their feelings.

Labour–management conflict resolution

After independence in 1945, labour unions were established by the diverse business organizations. To coordinate all the labour unions the Sentral Organisasi Buruh Seluruh Indonesia (SOBSI, Labour Central Organization for All Indonesia) was set up. At the beginning of the 'New Order', in 1966, the SOBSI was liquidated, based on the accusation that the organization was affiliated with the Indonesian Communist Party, which was liquidated by the 'New Order' government. In February 1973 a labour union was established, the Federasi Buruh Seluruh Indonesia (FBSI, Labour Federation for All Indonesia) which became the only labour union. All the other labour organizations were dissolved into the FBSI. The government did not tolerate the existence of many labour organizations (Uwiyono, 2001). FBSI was renamed as the Serikat Pekerja Seluruh Indonesia (SPSI, Worker Union for All Indonesia) in November 1985 (Simanjuntak 1992). Each private business organization is allowed to set up its own labour union, but the organization should inform the SPSI so that the new labour union can become a unit of the SPSI. The labour unions exist only for the private business organizations. The government-owned business organizations (Badan Usaha Milik Negara, BUMN) and all government offices have the KORPRI (Korps Pegawai Republik Indonesia, Civil Servants Corps of the Republic of Indonesia) who will speak up for the rights and defend the interests of civil servants. Strikes are forbidden in this context. A Collective Labour Agreement (CLA) should be stipulated as a result of negotiations between the management and union workers in each business organization, which should be able to prevent strikes. Conflict should be solved through 'musyawarah untuk mufakat' (deliberations to achieve common agreement). When no solution is found, several stages are available to come to an agreed resolution (Uwiyono 2001). The customs to resolve conflicts are stated in Act Number 22, Year 1957, about labour conflict resolution and the implementation of regulations. The first stage of conflict resolution is the negotiations between the management and the labour union of the organization. When no agreement has been achieved then the case will be presented to and discussed by the regional committee for the settlement of labour conflict (Penyelesaian Perselisihan Perburuhan Daerah, PPPD), the second stage. If the labour problem is still unsolved then the case will be presented to and deliberated by the central committee for the settlement of labour conflict (Penyelesaian Perselisihan Perburuhan Pusat, P4) until a solution is achieved, the third stage. During the second and third stages representatives of the management and the labour union actively participate in the deliberations led by the government representative from the Department of Labour. At this stage a final solution will be decided. Whether on not the solution is satisfying for either one or both parties, the management and the labour union representative, both have to accept the decision.

To prevent dysfunctional conflicts, all business organizations should implement the work culture ('budaya kerja') in their work organization. Guidelines to implement the work culture were created by the Office of the Minister of State on Empowerment of the State Apparatus (Civil Servants) in 1991.

According to the guidelines, the work culture should consider the interests of all stakeholders in the organization. Pancasila Industrial Relations (PIR) is part of the work culture. The employer and employees/workers should be seen as being members of a group working together as a team to achieve optimal results for the benefit of all involved, the organization, the owners (the government, or the shareholders), the management, the employees/workers themselves, and the customers. The core values that should be internalized by all employees (management and workers) are: togetherness (the feeling of being together to get the work done together); openness (open for new ideas, open for different and/or contradictory ideas); helping each other (the readiness and willingness to help each other in performing the duties); deliberations for common agreement (open and fair discussions to come to an agreement accepted by all members of the group). In the process of socializing and internalizing the core values, it is expected that the leader will set an example, able to motivate his people, and recognizing and empowering the capacities of his subordinates. This will than lead to managers and employees/workers who will have the feeling of mutual ownership of the organization ('Meloe handarbeni'), a feeling of common responsibility ('Meloe hangroekebi'), and an attitude of continuous learning based on regular self-evaluation ('Mulat sariro hangrosowani'). At that time, during the 'New Order' era, not many business organizations, private as well as state owned, had tried to implement the work culture in their organization, partly because they were not aware of the important role of a corporate culture in supporting the productivity of the business organization. Another cause could be the authoritarian character of the government instruction to implement the work culture in their organization. A third cause could be that the leaders of business organizations are doubtful whether the work culture is the right corporate culture for their business organization. To my knowledge, one of the few private organizations that have adopted the work culture as its corporate culture has developed into a large and successful business organization.

Implications for managers

To satisfy and to have good working relations with all stakeholders in the business organization the CEO should be very intelligent, imaginative, creative, self-confident, honest, and patient. The CEO should have the Leadership–Personality type of the Accomplisher (Crosby 1996), and most probably will face Trompenaars' (1994) dilemmas in the process of satisfying all stakeholders.

In serving the interests of the stockholders the CEO at the same time has to serve the interests of the government, especially the government officials the CEO has to deal with continuously, which can create several dilemmas that have to be solved to reconcile the problems. There will be the dilemma, for example, for obeying the rules, on the one hand, and following the special requirements of certain government officials, on the other.

In order to serve the interests of subordinates (managers, employees, workers), the CEO should create good working relationships with them, taking special care that subordinates are appointed from different ethnic groups, having specific values, customs, and habits. The CEO should build a strong and effective corporate culture together with them; should not make important decisions alone; and should build an effective work team who can assist in the decision making. The days of authoritarian leadership are over. The CEO should also be flexible in leading people. A collective leadership could be the alternative.

To serve the interests of suppliers and customers, the CEO should build effective communications and maintain good interrelations with them, identifying their needs and nurturing them (Crosby 1996). Managers employed in foreign business organizations, in particular, have to try to adjust themselves, without sacrificing their religious and national values, to the core business values of the foreigners (the CEO and managers).

Managers employed in business organizations with a dominant family corporate culture and a benevolent authoritative leadership should try to find ways to express their opinions and ideas, which they think would be best for the organization without hurting their superiors. Like the CEO, managers should build effective work teams with their subordinates, taking into consideration the possibly different work values of their subordinates who will be people from different ethnic groups.

Conclusions

Indonesia consists of about 200 ethnic groups, each having its own ethnic culture and its own language. The Indonesian language and the national curriculum executed in all primary and secondary schools have led to changes in the ethnic cultures and created a national culture. The intense interactions between Indonesia and other states have a significant overall impact on the national culture and on the economy of Indonesia.

The economy, which was not previously such a priority during the 'Old

Order', became very important and indeed a priority during the 'New Order'. The economic results were impressive. However, together with economic welfare, morality weakened. The monetary crisis followed by the economic crisis starting in 1997 also created a political and moral vacuum. The government has not yet succeeded in overcoming the crisis.

The remaining small-, medium-, and large-sized business organizations have to struggle on, not only to sustain their existence, but also to be able to grow enough to help the government overcome the economic crisis.

Finally, Indonesian managers should continue to become 'perpetual learners', working together in each business organization, and assist the CEO to become leaders (Crosby 1996), able to reconcile the dilemmas they face in their organizations (Trompenaars 1994).

References

Amir, M. S. (2001) *Adat Minangkabau* (Minangkabau Customs), Jakarta: PT Mutiara Zumber Widya

Anwar, M. A. and Prakarsa, W. (1992) 'Current and emerging trends in management education in Indonesia', Paper presented at the Annual Meeting/Workshop of the Pacific Asian Consortium for International Business Education and Research, Honolulu, January.

Anwar, N. (2002) 'Economic recovery from the crisis in 1997–1998', in M. Ikhsan, C. Manning and H. Soesastro (eds), *Ekonomi Indonesia di Era Politik Baru*, Jakarta: Penerbit Buku Kompas, pp. 33–50.

Azis, I. J., Thorbecke, E. and Thorbecke, W. (2002) 'The socio-economic impact of the Asian financial crisis on Indonesia', in M. Ikhsan, C. Manning and H. Soesastro (eds), *Ekonomi Indonsia di Era Politik Baru* (Indonesian Economy in the New Political Era), Jakarta: Kompas.

Budihardjo, A. (1991) 'Pengaruh sistem nilai manajer terhadap gaya kepemimpinannya' (The influence of managerial value systems towards their leadership style), Magister tesis, Jakarta, Universitas Indonesia.

Crosby, P. (1996) *The Absolutes of Leadership*, San Francisco: Jossey Bass.

Dananjaya, A. A. (1985) 'Pola system nilai manajer di Indonesia' (Value system of managers in Indonesia), Dissertation, Jakarta, Universitas Indonesia.

Dewi Setyorini (2002) 'Pengaruh sikap terhadap peran tradisional-non tradisional wanita dan Locus of Control terhadap motivasi berprestasi pada wanita pedagang batik etnis Jawa, Cina dan Arab di pasar Klewer kotamadya Surakarta' (The influence of the attitude towards traditional v non-traditional women and locus of control on the achievement motivation by Javanese, Chinese, Arab Batik women traders in Klewer marketplace in the City of Surakarta), Unpublished Masters Thesis, Faculty of Psychology, University of Indonesia.

Djokosantoso Moeljono (2002) 'Pengaruh budaya korporat terhadap produktivitas pelayanan di PT Bank Rakyat Indonesia' (The influence of corporate culture on the service productivity at the Indonesian People's Bank, Inc.), Dissertation, Universitas Gajah Mada, Yogyakarta.

Dwiatmadja, C., B.Neuijen, F. D. J., Grotenhuis, J. and Stroobach, Ph. G. (1997) 'Culture, management behaviour and employee performance', Unpublished report, Satya Wacana Christian University, Salatiga.

Hofstede, G. (1982) *Cultural Pitfalls for Dutch Expatriates in Indonesia*, Deventer: Kluwer.

Mann, R. I. (1994) *The Culture of Business in Indonesia*, Mississauga, Ontario; Gateway Books.

Mari, P. (2002) 'Facing the China challenge. Options for Indonesia and ASEAN', in M. Ikhsan, C. Manning and H. Soesastro (eds), *Ekonomi Indonesia di Era Politik Baru*, Jakarta: Penerbit Buku Kompas, pp.385 –400.

Mubyarto, M. (2002) 'Reformasi Ekonomi dari Orde Baru ke Indonesia Baru' (Economic reformation, from the New Order to New Indonesia'), in M. Ikhsan, C. Manning and H. Soesastro (eds), *Ekonomi Indonesia di Era Politik Baru*, Jakarta: Penerbit Buku Kompas, pp. 33–50.

Mursal, E. (1993) *Minangkabau, Tradisi dan Perubahan* (Minangkabau, tradition, and change), Padang: Angkasa Raya.

Poverty (2000) in *Statistik Indonesia* (Statistical Year Book of Indonesia), Jakarta: Badan Pusat Statistik, pp. 561–77.

Simanjuntak, P. J. (1992) *Masalah Hubungan Industrial di Indonesia* (The industrial relations in Indonesia), Jakarta: HIPSMI.

Sjahrir, M. (2000) 'Krisis Ekonomi Indonesia. Perlu Ekonomi Baru?' ('Indonesian economic crisis. Is a new economy needed?'), in M. Ikhsan, C. Manning and H. Soesastro (eds), *Ekonomi Indonesia di Era Politik Baru*, Jakarta: Penerbit Buku Kompas, pp. 33–50.

The Office of the Minister of State on Empowerment of the State Apparatus (Civil Servants), February 1991, Jakarta: Pedoman Pemasyarakatan Budaya Kerja.

Trompenaars, F. (1994) *Riding the Waves of Culture*, Singapore: Irwin.

Trompenaars, F. and Hampden Turner, C. (2001) *21 Leaders in the 21st Century*, Oxford: Capstone.

Uwiyono, A. (2001) 'Hak Mogok di Indonesia' ('The right to strike in Indonesia'), Dissertation, Faculty of Law, University of Indonesia.

6 Culture and management in Japan

Philippe Debroux

Introduction

The management system adopted by large Japanese companies after the war rests on two pillars: a labour–management compromise and a financial agreement that created a stable corporate governance system. The compatibility that was achieved between the needs, desires, values and expectations of employees and management created the conditions for the creation of competitive advantages in a number of industries until the 1970s (Abegglen 1976). Afterwards, when growth naturally slowed down, pressure started to develop between the business environment and the management practices and Japan entered a period that Hasegawa (1996) described as one of 'contrived' compatibility. From that time on companies were obliged to adjust the management system to keep as much of the compatibility as they could within the changing business environment. However, it has become increasingly difficult over time and the business system seems to have reached its limits.

Nobody would deny that Japan is in the midst of a severe crisis and that the management practices need a more drastic overhaul than was the case during the previous economic downturns.[1] Nevertheless, there is no reason to draw hasty conclusions. In 1945 the Japanese economy was almost completely destroyed and the Japanese people's standard of living had declined dramatically. Now, after a decade of sluggish growth, Japan remains the second-largest economic power, an affluent society enjoying a high standard of living, the first creditor nation in the world and still the best manufacturer in a number of strategic high-technology industries (Fingleton 1999). Present unemployment rates, although high in the historical perspective, are still relatively low by global standards. Japan is in a better position than it was fifty years ago to transform its business system into good condition. But this has to be done in a country where the lifestyle, patterns of thought and values drastically changed and diversified during the period. The features of the management system that were considered as key assets to create and sustain competitive advantages are now perceived as hindering structural reforms (Porter *et al.* 2000). The tentative reforms undertaken in companies led to different types of reaction. A feeling of insecurity and doubt permeates society (Nomura 1998). It induces conservatism and defence of vested interests in some quarters.

But the liberalization of the business system and opening up to the world is also creating a new dynamism transcending the generations. Japanese people desire to fulfil their self-achievement in social and professional life (Sugimura 1997). They want a more comfortable life with a better balance between private and working life (Economic Planning Agency 2000). Women express their desire for equality at home and in society. The rapid aging of the population is a great challenge, in economic but also in cultural terms, in a society for which the respect for seniority was always a key moral principle. The development of a new management framework will have to take into account such a mixture of economic and socio-cultural elements.

At least one element remains constant. The main wealth of Japan is in its human resources. Constant efforts to develop capabilities, knowledge and skills are required in a country almost devoid of any natural resources. This explains the central position occupied by education. It is, with marriage, employment and retirement, one of the four main preoccupations of Japanese people, reminding us of the durable influence of Confucianism. Japanese companies are now revamping their management system starting from this premise and devoting considerable resources in their efforts to acquire and diffuse knowledge and skill in the organization. The result will be different from the old one devised in the context of a country's reconstruction. But, it is likely to borrow from diverse influences to recreate a system encompassing the specificity, coherence and dynamics of the Japanese socio-cultural and economic environment.

Historical setting

The Japanese archipelago is often presented as a homogeneous world: a sole state and imperial dynasty since its origins in about the fifth century, a common language, no significant ethnical modifications since its origin. However, historians, anthropologists and sociologist insist on the multiplicity, the heterogeneity and the complexity of social relationships in Japan. The power struggle that ended with the takeover of political power by the warrior class at the end of the twelfth century is a turning point in Japanese history (Farris 1992). Subsequently, the Portuguese missionaries, relayed later on by the Dutch merchants, continued to explain that Japanese society was essentially of a warrior nature. Indeed, after more than a century of civil war there emerged a strong unified state led by the warrior class in the seventeenth century, with the imperial court playing a figurative role (Hunter 1984). The strengthening of the state allowed the diffusion all over the country of a sophisticated social system that had already appeared in the early history. The horizontal *mura* (village) structure, coming from western Japan, was integrated in an hierarchical structure inspired by the eastern model of the *ie* (house) to create a cohesive society centred on the patriarchal family (Nakane 1967).

The new regime rapidly decided to isolate Japan from the external world. So, the entry point into modernity that Japan took was different from that of Europe and the North America and this conditioned a different passage through the stages of industrial and technological development. But, globally, the Tokugawa period of relative closure did not stop internal dynamism and a fast economic and demographic expansion. Over time, the ranking and conditions, distinctions on which the warriors' power was based, were increasingly threatened by the social reality. The success of the big trading houses established business profit as an important social value long before the Meiji Restoration (Norman 1940). The Tokugawa period was also that of neo-Confucianism and Chinese studies. However, in contrast to China and Korea, no orthodoxy emerged. The neo-Confucian way of thinking diversified into diverse schools of thought. Intense intellectual activities flourished among a number of *samourai* and members of the bourgeoisie eager to assert their roles and values in society. This appeared notably in the interest in Western science and techniques, which familiarized Japanese people to the best of Western knowledge in the seventeenth century (Totman 1993). It may explain why, during the Meiji period, Japanese elites were able to assimilate over a period of about thirty years a modern company concept and organization that had been nurtured for centuries in Western countries (Fruin 1992). Economic modernization could not have taken hold so comprehensively and so rapidly from the Meiji period onwards without forces for change and modernization building up inside the society even before the country's opening up.

On that occasion, Japanese people again manifested their pragmatism and capacity for adaptation. Long-term employment, wages based on life stages and company unions were rational responses to the skilled labour shortage after the Russo-Japanese War and the subsequent development of heavy industry [2] (Taira 1970). The job rotation system developed in order to cope with absenteeism (Koike 1988). Thus, at the start of the twentieth century there emerged a number of key features of the modern Japanese management system. However, they were not given a normative social legitimacy during the pre-war period. There was little of the strong mutual organizational commitment that is the hallmark of post-war large Japanese companies. Management was of a 'top-down' nature organized under strict hierarchical lines. There existed little possibility of passing through the tight class structures and trade union activities were severely curtailed (Hazama 1997).

Economic background

In the aftermath of the Second World War, a welfare corporatist system in which large companies replaced the state in the role of wealth redistributor provided an economically workable and socially acceptable business system, fitting the post-war egalitarian social bias and the economic catch-up strategy (Dore 1973). Mixing pre-modern patterns of thought and modernity, this was predicated on job security for the regular members of the company and cooperative industrial relations. Building on the legacy of the Confucian culture in Japan, a system of well-defined networks of mutual obligations developed in a modern setting (Koizumi 1989). Management aimed at a steady expansion and emphasized long-term recognition of the economic and security needs of its members and their families. In return, the company could expect a strong organizational commitment helping to promote the long-term growth of the organization.

Standard theories of the firm, based on neo-classical economic analysis, seemed to be inadequate to explain the model of the Japanese company. In the Japanese economy, the motivations, mechanisms and institutions that rule demand, supply and equilibrium seemed to differ strongly from the neo-classical tradition. The preferences of a number of groups and associations took priority over what individuals normally create for themselves in an individual capacity. The system did not entirely eliminate the supply and demand laws and the need for economic equilibrium. However, selective alterations were large enough to affect performance characteristics and the potential of public and private organizations. Characteristically of a Confucian culture putting emphasis on the long-term perspective, Japanese organizations did not try to maximize profits as in a system based on competition and the market (Hofstede and Bond 1988). For managers, the rather flexible requirements towards profit were the necessary preconditions for preserving their leadership, stable employment and high wages for the permanent employees.

As a product of a group-oriented culture, the development of a multiple stakeholder system reinforced the networking among individuals and organizations. The stability of the principals could be ascertained from the mutual corporate control system coming from the institutionalization of long-term employment and collaborative industrial relations, from group business transactions and from cross-shareholdings in companies belonging to industrial groups (Dore 2000). Despite containing only about 20–25 per cent of the total salaried population, large companies have exerted a massive influence on employment practices, the markets, the civil society and even the family and its distinctive social composition during the last fifty years. Workers were confident that their jobs would be preserved and incomes would rise. This made it possible to avoid labour and other social conflicts and to increase steadily both savings and consumption. Japanese people were entitled to believe that they belonged to a large middle class. Wages and fringe benefit differentials remained large but the prosperity of large companies trickled down to some extent to smaller companies. The rationale of the system was socially legitimized. In an education system based on meritocracy, those who emerged with the best academic credentials went naturally to the best companies (Rohlen 1983). Female workers were treated on less favourable terms and conditions than males. But, on the whole, this was just the result of a distinctness of male and female roles in society accepted by the majority of men and women up until recently (Hunter 1993).

So, the success of the Japanese economy not only in terms of growth itself but also in terms of a rise in the standard of living of a growing segment of the population, despite the apparent sacrifice of key elements of the market mechanism, seemed to have vindicated the idea that business systems and social institutions are linked and organizational structures and strategies cannot be contemplated in isolation from their institutional contexts (Granovetter 1985). The Japanese 'communalist' system may have been a brake on the optimization of economic input. Nevertheless, it seemed to work efficiently against all odds, at least until recently. Nowadays, the company-centred ideology of welfare corporatism is under pressure. The Japanese economy and society have reached a high stage of maturity. The fertility rate is one of the lowest in the world and the population is aging rapidly. Japan achieved a 3.7 per cent growth in the decade after it broke into the big league of wealthy countries. However, it has followed the path of other developed countries (Ostrom 1999). Most econometric studies conclude that given the growth of the labour force, the projected rate of profitable investment and the expected increases in productivity, growth will settle in the range of 1–2.5 per cent a year (Economic Planning Agency 1999) but may be higher in a given year. By 2002, economic expansion was not much above zero, with unemployment around 5.5 per cent.

Societal culture

Japanese religions, as well as the world viewpoint they induced, have marked the culture of the archipelago since ancient times, but without imposing either unitarian dogmas or strict conceptions of the universe. Beliefs and ritual behaviour are turned towards multiple divinities, defined essentially in function of the place of residence (Reader 1991). People live under the protection of the *kami* (undifferentiated spirits or vital force) who assure the long-term existence and the prosperity of the community. The deep sociocultural transformations since the Meiji era have affected religious beliefs. As in most modern states, religion's influence, such as that of Confucianism or Shintoism, on society is clearly dwindling. Nonetheless, a number of specificities of Japanese culture remain: the pluralism of the cults, the heterodoxy and large variety of religious practices, the blurred distinction between the sacred and the secular worlds, and the relationships of reciprocity between human beings and their environment.[3]

It has become standard knowledge to say that Japanese people believe the self to be deeply embedded in social relationships. There is little confidence in the power of the individual to devise, control and execute his or her own destiny, especially if those plans run counter to prevailing external social and structural norms and conditions (Hamaguchi 1988). Throughout

Japan's history, social structures have generated a durable cohesion in all periods and places. Nowadays, the organization of many rural communities is still centred on traditional structures that govern group life. The group is composed of a complex system of local units of a secular or religious nature, sharing the objective of managing the communal assets and performing community services and obligations. Those communities are traditionally organized in a territory whose limits are both material and religious, with key places reserved for the important events of community life. To belong to such community is to enter into a network of solidarity and hierarchies. It is to be the heir and actor of the history of a specific place that confers identity, values and a sense of life (Berthon 1995). However, such rich social reality remains only in the least populated areas. Urban emigration since the high growth period of the 1960s has put an end to the slow transformation process of the local societies and destabilized them. The same phenomenon occurred also in the cities that were organized in local communities. The economic growth has displaced people, modified places and structures and almost destroyed local associative links.

To some extent it could be argued that post-war Japanese companies replaced the socialization process of the former periods. The corporate system created a genuine feeling of affectivity, belonging and trust between the members of the organization (Hayashi 1988). It developed a set of socially sanctioned rights and obligations for workers, companies and society at large. In so doing, it could satisfy the yearning for stability and the material needs of the workers while diffusing an ideology of work and of corporate relationships. For a while, it recreated mutual bonds of obligations that were legitimized by all the parties. Employees devoted their lives to the company to the point of sacrificing their social life in exchange for a predictable and secure career. They were induced to feel that something had to be given back in return for the long-term job guarantee and rising income. It made them accept working long hours and doing their best to improve their expertise. Meanwhile, their self-achievement needs could be somewhat sublimated by the success of the organization.

Now, what Aoki (1988) called the 'economic incentive mechanism' no longer works so well. Young Japanese people consider as outdated the collective ideals of the closed-knit organizations (Sugimura 1997). They do not want to be bound to a company and to sacrifice their private life to it. The content of the job is separate from activities outside the organization such as relations with family and friends, as well as leisure or volunteer-types of activities (Economic Planning Agency 2000). The control that the Meiji elites had exerted to limit Western influence to technical aspects (*wakon yosai*, namely 'Oriental Spirit, Western Technology') was not possible in democratic post-war Japan (Hunter 1984) but priority was given to the material needs. Now, gratifications limited to the external and material worlds do not seem to be sufficient for the newly affluent and highly educated Japanese society (Sugimura 1997). There is a strong need for a system allowing an expression of the inner world of the self, reflecting what can be called a 'contingent convergence' with the Western world in that respect.

Corporate culture

The concept of *unmei kyodotai*, literally translated as 'community of fate', which became the cement of the psychological contract inside Japanese companies, was grounded in economic rationality (Koike 1995). The post-war development project was aimed at regaining strength and prosperity in catching up with the most advanced countries. However, it was also a skilful socio-cultural construction redefining the meaning of work and the way individual employees relate to their company. Throughout working life, all practices have the purpose to construct and reinforce the affective, ethical and social foundations of belonging to a specific organization. Beyond economic rationality, the concept of a 'community of fate' was associated with the traditional Japanese culture that was supposed to give pre-eminence to the group and not to the individual (Hamaguchi 1988).

Japanese companies are capitalist organizations created for the long-term financial interest of all stakeholders. However, they are perceived as having objectives not based on purely economic individual interests and as being of a distinctly Japanese origin in their philosophy (Hamaguchi 1988). The features of exchange are expressed in both monetary and non-monetary terms. From recruitment to retirement, the whole person is to be considered and not only its economic value. The rights and duties of labour and management, and the consensual mechanisms of conflict resolution, began to be accepted as a given, closed to an official ideology or moral belief. Based on the presumed long-term presence of the members to the group, large Japanese companies became self-contained units, putting a strong emphasis on their history, unwritten rules, relationships, rites and systems (Hayashi 1988).

From an historical perspective, Japanese management can be regarded as an evolutionary product of 'rice culture', as suggested by Hayashi (1988). Group endeavour, diligence, consensual decision making and the lack of a strict division of labour can be regarded as practices that have evolved out of Japan's rice culture. In the company, members can count on the mutual support of the others with a high degree of interdependence. The scope of the internal relations is wide and pervasive and not just based on narrow interests. The tangibility of the responsibilities is subjective, implicitly under-stood and not public and easily observable. As Nonaka and Takeuchi (1995) explained, the acquisition and diffusion of knowledge in a Japanese company is mainly of the tacit type, as opposed to the explicit one. This is a characteristic of a high-context culture, where there is little emphasis put on explicit information diffused in a sequential manner (Hall 1976). In a Japanese organization, information is disseminated constantly all over the organization in an implicit manner. There is relatively little codification and access to the right information is personalized and contextual. In terms of time frame, the Japanese company developed as an open-ended and indefinite and not a close-ended and specific system. The possibility of trouble and problems is always anticipated as part of normality. They are supposed to be dealt with by cooperation and not governed by specific individual rights (Fliaster 1999).

Managerial behaviour

As presented by Aoki (1988), the management system features a decentralized internal information structure that facilitates horizontal communication between functional units whereby teams are able to resolve problems autonomously without the involvement of higher managerial levels. There is typically a close cooperation between the departments, particularly marketing and production, from an early stage of development (Aoki 1994). As such, it depends on the active cooperation of white- and blue-collar employees having broad integrative skills and problem-solving abilities and not just functional specialties (Koike 1995). Japanese managers have never been the broad generalists they are often believed to be. Middle managers have a coordinating role but after a few years they tend to specialize and pursue their careers in a relatively narrow field (Sato 1997). However, this does not preclude a high level of geographic and interdepartmental mobility in order to acquire organizational skills. Most of them acquire over time a large amount of experience in multi-functional teams, giving them the ability to have access to and make efficient use of the tacit knowledge required to operate in a high-context organization.

The qualities required in higher hierarchical positions may be acquired only through a long-term tenure in the organization. An understanding of the operating procedures, technology, subordinates' skills and personality, and customers' and suppliers' characteristics is necessary. Line managers also play the key role of mentor and careers adviser to their subordinates, while appraising them on a continuous basis. Shop-floor employees know about the details of production, senior managers provide the vision, and middle managers are the active intermediaries. In factories, there is closer interaction between management and skilled workers. Lam (1994) found that Japanese line managers maintain a stronger involvement in their area of technical expertise than do their British counterparts. Likewise, Lincoln *et al.* (1986) observed that, in terms of formal authority relationships, Japanese managers are more remote than their US counterparts, fitting the high power distance and respect of hierarchy characteristics of Japanese society (Hofstede 1991). However, when it comes to their actual behaviour, the position is reversed. Indeed, there is a strong respect for authority creating a clear chain of command. But it confirms Lam's observation of Japanese managers being 'player managers'.

Managerial values

During the post-war period, managerial ideology oscillated between two poles, i.e. that of management functionality and that of communality, but since the 1970s, the second pole of communality seems to have taken a dominant position. It was not supposed to be for ever. Managers, workers and union leaders had shared the pain of a long war and the material and spiritual deprivations that followed defeat. This explains why management supported and reinforced the long-term psychological contract with the labour force during the reconstruction phases and the high growth period of the 1950s and 1960s. Companies always tried to make the system more efficient by reinforcing its economic rationale through restriction of the advantages bestowed to workers in the 1950s. For many business leaders life-stage wages and the life employment system were only temporary measures justified by the circumstances. After economic and social recovery, a convergence with Western employment practices was expected to occur (Magota 1970). However, the community of fate that started as an artificial construction was a successful example of cultural modelling. It gained such a wide legitimacy in society at large that its tenets became difficult to challenge. The cornerstone of the structure, the life employment system, was never fundamentally challenged until the end of the 1990s. And the concern over human development continued to be translated into the practice of age-specific promotion, training and the remuneration system.

A move in a functional direction can now be observed. Reliance on capital markets and the shift towards a shareholder-centred corporate governance mean that employees cannot remain the privileged stakeholders. However, opinions diverge about the changes in corporate values this may entail. The Japan Employers' Federations Association (Nikkeiren 1995), the Corporate Governance Council of Japan (1998) and a number of top managers insist on the company's social responsibility vis-à-vis employees and society at large. Recently, however, the managerial elite, in asking for radical changes, has become more vocal (Keizai Doyukai 1999). It is argued that there is incompatibility between the psychological and emotional rigidity of lifetime membership of the corporate community and the attempts to increase performance through new incentives and control based on the contribution and/or abilities of individual employees. Changes not only of the functional features and institutions of the Japanese company but of the consciousness of the employees are required (Tanaka and Asakawa 2001).

Labour–management conflict resolution

Over the last fifty years, bargaining between labour and management took place on the understanding that employment was guaranteed. On this premise, management could make, sustain and if necessary change agreements with the company union. In exchange for integration into the wages-setting and redundancy systems, and as a counterpart for appropriate behaviour by companies, unions could guarantee cooperation by their members. Union leaders never got a say at board level, meaning that employee participation in the decision-making process always remained limited and not threatening to management control. True, as a last resort, unions could always use the weapon of the strike and companies could rely on pressure from organized business if the union was considered as not carrying out its side of the bargain. But, the leading paradigm was that of a coalitional entity where the bargaining parties seek to find cooperative game solutions (Aoki 1994).

Such relations could develop because the contents of the employment relations of the permanent workers have been traditionally homogeneous. Contracts are regulated by work rules promulgated by the employer, and the role of the individual contract is quite small. Nowadays, the individualization of the status and working conditions makes new rules necessary in such respects as clarification of the contracts' contents.

The courts play an important role in establishing the rights and obligations of labour and management through case laws, such as those regarding the right of dismissal (Ouchi 2002). The principle of just cause for dismissal during the post-war period made it very difficult to dismiss regular employees for economic convenience (Ouchi 2002). However, although it fitted the socio-economic environment, emphasizing stability in industrial relations, there is now an understanding that it has to be adjusted to the new management practices. In 2000, the number of civil suits involving labour relations brought to district courts reached a level of 2063, exceeding 2,000 for the first time (*Japan Labour Bulletin* June 2001: 5–6), and a figure three times higher than ten years ago. The number of collective disputes has tended to decrease but is offset by a growing number of individual cases due to the dismissals and forced retirements as a result of the business downturn and restructuring plans, harassment in the workplace and unpaid wages.

In a country with a tradition of conciliation out of court there is a shortage of legal expertise. Japan has no labour courts in which management and labour representatives serve as arbiters. As a consequence, proceedings on labour issues are slow, placing a heavy burden on the parties, especially the workers; that is why recent reform is focused on the participation of management and labour representatives as mediators attempting to resolve disputes before they are brought to court (Ouchi 2002).

Reform in the HRM system supposes the establishment of rules for employment adjustment. There is a push from domestic and foreign management associations for a loosening of the rules for dismissal. Companies complain that rulings restricting the employer's right of dismissal are an impediment to their activities and discourage them from expanding employment (Hanai 2001). Rengo, the largest labour union confederation, asks for the enactment of a labour contract law establishing rules for dismissal as well as for recruitment, transfers, job rotation and retirement (Rengo Website 2001). Courts' decisions on the issue of dismissal rely on justifications being socially and economically acceptable. Therefore, unless the social climate changes dramatically for the better, it is unlikely that decisions in favour of easier dismissal rights will be reached in general terms. But there is room for a more flexible approach in labour regulations. Workers' economic conditions and interests have diversified, so that the needs for legal protection and economic necessities are diverging. Some categories of workers, i.e. high-level professionals and core employees, now have a higher bargaining power than before because of the existence of a larger external labour market and better access to information. In their case, the assumption is that individual disputes ought to be resolved by the contractual parties, or a civil court (Ouchi 2002). Conversely, there is an need for better legal protective regulations for non- regular workers, those not covered by the existing regulations, such as teleworkers for instance, or part timers, temporary and dispatched workers who are covered by still unclear case laws. The law now allows local labour bureaux such as the Labour Standards Inspection Offices and the Equal Opportunity Mediation Commissions to take part in the resolution of the growing disputes concerning those categories of workers. They are allowed to collaborate and establish counselling desks, thereby creating a kind of 'one-stop service' to deal with general labour issues (*Japan Labour Bulletin* October 2001).

Implications for managers

Lifetime employment as a symbol of the post-war social and political norms as well as a prevailing economic rationality is put seriously into question. Until the end of the 1990s, companies' reluctant restructuring efforts were still partly the result of their remaining normative legitimacy, but the reform is accelerating. The necessity of the change induced by the economic crisis parallels the evolution of the labour market structure. The percentages of those working in professional and technical jobs, and clerical and related workers, are expected to increase. Their working conditions and lifestyle are quite different from those of factory workers in terms of time and place of work, expectation, behaviour and attitude in private and professional life. All those elements call for a reconsideration of a system based on the long-term accumulation of skills by regular male workers in an internal market.

Companies are using approaches oriented towards a more differentiated and flexible system that makes greater use of the external labour market and specific skills. They are moving towards more contingent types of internal relationships. On the whole, more clear-cut rules in term of mutual expectations, rights and obligations seem to respond to the expectations of both parties. This does not mean that life employment will disappear. The core of white-collar workers is likely to shrink further. But a small minority of them, considered as potential senior managers, are expected to stay in the company for a long time (Nikkeiren 1995). They will be joined by specialists in the managerial ranks. The appraisal and reward system does not change fundamentally for blue-collar workers (Watanabe 2000) and non-managerial employees. It remains fundamentally based on tenure and level of skill.

However, both categories of managers work more and more under appraisal and reward systems emphasizing individual performance and contribution (Kinoshita 2001). Already, the salary differential is growing rapidly at the managerial level (RIALS 2000) as companies devise new incentive and control policies for their managerial elites.

Since the revision of the law in 1997, stock option plans can also be offered as incentive tools. For the time being, they mainly involve managerial personnel although there are moves to extend them to lower categories of workers in the hierarchy (Fliaster 1999). Changes also include some forms of pre-selection in which the employees are differentiated earlier in their career according to their potential. Companies are considering maximum ages for certain managerial ranks in order to create enough promotion opportunities for their best young executives in a period of flattening of the hierarchy. Some are devising a multi-track career system where promotion is no longer confined to management positions but can also take place according to specific professional objectives. The fact that the plans are addressed mainly to young graduates confirms that, for the time being, large companies still prefer to train their future managers internally, rather than recruit mid-career specialists (Rebick 2001). Although recruitment at mid-career has increased and become formalized in quite a number of large companies, as a system it seems to be still a phenomenon driven by specific needs in limited circumstances. Therefore, it is likely to take time to be integrated into the organization as a casual feature of the recruitment of core employees. Other plans are also developed to keep in the company and offer acceptable career opportunities to managerial personnel preferring to stay in a given area or having to take care of their children and family. This is done in order to take advantage of the widening range of values to which workers subscribe and to respond to their growing heterogeneity of needs and expectations (Economic Planning Agency 2000).

Conclusions

Reform of the management system in Japan progresses but with many uncertainties. In some respects, companies face the same dilemmas as their Western counterparts. To introduce an instrumental concept of relationships in organizations that maintain most of their characteristics of a high-context corporate culture, and create a coherent working model, is likely to be difficult. The pressure from globalization is gradually forcing management towards a more ability-based system. However, incompatibility between rules' basic logic makes it difficult to 'pick and mix'. If the professed objectives of changing the consciousness of the employee at work are achieved, the current transition towards a new paradigm will affect not only operational aspects, but also the very essence of the company – that is, its basic behavioural norms, its goals and its vision. It will also impose changes on the unwritten rules of the games, i.e. the reality of organizational life, what behaviour and attitudes at work are rewarded or rejected, etc.

Some of the current changes in management practices are related to the present economic slump. But it is also reasonable to think that some kind of convergence with international standards is occurring in Japan, not only in the managerial and material aspects of people's daily lives but also in the patterns of thought of average Japanese people, as exemplified by their willingness to respond to and actively engage with new forms of social life.

The concept of community of fate may be outdated in many respects, but both management and labour, individually and through company unions, have participated in its conception and contributed to its development and success until now. Japanese organizations again need a system that fits the institutional and cultural characteristics of Japanese society. The current painful and seemingly haphazard process of change probably reflects this approach. In Japan there are elements that seem to indicate that companies are disposing of committed, cooperative, long-term-oriented employees. Then there are managers taking care of the long-term well-being of their employees, communicating with them actively and trying to upgrade their capabilities. It cannot be denied that workers and management have made the 'community of fate' a dynamic concept. A whole set of HRM policies has been put in place that is linked to corporate strategies and organizational systems. It has developed into something closer to the 'soft' developmental, humanistic approach in the sense given to the term by Storey (1995). However, at the same time the self-reflexive individual approach that is associated with the soft approach, caring about the career development of the human capital from both the management and individual workers' sides, was always missing in Japan. The current management problem may lie precisely there. As a product of affluence, the representation of the Japanese self is now experiencing a cultural transformation that places the individual at a higher position in the Japanese world-view. In the conservative and pragmatic Japanese social life, transformations and developments in the external material and institutional environments always precede transformations and developments in the inner world of cognitive experience. The time is probably ripe for a kind of cultural modernization in terms of thought and behaviour in Japanese society. It is unlikely to be directly based on religion as its imperatives have ceased to be the basis of culture in Japan. But it is likely to proceed with the same lack of dogmatism that has always characterized the Japanese religions, beliefs and world-view. They resulted from multiple influences, were of a syncretic nature, and never imposed a strict conception of the universe (Berthon 1995). Likewise, the management practices that will emerge are likely to be based on a mixture of thought but always reflecting the traditional pragmatic approach to their introduction and implementation.

Notes

1   The Japanese stock market followed Wall Street downwards in mid-summer 2002. It has remained in the doldrums.
2   This of course implies that the roots of the Japanese employment system pre-date the post-1945 period.
3   Cf. the role of Confucianism in China, see Chapter 2.

References

Abegglen, J. C. (1976) *The Japanese Factory: Aspects of its Social Organization*, Glencoe, IL: Free Press.

Aoki, M. (1984) *Information, Incentives and Bargaining in the Japanese Economy*, Cambridge: Cambridge University Press.

Aoki, M. (1988) *Information, Incentives, and Bargaining in the Japanese Economy*, New York: Cambridge University Press.

Aoki, M. (1994) 'The Japanese firm as a system of attributes: a survey and research agenda', in M. Aoki and R. Dore (eds), *The Japanese Firm*, Oxford: Oxford University Press.

Berthon, J. P. (1995) 'Religions, croyances et conceptions du monde', in *L'etat du Japon*, Paris: La Découverte.

Corporate Governance Forum of Japan (1988) 'Corporate Governance Principles – Japanese View (Final Report)'. Available online at: <http://www.ecgn.ulb.ac.be/ecgn/codes.htm> (accessed 12 September 2001).

Dore, R (1973) *British Factory–Japanese Factory: The Origins of National Diversity in Industrial Relations*, Berkeley, CA: University of California Press.

Dore, R. (2000) *Stock Market Capitalism: Welfare Capitalism*, Oxford: Oxford University Press.

Economic Planning Agency (1999) *Economic Survey of Japan*, Tokyo: Economic Planning Agency.

Economic Planning Agency (2000) *White Book on National Living Mode*, Tokyo: Economic Planning Agency.

Farris, W. (1992) *Heavenly Warriors: the Evolution of Japan's Military, 500–1300*, Cambridge, MA: Harvard University Press.

Fingleton, E. (1999) *In Praise of Hard Industry*, Boston: Houghton Mifflin.

Fliaster, A (1999) 'Redefinition of the essence of the corporation in the global era: crucial tasks of Japanese and German top management', in *Proceedings of the 16th Euro Asia Management Studies Association Conference, November 1999, Rotterdam*.

Fruin, W. (1992) *The Japanese enterprise system*, New York: Clarendon Press.

Granovetter, M. (1985) 'Economic action and social structure: the problem of embeddedness', *American Journal of Sociology* 91(3): 481–510.

Hanai, K. (2001) 'Easing rules against layoffs: no need to rush', *The Japan Times* December 24: 16.

Hall, E. (1976) *Beyond Culture*, New York: Doubleday.

Hamaguchi, E. (1988) 'Japanese management as a civilization', *MITI Journal* I: 46–8.

Hasegawa, H. (1996) *The Steel Industry in Japan: A Comparison with Britain*, London: Routledge.

Hayashi, S. (1988) *Culture and Management in Japan*, Tokyo: University of Tokyo Press.

Hazama, H. (1997) *The History of Labour Management in Japan*, London: Macmillan.

Hofstede, G. (1991) *Culture and Organization*, Maidenhead: McGraw-Hill.

Hofstede, G. and Bond, M. H. (1988) 'The Confucian connection: from cultural roots to economic growth', *Organizational Dynamics*, Summer:. 42–63.

Hunter, J. (1984) *Concise Dictionary of Modern Japanese History*, Berkeley, CA: University of California Press.

Hunter, J. (1993) *Japanese Women Working*, London: Routledge.

Keizai Doyukai (1999) *Dai 14 Kai Kigyo Hakusho* (14th Edition of the Company White Book), Tokyo: Keizai Doyukai.

Kinoshita, T. (2001) 'Chingin Seido no Tenkan to Seikashugi Chingin no Mondaiten' (Turning point in the wages system and issues associated to result-based wages), in *Yearly Report of the Japanese Association of Labour Sociology*, Vol. 12, Tokyo: Toshindo.

Koike, K. (1988) *Understanding Industrial Relations in Modern Japan*, London: Macmillan.

Koike, K. (1995) *Nihon no Koyo System* (The Japanese Employment System), Tokyo: Toyo Keizai Shimposha.

Koizumi, T. (1989) 'Management of innovation and change in Japanese organizations', *Advances in International Systems Management* pp. 245–54.

Lam, A. (1994) 'The utilization of human resources: a comparative study of British and Japanese engineers in the electronic industries', *Human Resource Management Journal* 4(3): 22–40.

Lincoln, J., Hanada, M. and Mcbride, K. (1986) 'Organizational structures in Japanese and US manufacturing', *Administrative Science Quarterly* 31(2): 338–64.

Magota, R. (1970) *Nenko-Chingin no Ayumi to mirai - Chingin Taikei 100 Nen-shi* (The past and future of the seniority wage system - 100 years of Japanese wages system), Tokyo: Sangyo R Chosa-sho.

Nakane, C. (1967) *Kinship and Economic Organization in Rural Japan*, London: Athlone Press.

Nikkeiren (1995) *Nihonteki Keiei no Shin-jidai* (A New Era for Japanese-Style Management), Tokyo: Nikkeiren.

Nomura, M. (1998) *Koyo Fuan* (Employment Fear), Tokyo: Iwanami Shinsho.

Nonaka, I. and Takeuchi, H. (1995) *The Knowledge Creating Company*, Oxford: Oxford University Press.

Norman, E. H. (1940) *Japan's Emergence as a Modern State*, New York: Institute of Pacific Relations.

Ostrom, D. (1999) 'The competitive debate comes to Japan', *Japan Economic Institute*, No. 24 (25 June): 1–6.

Ouchi, S. (2002) 'Change in Japanese employment security: reflecting on the legal points', *Japan Labour Bulletin* 1 January: 7–11

Porter, M., Takeuchi, H. and Sakakibara, M. (2000) *Can Japan Compete?*, Basingstoke: Macmillan.

Reader, I. (1991) *Religion in Contemporary Japan*, London: Macmillan.

Rebick, M. (2001) 'Japanese labour markets: can we expect significant changes?', in M. Blomstrom, B. Gangnes and S. La Croix (eds), *Japan's New Economy*, Oxford: Oxford University Press.

Rengo Website

<http//www.jtuc-rengo.or.jp> (accessed 6 November 2001).

RIALS (Research Institute for Advancement of Living Standards) (2000) 'Keieisha ankêto chôsa no gaiyô' (Summary of Survey on Corporate Governance to the Top Management, February 1999), in *IIRA 12th World Congress/Special Seminar on Corporate Governance and Industrial Democracy, Tokyo, 1 June*, pp. 20–8.

Rohlen, T. (1983) *Japan's High Schools*, Berkeley, CA: University of California Press.

Sato, H. (1997) 'Human resource management systems in large firms: the case of white collar graduate employees', in M. Sako and H. Sato (eds), *Japanese Labour and Management in Transition: Diversity, Flexibility and Participation*, London: Routledge.

Storey, J. (1995) 'Human resource management: still marching on, or marching out?', in J. Storey (ed.), *Human Resource Management. A Critical Text*, London: Routledge, pp. 3–32.

Sugimura, Y. (1997) *Yoi Shigoto no Shiso: Atarashii Shigoto no Rinri no Tame ni* (The Philosophy of Good Jobs: For a New Ethic of Work), Tokyo: Chuko Shinsho.

Taira, K. (1970) *Economic Development and the Labour Market in Japan*, New York: Columbia University Press.

Tanaka, S. and Asakawa, M. (2001) *Mazu, Nihonteki Jinji o Kae yo!* (Let us first change the Japanese-style Human Resource Management), Tokyo: Diamondsha.

Totman, C. (1993) *Early Modern Japan*, Berkeley, CA: University of California Press.

Watanabe, S. (2000) 'The Japan model and the future of employment and wage systems', *International Labour Review* 139(3): 307–33.

7   Culture and management in Malaysia

Wendy A. Smith

Introduction

Malaysia is an important case for the analysis of management and culture in Asia. No other country exemplifies such a strong example of the practicalities of managing cultural diversity, with three ethnically distinct communities, the Malays, approximately 60 per cent, the Malaysian Chinese, 30 per cent and the Malaysian Indians[1] and others, 10 per cent. This 'plural society' arose as a result of British colonial rule (Shamsul 1997a). The juxtaposition of two large and quite distinct socio-cultural entities, the Malays and the Chinese, means that managers and employees with quite different values and daily lifestyles must cooperate in the context of modern organizations, without a clear hegemony by one group's culture based on sheer numbers. Although the Malay culture, focused around the belief in Islam, has a degree of hegemony based on political factors and Malaysia's development planning imperatives, this is tempered with the 'Confucian dynamism' of Chinese culture, whose values are not unappreciated by the Malay ruling elite, but have been nevertheless incorporated into management cultures through a third-party avenue, the 'Look East Policy' (LEP) which focused on Japan and Korea.[2]

Malaysia consists of two components, separated by the South China Sea. To the west is Peninsular Malaysia, consisting of eleven states and stretching between southern Thailand and Singapore. To the east are the states of Sarawak and Sabah, in north Borneo.[3] As most modern industrial activity takes place in Peninsular/West Malaysia, the discussion in this chapter will focus on management in the former.

Malaysia has a population of 23.3 million, of whom 70 per cent are below the age of 35 and 57.3 per cent are urban residents. Malaysia is a constitutional democracy, with a bicameral parliament consisting of the House of Representatives and the Senate, presided over by the King, or *Yang di-Pertuan Agong*. Malaysians have an average life expectancy of 72 years and a literacy rate of 93.7 per cent. There were 5.0 people per telephone, 4.7 people per TV and 1.34 million Internet users. Until the Asian currency crisis of the late 1990s, the economy was booming, with a growth rate of over 8 per cent since 1988. By the mid-1990s, GDP growth had reached 9.3 per cent. However, this changed dramatically after 1997, when growth dropped to just over 2 per cent in October 1998. By 1999, GDP growth was showing a slow but steady recovery at 4.1 per cent, but this jumped to 10.6 per cent in 2000, and stabilized at 7.7 in 2001, with per capita GDP at US$10,700, annual exports and imports worth US$98 and 77 billion respectively, and a current account balance of US$12.6 billion. In fact, Malaysia weathered the crisis better than many of its South-East Asian neighbours.

Malaysia has achieved a reputation of economic and political stability, and, with its efficient corruption-free bureaucracy, is seen as a good base for foreign investment. Its post-independence development policies, beginning with the New Economic Policy (NEP), 1971–90, emphasized export-oriented industrial development. Hence it has had to rely heavily on foreign direct investment (FDI) for technology, capital and management software. Its efforts to attract FDI since this time have been successful owing to its well-developed infrastructure, established since the colonial days, of world-class ports, good-quality road and rail transportation systems, adequate electricity and water supplies, health care facilities and, more recently, innovative telecommunications projects. It actively promotes its educated, disciplined and trainable labour force in FDI publicity material and the government gives strong support to workforce training.[4] About 8 per cent of the labour force of 9.6 million are unionized, largely in industrial unions, although the government has been encouraging enterprise unionism since the early 1980s and has sought to limit the militancy of labour with successive amendments to labour legislation, as a further facet of its pro-FDI development policy.

Historical setting

Before the arrival of the Europeans in 1500, the traditional South-East Asian political units were riverine kingdoms, or sultanates. The sultans are still important in contemporary Malaysia as the custodians of Islam and Malay identity.

After successive waves of Buddhist and Hindu influence in the Malay world, by 1300 a non-violent brand of Islam became established in the region, brought mainly by traders and mystics, from the Middle East, South Asia and China. By the late 1300s, the newly Muslim Malacca sultanate became not only a dominant power in South-East Asia but also an entrepôt well known in the whole of Europe and East Asia. But its thriving trade and prosperity attracted European colonizers: the Portuguese captured Malacca in 1511, and it was taken over by the Dutch in 1641.

In the late 1700s the British, who had already established a strong position in India with the British East India Company, turned towards South-East Asia. In 1786, the British adventurer–trader Francis Light founded Penang. Stamford Raffles founded Singapore in 1819. In 1826, the British combined Penang, Malacca and Singapore under one administrative unit called the Straits Settlements. In 1874 the separate states of Perak, Selangor, Negeri Sembilan and Pahang came under an administrative unit called the Federated Malay States. Johore was added in 1914. The Federation of Malaya Agreement signed in 1948 finally unified all these states.

Although the Malay sultans agreed to have British residents as advisers, especially on matters of governance and land administration, they nevertheless insisted on keeping control over Malay religion and culture in their individual states, a control they still exert today.

The Industrial Revolution in Europe created a high demand for Malayan tin and, subsequently, rubber. In the early 1890s the British increased the production of these commodities and imported the necessary labour, mostly displaced peasants, from its other colonies: Chinese from South China for the tin mines, Tamils from South India for the rubber plantations and Javanese from Batavia for other plantations. These large groups of ethnically distinct workers persisted as separate communities, encouraged by British colonial policy, which used the method of divide and rule to maintain peace amongst them.

Malaysia's route to independence has its origin in the Second World War when Japanese forces occupied Malaysia. The Japanese success awakened the local population, especially anti-colonial Malay nationalists, to the fact that the Europeans were not invincible. During the Japanese occupation many Malay nationalists were given important positions in the administration, but the Chinese community received the brunt of Japanese cruelty, an approach already adopted in Japan's war with China. When the war ended in 1945 hostility between Malays and Chinese had been thus amplified, and during the interregnum, open inter-ethnic conflict occurred in Malaya for the first time, costing many lives.

After the British returned to Malaya, they faced increasingly intractable inter-ethnic and industrial conflict; in 1947 workers' strikes turned into violent encounters between workers and government forces. The Malayan Communist Party (MCP), although banned, took up arms and many from the government forces were killed. This led the British to declare a state of emergency, which lasted from 1948 until 1960.

In these circumstances of political, economic and social instability, the British achieved:

1   The restoration of peace and security, through the introduction of a number of stiff regulations such as the Internal Security Act (ISA) and the 'identity card' system. These are still in use in contemporary Malaysia.

2   The creation of an environment suitable for ethnic relations, through an 'ethnic bargain' under which ethnic-based political parties were formed,

the UMNO (United Malays National Organisation), the MCA (Malay(si)an Chinese Association) and the MIC (Malay(si)an Indian Congress), and then combined to form a team, the Alliance, later known as the National Front, which has been ruling the country since 1955. Later, the Independence Constitution legitimized the allocation of power, economic resources and socio-cultural space between the different ethnic groups, with a bargain being made of special privileges for the Malays in return for citizenship for the non-Malays.

3   The introduction of planned change through a scheme of five-year development plans which have become a permanent feature in Malaysia's nation- building policies,[5] each being an important platform for the allocation of resources and hence for the reinforcing of the 'economic bargain' amongst the different ethnic groups.

Economic background

From 1850 to 1940, British firms dominated the colonial economy, especially the import–export sector and the two mainstay industries, tin and rubber. Chinese entrepreneurs played a key supporting, rather than competitive, role as middlemen for the British, collecting produce for export and distributing and retailing imports. Chinese wage earners with sufficient savings also turned to trade because it presented opportunities for self-employment and upward mobility. These patterns of capital deployment and occupational preference can still be seen among Chinese management and shop-floor employees in large firms, and they have implications for organizational commitment and career outcomes.

In the colonial economy, two groups, the British (approximately 60 per cent) and the Chinese (approximately 30 per cent) controlled around 90 per cent of corporate equity ownership. The remaining 10 per cent ownership belonged to the Indians (approximately 7 per cent) and the Malays (approximately 3 per cent). The British and Chinese completely dominated the urban sector and part of the rural sector (the modern plantation agricultural sector). The traditional rural, private sector of subsistence rice cultivation was in the hands of the Malays.

The 'dual economy' of colonial Malaya was further complicated by this ethnic factor. As late as 1970, thirteen years after independence, after the 1969 racial riots brought things to a head, British capital still dominated the Malaysian economy: foreign (mainly British) ownership of corporate equity in Peninsular Malaysia was 63.3 per cent, the non-Malay (mainly Chinese) share was 32.3 per cent and the Malay share was a mere 2.4 per cent.

During the brief Japanese occupation period (1942–5) the economy stagnated, but the British reconstruction of war-torn Malaya benefited from the boom in the price of rubber resulting from the Korean War. When rubber and tin prices fell as a result of a decline in the world market, Malay had no choice but to adopt an import-substitution industrialization (ISI) strategy, recommended by the World Bank in 1954. The introduction of the Pioneer Industries Ordinance in 1958 signalled the government's intention to stimulate industrial development.

The ISI strategy did contribute to the development process in Malaysia but it soon came up against the limits of the domestic market. The anticipated reduction in unemployment and spillover of surplus production into the export market did not take place. The ethnic division between the urban Chinese entrepreneurs and the rural Malay peasants remained in place, with increasing dissatisfaction on the part of the Malays who felt they were being left behind, despite independence and economic progress.

The government was already planning to change the ISI strategy into an export-oriented industrialization (EOI) strategy in the late 1960s when the outbreak of the post-election ethnic riots on 13 May 1969 hastened the process because the tragedy was attributed to the economically backward position of the rural Malays. As a result, the New Economic Policy (NEP) of 1971–90 was introduced with two central aims: (1) to achieve national unity through the eradication of poverty and (2) to restructure society to eliminate the identification of race with economic function. These policy objectives were reflected in the five-year plan called the Second Malaysia Plan 1971–5, which placed emphasis on FDI-led EOI to generate high economic growth, and increase urban waged employment and business opportunities, mainly for the Malays.

After the first decade of the NEP, the Malaysian government realized that the export of manufactured goods was limited to a narrow range of products and it promoted heavy industries as a catalyst for higher economic growth. This policy was inspired by the perceived success of Japan and South Korea in their heavy industrialization. These changes were augmented by the introduction of a policy embodying work ethics and practical training schemes[6] – the 'Look East Policy' (LEP) of December 1981.

Despite this reintroduction of an ISI-type strategy at the mid-point of the NEP, growth was affected by the relatively weak performance of the heavy industries, and the limitations of a small domestic market. The government revived its EOI strategy and looked again at FDI as a source of growth. The Industrial Master Plan of 1986–95 introduced a new Incentives Act, which permitted complete ownership by foreign manufacturing enterprises on condition that they export more than 50 per cent of their output, and various other fiscal incentives. These had an immediate effect: from 1986 the average annual growth rate of the manufacturing sector, funded mainly by FDI, was 13.7 per cent.

The most significant development in the Malaysian economic sphere in the post-NEP period was the introduction of the National Development Plan (NDP) (1991–2000). The NDP maintains many of the important features of the NEP, especially relating to special rights for the Malays, but has a more open approach towards the economy as a whole, whereby participation of all ethnic groups is perceived as critical for development. The general EOI approach to industrialization is retained. However, there is clearly a strong push for ICT (Information and Communication Technology) and a knowledge-based K-economy with the active participation of the government through flagship projects such as the Multimedia Super Corridor and Putrajaya, the new administrative centre, as a city functioning via ICT.

Societal culture

Because Malaysia's population is made up of three culturally distinct groups it is difficult to speak of 'Malaysian culture'. Nevertheless, the accommodation, interpenetration and cross-fertilization of the three main cultural spheres have created a unique Malaysian mix, and there are elements, especially in the realms of leisure and consumer lifestyles, which can be said to be truly 'Malaysian' (Shamsul 1996). First, however, I describe the distinct cultures of the three main groups, in terms of the key indicators of language, dress, diet and religion.

The Malays are Muslim, speak the national language (*Bahasa Malaysia*) or English, dress according to the Islamic codes which emphasize modesty and head coverings for women, traditionally eat rice and curries and strictly avoid eating pork. The consumption of alcohol is also forbidden. All adult Muslims are required to pray five times per day and to fast, that is abstain totally from food and drink between first light and sunset each day of the lunar month of Ramadan. These and other religious requirements pose challenges for modern industrial production, especially in a multi-ethnic context.

The Chinese are Buddhist, Taoist or Christian. They speak the national language and the Chinese dialect of their kin group, plus Mandarin if they are Chinese educated, or English if educated in the English schools which existed prior to the establishment of the universal system of *Bahasa Malaysia* education in 1970. Younger Chinese speak *Bahasa* fluently too. Chinese dress in Western-style clothes, which in the tropical climate do not emphasize covering the whole body. Food preferences are predominantly for Chinese dishes, and one of the main meat ingredients is pork. The consumption of alcohol is an essential part of Chinese entertaining, doing business and demonstrating status.

Indians are generally Hindu or Christian or, if they are from the Sikh community, they follow the Sikh religion. There are also some Indian Muslims who have their own mosques. Indians speak mostly Tamil, but there are also smaller groups speaking Punjabi and other Indian languages, or English as well as the national language. Food is predominantly curry, Indian style, with the avoidance of beef or complete vegetarianism, depending on caste membership for those of the Hindu faith. The consumption of alcohol is widespread. Indian women wear the sari, Punjabi dress or Western-style clothing, and there is more emphasis on modesty.

What then are the areas where the differences in cultures are transcended? Common to all groups is the love of socializing informally with friends, neighbours or relatives and chatting while sharing food and drink. More formal, yet equally unifying, is the 'open house' tradition on major religious festival days (Armstrong 1988), where large quantities of food and drink are prepared for all comers on one's festival day, be it Chinese New Year, *Deepavali*, Christmas or *Hari Raya*. At these times, householders carefully provide food acceptable under the dietary restrictions of their friends and colleagues from other ethnic groups: Chinese go to the Malay section of the market to buy *halal* chicken (slaughtered in the Muslim way), for instance.

Urban residence in the new concrete block housing estates has homogenized many aspects of community lifestyles. Malays, Chinese and Indians live in close proximity in the single- or double-storey terraces and semi-detached houses. In such circumstances, the sound of Malays bathing at 6.00 a.m. for the pre-dawn prayer, or the smell of incense from the Chinese family altar, different cooking smells and the sound of popular songs in different languages from the houses next door make everyone's culture a daily reality. More than familiarity and acceptance of these entrenched cultural differences would be the common activities of all the residents – going by car to a local shopping mall, sending the children to after-school tuition classes or music lessons, visiting the night market to buy cakes and cheap audiotapes.

Class mobility is also a great homogenizer. At the golf and recreation clubs modelled on the old colonial drinking clubs of the British, individuals and families participate more as members of the middle class than as 'Malays', 'Chinese' and 'Indians'. They play golf with each other and their children swim together in the same pool. While dress codes, dietary restrictions, languages and appearances are still distinct, the underlying sense of being affluent consumers is what gives individuals their strongest sense of identity on these occasions.

While consumerist lifestyles have the most homogenizing effect upon the middle class, even for the new urban working class, who have less opportunity to mix across the boundaries of their ethnic communities, consumerism allows them to mingle as passive observers of the middle-class lifestyle in the shopping malls and expensive supermarkets (Smith 1999).

Perhaps the most striking characteristic of contemporary Malaysian society is the fact that its members, both middle and working class, are living with identities located simultaneously in the traditional past and in the most modern and post-modern global future.

While participating in modern urban organizations as salaried or waged employees, many Malays must maintain their relationships with poorer rural relatives. They must attend weddings and funerals and visit the sick in their native villages, as these people will be the ones who help them when a wedding or funeral needs to be conducted in their own middle-class nuclear family.[7] For Chinese or Indian salaried employees too, many are the first-generation members of their families to be employed in large organizations, having been born into small-business families or rubber plantation workers' families respectively. It is not possible for them to withdraw into the Western-style isolation of the urban, nuclear family in the space of one generation, and neglect their kinship and ritual ties with their communities of origin.

Corporate culture

It is difficult to generalize about a characteristically 'Malaysian' paradigm of corporate culture as three factors – British colonial organizational influences, the contemporary multi-ethnic communities and the effects of the pro-FDI economic development policy which attracted investors from many national cultures, especially the Japanese (see Smith 2002) – have created a very complex range of alternatives for organizational relationships and values.

Expatriate colonial management

British and other European interests ran the trading houses and rubber plantations that were the mainstay of the colonial economy of Malaya. Organizations were deeply hierarchical, with vertical status positions codified by education levels and by the ultimate barrier of race, which even took precedence over education. Traditions of labour management were established in the plantations, with a white planter at the apex and intermediary staff who were Indian but were of different ethnic origin from (and considered themselves to be superior to) the labour force of Indian Tamil plantation workers (Ramachandran 1994). The European planter's relationship with the plantation workers could be described as one of gruff paternalism, whereas the Asian supervisors often used brutal methods, both formal and informal, to control workers.

Remnants of the colonial traditions, concern for status differences reinforced by differences in race and skin colour can still be found in Malaysian labour management systems today, although they are decreasing rapidly as the principle of meritocracy based on wider access to educational opportunity takes over.

A more positive colonial legacy is the paternalist system of welfare benefits which is still a feature of Malaysian HRM policies.[8] Public service is seen as a desirable career especially by Malays and Indians, because of its association with security of tenure, the pension after retirement, transferable to a surviving spouse, allowances for housing, transport, even domestic help at the higher levels, medical treatment for the employee and often family members as well. There is therefore an expectation that employers in the contemporary private sector, even large foreign multinationals, will provide substantial welfare benefits as part of the corporate culture.

Chinese family business management

Members of the Chinese community in Malaysia have always preferred to be owners of their own business, however small, rather than employees. Chinese businesses in Malaysia closely follow the paradigm presented in the literature on Chinese family business in Hong Kong and elsewhere. (Redding 1990, also Chapter 3 in this volume). The management style in these organizations is characterized by the involvement of close family members in a business founded and controlled by a patriarchal figure.

As in Chinese business systems elsewhere, the reliance on *guanxi* (networks of useful personal relationships), *xinyong* (trustworthiness and creditworthiness) and quick responsiveness to new opportunities and challenges serve as key elements in Chinese corporate culture.

Malay patron–client management

Patron–clientage is one of the most important types of relationship in rural Malay peasant society. Poor people do not resent the presence of wealthy people so long as they perform their roles as patrons properly. They say: 'We are happy that there are rich people because they help us when we are in need.'[9]

These values have been translated into modern organizational contexts by the Malays, most of whom are first-generation urban middle-class professionals. Malay personnel managers find jobs for their relatives and the members of their rural village communities of origin. Hiring, even in large companies, is generally based on this patronage principle rather than being placed in the hands of anonymous employment agencies. When vacancies occur, notices are posted in the factory so that employees can urge their relatives or friends to apply. Thus even the lowliest employee can become a patron by providing a relative with a job.

Patron–clientage extends vertically across middle-class and working-class boundaries and has been used to create harmonious labour relations. An example is the case of a Malay personnel manager's personal friendship with the Malay union secretary of the same company. In cases of labour unrest, the manager was able to appeal to the secretary to cool down the situation so as not to make him lose face with the expatriate managers. At the same time, during the collective agreement negotiations the personnel manager exerted subtle efforts to make sure that workers received good benefits (Smith 1994; 1995). At a personal level, he made loans to individual Malay workers to enable them to buy motorbikes, when the company refused to set up a loan scheme. These loans were often not repaid.

Here patron–client values derived from peasant society were being used effectively in a modern organizational context to promote harmony and employee loyalty. On the surface, the organizational forms differed little from those in Western firms. Union procedures were followed; disciplinary procedures were followed. Yet underlying these formal structures was a complex system of multidimensional relationships which the expatriate managers did not appreciate.

Managerial behaviour

Institutional influences

Managerial behaviour, by both expatriate managers in MNCs and local managers, takes place in the context of the NEP, with its heavy emphasis on affirmative action for the Malays. On a formal organizational level, there were two major policy instruments within the NEP which significantly affected management policies and decisions during the two decades, the LEP and the Industrial Coordination Act (ICA) of 1974.

The ICA required that the ethnic percentages of the population at large be represented at all levels of the organization. Licence renewal is contingent upon annual reports of these figures. Previously, higher-level managerial and supervisory posts had been mainly held by Chinese. The only 'manager' role commonly held by Malays in the early NEP era was that of personnel manager, because the shop-floor workers were predominantly Malay. Until the mid-1980s, when the affirmative action policies designed to help Malays gain tertiary education in fields such as science and engineering began to bear fruit, there were not enough Malays to fill the large number of managerial positions opening up through foreign investment and rapid industrialization. To fulfil the conditions of the ICA, companies were forced to recruit large numbers of new Malay graduates and promote them to positions of responsibility too rapidly for their experience. This led to accusations of ethnic favouritism in promotions and also to a stereotype that the Malays were incompetent. Twenty years later, experienced and competent Malay managers are well represented in the management ranks, but they still remain more mobile than their non-Malay counterparts.

Malays were also clustered in the lowest ranks of the shop-floor workers. At this level too, HRM policies in individual firms were severely challenged by the ICA. In the NEP years, some Malay workers with little education had the capacity to be promoted up to the supervisory ranks formerly occupied by Chinese workers, on the basis of experience and in-house training. Now with seniority, these employees pose a dilemma to management, who would like to upgrade the educational level of their supervisory and junior management levels. But when firms which had hitherto operated an internal labour market, a legacy of the British era and also a facet of 'Look East management', were forced to recruit potential supervisors with higher secondary education, to upgrade the technical competence of the workforce in the face of market imperatives, this demoralized the veteran employees, who nevertheless had to swallow their loss of face. The growing sense of meritocracy, through dramatically increased education opportunities for all groups in Malaysia, and the recent statements by the Prime Minister[10] that the time of affirmative action for the Malays is now past, have challenged the old internal labour market paradigm.

Cultural influences – pre-modern superstition

Superstition also has its place in management decisions and actions. Underlying Malaysians' participation in the major world religions is a substratum of animism, a belief in the world of the spirits and magical influences. While much of this originates from the pre-Islamic Malay culture, all ethnic groups include an element of superstition in their world-views. For instance, not only Malays, but also Chinese and Indians consult Malay shamanic healers (*bomoh*) to solve their problems related to health, relationships and money. All factories have a little red spirit house some-where in the compound, where offerings are made by the Chinese to the spiritual protectors of the locality in return for their safeguarding the well-being of workers in the company.

Malay *bomoh* are also used by local and expatriate managers, for instance for the phenomenon of mass hysteria, experienced especially in the semicon-ductor factories, where large groups of young women work intensively on a three-shift system. As has been described by many researchers (such as Ong 1987), an attack of hysteria in one worker will trigger off the whole shop floor. Production has to be suspended, and usually the only remedy is to call in a *bomoh* to pacify the malevolent spirits of the area who are supposedly disturbing the workers. In this way, the most modern production techniques and a highly efficient and productive workforce coexist with a cultural overlay of religion and superstition.

Managerial values

Influence of ethnic values

Studies by management theorists comparing the cultural values relevant to organizational behaviour of the three Malaysian ethnic groups emphasize that there are similarities, such as the pan-Malaysian importance of 'face', politeness, the avoidance of conflict, multidimensional relationships with colleagues, respect for elders, extended family ties, and religious beliefs and superstitions (Asma 2001). These contrast with stereotypical Western values of individualism, assertiveness, informality, frankness, secularism, scientific rationality and privacy within the nuclear family context. However, in the long lists of ethnic values characteristic of each group, there are differences as well as similarities: the Chinese list also features factors such as wealth, success, diligence, entrepreneurship, thrift, education and food, whereas the Malay list contains more items linked to spirituality, feelings, rituals, apologetic attitude, indirectness, faith in God, *budi* (a system of reciprocal obligations) and so on (see the chapter on China in this volume, but the traditional traits may be more common in the overseas Chinese *Nanyang* communities – see the chapters on Hong Kong, Taiwan and Singapore). Many would argue that since the NEP, which encouraged Malays to enter the commercial sector, the ethos of the new Malay entrepreneurs now includes the Chinese values listed above. Indeed, a study by Asma and Lim (2000) shows that in comparison with 'Anglos' and Australians, Malaysian managers of the three ethnicities differ little in their values,[11] except in relation to the importance of religion, where the Malays scored significantly higher. The study by Westwood and Everett also showed 'strong similarities in value orientations between all groups' (1995: 31) but explained the paradoxical result for the sample of male Malay MBA students, who rated ambition high but achievement low, as being influenced by traditional cultural values in which 'a naked drive for personal achievement at the expense of others has low cultural acceptance' (1995: 25). In other words, modesty, sensitivity and refinement, as well as the fulfilment of one's religious duties, must be juxtaposed against mere individualistic striving.

Islamic work ethics

Much has been written about Confucian values in management (see Chapters 3 and 10 in this volume) and Japanese work ethics and these are both highly relevant to our discussion of management and culture in Malaysia. As part of the ideational component of national development strategy, Mahathir's administration has also emphasized Islamic values and work ethics in parallel with the 'Look East' values which summarize the Japanese/Chinese Confucian perspective. The slogan *Bersih, Cekap dan Amanah* (Clean/without corruption, Efficient and Responsible) was a very visible campaign within the public service in the 1980s. These values, supposedly arising from a Muslim/Malay cultural context, are indistinguishable from Japanese work ethics.

In order to understand Islamic work ethics (see the chapters 5 and 8 on Indonesia and Pakistan in this volume) it is important to see how the Islamic faith permeates the individual and community identities of Muslims. Based on records of the way the Prophet Mohamed conducted himself in daily life, the behaviour of Muslims, from the most basic survival actions, like procreation, eating, washing, etc., to the attitudinal and moral basis of social interaction, is codified in minute detail. Adherence to these practices is strongly emphasized in daily life to promote individual communion with God, *Allah*, and harmonious relations with others in the community, which is also seen as a way of experiencing the Divine. Hence in Islam, daily social life becomes spiritual practice, and the community of Muslims takes on a sacred quality transcending mere secular concerns.

Hence the performance of work is seen as a way of worshiping God and making spiritual progress (Bazargan 1980) and no task is too lowly for this to be the case (Khalil-ur-Rehman 1995). While high value is placed on diligence, at the same time, individual striving for profit and affluence, intrinsic to the capitalist system, is seen as antithetical to Islam, which offers a detailed system of distribution within the community, based on principles of equality and fairness (Anjum 1995). Some economic inequality is tolerated in the society, to promote the development of skills (Khalil-ur-Rehman 1995; Faruqi and Banna 1984), but this is tempered by the underlying principle of moderation and equality of opportunity in augmenting one's wealth. The overall sanction against amassing too much wealth is that, if one is devoting so much time to it that one neglects one's daily prayers and community obligations, then this is excessive. Similarly, the relationship between employer and employee is conceptualized as one of cooperation and siblinghood: employers are obligated to look after the welfare of their workers, give them safe working conditions and just compensation for their labour; employees are obligated to perform the work with due diligence and treat the job as if it were for their own enterprise (Khalil-ur-Rehman 1995). Thus, if they are pious in their observance of the faith, Muslim workers would ideally have a deep sense of commitment to work, a desire to improve community and societal welfare, and be creative, cooperative and loyal to their employer and the organization (Ali 1988; Abu-Saad 1998; Smith *et al.* 2001).

However, these ideas and concepts are ideal types operating in an exclusively Islamic community context. How they manifest in a foreign business organization, where the employers are non-Muslim and, moreover, where many co-workers are non-Muslim also, is an important issue. In Malaysia, accommodation by employers to the religious needs of their Muslim employees is sanctioned by law and custom and problems rarely occur.

Labour–management conflict resolution

Conflict resolution in Malaysia takes place in the context of trade union institutions arising from the British colonial era. Wage labour was introduced during the colonial period as a result of growing British capital investments in agriculture and mining, in the late nineteenth century. The proletariat in British Malaya were mainly Chinese and Indians and Malays played little part in trade unionism until the NEP era. Colonial labour regimes were harsh and the workers had much cause to organize. Although trade union activity in colonial times began in the towns among the Chinese proletariat, it developed through the strength of the National Union of Plantation Workers, formed in 1954. However, the lack of industrial manufacturing until the NEP era meant that Malaysian trade unionism was dominated by the primary sector in its initial stages, and when full-scale FDI-led industrialization progressed, the government needed to present an image of non-militant labour to the outside world. It set about revising labour law to this end.

Revision of Malaysian labour law

When Malaysia adopted its EOI strategy in 1970 it granted privileges to foreign investors by creating Free Trade Zones in which aspects of existing labour laws, such as the prohibition on night work for women, were waived. Also, the state effectively discouraged the formation of trade unions in 'pioneer' industries such as electronics.

In the 1980s, the Malaysian government legislated to weaken further the legal grounding of the union movement in response to the economic recession, and its desire to keep attracting foreign investment. The three central pieces of legislation in Malaysian industrial relations prior to the era of FDI were the Employment Act (EA) of 1955, the Trade Union Act (TUA) of 1959 and the Industrial Relations Act (IRA) of 1967. The EA, while outlining some minimum standards in relation to working conditions, leave and overtime rates, sets no minimum wage. It is problematic for the unions in that it also allows for dismissal of workers without notice on the ground of management-defined misconduct (Ayadurai 1993: 68; Grace 1990: 80).

The TUA legitimized unions by requiring their registration, but also set parameters for regulating their affairs. It is distinguished by the inordinate power it gives the Director-General of Trade Unions (until 1989, the Registrar of Trade Unions) to refuse registration to unions and set membership limits, solely on his or her judgement 'based on the statutory definition of a union as an association of workmen "within any particular trade, occupation or industry or within any similar trades, occupations or industries"' (Arudsothy 1988: 470). Appeal on this key issue of 'similarity' is to the Minister of Human Resources (formerly Minister of Labour) only. The TUA also prohibits the use of union funds for political purposes (Grace 1990: 80).

The IRA consolidated the system of compulsory arbitration by establishing the Industrial Court. It prohibits union officials from holding positions in political parties. The IRA also defines essential services as "all services and industries that have any connection with national defence and security of the country" and severely limits the right to strike in these sectors (Grace 1990: 81).

All three Acts were amended in 1971, following the establishment of the NEP. These amendments showed among other things the prevailing concern for national security in the wake of the race riots on 13 May 1969, and the desire to create a favourable industrial relations environment to attract FDI (Ayadurai 1993: 65). The IRA was revised again in 1976, but the most significant revision of all three Acts took place in 1980, tightening state control over labour matters in three main areas: amendments to the TUA limited union activities in the public sector, and broadened the definition of 'essential services' whose employees were not allowed to form trade unions; the Registrar was given even wider powers (he or she could now deregister a union for having acted against national interests, and could now refuse to register a union without specifying a reason).

Most significantly, the amended IRA severely curtailed the right to strike. Now, a strike requires the agreement of two-thirds of the union's members in a vote conducted by secret ballot. Political and sympathy strikes are declared illegal. No strikes can take place once a dispute is referred to the Industrial Court for arbitration. When a strike is deemed illegal, members of the union executive committee are each personally liable to a fine of MYR$2,000 and/or one year's imprisonment (O'Brien 1988: 163; Arudsothy 1990). Moreover, the 1980 amendments also extended the ban on forming unions in pioneer industries from five years to an indefinite period.

The NEP era saw the erosion of union power and the consolidation of managerial prerogative: promotions, transfers and dismissals became non-disputable issues. Under the LEP, in-house unions became the normative form of unionism (Ayadurai 1993: 65).

Implications for managers

Understanding the significance of diverse cultural practices creates a major challenge for foreign managers in dealing with their shop-floor employees and local managers. For local managers too, the management of an ethnically diverse workforce is complicated by the fact that social relations in most daily life contexts – at work, in the neighbourhood, in shops, in schools – are defined primarily in terms of ethnic identities. People relate to each other as Malays, Chinese or Indians, rather than as Malaysians. Given the dramatic cultural differences in all areas of social life, this is not surprising. However, it presents problems for management in organizing supervision and awarding promotions in an atmosphere of ethnic rivalry and suspicions of favouritism.

The Islamic faith of Malay workers and managers requires special managerial practices in employee deployment, leave policies and corporate culture socializing rituals. First, the mandatory attendance at the mosque for mid-day Friday prayers, which take over one hour plus travel time, is sometimes a problem for manufacturing plants. Male Malay employees may attend the mosque on a quota system, perhaps once in two weeks. Companies usually provide bus transport to the nearest mosque.

Muslims are also required to pray five times per day. Management make allowance for those who wish to pray during working hours by providing *surau*, or small prayer rooms, for their Muslim employees at the workplace.

The fasting month of Ramadan is another challenge for management, as it is very debilitating to go without food or drink during daylight hours, from about 5.45 a.m. until 7.30 p.m., in the tropical heat. Workers become sleepy, especially in the early part of the month when they are not used to the fasting. Pious Muslims claim that the fasting does not affect their capacity to work, and indeed everyone tries very hard to perform his or her work at normal levels, but management would expect a degree of reduced productivity.

Finally, it is mandatory for Muslims to make the pilgrimage to Mecca (*haj*) once in a lifetime. This requires about two months of annual leave. In some companies, collective agreements permit workers to accumulate leave; even so, such a long absence places a strain on production or supervisory requirements, and some companies discourage it. One foreign company told a senior manager who asked for leave to go on the *haj*: 'If we can do without you for two months, we can do without you for good'. However, he persisted in his plan and was still working with the company several years later. Since the NEP reinforced the Malays' awareness of their ethnic identity and generated a trend of expressing one's Malay identity through piety (Shamsul 1997b), it has become more common to perform the *haj* at an earlier age. Even working-class couples try to save money to go. (The all-inclusive cost is approximately US$2,000.) This new custom is a further example of the potential influence of religion on management planning.

The religious observances of the Chinese and Indian employees do not make such demands on management arrangements. However, the numerous holidays for the different religious festivals – *Hari Raya* (Malay), Christmas (Chinese and Indian), the Chinese New Year, *Deepavali* (Indian) – plus the national and state holidays, holidays for the King's birthday and the Sultan's birthday in each state, create numerous non-production days. It is mandatory for Malays to return to their villages for *Hari Raya*, so they take a week or more of annual leave at this time. One factory operating a continuous production process took the opportunity to have its annual shutdown each year at *Hari Raya* (Smith 1995). But this required it to employ only Chinese engineers, since Malays, being on leave, would not be able to conduct the overhaul of machinery during the shutdown. Not understanding this, the Malay-dominated union complained that Malays were being unfairly excluded from the engineering section. This example shows how management face the complex task of taking into account cultural factors while also defending themselves against the constant Malaysian preoccupation with suspicions of ethnic favouritism.

The food taboos defined by religious affiliation also create complications for management. Company canteens do not serve food with pork as an ingredient in deference to Muslims. Socializing of employees after working hours is also a problem. At gatherings of executives in the general manager's residence, it would be better to avoid not only pork but also beef dishes in deference to any Indian managers present. It would also be necessary to provide some vegetarian dishes. Drinking alcohol is a common element of corporate socializing and a major focus of Chinese social activity and international business negotiations, yet Malays cannot be seen to be involved in this.

As relationships in the Malaysian workplace are multidimensional, with supervisors taking into account the family circumstances of their subordinates, an awareness of the social outcomes of the NEP era is thus important for effective management. Foreign managers need to be aware that local employees, at both the management and unionized level, have a complex network of traditional roles and obligations to fulfil, which sometimes makes it difficult for them to perform according to the norms of a modern organization's timetable. For instance, shop-floor workers, obligated to attend the funerals of even distant relatives in the village, may state again and again that a grandparent has died, in order to get compassionate leave, and may forget that they have already claimed that four grandparents have died when they claim yet another special leave to attend a 'grandparent's' funeral. The strength of their traditional obligations does not mesh with the norms of Western-style kinship relations embedded in HRM practices in modern global organizations. A local manager would understand the worker's subterfuge, as he or she would have been in a similar dilemma, but a foreign manager may be outraged at the employee's 'dishonesty'.

Conclusions

The professional class of managers in modern organizations in Malaysia fulfil the standard managerial functions very competently, allowing Malaysia to perform well in a global economy, with a sustained growth rate which outranked that of many OECD nations, and an ability to recover well from the major financial crisis of 1997 (Rasia RasiaH 2001). Malaysia well deserves the title of a 'second-tier NIC' (Abdul Rahman 2001), and this is due not only to its abundance of resources, but also to the ability of the government to plan for economic development and manage the inherent tensions of the ethnically diverse society. Yet tribute must also be paid to the Malaysian employees themselves, both first-generation professional managers and the new working class, who have adjusted rapidly to the demands of industrial production in modern organizations and to the demands of urban, consumption-oriented lifestyles, while maintaining their complex set of relationships with their traditional communities.

Notes

1 Following local practice, the three ethnic subcategories of Malaysian citizens will be referred to as 'Malays', 'Chinese' and 'Indians' henceforth. These are census terms and the terms used by the people themselves.
2 Indian values have not had much impact on cross-cultural management dynamics in Malaysia yet as there are still very few Indian local managers and the Indian community as a whole, whilst maintaining its distinct culture in daily life, represents less than 10 per cent of the Malaysian population. See Chapter 4 for a discussion of their importance.
3 The first eleven peninsular states of the Federation of Malaya became independent on 31 August 1957. Subsequently, the Federation of Malaysia was declared

on 16 September 1963, when Sabah, Sarawak and Singapore were added. However, Singapore departed on 9 August 1965.

4 Young Malaysians entering the labour market have undergone at least eleven years of school education. A total of 15 per cent of public development expenditure is allocated to education under Malaysia's five-year development plans. Malaysia has 11 public universities, 6 private universities and 600 government and private colleges, as well as several polytechnic and industrial training institutes. In 1993, the government launched the Human Resource Development Fund to encourage training and skills upgrading in the private sector.

5 There have been nine more five-year plans since then, and the latest one, the Eighth Malaysia Plan of 2001–5, will focus on enhancing the knowledge content of the economy to increase production capacity in all sectors, with a focus on HRM and R&D to transform Malaysia into a K-economy (knowledge-based economy).

6 The LEP also included training schemes for Malaysian students to complete undergraduate degrees in Japanese universities after undergoing Japanese language training in Malaysia, and also for technical supervisors in Malaysian industries to visit comparable plants in Japan and Korea and undergo on-the-job training for several months. These experiences not only imparted academic or technical knowledge, but were also an excellent method of training in values and work ethics.

7 As yet, there are no commercially based wedding reception halls or funeral parlours for the Malays. These major rituals are conducted within the family context.

8 See *Salary and Fringe Benefits Survey for Executives 2001* and *Salary and Fringe Benefits Survey for Non-Executives 2000*, published by the Malaysian Employers Federation, with a summary available on their web page *www.mef.org.my*: 99 per cent of respondent companies provided medical benefits for their executives while 53.6 per cent (32.9 per cent for non-executive) also extended the facility to dependents. Personal accident insurance was more commonly provided to executives as compared with life insurance (82 per cent provided it to non-executives). Common loans provided include car loan, personal loan and computer loan.

9 For instance, a wealthy village family will lend plates and utensils to poorer families to allow them to conduct weddings, funerals and other major rituals of the life cycle, which always take place at home.

10 'Mahathir set for new attack on 'soft' Malays', *The Straits Times* 18 June 2002.

11 The value contexts tested were in relation to relationships, shame, group orientation, belief in God, respect for elders, polychronic time orientation and high-context communication.

References

Abdul Rahman Embong (2001) 'Beyond the crisis: the paradox of the Malaysian middle class', in Abdul Rahman Embong (ed.), *Southeast Asian Middle Classes – DemocrAtis Prospects for Social Change and Democritisation*, Bangi: UKM Press, pp. 80–102.

Abu-Saad, I. (1998) 'Individualism and Islamic work beliefs', *Journal of Cross-Cultural Psychology* 29(2): 377–83.

Ali, A. J. (1988) 'Scaling an Islamic work ethic', *Journal of Social Psychology* 128(5): 575–83.

Anjum, M. I. (1995) 'An Islamic Scheme of equitable distribution of income and wealth', *The American Journal of Islamic Social Sciences* 12(2): 224–39.

Armstrong, M. (1988) 'Festival open houses: settings for interethnic communication in urban Malaysia', *Human Organization* 47(2): 127–37.

Arudsothy, P. (1988) 'Labor law and industrial relations in Malaysia', *Labour and Industry* 1(3): 463–85.

Arudsothy, P. (1990) 'The state and industrial relations in developing countries: the Malaysian situation', *ASEAN Economic Bulletin* 6(3): 307–29.

Asma, A. (2001) 'Influence of ethnic values at the Malaysian workplace" in A. Asma and A. H. M. Low (eds), *Understanding the Malaysian Workforce: Guidelines for Managers*, Kuala Lumpur: Malaysian Institute of Management, pp. 1–24.

Asma, A. and Lim, L. (2000) 'Cultural dimensions of Anglos, Australians, and Malaysians', *Malaysian Management Review* December: 9–17, Kuala Lumpur: Malaysian Institute of Management.

Ayadurai, D. (1993) 'Malaysia', in S. Deery and R. Mitchell (eds), *Labour Law and Industrial Relations in Asia*, Sydney: Longman Cheshire, pp. 61–95.

Bazargan, M. (1979) *Work and Islam*, trans. M. Yusefi, A. A. Behzadnia and N. Denny, Houston: Free Islamic Literature.

Faruqi, al I. and Banna, al G. (1984) *Towards Islamic Labour & Unionism*, Cairo: The International Islamic Confederation of Labour.

Grace, E. (1990) *Shortcircuiting Labour: Unionizing Electronic Workers in Malaysia*, Petaling Jaya: Insan.

Khalil-ur-Rehman (1995) *The Concept of Labour in Islam*, Karachi: Arif Publications.

O'Brien, L. (1988) 'Between capital and labour: trade unionism in Malaysia', in R. Southall (ed.), *Labour and Unions in Asia and Africa*, London: Macmillan.

Ong, A. (1987) *Spirits of Resistance and Capitalist Discipline: Factory Women in Malaysia*, Albany, NY: State University of New York Press.

Rasiah, Rajah (2001) 'The political economy of the Southeast Asian financial crisis', in Abdul Rahman Embong (ed.), *Southeast Asian Middle Classes – Prospects for Social Change and Democratisation*, Bangi: UKM Press, pp. 46–79.

Ramachandran, S. (1994) *Indian Plantation Labour in Malaysia*, Kuala Lumpur: Insan.

Redding, S. G. (1990) *The Spirit of Chinese Capitalism*, Berlin: Walter de Gruyter.

Shamsul, A. B. (1996) 'The construction and transformation of a social identity: Malayness and Bumiputeraness re-examined', *Journal of Asian and African Studies* 52: 15–33.

Shamsul, A. B. (1997a) 'The making of a "plural" Malaysia: a brief survey', in D. Y. U. Wu, H. MacQueen, and Y. Yamamoto (eds), *Emerging Pluralism in Asia and the Pacific*, Hong Kong: The Chinese University of Hong Kong, pp. 67–83.

Shamsul, A. B. (1997b) 'Identity construction, nation formation, and Islamic revivalism in Malaysia,' in R. Hefner and P. Horvatich (eds.), *Islam in an Era of Nation States*, Honolulu: University of Hawaii Press, pp. 207–27.

Smith, W. (1994) 'A Japanese factory in Malaysia: ethnicity as a management ideology', in K. S. Jomo (ed.), *Japan and Malaysian Development*, London: Routledge, pp. 154–81.

Smith, W. (1995) 'The Japanese management system in Malaysia: a case study of a Japanese company overseas', PhD thesis, Monash University, Department of Anthropology and Sociology.

Smith, W. (1999) 'The contribution of a Japanese firm to the cultural construction of the new rich in Malaysia', in M. Pinches (ed.), *Culture and Privilege in Capitalist Asia*, London: Routledge, pp. 111–36.

Smith, W. (2002) 'Management in Malaysia', in M. Warner (ed.), *International Encyclopedia of Business and Management*, 2nd edition, London: Thomson Learning, pp. 3882–94.

Smith, W., Nyland, C. and Adlina, A. (2001) 'Islamic identity and work in Malaysia: Islamic work ethics in a Japanese joint venture in Malaysia', in C. Nyland, W. Smith, R. Smyth and M. Vicziany (eds), *Malaysian Business in the New Era*, Cheltenham, UK and Lyme, USA: Edward Elgar, pp. 189–202.

Westwood, R. and Everett, J. (1995) 'Comparative managerial values: Malaysia and the West', *Journal of Asia-Pacific Business* 1(3): 3–37.

8 Culture and management in Pakistan

Shaista E. Khilji

Introduction

The present chapter explores the nature and complexities of issues surrounding culture and management in modern-day Pakistan. This has become increasingly pertinent since certain factors such as the deregulation of the economy, initiated in 1990, and exposure to the thought processes of Western management styles, in particular American ones, have reshaped the organizational environment. A striking change has surfaced in the values espoused by a new generation of employees, reflecting a modern market economy (Khilji 2002b). The establishment and growth of organizations in the private sector (both local and multinational) has vitalized corporate culture, previously thought of as ineffective. This chapter analyzes the causes, effects and managerial implications of these changes.

In order to highlight those issues critical to the understanding of employee and management behavior in Pakistan, this chapter begins with a brief outline of the history of its people and provides a background of the economic development significant to the understanding of government initiatives, priorities and employee attitudes. Second, it describes the societal culture, which lays the foundation for the values people hold. Third, it identifies the managerial values used to inform corporate culture, management behavior and labor–management conflict resolution strategies applicable within organizations. It concludes by discussing implications for managers in these organizations.

Historical setting

Pakistan, with mountain passes in the north-west and the west, has long been used as the entryway to the subcontinent by migrating tribes, traders and invaders. First to arrive were the Aryans, who developed the rudiments of a religio-philosophical system which later evolved into Hinduism (*http://www.rpi.edu/dept/union/paksa* 2002). In the eighth century, Arab traders brought with them the teachings and practice of a new religion, Islam, which gradually took root through intellectual and spiritual conversion. In the centuries that followed, Muslim armies, Turks and Afghans, repeatedly invaded the subcontinent, each establishing their dynasties. The last and the greatest of the Muslim empires was the Mughul, from 1526 to 1858. It is remembered for the political, philosophical and cultural achievements reflected in the art and artifacts of both Pakistan and India[1] (http://www.geocities.com/pak_history/main.html).

In the sixteenth century, the Mughul officials permitted the British East India Company to trade with the subcontinent. Thereafter, their posts began to grow in both area and population. Armed company servants became effective protectors of trade and found themselves more and more involved in local politics. Within a hundred years, the British came to possess the most efficient military machine on the subcontinent (*http://www.rpi.edu/dept/union/paksa* 2002). As the Mughul Empire disintegrated, its power diminished. Subsequently, in 1857, it fell to the British who by this time had expanded their influence throughout the region. The British parliament transferred authority to the British crown, represented by the governor-general, and declared the subcontinent a British colony.

Colonial rule brought economic prosperity to the subcontinent. Agricultural output increased abundantly. A railway network was established. Trade expanded, as did industrial development. Socially and politically, however, the climate was conservative. "Divide and rule" tactics were used to run the subcontinent, resulting in the creation of an elite class, mainly feudal lords, the military and the bureaucrats running the government. Property was not in demand, due to inflated costs, and was bequeathed to pacify deposed chiefs and to reward locals who had been faithful and loyal to the British (Khilji 1999b). Racial criteria were used in a dramatic overhaul of the British Indian Army and for the recruitment for the Indian civil service. The number of British soldiers increased while that of the locals did not; in fact, they were excluded from artillery and technical services altogether. The Indian civil service was exclusively British; young men with a British classical education were recruited from overseas (*http://www.rpi.edu/dept/union/paksa* 2002). Due to their lack of appropriate training, they were ill-equipped to deal with this culturally distinct public; they could neither sympathize nor empathize with the masses (Khilji 1999b). As a consequence, dissatisfaction grew among the general public.

In addition, British rule (see Chapter 4) widened the gap between the Hindus and the Muslims (Lyon 1993). The thousand-year-long Muslim intrusion into the subcontinent had not been able to absorb Indian Muslims into the Hindu majority. British policies further aggravated the problem. The Muslims, as a result, developed the Two-nation Theory, an ideology describing Hindus and Muslims as two separate peoples and therefore demanding that the areas in which Muslims were numerically a majority, as in the north-western and eastern zones of the subcontinent, be grouped to constitute an independent state, Pakistan (Ahmed 1997; Ali 1990; Wolpert 1984). At the time, this concept was hailed as ridiculous, but by 1947, amidst opposition and resistance, the feeling among Muslims was so strong that the British decided to divide the subcontinent into two sovereign states, India and Pakistan, and leave (see Chapter 4).

Pakistan inherited from the British three strong administrative institutions needed to run the country effectively, namely the military, the bureaucracy and the feudal system. As is explained above, each operated on the basic principle of "divide and rule", which was probably appropriate for running a colony in the early twentieth century. However, unfortunately for Pakistan, since its inception representatives of successive governments have belonged to one of these three elite groups and have only had their own vested interests at stake. Hence, no sincere attempt was made to unshackle the society from its colonial structure. Instead, in an effort to monopolize and accumulate power, a tug-of-war among these elite groups continues to take place to this day (Amir 1999; Hussain 1999; Malik 1994), which explains why even after fifty-four years of independence the country has failed to develop democratic institutions. Meanwhile the public yearns for democratic order based on universal suffrage, equality, mundane sovereignty and accountability, all of which are clearly depicted in Islamic teachings and also reflect the goals of the very creation of the country. The ruling elite jealously guards existing state structures by applying methods varying from ideological rhetoric to coercion through state functionaries (Malik 1994).

Soon after Pakistan's independence, the USA became a significant foreign player in the politics and economics of Pakistan (Hussain and Hussain 1993), with periods of varying prominence. For example, with the Soviet invasion of Afghanistan in the 1980s, American aid for Afghani refugees, rehabilitation and defense purposes reached the US$2 billion mark (Khilji 1999b. It weakened after the Soviet Union disintegrated and its troops withdrew. In 1999, when Pakistan tested its nuclear capability in response to the Indians, economic sanctions were imposed. More recently, after the September 11, 2001 terrorist attacks on US soil, the USA seems to have gained renewed prominence in Pakistan's internal and external affairs. Its impact on social as well as organizational levels will be studied in later sections of the chapter.

Economic background

Since Independence, Pakistan has pursued liberal economic policies which sought to make maximum use of market mechanisms (Khilji 2002a). The only exception was the 1971–7 period of nationalization, which created a setback to the growth of the economy. The country that had developed a sound industrial base in the 1960s suddenly went into a slump. The problems were compounded by a low level of output and low employee morale (Mirza 1995). Consequently, in the late 1980s Pakistan began a program of market-oriented economic adjustment, which included privatization of inefficient and bureaucratic public sector enterprises and encouragement of foreign direct investments. In its initial years this was deemed a success as investors' interest was sparked and many new enterprises were established. At the same time multinationals that had long been operating with a low profile started reinvesting in the market through expansion of services or diversification of products. This created a healthy, profitable, and competitive business environment making the private sector more progressive than the public sector (Bokhari 1996; Unger 1999). However, shortly thereafter, a prolonged political instability stunted further private investment. In the past decade alone, five democratically elected governments were toppled on charges of corruption (Khilji 1999b). Each prime minister appointed a new cabinet and an entourage of advisers. Together they eliminated economic programs undertaken by previous governments. Although new programs were put into practice aiming to solve the same economic problems, they, too, were duly changed when the next government took office. No thought was given to the quantity of resources invested in formulating or implementing these programs. Other domestic problems, such as an influx of over 1.5 million Afghani refugees and ethnic and sectarian violence, have further worsened the economic situation in recent years (*http://www.usatrade.gov* accessed February 8, 2002).

Due to the interplay of the above-mentioned positive liberal economic policies and negative trends, Pakistan's economy has witnessed mixed progress. After growing at an average rate of 6 percent per year in the 1980s and early 1990s, real GDP growth dropped to 1.3 percent in 1996–7, 4.3 percent in 1997–8, 3.1 percent in 1998–9, 3.9 percent in 1999–2000 and 2.6 percent in 2000–1 (Government of Pakistan 2002; *http://www.usatrade.gov* accessed February 8, 2002). The present military government has identified economic reform along with improved governance as the two measures most urgently needed to restore the confidence of foreign and local investors which has been eroded by inconsistent policies and a lack of transparency in decision making, challenges very similar to those that exist in other developing economies. For example, the investment policy provides for equal opportunities for both domestic and foreign investors, has relaxed foreign exchange controls, allows full repatriation of capital, capital gains, dividend, and profits, offers a general policy of permitting foreign investors to participate in local projects on a 100 percent equity basis and provides full safeguards to protect foreign investment. Nonetheless, Pakistan, with a population of approximately 145 million, continues to offer a challenging market for foreign investors and exporters (*http://www.usatrade.gov* accessed February 8, 2002) mainly due to political uncertainty. The USA is Pakistan's biggest trading partner and it is also one of the largest contributors of foreign direct investment.[2] Other primary investors include European, Japanese, Middle Eastern, and South Korean firms (Government of Pakistan 2002).

The Pakistani economy is almost evenly divided between the commodity sector (49.7 percent) and the services sector (51.3 percent), with a large share of economic fortunes being closely linked to cotton and textile products (*http://www.usatrade.gov* accessed February 8, 2002). However, recently, some progress has been made in diversifying the economy. For example, the oil and gas sector is considered to be promising. The information technology and telecommunication services sectors are also growing rapidly because of aggressive deregulation and lower tariffs (*http://www.usatrade.gov* accessed February 8, 2002). The number of Internet users has grown to 1.2 million in the past four years alone, and this expansion continues with a large potential market available (CIA 2002).

The total labor force in Pakistan is estimated at 41.2 million, with approximately 2.4 million (or 5.9 percent) unemployed (Government of Pakistan 2002). If the underemployed population and the net migration rate (−0.84 migrants per 1,000 population; CIA 2002) were included, this rate would probably triple. The level of investment in human capital (Birdsall and Ross 1993; *The Economist* 1994: 106) in terms of education has been quite disappointing in Pakistan. The budget allocated to education does not exceed 2.25 percent of GNP because of the major portion that is reserved for defense purposes.[3] This is mainly due to long-standing unsettled border disputes with India. According to Haq and Haq (1998), Pakistan and India together spend over US$12 billion a year on defense. If these levels were cut by 5 percent a year over the next five years, it could release as much as US$22 billion in a peace dividend – over four times what is required for global universal primary education for the next five years (Haq and Haq 1998). As well, the education budget is disproportionately allocated: colleges and universities in urban areas have been expanded at the expense of elementary education in rural areas (Korson 1993). This, together with a high population growth rate of 2.1 percent (Government of Pakistan 2002; *http://www.usatrade.gov* accessed February 8, 2002) and the inability of the economy to provide job opportunities for both its educated and uneducated labor force, has created a paradoxical situation: an abundance of unemployed graduates and an increase of a million additional illiterate workers each year (Ahmad 1997). Several economists have examined this aspect and have concluded that Pakistan has forgone substantial income gains due to its low investment in education. This has also contributed to the country's reduced competitiveness in international markets (Amjad 1992; Birdsall and Ross 1993; *The Economist* 1994).

Most recently, the September 11, 2001 events and subsequent war in Afghanistan, have created new challenges and a climate of political complexity and deep vulnerability. According to the economic review report of the Pakistani ABN Amro Bank (quoted in Khan 2001), the impact unfolded in the form of a loss in revenue collection, in export orders, higher shipping and insurance costs, delays in clearing Pakistani consignments at various ports (*http://www.finance.gov.pk* 2002), an increase in the cost of imports, and deferment of foreign investment. Cancellation of air cargo flights by foreign airlines, the departure of expatriates from the country, and the suspension of visits by foreign buyers also disrupted trade flows (Aazim

2001). However, consistency of the economic reforms launched during the last couple of years increased foreign assistance and the effective management of exchange and monetary policies have helped the economy cushion the adverse impact to a certain extent. But the outlook on domestic growth has not shown any perceptible signs of improvement in 2001–2 fiscal year (Aazim 2002), due to a host of factors outlined above.

Societal culture

As was described previously, Pakistan's history is long and multicultural. From its very early days, the people of Pakistan were exposed to several foreign influences.[4] Hence, the contemporary Pakistani culture is considered to be an amalgam of the following: its Indian origins, religion, British colonialism, and American influences (Khilji 1999a; 1999b). The discussion in the next few paragraphs will outline the impact each of these has upon the structure of the society.

Although 97 percent of the Pakistani population is Muslim (Government of Pakistan 2002), a variance in allegiance to religion makes it as impossible to generalize about Pakistanis' attitudes toward Islam as it is to generalize about Americans' attitudes toward Christianity (Lyon 1993). There are people for whom Islam is the sole solution to the political, economic, and social problems of the country, who believe that Pakistan will never realize its full potential until Islamic laws are promulgated. There are others for whom Islam is present in a spiritual way, but who do not have the time or knowledge to raise such theological arguments; the religion is retained in their own private domains. Then there are people who have been born into the religion, but do not form conscious theories based on it. Furthermore, adding to the above diversity is the point that having lived under the influence of Indians for centuries, many of the local customs and traditions that form the structure of the society, such as the roles expected of women or the manner in which a child is raised, can be traced back to Indian origins. While Islam has caused changes in certain perceptions, for instance, evolved attitudes resulted in the elimination of the caste system, still, it has failed to affect many other aspects of daily life (cf. Chapter 5 on Indonesia and Chapter 7 on Malaysia, both Islamic states).

The family, kin, or *baradari* are the basis of the social organization, providing its members with both identity and protection (*http://www.lcweb2.loc.gov* accessed February 8, 2002). Obligations to family include both financial and ritual practices. The group of male kin plays a significant role in social relations; its members do not share earnings but rather the honor or shame of the individuals. A common proverb expresses this view: "One does not share the bread, but one shares the shame" (*http://www.lcweb2.loc.gov* accessed February 8, 2002). Family-like ties are also created with persons who are not biological relatives but who may be integrated socially into the group. These allegiances are abiding and generally take precedence over rules. As life is built within a group (Lyon 1993), there is a pattern of dependence which pervades all human contact, and people carry a strong need for security. The social system also requires surrendering to authority; originality and independence in decision making are met with disapproval (Khilji 2002a).

The British colonial rule also left some marks on the social structure (see Chapter 4 on India), the most important of which is the feudal elite of the country, who inherited ownership of large pieces of land gifted by the British. There are probably only 5,000 elite in a population of 145 million people, but the elite's political and social importance and wealth is disproportionate to its number. Just like its ancestors in the colonial era, the feudal elite symbolizes money, power, and status. Although over the past few decades this relatively small, educated elite is increasingly being displaced by an educated middle class, a quintessential change in attitude has not yet been achieved. It remains such that a rich or powerful person can easily get away with committing a crime, either through a bribe or *gaunxi*. The resulting two-track system has widened the gap between the haves (the elite) and have-nots (the general public). The best schools and other facilities are available only for the elite, while a majority of the public is still trying to obtain the basic necessities of life, such as electricity and clean drinking water. It is public opinion that there are no longer any checks and balances to curb the power of the influential (Hussain 1999).

As mentioned previously, American influences in terms of economic aid, foreign investment, and management education/training became significant only after independence, and peaked in 1980s when the Soviet Union invaded Afghanistan. Today affiliates of American business schools are seen in every neighborhood in major cities. Management faculties of government universities also follow American syllabuses. These have resulted in infiltration of American thought processes.

The above discussion reveals that fundamentally Pakistanis function within the general framework of a traditional family or kin situation and that they are frustrated by the social inequities, by the acts of vindictiveness targeted at each other by politicians, and by the failure of these same to deliver on their promises. Concurrently, there is a growing sense of materialism and consumerism (Jamal 1998; Khilji 1999b) which is commonly attributed to the American influence, as well as some other factors, mentioned above. In order to survive in a status-conscious society that offers scarce resources, people desiring to acquire material wealth have to compete with each other constantly, assisted by their extended families and any social power they may have.

Managerial values

Values represent basic convictions about what is important to individuals (Robbins and Langton 2000). These are perceptions about what "ought" and what "ought not" to be. Using Hofstede's (1991) five dimensions, Pakistani managerial values can be defined as collectivist, having high uncertainty avoidance, a high power distance, and a short-term orientation (Hofstede 1991; Trompenaars 1993). This implies that there is a general unquestioning respect for authority, people are integrated as cohesive groups, and they have an external locus of control. On the masculinity index, Hofstede (1991: 84) found Pakistanis scoring exactly at the half-way mark, i.e., possessing both masculine and feminine qualities, indicating that there is an equal degree of concern for quality and quantity of life. This includes hard-core values like assertiveness, acquisition of money, and competition, as well as softer values such as sensitivity and caring for others.

There are two problems associated with Trompenaars' (1993) and Hofstede's (1991) findings. First, these do not take into account the variations in employees' values across ages and types of organizations. Second, they are based on research that is from ten to thirty years old. Following a decade of a deregulation, increased globalization, and economic hardship, a striking change has surfaced in the values espoused by a new generation of employees. Although some societal values remain rooted in tradition, managerial values reveal changes reflecting a modern market economy (Khilji 2002a; 2002b). Khilji (2002b), in her recent survey of a large database of employees working in Pakistan,[5] has shown that both tradition and economic pressures are synergistically combined to form a set of unique values, some of which are supported by the societal culture and others by an economic ideology. The following points describe these new values.

1   There is a high level of masculinity due to growing materialism, economic hardship, and limited career opportunities.
2   There is a high level of collectivism while making a clear-cut distinction between in- and out-groups. Loyalty to the organization is low; organizations are considered to be the out-group. However, in-groups are formed with other co-workers and colleagues within organizations. Khilji (1999b) observed that ties to these in-groups are quite strong. For example, "group turnover," or the tendency of employees to leave "en masse" with their social group, is a common occurrence in organizations, resulting in high turnover rates.
3   There is low organizational commitment. Khilji (2002a) quotes a twenty-five-year veteran manager at a sample organization saying, "I am disappointed that the young employees are not committed to the organizations like we are. They join the organization with the sole purpose of learning or developing specific skills and then move on."
4   There is a low degree of uncertainty avoidance. People are open to taking risks because they have learned to survive in economic hardship and in a society that tolerates social inequity. The attitude "What could be worse than that which we have already faced?" prevails (Khilji 1999b).

5   There is an emphasis on extrinsic and financial rewards because income levels are vital. One manager in Khilji's sample (2002b) remarked, "Believe it or not, tons of employees have been leaving just for a couple of extra thousand rupees."
6   There is greater autonomy in doing tasks.
7   There is a low power distance, thereby improving communication patterns and allowing employees to participate in decision making.
8   There is achievement–orientation, such as the use of performance-led rewards.

The above values reveal a considerable shift from the conventional foundations. These, however, are not applicable across the workforce irrespective of age and background. Rather, the above list depicts the new values of the younger (i.e., less than 40 years of age, although more than 55 percent of Khilji's (2002b) sample was under 30 years of age) and highly skilled employees in private sector organizations. These employees have either been educated in the USA or been exposed to the American management thought process in business schools and training institutes in Pakistan, all of which follow American syllabuses, with no exceptions. They have access to the Internet and business magazines (such as *Fortune*), both of which help keep them informed about new developments in the management cultures in American companies. This represents the elite workforce of Pakistan.

Khilji (2002b) observed that the older and more senior managers are comfortable with the traditional values, as described by Hofstede (1991) and Trompenaars (1993). This creates specific dilemmas in organizations, since managers and employees stand divided on the basis of their different value systems. Challenges involved in managing such dilemmas will be explained in a later section of this chapter.

Corporate culture

The corporate culture in Pakistani organizations varies from the public to the private sector. Up until the early 1990s when the economy was regulated, PSEs (Public Sector Enterprises) monopolized the organizational scene. The culture within PSEs remains a replica of the colonial era: bureaucratic, centralized, and inflexible. These organizations have a high power distance and are typically authoritarian, meaning that the decision-making authority is located at the top management level. There is limited employee autonomy; top-to-bottom communication is minimal and bottom-up communication is nonexistent. Employee involvement is a foreign concept (Khilji 2001). In large PSEs, decisions are made by government-appointed committees (Klein 1992). Managers are often forced to hire staff not necessarily on the basis of merit, but on the recommendations of their committees or unions. Seniority-based remuneration is practiced. Scope for creative management is limited because of rigid rules and regulations. Employees' initiative is not encouraged due to poor incentives. Wages and salaries are not competitive with those of multi-nationals (Khilji 2002a). Management has failed to develop or implement systems that are fair, that assess training needs, and that are linked to career development plans of individual employees (Qureshi 1995).

Some organizations in the private sector which flourished from the mid- to early 1990s are more progressive. Khilji (1999a) explains, "Pakistani organizations and their cultures are undergoing a dramatic change. A deregulation of the economy has added impetus; private local organizations are being set up and multinationals are expanding. It has indeed added a fresh perspective." According to a recent survey published in *The Economist*, "There are remarkable examples of the private sector taking over the duties of the corroded public sector and performing them well" (Unger 1999). At least two forces can easily be identified as agents of change in this process: American influences that have gained significance in the workplace through educational and training institutions; and multinationals whose growth was encouraged in order to introduce modern corporate cultures when confidence in local organizations (PSEs) was notoriously low. In one example, the ex-prime minister appointed a Citibank-trained Pakistani and his team, all of whom had vast experience with multinational banks, to rescue the biggest nationalized bank from a crisis and to modify its management culture.

A selective few private sector organizations have adopted a participatory style of management with success. Power distance in these organizations is quite small. Collectivism of employees is being used to instill a team-based structure and to promote organizational commitment. Employees are involved in decision making. At the moment, this new culture has been adopted by a handful of organizations; however, there are several more that are also moving toward redesigning their structures to reflect a modern and flexible culture.

Management behaviour

As has been discussed previously, at least two distinct sets of values prevail in Pakistani organizations. This is of significance at micro levels, especially when organizations, in the public as well as the private sector, are undergoing transformations in terms of structures, cultures, and management practices. Since values lay the foundation for organizational behavior, duality of values will be used to discuss the management behavior in these organizations.

Data from Khilji's (2002b) research, the most recent piece available, is used to investigate the impact of the cultural transformations which target management practices, including key HR functions such as performance evaluations, rewards disbursal, training, and development, in order to develop flexible, participatory, communicative, and achievement-oriented cultures, reflecting the values of a new generation of employees. Despite a commonality of objectives across these organizations, the individual outcomes vary. The following discussion illustrates that the success of the desired management behavior in these organizations is determined by their managerial values. In a country such as Pakistan, where employees carry two distinct sets of values that are conflicting in nature, the following situations are found, which are useful in understanding management behavior:

1   *The values of senior and HR managers do not match with the new sets of values targeted by the organization*: in these organizations, change is piecemeal, haphazard, and can only be seen on paper. There is also little understanding at the management level of the changed values of the new generation of employees. Hence, commitment to transforming the organization is low. If changes are being made, it is because of market trends. The result of this is that prevailing centralized and bureaucratic organizational structures hinder an effective flow of communication, and at times employees are not even aware of the cultural changes being targeted by senior managers. In one example, in a move to become performance oriented and participatory in style, an open feedback appraisal system is adopted. The policy requires managers to involve individual employees in the process and to seek feedback from them by providing an opportunity to discuss their strengths and weaknesses for their career development. The policy also aims to protect the interests of the employees in case of a disagreement with managers, and provides both of them the right to refuse to sign off the appraisal, as well as the right to repeal, thus allowing intervention from HR managers and senior managers. However, in practice, managers with old value systems either show their employees the assessment once it has been written down, expecting them to sign it off, or simply inform them of it, not giving them the chance to provide feedback on their appraisal. Sometimes managers do not even make a regular assessment of their employees. In other cases the top management itself has flouted the policy of fair intervention. Employees are often victimized for taking steps to uphold the written policies. In actuality the practice reflects the old norms, i.e., informing the employee of his or her evaluation after it has been sent off to the HR department for consolidation. In these organizations, employees are quite dissatisfied, and have a high level of frustration with existing managerial behavior. One employee remarked, "There is nothing wrong with our management policies; in fact some of them are praiseworthy. The problem lies at the heart of the managerial values that do not support transformation of this kind." Another commented, "Everyone here is so disillusioned with the current management behavior. It is so primitive!"

2   *The values of some functional managers match with the desired values*: in these organizations, with some managers' behavior reflecting the goals, it is easier to follow the written policy. Employees working for these

managers are quite satisfied and have developed strong bonds with them. One employee remarked

> When I consider leaving (this organization), I think of the immense support I get from my manager. He has created a learning environment for us by offering us autonomy and by involving us in decision-making. I am not sure if I want to give that up.

3   *The values of senior and HR managers match with the new values*: in these organizations, commitment from top management translates into effective organizational cultural transformations. What distinguishes these organizations is that top management understands the new values of employees and gradually changes the culture to follow suit. The core organizational characteristics of little autonomy, limited communication, and a high power distance are eliminated. All employees become fully involved in policy formulation and change: presentations are made at all levels, and responses and feedback are evaluated, impacting decisions. Employees receive online access to manuals to ensure understanding. Managers are trained to assess uniformity in following policy guidelines. Employees are encouraged to approach the HR department directly in the case of a problem, such that any deviation from policy is brought to its awareness. Here the values of functional managers match with employees' values. Managers do not feel threatened by sharing their power because senior management has taken great pains to ensure that they understand and adopt the positive elements of this kind of culture. The resultant satisfaction among employees is quite high. These organizations prove to be the most profitable in their industry. Another characteristic that distinguishes them from competitors is that their workforce is young. In one of these organizations, the most successful of all in the sample, the chief executive is in his late 30s and the average age is around 32 years old.

The above discussion illustrates that management behavior not only is the outcome of a manager's own value systems; it can be enforced by organizations that are committed to developing a unique value set across their various offices and functions.

Labor–management conflict resolution

British bureaucratic structures persisting after independence have introduced many elements of rationalized systems including a large number of laws regulating HRM practices: The Workmen's Compensation Act 1923, Payment of Wages Act 1936, Social Security Ordinance 1965, Companies Profit Act 1968, and Industrial Relations Ordinance 1969. Broadly, these laws deal with the provision of a safe and healthy working environment, the employer's liability in case of injury caused by accident, various welfare measures for workers, the employee's fair share in the company's profits, and the employer's contributions toward the social security funds. All organizations, irrespective of origin and industry, are required to abide by these laws. For example, the termination of a regular employee is not permissible for any reason other than misconduct. In the case where an employee is aggrieved by the termination of his or her services, by discharge or dismissal, that employee has the right to apply to a committee for the redress of his or her individual grievance. In the past, many organizations were taken to court by dismissed employees. Not only did it tarnish their image in the market, but the majority of court decisions favored the employee and, in some instances, organizations were asked to reinstate the employee. Consequently, organizations hesitate to dismiss an employee unless gross misconduct is repeatedly observed. In such a case, a full internal investigation into the cause is launched before dismissal takes place (Khilji 2001).

The labor history of Pakistan is characterized as a mix of labor concessions and repression, in the form of four different labor policies. The first labor policy aimed at protecting the interests of the workers and employers; the second emphasized that labor must deliver the goods and there should be no strikes or lockouts; and the third paved the way for the enforcement of Industrial Relations Ordinance 1969. For the first time, then, minimum wages were fixed. Finally, the fourth labor policy, introduced in 1972, included comprehensive measures for strengthening trade unions (Saeed 1995). It, at the same time, "brought to new heights the familiar mix of labour concessions and repression that have characterized the Pakistani labour history" (Chandland 1995: 69). Unions received political patronage and the interests of workers were not necessarily represented. In 1977 the military regime banned strikes and lockouts, as well as student unions and the registration of trade unions of some corporations, such as Pakistan International Airlines and Pakistan Television. At the same time, politicization of the labor unions in public sector organizations reached notorious levels in an attempt to gain more power (Khan 1989). Successive governments of the 1990s failed despite their promises to implement comprehensive new policies, and political patronage of the unions reached new heights, such that in Pakistan unions are instantly equated with corruption and misuse of power by employees and management, alike.

In 1997, the government introduced a new policy, Article 27b, to free the work environment from the influence of the unions. As a result, the power that the unions once enjoyed and exploited is curbed, and their impact on PSEs in Pakistan is reduced to an insignificant level. New private sector organizations and multinationals now discourage employees from forming unions. Some organizations take extra caution, either by obtaining an "undertaking" from new employees stating that they will not involve themselves in union activities of any kind, or by assigning titles of "officers" to clerks and computer operators to legally prevent them from forming a union (Khilji 2001).

Implications for managers

The duality of values, as shown above, is difficult to understand and, as such, poses several unique dilemmas for managers committed to developing effective organizational cultures in order to remain competitive. With the increasing dominance of market mechanisms in businesses there is a considerable demand on them to come to terms with new ways of conceptualizing work, organizational processes, and approaches. Managers in Pakistan need to deepen their understanding of values as they reprioritize their organizational systems. The opportunities to learn and undertake challenging tasks align strongly with today's organizational climate of rapid change and aggressive competition (Chatterjee and Pearson 2000).

There appears to be immense potential for managers to use teamwork since Pakistani employees tend to develop strong bonds with their co-workers. Although the encouragement of the development of social ties amongst employees is often cited as the major cause of "group turnover," managers can significantly reduce the occurrence of this problem. By creating closely knit teams to carry out particular projects, organizations can increase the likelihood that the teams will remain intact for the length of the initiative. Employees who would hardly think twice about abandoning an organization find it very difficult to walk out on their teammates (Cappelli 2000). Teams have another added benefit: studies have shown that they increase employees' commitment to their work. After all, commitment is far easier to establish among employees than between an employee and an abstract entity such as an organization.

Recently, PSEs have hired a younger cohort of employees in order to vitalize their corporate culture. This presents a greater challenge for managers since they are faced with managing two sets of conflicting values, as has been observed in private sector organizations (Khilji 2002b). Younger employees recognize the importance of involvement-oriented and participatory management behaviour. There appears to be significant room for management to become more progressive as the economy develops, structures of macro institutions and organizations change, employees take on bargaining positions, and managers recognize the need to develop their potential in order to survive in a competitive environment. On a positive note, in organizations where these dilemmas have been dealt with, a unique set of values has been one of the driving forces of the success.

Conclusions

The above discussion highlights that the people of Pakistan are open to foreign influences and change. Their traditional core societal values have been an amalgamation of many foreign ideas. And more recently, forces such as globalization, the Internet, and the infiltration of management education together have led to the development of new sets of managerial values among a younger cohort of employees. These values reflect the characteristics of a modern economy. As such, organizations are caught between the preservation of their core cultural values and the need to modernize in an era of globalization in order to be progressive and to satisfy the younger workforce. Some Pakistani organizations have departed from the old centralized and bureaucratic structures; this change has been able to motivate employees and enhance their satisfaction significantly. This supports the argument put forth by McGaughey and De Cieri (1999) that cultural values are not static, as well as the convergent view, i.e., that as the world becomes more global, management practices will converge to a similar model (Raltson *et al.* 1997).

In the wake of these cultural changes, further studies must be conducted to obtain a better understanding of cultural dynamics and of the imperatives of the economic reform agenda in countries such as Pakistan. These studies must be designed to outline the numerous changes taking place, both in the minds of people and in organizations, to describe their impact on management behavior, and to evaluate their effectiveness in terms of employee satisfaction and organizational commitment.

This chapter illustrates that Pakistan has much to offer to foreign investors in terms of its liberal policies, a large consumer market, and its educated elite workforce, which proves to be quite at ease with Western values. Managers in various organizations have taken on the challenge of adopting new value systems and seem to be doing quite well on their own. However, political and economic uncertainty may be delaying progress. Government's sincere initiative and consistent commitment to the economic reform process are required to bring Pakistani organizations and employees to the forefront of world markets. Without these, Pakistan will continue to make little progress, to the great dissatisfaction of its people.

Notes

1   One of the most renowned and remarkable monuments of the Mughul dynasty is the Taj Mahal at Agra.
2   In 2000, Pakistan imported more than $646.5 million worth of US products, while Pakistan's exports to the USA amounted to $2.12 billion (*http://www.usatrade.gov* February 8, 2002).
3   During the 2000–1 federal budge, Rs130,819 million was allocated for defense purposes and the amount for development was estimated at Rs 72,164 million (*http://www.finanace.gov.pk* 2002).
4   Even the national language of Pakistan, Urdu, is derived mainly from Arabic, Turkish, and Persian vocabulary.
5   The database included a sample of over 500 demographically diverse employees (in terms of education, gender, and age) from a number of industries including financial services and the hi-tech sector.

References

Aazim, M. (2001) "State Bank warns of lower GDP growth," *Dawn* 30 November. Available online at: <http://www.dawn.com>.

Aazim, M. (2002) "Domestic growth shows no sign of improvement," *Dawn* 21 March. Available online at: <http://www.dawn.com>.

Ahmad, M. (1997) "Education," in R. Raza (ed.), *Pakistan in Perspective 1947–1997*, Karachi: Oxford University Press, pp. 238–75.

Ahmed, A. S. (1997) *Jinnah, Pakistan and Islamic Identity: The Search for Saladin*, London: Routledge.

Ali, K. (1990) *A New History of Indo-Pakistan Since 1526*, London: Columbia Press.

Amir, A. (1999) "Out of breadth already," *Dawn* 10 September 1999.

Amjad, R. (1992) "The employment challenges for Pakistan in the 1990s," in A. Nasim (ed.) *Financing Pakistan's Development in the 1990s*, Karachi: LUMS, pp. 53–73.

Birdsall, N. and Ross, D. (1993) "Under-investment in education: how much growth has Pakistan forgone?" *Pakistan Development Review* 32(4): 452–9.

Bokhari, F. (1996) "Loss of faith?" *The Banker* 146: 73–6.

Cappelli, P. (2000) "A market-driven approach to retaining talent," *Harvard Business Review* pp. 103–11.

Chandland, C. (1995) "Trade unionism and industrial restructuring in India and Pakistan," *Bulletin of Concerned Asian Scholars* 27(4): 63–78.

Chatterjee, S. R. and Pearson, C. (2000) "Indian managers in transition: orientations, work goals, values and ethics," *Management International Review* 40(1): 81–95.

CIA (2002) *The World Fact Book*, Pakistan. Available online at: <http://www.cia.gov/Pakistan> (accessed February 8, 2002).

Government of Pakistan (2002) *Economic Survey 2000–2001*, Islamabad: Ministry of Finance. Available online at: <http://www.finanace.gov.pk> (accessed February 8, 2002).

Haq, M. and Haq, K. (1998) *Human Development in Asia*, Karachi: Oxford University Press.

Hofstede, G. (1991) *Cultures and Organizations*, London: HarperCollins.

Hussain, I. (1999) "Democracy in doldrums," *Dawn* 16 October 1999.

Hussain, M. and Hussain, H. (1993) *Pakistan–Problems of Governance*, Lahore: Vanguard Books.

Jamal, A. (1998) '*Can we learn something from the perceptions and consumption practices of transnational South Asia communities living in the west?*' Inaugural Conference of the Asia Academy of Management, Hong Kong.

Khan, M. Z. (2001). 'Afghan crisis has put economy at risk: report'. *Dawn*: 30 November. Available online at:
<http://www.dawn.com>.

Khan, S. Y. (1989) 'Trade union revival: Are we moving in the right direction?' *Pakistan and Gulf Economist:* 12–15.

Khilji, S. E. (1999a) *Management in Pakistan*, London: Thomson Learning.

Khilji, S. E. (1999b) "An empirical study of human resource management in a developing country – the case of Pakistan," *The Judge Institute of Management Studies*, Cambridge: University of Cambridge, p. 252.

Khilji, S. E. (2001) "Human resource management in Pakistan," in P. Budhwar and Y. Debrah (eds), *Human Resource Management in Developing Countries*, London: Routledge, pp. 102–20.

Khilji, S. E. (2002a) "Modes of convergence and divergence – an integrated view of multinational practices in Pakistan," *The International Journal of Human Resource Management* March: (2).

Khilji, S. E. (2002b) "Conflict and contentment – assessing the significance of national culture in the development of organizational culture during times of change," *International Society of the Study of Work and Values*, Warsaw.

Klein, M. U. (1992) "Commercial banking in Pakistan," in A. Nasim (ed.), *Financing Pakistan's Development in the 1990s*, Karachi: LUMS, pp. 388–413.

Korson J. Henry (1993) *Contemporary Problems of Pakistan*, Oxford: Westview Press.

Lyon, P. (1993) "Epilogue," in P. James (ed.), *Pakistan chronicle*, London: Hurst.

Malik, I. H. (1994) "Governability crisis in Pakistan – problems of authority, ideology and ethnicity," *Roundtable* 33: (2).

McGaughey, S. and De Cieri, H. (1999) "Reassessment of convergence and divergence dynamics – implications for international management," *The International Journal of Human Resource Management* 10(2): 235–50.

Mirza, S. A. (1995) *Privatization in Pakistan*, Lahore: Ferozesons.

Qureshi, Z. I. (1995) *Management in South Asia*, California: Greenwich.

Raltson, D. A. *et al.* (1997) "The impact of national culture and economic ideology on managerial work values – a study of the US, Russia, Japan and China," *Journal of International Business Studies* First Quarter: 177–200.

Robbins, S. and Langton, N. (2000) *Fundamentals of Organizational Behavior*, Toronto: Prentice Hall.

Saeed, K. A. (1995) "In search of a new labour policy," *Pakistan and Gulf Economist* 14: 6–11.

The Economist (1994) "Pakistan's real poverty," 330: 38.

Trompenaars, F. (1993) *Riding the Waves of Culture*, London: The Economist Books.

Unger, B. (1999) "India and Pakistan – a survey,' *The Economist* 22–28 May.

Website

<http://www.finance.gov.pk> (accessed February 8, 2002).

Website

<http://www.geocities.com/pak_history/main.html> (accessed February 8, 2002).

Website

<http://www.rpi.edu/dept/union/paksa> (accessed February 8, 2002).

Wolpert, S. (1984) *Jinnah of Pakistan*, New York: Oxford University Press.

9 Culture and management in the Philippines

Jan Selmer and Corinna de Leon

Introduction

About 77 million people live in the Philippine archipelago where more than 70 mutually unintelligible languages and dialects are spoken. The national language is Tagalog, originally the dialect of the Luzon region, but the English language was introduced to the islands by American occupiers in the early 1900s (Karnow 1989). Despite an increasing preference for the local language (Lopez 1998), Filipinos are still educated in English as well as Tagalog, comprising one of the largest English-speaking countries in the world. Augmenting the Westernization initiated by a distinctly Spanish heritage, Americanization has penetrated deeper into the Filipino society than into any other Asian country. 'The influx of American ideas and social patterns in a broad range of institutions and the Filipinos' receptivity to them are well-known' (Arce and Poblador 1977: 6). Consequently, the Philippines is unique as a Christian, English-speaking democracy in Asia (Blitz 2000; Engholm 1991; Lopez 1998).

Despite its veneer of Westernization, the style by which managerial practices are devised and implemented in the Philippines is easily identifiable as distinctively Filipino. Filipino management is based on an intricate system of indigenous core values that emphasize social acceptance. So far, the onslaught of globalization is less evident than elsewhere, since indigenous cultural imperatives remain as the powerful social dynamics that govern Filipino managerial behaviours.

The purpose of this chapter is to describe management in the Philippines, by identifying it's fundamental characteristics. The intention is to highlight the enduring and distinguishing features of Filipino management and its determining circumstances. Drawing on a multitude of mostly domestic sources for secondary data, this chapter attempts to provide a generalized portrayal of typical behaviours. This discussion includes relevant historical developments, economy, societal and corporate culture, managerial behaviour and values, as well as labour–management conflict resolution. Based on the broad description of a complex society, implications for managers are discussed and conclusions are drawn.

Historical setting

Foreign contact began in the tenth century through the Chinese traders who introduced their customs to the indigenous tribes (Junker 1999). For the next five centuries, there was extensive trade also with Arabs, Malays and Siamese. In 1521 the cluster of islands was 'discovered' by Ferdinand Magellan of Spain, when his fleet landed on Limasawa. The Philippines was a Spanish colony for almost 400 years, during which it was sporadically 'invaded' by the Portuguese, Dutch and English traders (Arcilla 1994). The rule of the Spanish throne ended on 12 June 1898 when the Philippines was ceded to the American government for 20 million dollars, as part of the settlements of the Spanish–American War. (Roces and Roces 1985; Wolf 1991).

Westernization of Filipino society occurred at a rapid pace, mainly through the exceptional zeal of Spanish friars at converting the Filipinos to the Roman Catholic Church (de la Costa 1961). Large churches were built throughout the country, which became the centre of town development and the gathering point (*plaza*) of community activities. The native customs were modified by the civic regulations which fostered the integration of the Spanish culture: for example, the registration of families under Spanish family surnames, the education of native intellectuals in the Spanish language, the adaptation of Spanish manners and clothing.

The forty years of American occupation further modernized the Philippines through Westernization (Blitz 2000). The American system of public education was developed successfully by American teachers, with English as the medium of instruction. An American-styled democratic government was instituted, with a president as the executive, the Senate and Congress as the legislators, and a Supreme and Appellate Courts as the judiciary. During the Second World War, the Japanese Army occupied the Philippines for three years. In 1945 the American government recognized the independence of the country, and a constitution was promulgated.

The Republic of the Philippines was proclaimed on 4 July 1946, with Manuel Roxas as the first president. Ferdinand Marcos was president for more than two decades, after election in 9 November 1965. He was re-elected in 1969, but, as the Constitution did not allow a third term, he declared martial law in September 1972. Marcos's one-man rule lasted for thirteen years, creating economic and political crises that resulted in national impoverishment (Villegas 2001).

A highly popular political rival of Marcos, Benigno Aquino was assassinated on 21 August 1983, on his return from long exile in the USA. Widely perceived as a martyrdom to democracy, the incident accelerated political change. Anti-Marcos mass rallies gathered momentum, and the opposition won about one-third of the contested seats in elections for the National Assembly. In 1986 Aquino's widow, Corazon, contested Marcos in presidential elections that were made possible only through the constitutional changes dictated by Marcos. While Marcos's victory was under dispute, a military revolt in Manila was led by top officials of the Marcos government, one of whom was Brigadier General Fidel Ramos. Supported by the powerful hierarchy of the Catholic Church, the mutiny propelled massive public protests for the ousting of Marcos. Later referred to as the 'People Power Revolution' (Mercado 1986), this historical event concluded after a few days when Marcos fled to exile to Hawaii where he died in 1989.

Corazon Aquino was officially recognized as the President of the Philippines in February 1986. Despite several military coups, she served the full term of six years. Her government is credited with the restoration of democratic institutions, the Senate and Congress. Under her authority, an ad hoc Constitutional Convention promulgated several major changes in the Philippine Constitution, one of which was the extension of the presidential term from four to six years but prohibited successive *re-election*. Fidel Ramos, a People Power hero, was elected president in May 1992, supported by a coalition of political parties. Although he governed during a period of economic growth and political stability, popular support for Ramos was not enough to push through another constitutional change to permit his re-election.

The opposition politician Joseph Estrada was elected president in May 1998. Known as 'Erap' (the inverse of *pare* which in Tagalog means partner), he was a highly popular ex-movie actor who had been the Mayor of San Juan, a prosperous town in Metro Manila. After a series of political blunders and escalating scandals, Joseph Estrada became in 2000 the first president in the history of the Philippines to be impeached. After a tumultuous three-month trial that was publicized in full by all media, anti-Erap public protests escalated. Angered by attempts of Estrada supporters in the Senate and Congress to negate the impeachment, widespread upheaval on the streets of Manila forced Erap out of office. 'People Power II' was victorious when Estrada was officially removed from the presidency by the Supreme Court, confirming the validity of the impeachment process.

As a member of the political party led by ex-President Ramos, Gloria Macapagal-Arroyo had been elected vice-president in 1998, alongside President Estrada. Arroyo was sworn in as the acting president on 20 January 2001, effectively ending the rule of the Estrada-backed opposition. In early March, the Supreme Court handed down a unanimous decision stating that Gloria Macapagal-Arroyo is the constitutionally designated President of the Philippines until June 2004 (Villegas 2001).

Economic background

After the Second World War until about the 1970s, the economic development of the Philippines was second only to Japan, in the Asia-Pacific region. By the middle of the 1980s, the promise of the Philippines as a prosperous Asian economy was thoroughly jeopardized by the Marcos regime. More than twenty years of inward-looking, protectionist, ultra-nationalistic and interventionist economic policies had completely dismantled the gains of earlier progress (Villegas 2001). The country acquired the most unflattering reputation in what had become the world's most dynamic region, derisively called the 'sick man of Asia'. The fall of the Marcos dictatorship in 1986 restored political freedom, enabling succeeding presidents to correct unfavourable economic measures. After the disastrous performance in the first half of the 1980s, the country has posted periods of respectable growth.

Deregulation, liberalization and privatization have all been championed by the Aquino, Ramos and Arroyo governments, limiting the stranglehold of mercantilism, protectionism and state intervention (Villegas 2001). Tariffs have been reduced considerably, so that the Philippines is regarded now as one of the most open economies in Asia (Kuruvilla *et al.* 2000). The main thrust has been the development strategy of export-oriented industrialization.

Foreign direct investment increased substantially in the 1990s, and so has the share of manufactured goods of total exports. As the savings rate is quite low (below the investment rate), foreign capital compensates for the lack of domestic capital. The Philippines depends on foreign capital sources not only to develop the export economy, but also to finance many government projects (Skene 2002). Since 1992, many foreign firms have built infrastructure projects like the North Luzon Expressway and the EDSA Light Rail Line (Tan 1996) and electricity generating plants.

New economic policies seem to work. During the East Asian financial crisis in 1998 when other countries suffered a 5–13 per cent decline in their GDPs, the Philippines' GDP only had a slight drop of 0.5 per cent. Again in 2001 when most of the East Asian economies experienced GDP declines, the Philippines showed its resilience by altogether avoiding a recession, with a GDP growth of more than 2 per cent. Agriculture and services were the sectors that contributed most to this outcome. Agricultural production grew by 1.9 per cent, accounting for roughly 20 per cent of the country's GDP and 40 per cent of its workforce. Transport and telecom services delivered double-digit growth rates at the beginning of 2001 (Villegas 2001).

The 1997–8 financial crisis in Asia and the political turmoil of the Estrada government (1998–2000) seriously threatened the survival of the nation. Nonetheless the Philippine economy may still regain the economic stability achieved during the Ramos government (1992–8). An average of 4.2 per cent of GDP growth is projected for 2004, when presidential elections will be held at the end of the term of the incumbent Arroyo (Villegas 2001). President Arroyo is evidently supporting the liberalization of the Philippine economy, as well as attempting to reduce widespread poverty through investments in education and reform in landownership.

Currently, major industries in the Philippines are food, electrical machinery and chemicals/chemical products. Agro-based products, mineral products and fruits and vegetables are the major exports (Westlake 1999). For the future, information and computer technology are considered to be the long-term drivers for the economy. A long-stalled land-reform programme may be accelerated, which breaks up large landholdings for wider-based property ownership. There are plans to simplify the tax code. Further, the government is eliciting the participation of the private sector in infrastructure development (Westlake 2001).

Societal culture

Traditional values arose from small agrarian villages that were organized along tribal kinship patterns, comprising a social configuration in which the institutional and cultural fabric was the extended family. Cutting short the victory of his arrival in the Philippines, Ferdinand Magellan was killed during a battle with the tribe of Lapu Lapu, when the Spaniard took the side of Rajah Humabon in a kinship feud (Arcilla 1994; Junker 1999; Roces and Roces 1985). Until now, Philippine politics has been characterized by the rivalry between families who have retained political control over a city/province/region for many generations, in which there is little importance given to ideological issues.

The emergence of Filipino identity can be traced to the *illustrados*, the local educated elite during the Spanish colonial period (Arcilla 1994). Exemplified by the national hero Dr Jose Rizal, the *illustrados* belonged to the wealthy echelons of the native middle class, most with ethnic Chinese ancestry. The Chinese–Filipinos comprised the leadership of the Katipunan, the revolutionary organization which continued the armed struggle for Philippine independence against the Spanish and the American governments from 1896 to 1913 (Linn 2000; Mojares 1999; See and Go 1996).

Despite wealth and education, the *illustrados* were *indios* (natives) who were not fully accepted into the Hispanic society, the members of which distinguished themselves as *penninsulares* (born in Spain) or *insulares* (Spaniards born in the Philippines). Nonetheless the *illustrados* were fluent in the Spanish language and were accustomed to Spanish ways, since many lived and studied in Spain for many years (Arcilla 1994). The myriad of cultural influences on today's society can be summarized as 'three hundred years in a convent and fifty years in Hollywood' (Engholm 1991: 23) with regular sojourns in Chinatown. Unlike in other South-East Asian nations, racial backgrounds have intermingled in the Philippines to the extent that present-day Filipinos are proud to be considered mixed blood (*mestizo*).

Through intermarriage with Filipino women, Chinese immigrants reinforced the family structure of the native society with their hierarchical authoritarianism (Roces and Roces 1985). The strong sense of community, loosely referred to as *bayanihan*, was not directly challenged by the widespread conversion to Spanish Catholicism. The centuries as a Hispanic colony resulted in an integration of Western Christian values with the indigenous cultural imperatives, the main dynamic of which was social acceptance. Decades of exposure to American democratic government, free enterprise and liberal education cemented social institutions that had Westernized structures, but in essence the national character remained unique. The complex Filipino culture is more easily grasped if seen as the amalgamation of four disparate cultures: indigenous Filipino, Chinese, Hispanic and American.

The main characteristic of Filipino societal culture is collectivism (Hofstede 1980), whereby collective identity arises from a strong sense of group belonging fostered by the need for social acceptance (de Leon 1987). The core value of *amor propio* protects the Filipino from the loss of social acceptance. *Hiya* delineates behaviour as socially acceptable or unacceptable. *Utang-na-loob* strengthens the bonds of social acceptance through mutual reciprocity. *Pakikisama* is derived from the notion of *bayanihan* (community), fostering cooperation (*pagtutulungan*) through a sense of togetherness. Collective identity is paramount among Filipinos, in that individual interests are subordinated in the kinship orientation of the extended social network (Silos 1985).

During the Spanish colonization, Westernized religious tenets were superimposed on the *kin* relationships that comprised the traditional social system. The indigenous blood-brother bond coincided with the *compadrazco* (godfather relationship) fostered by Catholicism. A Filipino's extended family was expanded further into a social network through the inclusion of *compadres*, non-kin who were initiated into godparenthood at baptismal or wedding ceremonies. An *inaanak* (godchild) acquires a *ninong/ninang* (godfather/godmother) who become *compadres* of the parents.

The traditional values have survived in contemporary Filipino society, although to a lesser extent in urban rather than rural areas. The hallmark of contemporary Filipino society is the universe of kinship groups, in which group pressure is brought into play throughout the various layers of the social hierarchy. The enlargement of a kinship network based on bloodlines occurred through the multiplication of *compadres* as quasi-relatives.

The kinship structure puts group pressure not only on its members, but also on other groups who may pose a threat by harming a member. As each person is an outward extension of their kin group, individual shame or blame involves the whole network (Andres 1991; Engholm 1991; Roces and Roces 1985). The group-conscious Filipinos expect trustworthiness from all with whom they have a relationship, and tend towards distrust of all others.

Since family membership was crucial, exclusion from the group became a Filipino's worst anxiety (Engholm 1991; Jocano 1989; 1997). Social acceptance and group membership remain central to the way modern Filipinos think, believe, feel and act (Jocano 1989; 1997). As such, social norms promote social relationships: for example, respect for elders, deference to superiors and kindness or tolerance to underlings.

Corporate culture

Although Filipinos give the impression of being highly Westernized, a distinctive Filipino management style is kept in place by indigenous values.

The predominant corporate culture is derived from social traditions on the importance of kinship, which have been influenced but not substantially changed by the integration of Spanish Christianity, American liberalism and Chinese mercantilism. Family connections are relied upon for almost all business situations, be it a small family-owned enterprise or a large publicly listed corporation. Group membership is used to procure various favours, from tax breaks and kickbacks to lucrative business contracts.

It has been estimated that about eighty individuals control 450 of the country's major corporations, and six families control 90 per cent of the economy. Without access to this elite group of business people who can ease one's entrance into the cohesive network of interrelationships, there is little hope of success.

The social status of a particular kinship network is exhibited by the prominence of the godparents of the baby or the wedding couple. As it is commonly accepted and widely practised that one's *ninong* or *compadre* has higher status, distinguished members of high society can have hundreds if not thousands of godchildren. Community leaders are sought after as godparents even by those with whom their social relationship is tenuous, since the *compadre* network is the main channel for ensuring the child's future and extending the parent's political clout, business connections or job references.

Early social studies pointed out that the peculiar characteristic of Filipino collectivism is high segmentation, through the division of society into mutually exclusive in-groups (Lynch 1970). The awareness of *tayo* (us with you) as opposed to *kami* (us without you) results from loyalty to one's primary group and a disregard for non-members (Hollnsteiner 1981; Silos 1985). Such group-centredness explains the inevitable rivalry between various *barkada* (in-groups). Filipino bureaucrats are under constant pressure to respond to their group members and ignore others, including their bosses (Engholm 1991; Roces and Roces 1985). The presence of factionalism stresses the importance of intragroup cooperation and intergroup conflict in Filipino organizations (de Leon 1987).

To further understand corporate culture in the Philippines, the Filipinos' sense of fatalism (*suerte*) has to be considered as a central societal mechanism. Lacking a direct translation, *bahala na* is a crucial value that underlines the escapist nature of the Filipino personality (Andres 1988). *Bahala* (or *pagwawalang-bahala*) is generally manifested through various concepts: *pasensiya* and *pagtitimpi* refer to resignation to and acceptance of failures or shortcomings; and *pagtitiis* enables one to endure difficulties of life without complaint, by adapting to misfortune with resiliency.

Pagwawalang-bahala is manifested as well through several counter-productive behaviours: Filipino subordinates tend to overdepend on and defer to authority, by viewing others as arbiters of one's fate; and concurrently, Filipino bosses believe in maintaining control (Gonzalez 1994). Maintaining the status quo is preferred by all, 'perpetuating the things that have worked in the past' (Gonzalez 1994: 146) and attributing past misfortunes to fate (Abadesco, cited in Suleiman 1994). *Ningas-cogon* is the tendency for an initial outburst of enthusiasm, followed by an equally abrupt loss of interest in the endeavour. Since a Filipino considers personal control of events as limited, he or she believes one's best efforts would have little impact on the overall organizational performance. Since *bahala na* predisposes Filipinos to entrust outcomes to the whimsy of destiny, the corporate culture provides equal justification for inefficiency as well as productivity, and for failure as well as success.

The Filipino believes that fate eventually saves one from shortcomings and that 'there is always a tomorrow' which may reverse one's fortunes (Abadesco, cited in Suleiman 1994). 'Filipino time' refers to traditional propensity to be late for appointments. Among Filipinos for whom time is elastic and deadlines are absent, a strict sense of punctuality, regularity and timekeeping is difficult to instil and enforce in organizations. The '*manana* (tomorrow) habit' permits Filipinos to procrastinate without a sense of urgency.

Managerial behaviour

Filipino culture cultivates great respect for fellow humans, regardless of rank or status. Typically a beggar's supplication is rejected with the polite phrase of '*patawarin po*' ('forgive me, sir'). When service is required by customers, salesmen or waiters are called euphemistically as 'boss, boss'. Elders are respectfully referred to as '*Tito/Tita*' (uncle/aunt), even when the parties have no blood relations.

Filipinos take great care to protect others from *hiya*, mainly through the avoidance of overt conflict. Aggression is evaded, because the Filipino seeks to honour the dignity of the other person (Jocano 1989; 1997). Preventing the occurrence of *hiya* is more important than telling the truth. Filipinos may perceive what constitutes constructive criticism in Western organizations as insults. Objective feedback and standard performance evaluation can cause a Filipino to experience shame and lose self-esteem. To prevent the *hiya* of their superiors, Filipino workers are reluctant to say 'no' to any request or instruction, such that the Filipino 'yes' has many nuances, including the implicit 'no' (Andres 1985).

The available literature confirms that cultural values have a profound impact on management practices in the Philippines (Gonzalez 1994). The Filipino manager is typically person oriented and committed to maintaining smooth interpersonal relationship with subordinates, fellow managers, supervisors and even competitors. At the workplace, there is little hesitancy to mix informal matters with official issues, pleasure with duties, social interaction with work discussion – so much so that employees find it difficult to differentiate the organizational from the personal (Andres 1988). Whereas a Western manager designs work around equipment and the production process, a Filipino manager prefers to view machines and systems as simply extending a person's abilities.

Personalistic considerations are seldom separated from task issues, because human capital is often given priority over profitability. Practitioners of organization development (OD) in the Philippines tend to address 'individual or interpersonal needs, where in other countries it might focus on the total organizational structure' (Suleiman 1994). A prominent business leader described the ideal Filipino manager thus: 'In the final analysis, what makes us motivate people is our genuine interest in them as individuals' (Buenaventura, reported in Ortigas 1994: 70).

Intertwined with their person orientation, Filipinos would give serious deliberation to the moral dimensions of managerial behaviour (Andres 1985). They are compelled not only to consider the earnings of the enterprise, but also to have conscientious regard for a fellow human being. In lieu of organizational growth, Filipino OD practitioners tend to focus on the humanistic goals of helping individuals cope with problems and develop abilities (Suleiman 1994). A sense of gratitude to a person who supported the company during previous difficult times may give a Filipino manager enough reason to retain an employee whose skills are no longer needed. The ideal Filipino predilection would be to subsume work performance to the welfare of the worker and the worker's family (Fajardo 1994), as a sense of reciprocal loyalty between managers and employees should be paramount.

On the other hand, the primary value for *pakikisama* requires the Filipino to make sacrifices in personal welfare for the sake of the group (Engholm 1991). There is a natural willingness to share whatever one has with others in one's circle of relationships. It has been observed that Filipinos prefer to work in groups, whereby face-to-face interaction increased productivity (Gatchalian, reported in Andres 1985). Filipino workers specified helpful cooperation (*pagtutulungan*) as the desired characteristic of work relationships, because it motivates job efficiency and increases job satisfaction. Social acceptance and fear of rejection were shown to be critical factors of work satisfaction among Filipino managers, explained by the desire to preserve social harmony within the work organization (Marzan 1984).

In comparison with managers from other Asian countries (Singapore, Thailand, Indonesia, Malaysia), Filipinos expressed high fulfilment in social needs (Oltramare 1986). The collective identity so central to the Filipino psyche operates through the informal, fluid and interdependent personal networks within the larger organizational and social systems. Filipinos working in groups had higher morale, lower absenteeism and lower turnover (Andres 1985). The camaraderie and loyalty of the group, expressed through *pakikisama* and *pagtutulungan*, are the primary motivators in Filipino organizations (Jocano 1984; Ordonez 1982).

Filipino values underlie the participative nature of managerial decision making, seemingly democratic but essentially socially harmonious.

Pagsangguni means 'to consult', a social value for seeking and encouraging others' opinions. Filipinos expect their views to be heard and respected on all matters, because normative interaction should emphasize social acceptance and foster collective identity. *Pagkakasundo* is a cultural mechanism towards group consensus, as mutual agreement is preferred in all situations. Filipino culture is not confrontational but consensual in orientation, as any violation of the core principles of *smooth* interpersonal relationships should be avoided. Since decisions are made only after consultation, a Filipino believes participative decision making is a mechanism for validating the importance of one's role in the organization.

Modes of communication are also peculiarly Filipino, even in the formal organizational setting. Filipinos expect not only to be consulted but also to be persuaded by others, so as to be given a sense of belonging (Andres 1988; 1991). *Paghihikayat* means 'to persuade or to convince', specifically referring to friendly argumentation (often with the use of humour) to facilitate a meeting of minds. The consciousness of a collective identity is the underlying motive as to why Filipinos use banter as a preface to evidence, avoid going directly to the point, and are almost always ambiguous (de Leon 1987). Ideas are presented as tentative and flexible, to enable one to change one's opinion without personal humiliation. When Filipinos move from an original viewpoint (usually presented as an innuendo) to achieve compromise, they are attesting to group cohesiveness (*pakikisama*) and preventing loss of face (*hiya*) for everyone including themselves.

The corporate culture tends to be elitist, since Filipinos assume that rank has its privileges and rules have exceptions (Gonzalez 1994). Filipino managers 'view themselves as more deserving of respect, approval and reward than lower level employees' (Dowling 1994: 116). Filipino managers assume that their opinion carries greater weight than that of others, as they are the knowledgeable and responsible authority. Nevertheless managers usually make an effort to listen to and acknowledge subordinates' views before the final directive, to maintain their paternalistic image. While espousing 'the values of trust, collaboration, and power sharing ... they still follow traditional authoritarian values' (Abadesco, cited in Suleiman 1994). Four types of distinctive Filipino leadership styles can be identified: *pakiramdam* ('feeling the other'), *takutan* (fear), *kulit* ('much ado about something'), *patsamba-tsamba* ('guesswork') (Andres 1988).

Pakiramdam is a management style that relies on subordinates' anticipation of the boss's work requirements (Andres 1988). This type of passive leadership motivates employees through camaraderie and friendly innuendoes. The staff attempt to 'align with the right person' (Gonzalez 1994: 146) by surmising the manager's implicit expectations, irrespective of the relevance to organizational objectives. As the lack of explicit directives provides little guidance, the subordinates restrict performance to what is deemed acceptable, doing no more and no less to play safe. Obviously, *pakikiramdam* results in a lack of initiative and a dearth of innovation.

On the other hand, *takutan* is a leadership style that puts the onus on the manager who relies on coercion, arrogance and hostility. As threats and punishments are the *modus operandi*, the manager motivates subordinates to obey without argument or complaint. This type of Filipino executive tends to sermonize or lecture the staff, because a monologue emphasizes authority and prevents questions. In the Philippines, there is 'a belief that strong and stable organizations populated by loyal conformists ... do not value diversity or dissent' (Gonzalez 1994: 146). *Takutan* is easily explained by the managers' view that professionalism 'requires social distance between themselves and the "ranks"' (Dowling 1994: 116). Such blatant exhibition of traditional authoritarianism is permissible within the Filipino context, as subordinates prefer to avoid conflict with superiors and to ensure their social acceptance within the work group.

Kulit veers towards micro-management, as the superior consistently checks on the details of the work assignment. Such a Filipino leader hesitates to delegate, requiring frequent feedback. The lack of trust may be masked by the egalitarian manner of the boss, attempting to oversee subordinate's performance by appearing to share (*pakikisama*) staff workload. As this style of leadership is often attributed to a manager's prerogative or personality quirks, Filipino subordinates comply without much resentment (*pagtutulungan*). The staff accept if not respect such a leader, simply because the burden of efficiency is eased and the need for productivity is excused by the undeniable accountability of their superior.

Patsamba-tsamba refers to a manager who works without any clear strategy or structured procedure. As goals and objectives are undefined or disregarded, success or failure is left to fate (*bahala na*). Without explicit directives from their superior, subordinates have no option but to rely on trial and error. Often this type of Filipino manager puts a priority on flamboyant actions rather than rational decision making, tantamount to betting on luck. The manager's 'muddling through' creates a chaotic corporate culture, with the staff confused on job requirements and the organization inefficient in its operations. Although the risky spontaneity inherent in *patsamba-tsamba* is disastrous for long-term productivity, such a managerial style is often seen in Filipino organizations (Andres 1988).

Managerial values

Early studies found that the prevalent management style in the Philippines was authoritative–benevolent (Silao 1981; Tan 1981a; 1981b; Villanueva 1981). Such evidence corroborated Hofstede's (1980) observation that paternalism occurs from a large power distance, a characteristic of Filipino culture. Authoritarianism is acceptable because subordinates expect paternal care in return for filial loyalty (Silos 1985; Gonzales 1994).

It is customary for Filipinos to be employed or promoted through social pressure or *lagay* ('grease money'). Skills and capabilities are given little consideration, because the person who is backed by an insistent supporter or who offers the highest 'agent's commission' succeeds (Dowling 1994). The approval for a request is eased through the personal network directly to the decision maker or to an insider with access. So-called friends of friends can hasten the processing of documents, get the special attention of managers, or facilitate an indirect *areglo* (arrangement) for the payment of *lagay*.

The nepotism inherent in Filipino managerial practices is an outgrowth of the *compadre system* ingrained in Filipino society. For example, *lusot* facilitates job applications (Andres 1985), referring to the process in which aspirants make use of their connections or *compadres* to reach power brokers in the organizational hierarchy. 'It is the exceptional manager who does not find himself pressured by a valued client, a senior officer, or a *compadre* into employing a relative' (Dowling 1994: 119–20). Apart from official references (police clearances, certifications of employment, diplomas), personnel recruitment also requires informal screening of applicants, by tapping personal links inside the company. Consequently, applicants' reputations benefit from pre-existing social relationships with others within the firm, and the organization's risk is lowered by the informal guarantees issued by the applicant's group connections (Amante 1993; 1994).

When existing staff recommend an applicant for an entry position, an implicit contract or bond known as *palakasan* or *kakilala* is created. Supported by the paternalistic managerial style, the new recruit is under the tutelage and responsibility as well as protection of such persons or factions. A breach of trust would lead to *samaan ng loob* (hurt feelings), an emotional tension between two parties which would jeopardize the implicit reciprocity. The network of overlapping bonds could lessen staff-monitoring costs, as the subordinate's good performance is personally guaranteed by supervisors. The Filipino cultural values of *utang na loob* and *hiya* will ensure that the new workers will honour their social obligations by exhibiting good performance; for example, refraining from striking or displaying unproductive behaviours. The bond of mutual obligation would predispose new workers to exercise caution (*kusang loob*) in all aspects of their work environment, to prevent the loss of face (*hiya*) of their guarantors (Amante 1993; 1994).

Labour–management conflict resolution

Insights into the nature of industrial relations may be gleaned from the Philippine Labour Flexibility Survey (PLFS), a national survey of a random sample of 1,311 industrial firms in construction, trade and manufacturing (Standing 1992). The findings of the PLFS showed that just over 40 per cent of the surveyed establishments were unionized. Union membership ranged from 9 per cent in the construction industry to more than 58 per cent in basic metals manufacturers, the share increasing with the size of the firm. Of all unionized firms, about 69 per cent had industrial (or independent) unions. Company (in-house) unions were more frequent in medium-sized rather than in either small or large establishments.

According to the PLFS, about 29 per cent of the firms had a labour–management council (LMC), a feature peculiar to Philippine industrial life. Owing to years of political instability and relatively slow economic development, labour protests are generally seen to be detrimental to progress. To lessen the power of unions to incite strikes, there has been a vigorous government campaign to promote LMCs at the firm level as a viable alternative to labour unions. Both employers and employees are represented on the LMC, which can decide on major policies affecting workers' rights and obligations (Ang and Palanca 2000; Standing 1992).

Industrial relations are to a large extent regulated by the state. There are laws guaranteeing workers' right to collective bargaining, for union registration, for certification elections, and for compulsory and voluntary arbitration (Ang and Palanca 2000; Macapagal 1993). During the dictatorship of President Marcos, the prohibition of strikes was an explicit government policy. After the People Power Revolution of the late 1980s, President Aquino attempted to remove the more repressive thrust of Marcos's labour policy. Since then, industrial relations experts have argued that government interference in labour–management issues should be lessened, especially decrees on minimum daily wage should be withdrawn to permit negotiations at the company or union levels (Salazar 1994).

However, new labour laws have not substantially changed the nature of labour–management relations in the Philippines. Although successive governments in recent years have been democratic, violations of labour rights have not been eliminated but have simply become more covert (Skene 2002). The apparent improvements in labour practices have not encouraged a stronger labour movement, nor stabilized industrial relations.

On the contrary, abating the rules governing the formation of unions has widely fragmented the labour movement. Labour federations are being reorganized into so-called labour centres, the largest of which are the Trade Union Congress of the Philippines, Lakas Manggagawa Labor Centre and the Kilusang Mayo Uno. Currently, there are about 8 national centres, 155 national federations along a myriad of political lines, and more than 5,600 independent local unions (Skene 2002).

The weakness of the labour movement is hidden within the massive institutional structure. As of 1998, only 10 per cent of the workforce was composed of members of trade unions and even fewer were included in collective bargaining agreements (Ang and Palanca 2000; Kuruvilla 1996). The unions rely on government decrees on the minimum daily wage as a floor for collective bargaining, usually resulting in small increases that do not meet the basic survival needs of the common *tao* (man). The clout of the labour movement is curtailed by the law's restrictions on strikes, the government's crackdown on illegal strikes, and employer's replacement of striking workers. To circumvent legal protection of job security, casual workers are preferred to permanent employees. Subcontracts of labour have increased five times, hastening the demise of union power (Kuruvilla 1996).

Owing to the institutional restructuring by the American colonial government during the first half of the twentieth century, the Philippines inherited a rich body of labour legislation that is supported by government and private sector initiatives. Yet the ambitious legal framework may not indicate how labour–management conflicts are being resolved in practice. During a period of extended economic and political problems, further deterioration can be expected in union strength, real wages, job security and labour standards.

Despite the person orientation and group-centredness of the society, economic and political factors have a substantial impact on industrial relations in the Philippines. Imminent economic decline and recurring political turmoil have inhibited the Filipino workers' enthusiasm for labour protests, possibly explained by their penchant to be long suffering (*pagtitiis*). Bolstered by their fatalism (*bahal na*) and their sense of cohesiveness (*pakikisama*), harmonious acceptance of the status quo prevails over the divisiveness of labour–management conflict.

Implications for managers

Among Filipinos, the personal is a crucial element of most work situations. Managers are expected to maintain reciprocity with their subordinates, based on the exchange of personal loyalties and mutual obligations. Social relationships have to be established before work can commence, deals can made and business can prosper. Furthermore, actions at work are not separated from the person who is performing them, intermingling the objective with the subjective and the formal with the informal. Impartial business decisions that are unfavourable to an individual can easily be regarded as a biased personal attack. In summary, the Filipinos' laudable humanistic and moralistic orientation can become detrimental, as comprehensive rational management may be reduced to excessively narrow-minded personalistic interaction.

Hiya (a sense of shame) is a powerful rule of conduct, a norm prescribing that social harmony is possible only if no one is made to lose face. Most Filipinos tend to be sensitive to personal slights or implicit insults, described as '*balat sibuyas*' (onion skinned). When public shame is experienced, the Filipino will not easily agree to any arrangement that resolves the conflict, as his or her personal dignity would be at stake. Holding hard and fast on one's stated position is a face-saving mechanism, so much so that litigation can last for years in the Philippines. In summary, the Filipino organization is hampered not only by conflict avoidance, but also by inadequate social mechanisms for conflict resolution.

One may wonder whether the impact of Filipino values on management behaviour fosters efficiency through social harmony, or enhances the latter at the expense of the former. The momentum within Filipino society is derived from the trustful expectation that relationships are always mutually beneficial. As Filipinos place a high premium on maintaining smooth inter-personal relationships, conflict is perceived to be a dangerous pitfall rather than an opportunity for change. Furthermore the fatalistic belief that everyone is controlled by forces beyond their control results in satisfaction with the status quo, a lack of foresight and a deficiency in planning. Relatively low labour productivity is an enduring problem in the Filipino economy.

Family obligations or in-group benefits are promoted over institutional or community interest, because personal relationships must be preserved. Taking the constructive view, kinship patterns that promote social harmony can become a tool for promoting organizational commitment. Harnessing the dynamics of collectivism inherent in the culture would be to the advan-tage of the firm. Observing that 'management by objectives' is hampered in Filipino organizations by its focus on the individual, it has been suggested that 'Filipino managers should think of peer groups as the basis of a more meaningful system of planning, implementation, evaluation and control' (Morales 1994: 134.). Since Filipinos naturally subsume personal gain to the common interests of their group, it would be beneficial if management were to create a corporate culture wherein the organization is seen as a unified extended 'family' (Andres 1985; Ang and Palanca 2000; de Leon 1987; Jocano 1989).

The networks of interrelationships of kin and quasi-kin provide 'a built-in survival system' not only in the Philippines, but also in all other countries where Filipino communities can be found (Root 1997; Sanders 2002). The success and high productivity of Filipinos working abroad is well known, in that examples abound from extremely diligent domestic helpers to highly successful business professionals (Ang and Palanca 2000; San Juan 1998). In the USA, the poverty rate among ethnic Filipinos is almost negligible (about 1 per cent), lower than all other social categories (Ang and Palanca 2000; San Juan 1998). Physically removed from the social pressures found in the home country, these immigrants find that indigenous values can motivate a strong work ethic. There is ample evidence that given a supportive environ-ment, Filipinos want to do their work well and for the right reasons are willing to put in the extra effort to complete the task (Gonzalez 1994).

Conclusions

The future development of Filipino management cannot be readily foreseen. The wave of rapid globalization will not stop at the shores of the Philippines, and the influx of worldwide changes will eventually influence the nature of Filipino business and management. Coinciding with the opening of markets, deregulation of trade was initiated by ex-President Ramos and is vigorously pursued by President Arroyo. In the highly competitive environment, exacerbated by the entry of the People's Republic of China into the WTO, survival of the economy requires that the conduct of business assumes an international perspective and acquires cross-cultural sensibility.

Centuries earlier, business in the Philippines flourished mainly through highly centralized family corporations in which most key positions were reserved for family members. There has been an increase in autonomous business enterprises that are patterned after Western corporate structures, with skilled professional managers (Ang and Palanca 2000). However, as indigenous values in the Philippines have proven to be resilient, it is highly unlikely that comprehensive changes in corporate culture and management behaviour will occur in the near future.

The unspoken but cogent code of conduct poses a serious dilemma for Filipinos, as business becomes more global. Although Filipino managers are easily perceived as Americanized, the nuances of their behaviour are easily understood only in the context of complex cultural imperatives. Upholding kinship loyalties (e.g. the *kakilala* system of recruitment) might be perceived as nepotism. Gift-giving to express gratitude for past favours (*utang-na-loob*) could be considered as bribery. Power sharing within a wide network of friends and *compadres* might be seen as corrupt cronyism (Ang and Palanca 2000). Many business practices are viewed negatively as counter-productive, if Filipino managerial behaviour and values are not seen as essentially culture bound.

A casual visitor to the Philippines may quickly conclude that the society is thoroughly Westernized in manner and attitude. Since nothing could be farther from the truth, anyone dealing with Filipinos in business or otherwise needs to be familiar with the complex value system that intertwines the indigenous Filipino, Chinese, Spanish and American cultures. Looking beneath the veneer of societal openness and cultural flexibility, there is a uniquely Filipino way of acting in most situations. As seemingly simple behaviours are essentially complicated in intent, an appreciation of the Filipino nature is basic to any understanding of management in the only Christian, English-speaking democracy in Asia.

References

Amante, M. S. V. (1993) 'Human resource management in Japanese enterprises in the Philippines: issues and problems', *Asia Pacific Journal of Management* 10(2): 237–45.

Amante, M. S. V. (1994) 'Pay and employment approaches in the Philippines: study of Japanese, Filipino-Chinese, Western-owned firms', in M. S. W. Amante (ed.), *Human Resource Approaches*, Quezon City: UP SOLAIR/Japan Foundation.

Andres, T. D. (1985) *Management by Filipino Values*, Quezon City: New Day Publishers.

Andres, T. D. (1988) *Managing People by Filipino Values*, Quezon City: Publishers' Press.

Andres, T. D. (1991) *Human Resource Management in the Philippine Setting*, Quezon City: New Day Publishers.

Ang, R. P. and Palanca, E. H. (2000) 'Management in the Philippines', in M. Warner (ed.), *Regional Encyclopedia of Business and Management: Management in Asia Pacific*, London: Thomson Business Press.

Arce, W. F. and Poblador, S. (1977) 'Formal organizations in the Philippines: motivation, behavior, structure and change', *Philippine Studies* 25(1): 5–29.

Arcilla, J. S. (1994) *An Introduction to Philippine History*, Quezon City: Ateneo de Manila University Press.

Blitz, A. (2000) *The Contested State: American Foreign Policy and Regime Change in the Philippines*, Lanham, MD: Rowman and Littlefield.

de la Costa, H. (1961) *The Jesuits in the Philippines, 1581-1768*, Cambridge, MA: Harvard University Press.

de Leon, C. T. (1987) 'Social categorization in Philippine organizations: values toward collective identity and management through intergroup relations', *Asia Pacific Journal of Managemen* 5(1): 28–37.

Dowling, J. M. (1994) 'Transactional analysis in Philippine organizations', in C. D. Ortigas (ed.), *Human Resource Development: The Philippine Experience*, Quezon City: Ateneo de Manila Press.

Engholm, C. (1991) *When Business East Meets Business West: The Guide to Practice and Protocol in the Pacific Rim*, New York: John Wiley.

Fajardo, L. B. (1994) 'The personnel manager then and now', in C. D. Orgtigas (ed.), *Human Resource Development: The Philippine Experience*, Manila: Ateneo de Manila University Press.

Gonzalez, R. L. (1994) 'Corporate culture modification', in C. D. Ortigas (ed.), *Human Resource Development: The Philippine Experience*, Quezon City: Ateneo de Manila University Press.

Hofstede, G., (1980) *Culture's Consequences: International Differences in Work-Related Values*, Beverly Hills, CA: Sage.

Hollnsteiner, M. R. (1981) 'Philippines organizational behavior: pesonalism and group solidarity', in N. N. Pilar and R. A. Rodriguez (eds), *Readings in Human Behavior in Organizations*, Quezon City: Ateneo de Manila University Press.

Jocano, F. L. (1984) 'Culture-bound approach to Philippine industrial relations: a search for an indigenous model', *Philippine Journal of Industrial Relations* 6(1–2): 109–23.

Jocano, F. L. (1989) 'Module VI: Integrating Filipino values in managing industrial relations', in J. C. Gatchalian, M. M. Gatchalian, B. C. Gonzales, R. F. Resurrecion and F. L. Jocano (eds), *Handbook on Labor-Management Cooperation: LMC for Philippine Setting*, Metro Manila: Institute for Labor Studies.

Jocano, F. L. (1997) *Filipino Value System: A Cultural Definition*, Metro Manila: Punlad Research House.

Junker, L. L. (1999) *Raiding, Trading, and Feasting: The Political Economy of Philippine Chiefdoms*, Honolulu: University of Hawaii Press.

Karnow, S. (1989) *In Our Image: America's Empire in the Philippines*, New York: Ballantine Books.

Kuruvilla, S. (1996) 'Linkages between industrialization strategies and industrial relations/human resource policies: Singapore, Malaysia, the Philippines, and India', *Industrial and Labor Relations Review* 49(4): 635–57.

Kuruvilla, S., Erickson, C., Anner, M., Amante, M. and Ortiz, I. (2000) *Philippines: Corporate Social Responsibility and Working Conditions*, Bangkok: International Labour Organization.

Linn, B. A. (2000) *The Philippine War, 1899-1902*, Lawrence, KS: University Press of Kansas.

Lopez, A. (1998) 'No English, please: Estrada's Filipino direction', *Asiaweek* 24(40): 32.

Lynch, F. (1970) 'Social acceptance reconsidered', in F. Lynch and A. de Guzman II (eds), *Four Readings on Philippine Values*, Institute of Philippine Culture Papers No. 2, Quezon City: Ateneo de Manila University Press.

Macapagal, D. (1993) *Constitutional Democracy in the World*, Manila: Santo Thomas University Press.

Marzan, C. V. (1984) 'Preferences and job satisfaction in selected domestic private commercial banks', MBA thesis, Ateneo de Manila University.

Morales, A. R. (1994) 'Management by objective as O.D. strategy in the Philippines', in C. D. Ortigas (ed.), *Human Resource Development: The Philippine Experience*, Quezon City: Ateneo de Manila University Press.

Mercado, M. A. (1986) *People Power: The Philippine Revolution of 1986*, Manila: The James B. Reuter, S.J., Foundation.

Mojares, R. B. (1999) *The War Against the Americans: Resistance and Collaboration in Cebu, 1899-1906*, Quezon City: Ateneo de Manila University Press.

Oltramare, N. (1986) 'A comparative profile of managers in ASEAN', MBA Advanced Study Project, School of Postgraduate Studies, National University of Singapore.

Ordonez, R. M. (1982) 'The behavioral skills of the ASEAN manager', *Occasional Papers*, No. 3, Metro Manila: Asian Institute of Management.

Ortigas, G. Z. (1994) 'The human resource executive as a strategic manager', in C. D. Ortigas (ed.), *Human Resource Development: The Philippine Experience*, Quezon City: Ateneo de Manila University Press.

Roces, A. and Roces, G. (1985) *Culture Shock: Philippines*, Singapore: Times Books International.

Root, M. P. P. (ed.) (1997) *Filipino Americans: Transformation and Identity*, Thousand Oaks, CA: Sage.

Salazar, M. V. (1994) 'New dimensions in industrial relations', in C. D. Ortigas (ed.), *Human Resource Development: The Philippine Experience*, Manila: Ateneo de Manila University Press.

Sanders, A. (2002) 'Filipinos are skirting poverty trap', *San Francisco Examiner* February 27.

San Juan, E. (1998) *From Exile to Diaspora: Versions of the Filipino Experience in the United States*, Boulder, CO: Westview Press.

See, T. A. and Go, B. J. (1996) *The Ethnic Chinese in the Philippine Revolution*, Manila: Kaisa Para sa Kaunlaran.

Silao, J. V., Jr (1981) 'The management system of Manila Doctors' Hospital', MBA thesis, Ateneo de Manila University.

Silos, L. R. (1985) 'The basis of Asian and Western organization', *Occasional Paper*, No. 13, Metro Manila: Asian Institute of Management.

Skene, C. (2002) 'The impact of external constraints on labour rights: the case of the Philippines', *International Journal of Human Resource Management* 13(3): 484-500.

Standing, G. (1992) 'Identifying the "Human Resource Enterprise": A South-East Asian experience', *International Labour Review* 131(3): 281–9.

Suleiman, I. K. (1994) 'Organization Development (OD) in the Philippines', in C. D. Ortigas (ed.), *Human Resource Development: The Philippine Experience*, Quezon City: Ateneo de Manila University Press.

Tan, A. (1996) 'Growth of 7 per cent, but inflation worries', *Asia Today* October.

Tan, D. A. (1981a) 'The management system of the Far Eastern University-Nicanor Reyes Medical Foundation Hospital', MBA thesis, Ateneo de Manila University.

Tan, E. C. (1981b) 'The management of the Daniel Romouldez Memorial Hospital', MBA thesis, Ateneo de Manila University.

Villanueva, M. A. (1981) 'The management system of Medical Center Manila', MBA thesis, Ateneo de Manila University.

Villegas, B. M. (2001) *The Phillipine Advantage*, Manila: University of Asia and the Pacific.

Westlake, M. (ed.) (1999) *Asia 2000 Yearbook*, Hong Kong: Far Eastern Economic Review.

Westlake, M. (ed.) (2001) *Asia 2002 Yearbook*, Hong Kong: Far Eastern Economic Review.

Wolf, L. (1991) *Little Brown Brother: How the United States Purchased and Pacified the Philippines*, Singapore: Oxford University Press.

10 Culture and management in Singapore

Charles M. Hampden-Turner

Introduction

Singapore is, in many respects, one of the strangest, yet one of the most spectacularly successful, economies in the world . As recently as 1966, its citizens had a gross domestic product of $600 per head (Peebles and Wilson 1996). By 1997, this had passed $29,000 and Singapore was among the six wealthiest economies in the world (see Swee 1995). This ascent from rags to riches is unprecedented in economic history.

Nor is Singapore merely an economist's prodigy. For those of us asking whether economic development is sustainable, or whether the degradation of the environment and large gaps between rich and poor are the prices to be paid for quick development, the answer given by Singapore is both positive and reassuring. Although densely populated with 3.5 million people and no more than 271 square miles (702 square kilometres), Singapore is beautifully landscaped and maintained. It *is* possible to grow fast economically while caring for one's people and the environment, to largely eliminate poverty, to maintain a very low crime rate and to avoid racial and civic disorder.

Singapore has made it from the Third World to the First World in thirty years or less. Not a bad record for a city-state which was considered non-viable when pushed out of the Malaysian Federation in 1965 only two years after the Federation was formed. Even today it is virtually undefendable in a military sense and must rely on commercial relationships for its strength and on Malaysia for its water.

All of this owes much to a single political leader and now Senior Minister, Lee Kuan Yew, who negotiated the end of Singapore's colonial status and became the nation's Founding Father. His PAP (People's Action Party) has ruled continuously since the nation's birth, with very scant opposition or none at all.

Historical setting

Singapore island is strategically situated where the Pacific Ocean meets the Indian Ocean at the tip of the Malaysian peninsula, giving access between

Malaysia and Indonesia to the South China Sea. It was populated by fishermen and pirates from the eleventh century onwards. Its name, Singapore, is Sanskrit for 'Lion City' and owes its name to the once abundant creatures in the locality. Huge effigies of lions decorate the city to this day.

The city was called Tumasik until sacked by Javanese invaders in 1377. In the early nineteenth century it was discovered by an agent of the British East India Company, Sir Stamford Raffles, who saw the immense strategic significance of Singapore to British trade routes (see Collis 2000). In 1819 he gained possession of Singapore through an agreement with one of the Sultans of Johor (now Malaysia). It is of significance that Singapore was peaceably acquired, unlike Hong Kong, and that Raffles was by all accounts an extraordinary person, a veritable Renaissance Man.

The 'Raffles effect'

Very few non-white ex-colonial countries harbour affection for their one-time rulers, but Sir Stamford Raffles (1781–1826) was a very fortunate exception to this rule. A fierce political enemy of slavery, he was a linguist, an orientalist, an author, a zoologist and a collector of rare plants, elected to Britain's exclusive Royal Society towards the end of his short life. Above all, he was a great humanitarian, intervening again and again to prevent punitive measures against the peoples he had come to study and admire. He was largely responsible for awakening European interest in 'the Far East' as we still (rather ethnocentrically) call it.

Above all, he founded the trading post, port and town of Singapore and drew up the maps that survive to this day and have special demarcated areas for Chinese, Malays and Indians, whose indigenous cultures he studied and wished to survive. He freed all African slaves left over from Dutch rule and even founded schools for their education and that of their children. There is extensive communication between Raffles and William Wilberforce, the leader of Great Britain's anti-slavery movement. In it Raffles foresees a 'great co-mingling of the wisdom of East and West'.

At a stroke and without authorization from London, which came months later, he had opened up the China trade with Great Britain via Calcutta. So great was the rejoicing among merchant traders and the City of London that the politicians accepted the *fait accompli*, despite Dutch objections.

The spirit of Raffles still infuses Singapore. The famous Raffles Hotel and restaurant, a white colonial mansion with a marvellous ambience of tranquillity and civility, stands as a memorial to his statesmanship. His name finds its way into innumerable streets, clubs and landmarks. 'Raffles Class' (business class) on Singapore Airlines rightly commemorates a man of action, not an aristocrat or overlord travelling first class. Raffles represents the culturally inherited British characteristics that appear to have served Singapore so well.

The Lee Kuan Yew influence

But by far the strongest influence on the history and culture of Singapore is that of its founder and, until recently, its First Minister, Lee Kuan Yew, now formally retired, but still very influential as Senior Minister. He attended Cambridge University in the immediate post-war period, reading law, and met his wife, a fellow Chinese student, both of whom received first-class honours, with stars for special distinction.

He returned to Singapore as a lawyer to help represent (moderate) trades unionism in its negotiations with mostly British employers. Malaya, later to become Malaysia, had been in serious conflict with communist insurgents of Chinese ethnicity since the late 1940s. He had quickly to decide his position. Was he a Chinese communist, or a believer in the partnership of labour and capitalism? His experience of Cambridge, of the British common law tradition, and of the Attlee Labour government in the post-war UK, where the disciplined and orderly habits of a population at war had not yet ceased, all inclined him towards partnership and helped shape his social reform agenda.

Trained in constitutional law and with a mind which his colonial masters soon learned to respect, he took a leading role in the negotiations which formally sealed Singapore's independence from British rule, although the UK retained armed forces in Singapore for a period after independence and helped the fledgling republic resist communist pressures. The Peoples' Action Party founded by Lee Kuan Yew swept to victory in the first elections, heavily defeating the communists, and has won elections easily ever since.

He was a great admirer not only of British legal tradition but of its civil service, a highly professional body recruited from clever young people at the best universities, largely free of corruption and with a strong public service ethos, which put the nation first and private interests second.

It is important to grasp that the Singaporean Chinese elite of that time spoke English not Chinese. Although the Senior Minister has been at pains to study Mandarin, his first language, and that of the government elite in general, was and remains English.

Most of Singapore's present cultural characteristics spring from the experience of their long-time leader, the strict rule of law, economic egalitarianism, educational and administrative elitism, resolute anti-communism, incorruptible civic virtue, and Chinese family-type moral virtues, with father figures leading both nation and families. (Television commercials promote romance, marriage, children and stable, long-term relationships.)

Economic background

We understand little of Singapore's 'Third Way' between socialism and capitalism unless we look closely at the nation's industrial policy. Industrial policy gets a bad press in most Western countries, outside France, because of the wide distances, both geographical and political, between government and people. It is usually seen as a form of command economy, in which governments tell industries what they should do. The flexibility and self-organization of the market economy is seen as far superior to economic imperatives dictated from above.

In fact, Singapore is not a command economy in this sense at all and has few if any nationalized industries with monopoly powers. There are a diminishing number of GLCs (Government-Linked Companies) whose performance has not in general been exemplary and whose influence is declining, but one of the secrets of Singapore's success is the refusal of government to cater to special interests, a characteristic it once shared with British-administered Hong Kong. These *are* 'level playing fields', or at least a closer approximation to this than is often achieved by the lobbying systems in Western democracies, where influence can be bought *à la* Enron.

Singapore is less a command economy than 'a facilitated development economy'. How do you facilitate economic success without favouring one enterprise over another or 'picking winners' to use the fashionable epithet? One obvious way is to rate all business by its 'knowledge intensity,' and to give preference to 'high-end' products, that is products that require large amounts of knowledge to develop, manufacture, distribute and use. To require industry to be complex and its products therefore scarce, profitable and educational is more a condition of economic freedom than an infringement.

The government has discretion to let into the island nation or to keep out a large variety of businesses from abroad, including leading global players with world-class products. An English-speaking enclave in the middle of Asia, with perhaps the best port facilities in the world and an IT infrastructure second to none, is an extremely popular location for leading companies. Anyone who wants to be represented in that part of the world is very likely to choose Singapore.

It follows that the government is able to extract major concessions from this surfeit of applicants. Instead of bribes and militias ready to beat up the indigenous workforce in exchange for protection money, Singapore seeks products that will help to educate all those workers in foreign companies, along with training facilities and on-the job instruction that will render Singaporeans more employable.

Almost alone in the world the Singaporean government penalizes employers who pay low wages. Pay below a certain benchmark decreed by government and employers must pay a training levy into a central fund that reskills workers left behind in their earnings. The calculation is *not* to promote wage inflation, but to raise productivity via skill enhancement even faster than wages, so as to reward both shareholders and employees.

Great care is taken when large MNCs are invited to locate in Singapore, to train the skilled workers and engineers in sufficient quantities. That way their salaries and wages will not be bid up by skill shortages. Foreign businesses are not only welcome in Singapore; if the national value added per person is raised thereby, they are invited to join a cluster of similar businesses in the same region of the city. There is a shipping cluster, an electronics cluster, a media cluster, a financial services cluster, an aeronautics cluster, a precision engineering cluster and so on.

The phenomenon was described by Michael Porter in his book *The Competitive Advantage of Nations* (1992), who pointed out that clusters formed spontaneously in Silicon Valley, Milan, Detroit, etc. Within two years Singapore was creating them deliberately. The EDB (Economic Development Board) is perhaps the most alert and creative facilitator of business in the world.

Clustering is supposed to increase cross-fertilization of talent and creativity within an industry, pushing up standards through competition *and* cooperation and drawing on the same pool of escalating expertise to service all players. More people are attracted to Saville Row to buy suits, to Charing Cross Road to buy books, or to Madison Avenue to buy advertising, than are attracted to the individual enterprises. The cluster acts as a magnet to buyers and an incubator of talent.

Singapore is careful to avoid sending away companies that wish to locate there but cannot be accommodated. If Pepsi Cola wants to locate a bottling plant, this can be sited in Ho Chi Minh City or Bangkok with Singapore's assistance, while the Asian HQ *is* allowed into Singapore, since work more complex than mixing water with syrup is performed there. Such a policy creates a 'knowledge ladder' with Singapore several rungs higher than its neighbours, earning money by the relative rarity of its knowledge.

Like Japan, Singapore is virtually without raw material resources. What it does have is the brains between the ears of its own people and to that end it teaches, trains, even drills its inhabitants from kindergarten onwards. Because mothers have themselves been well educated and because many stay at home while their children are young, Singaporean families are powerfully 'supervised' by resident mothers and children earn love by scholarly endeavours. School homework assignments are put out over the Internet and can be accessed via television, not just computer.

While some 80 per cent of Singaporeans were initially consigned to public housing, the right to buy an apartment from the wages (compulsorily) saved has turned the nation into property owners who can rent or sell their entitlements.

Two other big boosts to the Singaporean economy were its early financial centre and its superlative port facilities. Lee Kuan Yew tells of mapping financial centres across the globe. In the 1960s first Zurich opened, then London, then New York, then San Francisco, after which the sun set on world finance until Zurich opened again next day. Establishing Singapore (and Tokyo and Hong Kong) as financial centres would mean that global capitalism never slept, a fact that he woke up to in the early 1060s when he established a stock market with the help of the Bank of America.

Another aid to economic take-off was Singapore's very modern port facilities. It not only pioneered the revolution in containerized cargo handling in East Asia, it modelled the holds of all incoming ships on computer software and reduced turnaround times to a matter of days or even hours. Fly low over Singapore harbour today and you will see as many as fifty ships waiting to anchor. It is the busiest and most efficient port in the region.

Societal culture

Singapore is perhaps the world's purest meritocracy. This is most important to the nation's sense of order and fairness. While the British civil service tradition gave the process a jump start, it has far deeper roots in the Chinese culture itself. The Tang Dynasty, which ruled China for nearly 300 years, from 618 to 907, had installed a system of civil service examinations, exchanging aristocracy by birth for aristocracy by talent. This was much expanded and institutionalized by the Sung Dynasty which ruled China until the Mongol invasions of the thirteenth century. These are the world's oldest meritocracies by far, built on a philosophy of neo-Confucianism and the ideas of Chu His.

Scholarship is also very important in the culture of the Chinese diaspora. Once you migrate you can carry with you on your journey neither land nor real estate, nor many physical possessions, but mostly your own skills, training and intellect which you pass on to your children and community (see George 1992). Education plus business acumen are the migrant's means of survival. All over the world, but most noticeably in the USA, students of Chinese background have gained places in top institutes of higher education in numbers far exceeding their proportion of the local populations. Moreover they tend to choose 'hard' subjects – engineering, mathematics, physics – where answers are demonstrably true or false and do not depend on the teacher liking minority students or exercising judgements in their favour. Unambiguous merit can thus fight discrimination.

However, in Singapore with its 72 per cent Chinese population, high levels of scholarship go to legitimisze the strong influence of Chinese culture. Yet a major split remains between the English-speaking Chinese elite, of which Lee Kuan Yew is himself an example, and the mainly Mandarin- and Cantonese-speaking Chinese. English, plus their own ethnic language, are the two languages which all Singaporeans learn, whether Malaysian, Indian or Chinese. This makes English the governing language, as well as the international language, and other languages those of various ethnic origins. This has given rise to what the authorities call 'Chinese chauvinism' and what its exponents might call 'Chinese heritage'.

The politics were played out around the city's two principal universities, the National University of Singapore with its colonial origins and strictly English-language teaching, and Nanyang University, built, it is said, out of the contributions of humble prostitutes and rickshaw men seeking a genuinely Chinese university. After student disturbances in the 1970s in which the First Minister was jostled by rowdy demonstrators, students were arrested and the university closed. Contracts to remove its famous gates were not bid on, so strong was the feeling in the city at large.

When the university reopened it was under a new name and the departments teaching humanities and social science subjects were not restored. It was from these that most demonstrating students had originated. There is clearly a pattern here. Meritocracy in 'hard' rather than 'soft' subjects is a way of maintaining social order and engineering science and business subjects do not simply spur the economy, they help maintain that order. Singaporean culture prefers questions to which there are clear and precise answers known to teachers and authorities in advance. The hard disciplines are better for discipline in general.

Merit does, of course, make possible an hierarchical ordering. Every year there are established from student achievements President's Scholars, Armed Forces Scholars and Merit Scholars in a descending order of excellence. It is usually possible to predict the future rank of a civil servant or an army officer from how he or she did in this order of educational attainment. Meritocracies do not like surprises; they like potentials to fulfil themselves on schedule and so they do. Early educational attainment is a self-fulfilling prophecy.

In 2000, 'The World Competitiveness Report' (Table 10.1) inquired as to what extent the values of different national cultures supported competitiveness. Not unsurprisingly, given the foregoing discussions, Singapore headed the list. The culture's major energies are mobilized for economic development.

Table 10.1   Extent to which the values of society support competitiveness

1	Singapore	8.46	24	Turkey	5.82
2	Hong Kong	8.12	25	France	5.74
3	Malaysia	7.63	26	Thailand	5.68
4	Japan	7.37	27	Denmark	5.68
5	Chile	7.19	28	India	5.54
6	Canada	7.06	29	UK	5.53
7	Finland	7.01	30	Austria	5.50
8	Israel	7.01	31	Brazil	5.43
9	Switzerland	6.98	32	Indonesia	5.50
10	Iceland	6.92	33	Czech Republic	5.17
11	Belgium	6.77	34	Italy	5.12
12	Korea	6.69	35	Portugal	4.94
13	New Zealand	6.60	36	China	4.89
14	USA	6.54	37	Columbia	4.89
15	Taiwan	6.53	38	Argentina	4.88
16	Ireland	6.46	39	Mexico	4.83
17	The Philippines	6.25	40	Spain	4.68
18	The Netherlands	6.13	41	Greece	4.38
19	Australia	5.93	42	Hungary	4.11
20	Norway	5.91	43	Russia	4.08
21	Luxembourg	5.90	44	Poland	4.05
22	Germany	5.87	45	South Africa	3.71
23	Sweden	5.83	46	Venezuela	2.90

Whether all this deliberateness is effective in promoting entrepreneurship is a topic to which we will now turn.

Corporate culture and managerial behaviour

It is hardly surprising in view of the emphasis on meritocracy that Singapore has not produced as many entrepreneurs as other overseas Chinese communities, like Hong Kong, Malaysia, Indonesia, Taiwan, the USA and Canada. Indeed Singapore produces fewer entrepreneurs per head of population than almost all advanced economies. Only Belgium and Japan fare worse. A recent report from California traced one-third of Silicon Valley's wealth of $58 billion to Chinese and Indian immigrants to the USA post-1970.

If low levels of entrepreneurship cannot be traced to Chinese culture, there has to be something distinctive about Singapore which fails to encourage what overseas Chinese typically do well. My view is that meritocracy impedes entrepreneurship and is a distinctively *different* way of generating wealth – a very successful way, but still antithetical to entrepreneurship. Consider the following contrasts.

Merit scholars tend to live at the *top* of the abstraction ladder, being adept at the highly codified symbolic worlds of their favourite disciplines, but entrepreneurs must deal with concrete realities as well, completing every humble detail, getting real goods to real people in real time.

The merit scholar achieves excellence *as educational and government authorities define this*, but the entrepreneur *redefines* excellence and goes on to achieve it. The merit scholar is typically *right first time* having correctly deduced data from initial theory, but the entrepreneur makes several *errors followed by corrections* to achieve intended results by successive approximations to an ideal. The merit scholar discovers *already-established answers* while the entrepreneur *invents and poses new questions*. The first *prefers hard sciences* where such answers are to be found. The second *needs soft skills* to motivate and persuade others.

The merit scholar typically *develops early*, completing most steps of his or her schooling at a young age, egged on by the applause of parents and teachers. The entrepreneur is typically a *late developer*, if only because you need education in more than one discipline if you are to make creative connections between these. Moreover, it is not possible to 'move knowledge around' and resynthesize it until that knowledge has been accumulated, so that the pay-off of creativity develops relatively later, in one's late twenties onwards. Many entrepreneurs have first succeeded in their middle years or later.

Many top scholars receive their education at government expense in return for a bond that they will return and repay the taxpayers through several years of service. This has the unfortunate effect of preventing those sent, say, to MIT from exploiting opportunities discovered there and starting businesses.

Could it be that Singapore is 'too fair' to be an entrepreneurial culture, opening up opportunities for all its citizens? The reason for suggesting this is that many, even most, entrepreneurs in history have been *disadvantaged*. British entrepreneurs were non-conformists in religion, which effectively barred them from important posts. French Huguenots were a persecuted Protestant minority, while many Taiwanese entrepreneurs were displaced by China's retreating nationalist army. Japanese entrepreneurs are often of Korean ancestry. Hong Kong entrepreneurs were under British colonial rule; and in countries where the Chinese are a minority many avenues of advancement are closed to them. Entrepreneurs have an element of disorder in their lives, 'making it' in third careers or fifth attempts and frustrated in early aspirations.

Above all entrepreneurs do not seek to qualify themselves for existing posts or climb career ladders. They build these ladders in the first place, occupying the top rungs.

In one sense Singapore has no recognizable 'corporate culture' of its own, although it has a societal culture as we have seen (see Mabubani 1993). The reason for this is that many of the world's top companies in high tech are located in Singapore and Singaporeans work for these companies, so that there are as many 'corporate cultures' as there are foreign companies and each company brings its own ethos to Singapore. This fact gives us an important insight into how and why Singapore has been so successful. Essentially, it *imports* largely American high tech around which the entrepreneurship, the competitiveness and the competition with rival technologies has already taken place. These products are 'winners'. They have already achieved world-class status so that the phase of initial struggle is over.

What Singapore now adds to the equation is a *very* well-trained workforce and process engineers educated in advance about this technology and sufficiently skilled to produce and distribute it locally. All companies must go through a competitive phase to discover which product or idea is the best, followed by a cooperative phase in which they organize swiftly and effectively around the winning product and sell it as widely as possible. Singapore is brilliantly successful at this *second* phase, but not at the first phase, which helps explain not only its lack of entrepreneurs but why so few Singaporean companies have world brands of any repute.

One has only to compare the output from graduate schools of *process* engineers with the number of *research engineers* to note the emphasis on refining existing products invented abroad. And this is in a culture where 75 per cent of the male graduate population choose to major in business, engineering or economics, all geared directly to economic development. Some would say that Singapore's society was hollow of enthusiasm for what most of us regard as 'culture': the arts, the humanities, the search for scientific truth.

Managerial values

Geert Hofstede (1980) found Singaporean managers to be high in power distance; in other words, they regard it as legitimate that their top managers and government officials are considerably more powerful than they are. East Asian countries are all high on this dimension, Singapore slightly less so than others.

It is this which allows the government to follow an economic development policy without deferring to private interests or special pleading. There are no constituencies to be placated. Singapore also scores high on uncertainty avoidance and the ladders of merit climbed steadily by bonded scholars are ways in which uncertainty is avoided while allowing talent to be mobilized. Avoiding the conflicts around innovation and entrepreneurship, while refining winning Western products, is another way of keeping uncertainty at bay.

On the Trompenaars–Hampden-Turner dimensions, Singapore scores mainly on the Western side of East Asian values, almost as if it were mediating between East and West (see Bedi 1993). Hence on the 'traffic accident dilemma' in which you must either tell the truth in court that your best friend was speeding when he injured a pedestrian, or lie on his behalf, remaining true to friendship, only 33.84 per cent of Singaporeans would lie, compared with 63.53 per cent of Korean managers and 13.11 per cent of American managers. Singapore and Malaysia are the most 'Western' in their scores (Table 10.2).

Singapore is famous in this regard for the strictness and impartiality of its laws, which are administered without fear or favour. A lieutenant-colonel in the army was recently jailed for two weeks for leaving an out-of-date parking ticket on the shelf above the dashboard of his car to allegedly 'deceive' the parking attendant. Singapore has taken 'zero tolerance' to new heights. In a society where you can be fined or imprisoned for holding a mobile phone to your mouth while driving, very few inhabitants attempt anything

Table 10.2 'Would I testify for my friend?' (percentage agreeing)

1	Korea	63.53	14	Brazil	28.81
2	China	48.50	15	Germany	21.29
3	Indonesia	48.24	16	Italy	20.88
4	Hong Kong	46.43	17	The Netherlands	18.93
5	Thailand	43.09	18	UK	17.17
6	Japan	38.22	19	Canada	16.28
7	Taiwan	38.00	20	Ireland	15.14
8	The Philippines	37.61	21	Australia	13.54
9	Belgium	34.62	22	USA	13.11
10	France	34.58	23	Sweden	13.05
11	Singapore	33.84	24	New Zealand	12.97
12	Malaysia	31.91	25	Switzerland	10.71
13	Spain	29.83	26	Norway	8.20

approaching a real crime. Other offences include chewing gum, not flushing the toilet, spitting and smoking in prohibited areas. Those who obey the law in minor respects can be counted on never to break it in major respects. Lee Kuan Yew recalled a visit to London in 1947, where a newspaper vendor had left his cloth cap full of coins by his newspaper stand. People were dropping the correct money into his hat and helping themselves to newspapers. He decided then and there that Singaporeans must behave with the same responsibility in minor affairs.

Given the cooperative and facilitative role that Singapore plays to world capitalism, we would expect that it would retain its Chinese communitarian traditions. Until and unless it joins the competitive struggle involved in innovation, it remains the midwife of others' labours. This is indeed what we find. Asked if the purpose of work was personal freedom or 'continuously taking care of the needs of your fellow man' (Table 10.3), 57.5 per cent of Singaporeans voted for the latter, compared with 38.3 per cent of Brits and 30.49 per cent of Americans, the two cultures that pioneered entrepreneurial capitalism. Singapore is close to other Chinese communities, namely Taiwan, China, Hong Kong.

Note, that while Singapore is pulled towards Western values on the universalism–particularism dimension, in part by the Senior Minister's own training in law and the adoption of English common law traditions, it is not so much drawn towards Western individualism. Indeed Singaporean politicians and commentators remain critical of human rights doctrines. From their point of view an orderly community which meets the needs of its members is the first priority, while greater freedom will come in time from the entire society becoming middle class or near middle class.

In a recent interview Lee Kuan Yew has stated that the case for democracy is essentially similar to the case for participation in the workplace (see Lee 2000). As people grow smarter and work becomes ever more complex, multiple viewpoints must be considered. Hence democracy too is seen as a

Table 10.3 'Continuously taking care of one's fellow man even if obstructs freedom' (percentage agreeing)

1	Japan	61.32	14	Italy	49.18
2	Hong Kong	60.71	15	Germany	46.73
3	Thailand	60.49	16	Norway	45.36
4	The Philippines	60.44	17	Belgium	43.15
5	Brazil	59.49	18	Sweden	40.20
6	China	58.93	19	Australia	38.66
7	France	58.89	20	UK	38.33
8	Taiwan	58.80	21	Spain	37.02
9	Singapore	57.67	22	The Netherlands	35.19
10	Korea	56.07	23	Switzerland	33.70
11	Malaysia	55.48	24	USA	30.49
12	Indonesia	53.31	25	New Zealand	30.23
13	Ireland	49.31	26	Canada	29.80

contributor to economic development provided it is not premature, as in India and the Philippines, where the Senior Minister believes it has promoted chaos and has impeded economic growth. Is Singapore perhaps a new type of entity, a corporate state? Is democratic participation but a means to an end?

Many critics of Singapore complain that it has yet to meet the prime test of democracy, the willingness to hand over peaceably the power of government to an opposition party. Whether we should blame Singapore's government for not handing over power, or praise its government for being so outstandingly successful that no opposition capable of governing has ever emerged, is an interesting question. Should a government which has wrought this economic miracle be ousted? The voters do not seem to think so. The PAP has been returned with overwhelming majorities in successive elections.

On the other hand opposition politicians face being sued for libel for what, in Western democracies, would be considered rude exchanges and unfounded allegations. Since the plaintiffs use taxpayers' money, while the defendants must fund themselves, and since Lee Kuan Yew has yet to lose in court after more than a hundred encounters, the right to oppose is circumscribed to say the least and opposition is rarely regarded as loyal to the state.

A third cultural dilemma concerns specificity vs. diffusion. To what extent does a culture put specific goals and objectives to the fore and to what extent does it rely on diffuse relationships and more holistic impressions?

Hampden-Turner and Trompenaars (1997; 2000) measure this by asking: is a company a set of tasks, payments, machines, objectives, etc., or a web of social relationships? The tasks etc. are specific, the webs diffuse. Cultures answered as in Table 10.4.

Singapore is on the diffuse end but not markedly so. More significant is the Singaporean attitude to leadership (see Bedi 1993), wherein the good leader is continuously facilitating and helping the work of subordinates, *not*, as is more usual in the West, setting them objectives and leaving them alone

Table 10.4   'Company as social relationships' (not specifics) (percentage agreeing)

Thailand	70.37	The Philippines	57.14
Norway	65.98	Australia	56.74
New Zealand	64.47	Belgium	54.84
Korea	63.58	China	53.73
Ireland	62.68	Spain	53.39
Japan	61.62	Germany	52.84
Taiwan	60.55	Italy	52.01
France	59.96	Canada	51.26
Indonesia	58.55	Sweden	49.47
Singapore	58.35	UK	48.89
Malaysia	57.59	Hong Kong	48.21
Brazil	57.35	USA	44.82
Switzerland	57.20	The Netherlands	43.77

for a while to get on with it. The omnipresence of Singaporean supervision is revealed in this question (Table 10.5).

A fourth set of dilemmas measured by Hampden-Turner and Trompenaars (1997; 2000) is inner-directed vs. outer-directed. To what extent do managers feel that they are self-directed from within and to what extent do they feel they are 'hitching a ride' as it were, on the tide of world events? Given Singapore's policy of inviting foreign companies into the city and sharing their future fortunes, we might expect more outer direction than inner, the feeling of being caught up in some larger game. That is what we find. Singapore is not as 'swept up' into the wider world as is China, but a sizeable minority do feel that they are propelled by external forces (Table 10.6).

Table 10.5 'Gets his group of subordinates working well together … helps them solve problems' (percentage agreeing)

Singapore	55.50	Australia	26.40
Hong Kong	55.36	Italy	25.29
Japan	53.95	UK	24.43
The Philippines	53.85	Spain	24.35
Korea	47.67	Ireland	23.40
Indonesia	46.69	Germany	22.51
China	42.86	Sweden	22.40
Malaysia	41.12	New Zealand	21.86
Taiwan	40.27	Norway	20.62
Thailand	39.90	The Netherlands	19.73
Belgium	31.61	Canada	19.27
Brazil	30.74	USA	16.10
France	29.96	Switzerland	15.87

Table 10.6 Accepts: 'Sometimes I feel I do not have enough control over the direction my life is taking'. Rejects: 'What happens to me is my own doing' (percentage agreeing)

China	60.89	The Netherlands	25.11
Singapore	42.66	France	23.89
Japan	36.61	Brazil	23.75
Hong Kong	33.97	Ireland	23.08
Germany	33.47	UK	22.47
Korea	31.79	Spain	21.83
Indonesia	29.58	Switzerland	20.83
Taiwan	29.40	Canada	19.06
Malaysia	29.02	Australia	18.40
Sweden	28.18	USA	17.29
Belgium	28.12	Norway	14.46
Italy	27.97	New Zealand	13.79
Thailand	27.16	The Philippines	11.76

Table 10.7   Accepts: 'It is not always wise to plan too far ahead because many things turn out to be a matter of good or bad fortune anyhow'. Rejects 'When I make plans, I am almost certain I can make them work' (percentage agreeing)

Japan	55.97	Korea	23.70
Hong Kong	49.21	Thailand	23.46
Malaysia	47.72	Ireland	21.68
China	43.77	Italy	20.79
Singapore	42.43	Spain	20.52
The Philippines	32.22	The Netherlands	17.39
Indonesia	31.44	UK	16.73
Belgium	27.49	New Zealand	16.28
Taiwan	27.35	Switzerland	15.00
Sweden	27.01	Norway	13.05
Germany	26.10	Australia	10.84
Brazil	25.57	USA	7.39
France	24.90	Canada	5.19

This makes planning difficult and responding quickly essential. On this issue too, Singaporeans tend to be more reactive than other business cultures (Table 10.7).

It is clear that the pioneer industrialists and entrepreneurs in the USA, Canada, Australia, New Zealand and the UK idealize 'having their own way', while Japan, Hong Kong, China, Malaysia and Singapore admit to joining the plans of others. In fact, the whole world system is so complex and so dynamic that we *all* have to react, whether or not we like to admit it.

Labour–management conflict resolution

What with the Senior Minister himself being a labour lawyer in his early practice, unions have been largely coopted into management and 'company unions' are the rule. In fact, Singapore has removed the major thorn around which managers and unions bargain: the issue of wages. In its place is the advocacy of participation in the workplace.

Trade unions and managers in the West bargain about scarcities: how much of the surplus generated by business should go to shareholders and how much to unionized employees? Singapore, as we have seen, punishes low wages, prevents companies benefiting therefrom, by levying a training tax and makes skill enhancement part of every employee contract.

Skills are increasing faster than wages and the higher productivity generated therefrom is shared between workers and companies. The bargaining is not about scarcities, but mutually generated abundances, which, if all goes to plan, will leave workers more skilled and employable, and will leave companies with higher levels of productivity and knowledge intensity. Singapore boasts of the world's number 1 workforce.

There are virtually no strikes but there are pressure tactics. One device is to withdraw certain forms of cooperation, before switching these on again at renewed levels of intensity. The purpose is to send 'a message' about how much more happy workers can produce than unhappy ones.

Not everything in Singapore has been so rosy lately. While the nation survived the worst of the Asian crisis, there was a hefty across-the-board wage and salary cut with the burden shared across income ranges. Singapore has suffered more than most in the current US downturn, in part because it is heavily dependent on US corporations, which tend to cut their overseas activities more than their domestic ones, and partly because it was heavily invested in electronics, e-commerce and the New Economy, which recently took a knock. The policy of cutting straight for the leading edge is not without its dangers.

Implications fro managers

Singapore is a vibrant, sustainable, dynamic economic experiment which may 'show the way' to economic development for China and much of South-East Asia. It is one of the best possible environments to be located as a manager. The support given to enterprises is overwhelmingly positive.

In one sense it does 'too much for you', speaks your language in every sense of the word and so protects you from meeting those of East Asian culture who are very different from you and require much more effort to engage. Nor are Singaporeans universally popular in South-East Asia. Their wealth is envied and the confidence that comes with it resented. The idea that overseas Chinese are welcome in China and can be effective there should not be taken for granted. You can live and work in Singapore without being exposed to major differences and so may fail to learn as fast as you would elsewhere.

Conclusions

Singapore has itself reached a watershed (see Chua 1995). Its policies thus far have been that of a 'catch-up economy' coming from behind, a late developer, using the coat tails of advanced economies and helping to refine, manufacture and distribute their inventions in Asia.

The question must now be faced. 'What does a catch-up economy *do* now that it has caught up?' One option is to start to innovate and create new products like other advanced economies (see Yah 2001). Yet this will require a major culture change in Singapore, where nearly all work and study is 'applied' to economic development.

Creativity and innovation requires some slack, some disorder, some ferment and casting around before the best solution is discovered (see Schein 1997). Does Singapore have a culture that encourages entrepreneurship (see Quah 1990)? The present evidence says not. Can it change and adapt as it has so often before? Perhaps, the jury is out. The problem ironically is *just how successful* the catch-up system has been. Nothing so spectacularly effective is easily put aside. Cultures tend to overplay their winning combinations with diminishing returns. Singapore confronts some fateful decisions about its future.

References

Bedi, H. (1993) *Understanding the Asian Manager*, Sydney: Allen & Unwin.

Chua, C.-Y. (1995) *Communitarian Ideology and Democracy in Singapore*, London: Routledge.

Collis, M. (2000) *Raffles: The Definitive Biography*, Singapore: Graham Bash.

George, R. L. (1992) *The East-West Pendulum*, New York: Woodland-Faulkner.

Hampden-Turner, C. M. and Trompenaars, F. (1997) *Mastering the Infinite Game*, Oxford: Capstone.

Hampden-Turner, C. M. and Trompenaars, F. (2000) *Building Cross Cultural Competence*, Chichester: John Wiley.

Hofstede, G. (1980) *Culture's Consequences*, Beverly Hills, CA: Sage.

Lee, K.-Y. (2000) *From Third World to First*, Singapore: Times Media.

Mabubani, K. (1993) *The Dangers of Decadence in the Clash of Civilizations*, New York: Council of Foreign Relations.

Peebles, G. and Peter, W. (1996) *The Singaporean Economy*, Cheltenham: Edward Elgar.

Porter, M. (1992) *The Competitive Advantage of Nations*, New York: Free Press.

Quah, J. S. T. (1990) *In Search of Singapore's National Values*, Singapore: Times Academic Press.

Schein, E. H. (1997) *Strategic Pragmatism*, Cambridge, MA: MIT Press.

Swee, C.-K. (1995) *Wealth of East Asian Nations*, Singapore: Federal Publications.

'The World Competitiveness Report' (2000) Geneva: IMD.

Yah, L.-C. (2001) *Economic Essays*, Singapore: World Scientific.

11 Culture and management in South Korea

Chris Rowley and Johngseok Bae

Introduction

Examining management and culture in South Korea (hereafter Korea) is important for several reasons. Management plays a role in business, economic development and society, but does not exist in a vacuum. Famous work indicates management variations stemming from culture (Hostede 1991). In contrast to the universalism of convergence and contingency views, underpinnings from, and interactions with, culture (along with institutions) remain crucial to understanding management and behaviour. For example, post-1960s Korea rapidly developed from a poor agricultural society into a rich, industrialized 'Asian Tiger' economy.[1] Then the 1997 Asian crisis hit and 'the miracle on the Han River' seemed more of a 'mirage'. However, performance recovered, unlike many economies in the region. Within this roller coaster ride of development, the role of management and culture has changed from being eulogized as a 'saint' to castigated as a 'sinner'. Furthermore, culture may produce paradoxical outcomes, and is often seen and portrayed as ingrained, deep and slow moving, while management and its practice may well need to be less so. These differentials may produce incongruence between cultural norms and management practice.

The format of this chapter is as follows. The crucial historical setting is followed by an overview of the economic background. Culture, societal and corporate, is dealt with in the subsequent two sections. The next parts cover management in terms of values, behaviour and labours conflict resolution. Final sections on the implications for management and conclusions complete the picture.

Historical setting

The 'Three Kingdoms' (39 BC onwards) were united in the Shilla Dynasty (from 668) and the Koryo Dynasty (935 to 1392) followed by the Yi Dynasty, ended by Chosun's annexation by Japan in 1910. The colonization experience, along with forced introduction of the Japanese language, names and labour, inculcated 'quite strong nationalist sentiments which in due course turned out to be a central psychological impetus for the economic miracles' (Kim 1994: 95). While colonized, Koreans were restricted to lower positions in organizations and excluded from managerial roles. Other Japanese influences included infrastructure developments, industrial policy imitation, application of technology and techniques of operations management and via Korean émigrés (Morden and Bowles 1998).

After 1945 came partition, with US military governance until the South's independence government in 1948 and then further widespread devastation with the Korean War from 1950 to 1953 (see Vietnam chapter for similarities). A large US military presence, with tensions with the North, remain. Many Koreans studied the American management system, especially as most overseas students went to the USA. This had impacts on managerial, business and academic outlooks and views, perspectives and comparisons, and possible sources of practices and examples. Korea's twenty-five years of authoritarian and military rule ended in 1987. Also, many executives were ex-officers, while most male employees served in the military and had regular military training, and companies even maintained reserve army training units.

This North-East Asian country, once known as 'The Hermit Kingdom', now occupies almost 100,000 square kilometres of the southern Korean peninsula (6,000 miles (9,600 km) from the UK). Korea's very homogeneous ethnic population rapidly urbanized and grew, more than doubling since the 1960s, from 20.2 million (1966) to 47.3 million (2000). Of these, nearly 10 million are in the capital, Seoul (more than double its 1966 level of 3.8 million), the dominant centre for political, social, business and academic interests.

Economic background

Korea's nickname of 'the country of the morning calm' became increasingly obsolete with the cacophony from continuous construction (Rowley 2002). From the 1960s Korea was rapidly transformed from a poor, rural backwater with limited natural or energy resources, domestic markets and a legacy of colonial rule and war with dependence on US aid. Korea became one of the fastest growing economies in a rapidly expanding region. GDP real annual growth rates of 9 per cent from the 1950s to the 1990s (with over 11 per cent in the late 1980s) took GDP from US$1.4 billion (1953) to US$437.4 billion (1994) (Kim 2000). Per capita GDP grew from US$87 (1962) to US$10,543 (1996) and GNP from US$3 billion (1965) to US$376.9 billion (1994). From the mid-1960s to the late 1990s annual manufacturing output grew at nearly 20 per cent and exports over 25 per cent, rising from US$320 million (1967) to US$136 billion (1997) (Kim and Rowley 2001). Korea became a large manufacturing exporter in both more 'traditional' (steel, ships, cars) and 'newer' (electrical, electronics) sectors (see Japan chapter for similarities) and the world's eleventh largest economy, joining the

OECD in 1996. Employment grew and unemployment levels declined to just 2 per cent by the mid-1990s.

This developmental, state-sponsored, export-orientated and labour-intensive model of industrialization[2] (Rowley and Bae 1998a; 1998b; 1998c; Rowley *et al.* 2002) was reinforced by exhortations and motivations, often with cultural underpinnings, such as 'national goals'. These included the need to escape the vicious circle of poverty, achieve economic superiority over 'The North', compete with Japan, repay debts and elevate Korea's image and honour.

Chaebol

These leading lights and drivers of the economy were family founded and owned and controlled large, diversified business groupings with a plethora of subsidiaries, as indicated by their Korean label, 'octopus with many tentacles'. They were held together by cross-shareholdings, subsidies and loan guarantees in opaque fashion with competitive tension, distrust and rivalry between *chaebol* (Morden and Bowles 1998). Much of the large business sector was part of a *chaebol* network and it exerted widespread influence over other firms, management practices and society (see Japan chapter for similarities). It was underpinned by a variety of elements (Rowley and Bae 1998c) and explained by a range of theories (Oh and Park 2002). For some, the state–military links and interactions with the *chaebol* were the most important external factor, producing politico-economic organizations substituting for trust, efficiency and the market (Oh and Park 2002). The state-owned banks (with resultant reliance for capital) promoted *chaebol* as a development strategy and intervened to maintain quiescent labour. These close connections have been damned as nepotism and 'crony capitalism'.

There were more than sixty *chaebol*, although a few dominated. At their zenith in the 1990s the top five (Hyundai, Daewoo, Samsung, LG, SK) accounted for 9 per cent of Korea's GDP, and the top thirty for 15 per cent of GDP, spread across 819 subsidiaries and affiliates. Some became major international companies in the world economy, engaged in acquisitions and investments overseas, dominated by the USA and China (Chung *et al.* 1997). Samsung Electronics, LG Electronics and LG Chem are among Korea's biggest investors in China, with Hyundai Motor announcing a US$250 million investment in a joint venture car factory in early 2002. We now give illustrative sketches of three important *chaebol*.

Hyundai began in the 1940s as a car repair shop, moving into construction, building the first cars in Korea in 1968 and ships. By 1998 its sixty-three subsidiaries also included heavy industry, machinery, chemicals, electronics, banking, finance and other services. It was so powerful it was dubbed the 'Republic of Hyundai', with 1996 sales of US$92.2 billion, over 200,000 workers and ranked amongst the world's largest car, construction and semiconductor producers. However, its post-2000 dismantling has seen the disaffiliation of the motor, engineering and construction, semiconductor and heavy industries parts, pushing it out of Korea's top twenty largest groups. For Hyundai Engineering's vice-president, 'The Chung family has withdrawn from the business. We're no longer a family-run company' (in Ward 2002b). Nevertheless, one of the most successful spin-offs, Hyundai Motor, with record profits of US$888 million in 2001, remains part of the Chung dynasty. The family owns a 22 per cent stake, retaining links by 'blood' (in Ward 2002b) to the Hyundai Group, still composed of diverse subsidiaries: Securities and Investment Trusts; Merchant Marine; Elevator Corporation; Asan; and Logistics.

Samsung,one of the oldest *chaebol*, has roots in the Cheil Sugar Manufacturing Company (1953) and Cheil Industries (1954), although it started as a trading company in 1938. It developed from a fruit and sundry goods exporter into flour milling and confectionery. Over the post-war decades it spread to sugar refining, textiles, paper, electronics, fertilizer, retailing, life insurance, hotels, construction, electronics, heavy industry, petrochemicals, shipbuilding, aerospace, bioengineering and semiconductors. Sales of US$3 billion and staff of 45,000 (1980) ballooned to US$96 billion and 267,000 (1998) (Pucik and Lim 2002). Samsung Electronics alone had twenty-one worldwide production bases, fifty-three sales operations in forty-six countries, sales of US$16.6 billion and was one of the largest producers of dynamic random access memory semiconductors by the late 1990s. By 2002 Samsung still claimed global market leadership in thirteen product categories, from deep-water drilling ships to microwave ovens, television tubes and microchips, and with a target actually to have thirty world-beaters by 2005.

Lucky Chemical Company, founded in 1947, manufactured facial creams, then toothpaste and soap. Goldstar was founded in 1958 and went on to produce radios, telephones, fans and consumer electronics, the first refrigerators and televisions built in Korea, computers, semiconductors and microprocessors. In the 1970s media, advertising, engineering and petrochemicals were added. LG Electronics alone had sales of US$9.3 billion and 22,800 staff in early 2000. Its 59 branches, 18 sales subsidiaries and 31 manufacturing subsidiaries spanned 171 countries, with 26 R&D facilities in Korea (Kim 2000).

The Asian crisis

It seemed the sun would never set on Korea's expansion. Yet it did as the 1997 Asian financial crisis spread. In 1998 came falls in GDP of −5.8 per cent, GNP of two-thirds, currency of 54 per cent against the US dollar, the number of establishments by 14 per cent (68,014) and 1 million jobs were quickly lost (Korea National Statistical Office). The stock market plunged by 65 per cent between June 1997 and June 1998, with problems and bankruptcy for *chaebol* and the banks. The low unemployment rate almost

tripled to 8.6 per cent (2 million) by February 1999. Wage rates declined by
−2.5 per cent (nominal) and −9.3 per cent (real) in 1998. This economic
collapse led to much anxiety and incomprehension among commentators,
policy makers, management, workers and the public as to how quickly and
totally things had seemingly gone wrong, and why. Management and
culture, amongst other suspects, were quickly implicated and paraded as
having a role in this downfall.

However, the economy rapidly recovered. GDP grew by 10.7 per cent in
1999 and growth has continued. By 2000, GDP was US$461.7 billion, per
capita GDP US$9,823 and GNP US$459.2 billion. Some *chaebol* weathered
the crisis and made record profits. Yet this recovery may be a chimera and
fragile.[3] Korean companies remain plagued by adverse publicity,
bankruptcy, state bailouts and opaque operations. High-profile examples
include Daewoo's huge debts and accounting fraud, Ford's abandonment of
interest in Daewoo Motor (after six months) in September 2000, followed by
the inordinate length of subsequent negotiations with GM (in 2002). Others
include lengthy talks between Hyundia's securities and AIG (eighteen
months), Seoul Bank and HSBC and Deutsche Bank (three years) and the
Hynix and Micron saga. These indicate problems, especially those that may
be more deep seated or hidden.

Then there is the 'demographic time bomb'. There is an aging population
and workforce. In 1990 the economically active population aged 15–19 was
639,000, by 1995 it was down to 441,000, while over the same period the
numbers aged 40–54 increased by 8 per cent (Lee 2000). Of course, such
forces are not restricted to Korea (see chapter 6, on Japan), but the implications for management are stark given some of the traditional aspects of
society, not least its homogeneity and exclusiveness. This brings us to societal culture.

Societal culture

'Societal culture' is important, even for some non-culturalists. Indeed,
cultural underpinnings have consequences for institutional environments,
which for Whitely (1991) were via the systems of: (1) authority relations,
importance of personal ties and conception of appropriate behaviour; (2)
trust, reciprocity, obligation and enterprise loyalty and commitment; (3)
organization and practices of political and bureaucratic state elites, policies
and finance. Thus, even if one takes a more institutional perspective, it needs
grounding in cultural contexts. This can result from the dynamic interaction
among political, economic, social and cultural factors and 'the selective
adoption, absorption and assimilation of some foreign elements; and the
selective abandonment, modification and utilization of others' (Kim 1994:
103). This selectivity occurs through the culture or political decisions.

Traditional social values have been identified in Korea (Lee 1997). These
include: absolute loyalty of subjects to sovereigns; close relationship between

father and son; separate roles of women and men; precedence of the elder over the younger; mutual trust among friends; unequal inheritance in favour of the eldest son; ancestor worship and emphasis on family members in a direct line. We return to these in the next section in terms of their management impacts. Where do these values come from?

As we have seen, Korean society experienced many influences (see Vietnam and Japan chapters for similarities). Additionally, Korea's religious and philosophical influences include Buddhism (from 372, and especially 935 to 1392) and Confucianism, the state religion for over 500 years from the fourteenth to the early twentieth century. Confucianism, from its inception in China, evolved. There was the 'high' Confucianism of the elite, which was 'of a philosophical nature, providing the ideological-normative foundation for statecraft and governance, state control and individual self discipline' (Kim 1994: 96), and then there was the 'low' Confucianism of ordinary people, a secularized version in contemporary Asia (Kim 1994: 96). This included values such as: positive attitudes to the affairs of the world and faith in the transformability and perfectibility of the human condition; importance of self-cultivation; lifestyle of discipline and desirability of hard work and frugality as social discipline; duty; consciousness in the form of reciprocity of respect and authority and public accountability; centrality of overriding concern for the family in social harmony and stability; political order as a moral community; necessity of government leadership; disinclination for civil litigation (Kim 1994: 96). This influence can be seen in Korean society's rigid Confucian code of personal and social behaviour and feudal system, maintained by a hierarchical, authoritarian structure, rigidly stratified from top to bottom (Kwon and O'Donnell 2001). There were the *yangban* (the upper or ruling class), the *jungin* or *seoin* (middle class), the *sangmin* (peasant farmers and craftworkers) and the *cheonmin* (underprivileged class).

Confucianism's fundamental influence remains in contemporary Korean society (see Vietnam chapter for similarities). Confucianism guides daily life, with the social mores, values, ways of thinking and modes of conduct centred on family life, with hierarchy, seniority and traditions paramount. This includes respect and esteem for educational attainment (see Japan chapter for similarities). This is indicated by high levels of literacy and the numbers graduating from high school. Also, respect and deference is still paid to professors by their students (stopping and bowing and forms of address) and companies (used as consultants). Education was regarded as one of the best and shortest ways for attaining upper social status and the better way for *jasusungga* ('making one's own fortune'), one reason why such large amounts are spent by parents on children's education. There was extensive investment in education: for instance, in terms of the share of education expenditures of central government to GDP, Korea spent 3.6 per cent in 1982, 3.2 per cent in 1990 and 3.2 per cent in 2000.

Beneath the Korean people's ways of thinking and values lie a mixture of easy-going and optimistic behaviours of Confucianism on the one hand (for instance, even after the Asian crisis people believed that everything would be well in the future), and hard work, *'palli-palli'* (quickly–quickly), high achievement, and a goal-oriented perspective, on the other. Reasons for the latter include experiences of invasions, difficult circumstances and predicaments, and rapid economic development policies.

Koreans remain very proud of their country. This was seen in the post-1997 crisis IMF bailout, which was popularly perceived as a national humiliation and loss of face, while people donated gold and jewellery to national funds. Furthermore, Korean society was very exclusive towards other countries, people and cultures. One reason is due to the homogeneous population composed of a single ethnic group. A second factor is the tradition of an agrarian society, characterized by passive, closed and dependent views. Contributing to these was Korea's climate (like that of Japan and China) favouring rice cultivation. This was labour and time intensive and occurred along rivers and deltas in communities relatively isolated by mountains and distance. This also encouraged cooperation and close-knit groups dependent on each other in the community for survival, with collectivism and inter group responsibilities. A third reason is the antagonistic memories and feelings against foreign interventionist powers. For some, this 'one-race–one-culture' mentality produced insensitivity.

In contrast to these societal and cultural aspects and challenging exclusiveness are other developments, such as experience of education or work in the West, business internationalization, recent influx of foreign capital, ideas of importing management 'best practice' and opening up to global (American) cultures (Bae and Rowley 2001). Indeed, in the early 1990s the administration explicitly employed a *segyewha* (globalization) policy facilitating more communications and interactions with foreign countries. Companies adopted similar policies, sending employees to other countries for exposure to foreign cultures.

However, cultures often remain robust and slow moving. Furthermore, there have been some reactions against Western cultures, with enhanced power of Korean culture, especially within Asia (Ward 2002a). Paradoxically, it is argued that this resurgence partly 'reflects changes in the country's make-up. Society is becoming more modern and less formal' (Ward 2002a).

Corporate culture

There is interaction between social values and corporate culture. The impacts of the traditional social values noted earlier on corporate cultural characteristics are seen in Table 11.1.

The corporate culture of Korean companies is differentially viewed as the most collectivist by Westerners, but more individualistic by the Japanese (Cho and Yoon 2002). This is explained by 'Dynamic Collectivism', an elaboration of traditional notions of collectivism, which 'applies collectivist norms for in-group members and individualistic ones for out-group

Table 11.1   Impacts of traditional social values on corporate cultural characteristics

Traditional social values	Impact	Corporate culture characteristics
Absolute loyalty of subjects to sovereigns	⊠▷	Owner management's authority, paternalism
Close relationship between father and son	⊠▷	*Inhwa*, belongingness, kinship-based relations
Separate roles of women and men	⊠▷	Hardworking, devotion to company (especially male workers)
Precedence of the elder over the younger	⊠▷	Hierarchical relationships among staff, seniorityism
Mutual trust among friends	⊠▷	Trustworthy relations among peers, collectivism
Unequal inheritance in favour of eldest son, ancestor worship, emphasis on family members in a direct line	⊠▷	Kinship-based ownership/succession; *Yongo*ism (blood, geography, education based connections)

Source: Adapted from Lee (1997).

members' (Cho and Yoon 2002: 71). As a consequence, it reinforces the boundary between in- and out-groups and intensifies competition, which makes Korean society more dynamic and competitive. This is built into corporate culture through the interplay between internal mechanisms (learning, selection and attrition) and the environment based on external forces. These forces were: (1) 'Culture Legacy', traditional culture embedded in Confucian values, with five key components (emotional harmony, hierarchy, discrimination against out-groups, networking, high-context orientation); (ii) 'Social Climate', the socio-political situation created by the state and economic development stance; (iii) 'Corporate Leadership', with paternalism and authoritarianism. Their interaction with internal culture management produced 'Dynamic Collectivism's' three dimensions: 'In-Group Harmony'; 'Optimistic Progressivism'; 'Hierarchical Principle' (Cho and Yoo 2002). We return to these later.

To investigate corporate culture further we employ Cameron's (1978) competing values framework and culture quadrant (Quinn 1988). 'Group Culture' contains: (1) a very personal place, like an extended family; (2) head of unit is a mentor or sage; (3) the 'glue' is loyalty and tradition; (4) emphasis on human resources. 'Developmental Culture' consists of: (1) a very dynamic and entrepreneurial place; (2) head of unit is an innovator or risk taker; (3) the 'glue' is commitment to innovation and development; (4) emphasis on growth and acquiring new resources. 'Rational Culture' includes: (1) great production orientation; (2) head of unit is a producer or technician; (3) the 'glue' is tasks and goal accomplishment; (4) emphasis on competitive actions and achievement. 'Hierarchical Culture' covers: (1) a very formalized and structured place; (2) head of unit is a coordinator or an organizer; (3) the 'glue' is the formal rules and policies; (4) emphasis on permanence and stability.

Using this instrument we surveyed (in 2000) 103 companies operating in Korea (41 indigenous, 28 American, 10 Japanese, 24 European). Although these are not representative of each group, interesting results emerge (see Table 11.2). Overall, an ANOVA test indicates that all the competing value quadrants, except 'Group Culture', are statistically significant at the conventional level. In the case of 'Group Culture', all company groups have similar levels of the value regardless of country origjn. The *post hoc* test (Tukey test) shows that American subsidiaries, compared with Korean or Japanese ones, have higher values at both 'Developmental Culture' and 'Rational Culture'. The reverse is true for 'Hierarchical Culture', where firms from Asian countries, on average, have higher values. European subsidiaries are in the middle, between oriental and American firms. Both Korean and Japanese firms have higher values at group and hierarchical levels vis-à-vis developmental and rational values, while the reverse is true in American firms.

There is an increasing diversity of business ownership in Korea, but corporate culture in the *chaebol* is important. It retains its high profile and strong, influential and normative nature, with roots in the family and military. The founders' beliefs permeated whole organizations, replicated and reinforced by scions of families, and practices such as long in-house induction with employees staying at training centres, where they are inculcated in company history, vision and songs (Kim and Briscoe 1997). Some *chaebol* dominate localities, even leading to company towns, such as Woolsan (Hyundai) and Pohang (POSCO), housing and servicing large numbers of employees.

Examples of corporate culture change

Given the above, how do cultures change? Park (2002) examined corporate culture change campaigns in Korea and reasons for problems and effectiveness. These include the need to secure qualified campaign managers and consistency with overall organizational strategy.

Table 11.2 Cultural differences among Korean indigenous firms and foreign subsidiaries

Culture type	Korean (N = 41)	American (N = 28)	Japanese (N = 10)	European (N = 24)	ANOVA F value	ANOVA Sig.	Post hoc test (Tukey)
Group	3.54	3.58	3.43	3.51	0.177	0.912	All groups no difference
Developmental	3.37	3.69	2.88	3.31	2.96	0.036	American > Japanese
Rational	3.41	3.99	3.20	3.68	5.67	0.001	American > Korean = Japanese
Hierarchical	3.48	2.91	3.60	3.25	6.65	0.000	Japanese = Korean > American

For further detail we use examples of corporate culture change. Samsung had two distinguishable stages from its establishment. Lee Byung-Chull, the founder, remained as the top leader until the mid-1980s, with 1983–92 a transition period for the handover to his son, Lee Kun-Hee. From the beginning a rational and bureaucratic internal process was emphasized. High rationality and low risk taking were important values. Rules and regulations, thorough analysis and evaluation, hard work and well-planned processes were Samsung's core capabilities. These values were necessary and sufficient during the high growth stage under low-uncertainty environments. However, Lee Kun-Hee's Frankfurt Declaration (1993) launched the 'New Management' movement through restructuring and radical organizational, including cultural, change. Through this process he refocused Samsung's direction from 'quantity-oriented, domestic-centred, rationality' towards 'quality-oriented, global player, risk-taking' values. He stated the need to 'change everything except the wife and children'. He encouraged top management to take risks, autonomy and diversity. Samsung's style moved from a 'look even at a stone bridge before one leaps' ('act with utmost caution') to a 'leap if you see just a wooden bridge without being afraid' approach. The resultant value and cultural conflict was seen as a 'necessary evil' for reorientation of the organization. Earlier values now had inertia, changing core capabilities to rigidities. Another issue related to its 'Single Samsung' approach. Although affiliates had different environments and dominant logics in each industry, Samsung wanted common, universal change. Yet, some firms may need to keep earlier cultures, or have different speeds and scope of change, to this.

LG Group had similar experiences. *Inhwa* (harmony) and solidity were core values, and such values as 'respect and love among LG members', 'tolerance and trust' and a 'sense of unity and cooperation' were stressed. These values had served as core capabilities by enhancing LG members' loyalty and devotion and were taken as key factors in growth. However, it was argued that over time these values made LG people more conservative, with passive and easy-going attitudes and behaviours. *Inhwa* sometimes meant lenient evaluation and overlooking faults. In the late 1980s, an LG survey showed that about 60 per cent of members recognized LG as a humane and conservative organization, and less than 2 per cent perceived it as having a high progressive spirit (Lee 1997). It also indicated that 80 per cent wanted to move towards a more 'competitive company' no matter how difficult. To redress these rigidities a 'Vision Team' was launched to change its core values. In February 1990 the chairman, Koo Cha-Kyung, declared two new core values: 'creating value for customers' and 'management based on esteem for human dignity'. Simultaneously, LG Group emphasized autonomy to respond quickly to uncertain environments. Recently it promoted its image using 'Digital LG', but its earlier values are inertial for the cultural transformation.

Management values and behaviour

Korea's background and milieu influenced management values and behaviour. In-group harmony has been found to be the most important managerial value for Korean firms (Chung and Lee 1989). For the sake of this, people sacrifice their own goals for collective ones, and in return companies take care of employees and management helps subordinates save face (Cho and Yoon 2002). Together with this there is the hierarchical principle, which reinforces particularistic relationships among members (Cho and Yoon 2002).

A survey (in the late 1980s) of eighty-eight large Korean companies in twelve different industries showed various core values in their vision statements (Lee 1997). This found: *inhwa*, solidarity and cooperation (46.4 per cent); devotion and hard work (44.2 per cent); creativity and development (41.2 per cent); honesty and credibility (28.8 per cent); quality, technology and productivity (16.9 per cent); responsibility (16.9 per cent); progressiveness or enterprising spirit (14.3 per cent); national wealth through business (14.3 per cent); rational and scientific approach (10.4 per cent); and sacrifice, service, etc. (6.9 per cent). More recently, firms began to emphasize creativity, competitiveness, diversity, customer satisfaction, value creation, and so on. The common concepts, meanings and resultant managerial behaviours and managerial characteristics are outlined in Table 11.3.

Where do these values come from? As we have seen, these include Japan, the military and Confucianism. Thus, Korean organizations 'are like families as well as armies' (Cho and Yoon 2002: 79). In particular, Confucianism's influence on the values, attitudes and norms of Koreans 'spilled over to the fundamental underpinnings of the Korean management system and human relationships within Korean companies' (Song 1997: 192).

The influence of hierarchical traditional family systems impacts on management behaviour. This includes business strategies, organizational structures and Human Resources Management (Cho and Yoon 2002). Companies were centralized and hierarchical with formal structures and vertical organizational principles[4] and family-style relationships. The hierarchical principle made for more predictable behaviour, obligations and indebtedness contributing to vague roles between personal and public relationships (Cho and Yoon 2002). Founders organized and managed on the basis of principles governing family life. There was both authoritarianism and paternalism, with companies as 'parents' and employees as 'family'; often they actually were, of course (for similarities see Vietnam chapter). There was kinship-based recruitment from extended clans (*chiban*) or regions, which dominated positions of power, and kinship-based relationships with owners (*hyulyon*). Ideas of harmony and family-orientated HRM took seniority as the primary factor, with special allowances for family matters, from marriage and parents' 60th birthdays to funerals (Cho and Yoon 2002).

However, during the twentieth century people began to disregard leaders.

Table 11.3 Characteristics and paradoxes of culture and management in Korea

Cultural influences	Concepts	Meanings	Management behaviours and managerial characteristics	Paradoxes
	Inhwa	Harmony, solidarity	Company as family-type community	Sharp owner–manager–worker distinctions
	Yongo	Connections: hyulyon: by blood jiyon: by geography hakyon: by education	Recruitment via common ties, solidity within inner circles, kinship-based relationships with owners	Bounded collectivism and exclusivism
Confucianism (family)	Chung	Loyalty, subordinate to superior	Paternalistic approach and taking care of employees and their families	Emphasis on hierarchical ranks, authoritarianism in leadership
	Un	Indebtedness to organization/members	Respect, tolerance, patience adhered to in business	Loyalty/cooperation to individual not organization
	Uiri	Integrity to others in everyday life	Long-term relationships (e.g. lifetime employment)	Personal entertainment, gift giving, transaction opaqueness
	Gocham	Senior in service, an 'old-timer'	Seniority-based rewards and promotions	Tension between seniority and competence/ability
Japan	Kibun	Good mood, satisfactory state of affairs	Maintain harmony, not hurting someone's kibun	Performance management tensions
	Sinparam	Exulted spirits	Management and making efforts by sentiment-based motivation rather than rational understanding	Delinquency and low commitment without sinparam
Military	Han	Resentment/frustration felt over unjust or inequitable treatment	Confrontational and militant labour relations (e.g. employment adjustment tensions)	Passiveness, negativism and suppression
	Chujin	Propulsion, drive, get through something	Can-do spirit, strong driving force, rapid accomplishment of plans/goals	Lack of rational evaluations and omitting due processes
	Palli palli	Quickly quickly	Speed of action	Quality, reflection
	Sajeonhyupui	Informal consensus formation prior to making final decisions	Collaboration and participation of stakeholders in decision making	Team ethos impacts, slow decisions, impediment to empowerment

Source: Adapted from Song (1997), Morden and Bowles (1998) and Rowley (2002).

In addition, as leaders have been increasingly publicly exposed as dishonest and corrupt, this sort of trend was reinforced. The trend also helped to generate a sense of equality among people. Equality in Confucianism is perhaps a necessary condition for *inhwa* (harmony).

A group-orientated approach is also often noted (for similarities see Vietnam chapter). However, practices endorsed by Confucianism made in-group members mutually interdependent and emphasized *inhwa*, making the out-group boundary more salient and contributing to strong competition with other groups. This helps explain why 'the delegation of authority, often espoused formally, is ineffective and why bottom-up and lateral communications are consistently promoted only to fail' (Cho and Yoon 2002: 79).

The high regard for education can be seen in management behaviour, encouraging and supporting a skilled and well-educated workforce with heavy investment in human resource development. The *chaebol* put a strong emphasis on this, with large, well-resourced and supported training centres. These provided induction and a variety of ongoing training programmes. In 1995 Samsung spent US$260 million on training, Hyundai US$195 million, Daewoo and LG US$130 million each (Chung *et al.* 1997).

Another management behaviour concerns mergers and acquisitions. The protracted negotiations with Western companies post-1997 we noted earlier displays this. While there are historical, technical, structural and trans-parency reasons, culture also has a role. This is in terms of the process itself, with concepts such as 'face' and 'shame', along with xenophobia. For example, Koreans rarely see negotiations as 'win–win' propositions, but 'zero-sum' games, implying that 'Any agreement means they have conceded too much' (*The Economist* 2002: 61). Along with negotiators being criticized in the press for being 'easy' on foreigners, this all produces 'paranoia and posturing by Korean negotiators' (2002: 62), who, to prove toughness, frequently storm out of meetings.

Contrasting company examples of management values and behaviour

Samsung and Hyundai are different in terms of not just cultures, but also management styles, decision-making processes, risk propensity and HRM. Traditionally, Samsung tried to minimize strategic risks, using well-estab-lished decision-making systems, utilizing professional staff and pursuing standardization and formalization, emphasizing rationality, analysis and cause–effect relationships. Hyundai showed high-risk propensity and emphasized intuition, totality and contexts, and in decision making a lower utilization level of professional staff, less standardization and formalization. As a result, Hyundai has been more tolerant towards cause–effect ambiguity and non-specificity of goals and minimized its efforts for the acquisition and analysis of information.

These differences are directly related to their founders: Lee Byung-Chull of Samsung and Chung Ju Yung of Hyundai (Lee 2002). First, Lee gave a high priority to the pursuit of rationality. He argued that Samsung people should pay attention to scholars' views even if they were far from reality, emphasizing scientific judgements and logical reasoning. Next, he was very analytical and cause–effect oriented. For this he stressed philosophy and principles, prior research, thorough planning and well-established systems based on core ideologies. Finally, Lee was a 'risk averter', as mentioned above, with a 'do not even embark on a new business without 100 per cent confidence' approach.

Chung had quite different values and styles. Unlike Lee, he disliked sticking to theories, rationality, common sense, fixed stereotyped ideas and logical thinking. He discouraged people from clinging to textbook approaches or theories taught in schools. He was a 'crisis generator', believing that this helped learning and building up organizational capabilities (Kim 1998). He was also very intuitive (Lee 2002). In addition, he was a 'risk taker'. Without adventures, Chung said, people and organizations would be at a standstill, then lag behind, and finally fall down. He also believed adventure would inject fresh vigour into the inertial organization.

Why do such firms differ? Carroll (1993) examined several perspectives: individual (dispositional and situational), organizational (spin-offs and internal change), environmental sources and organizational blueprints. Our example is related to individual sources. These individuals' (Lee and Chung) values and styles affected organizational characteristics by influencing strategic choice (Hambrick and Mason 1984) and structure (Miller and Dröge 1986) and by mediating contextual variables to organizational behaviour (Child 1972). Thus, individual founders' values and behaviour were eventually embodied into organizational structure, culture, decision-making processes, systems, and so on. However, this organizational architecture has double-edged features: a well-aligned architecture is a source of competitive advantage, but it slowly becomes organizational inertia which hinders transformation for further development and growth.

Example of management behavioural change

Changes in management (Rowley 2002) are contrasted in Table 11.4. A key area concerns employment, where much has been propounded on breaking with lifetime employment and seniority-based reward systems. These are seen as costly, 'inflexible', unfair and a drag on motivation and economic development. There are concerns that junior, younger workers were paid less, and older workers more, than their respective contributions. These characteristics were seen to stifle recognition and reward differential performance. In contrast, the flexible labour market model generated employment and rewarded performance. Therefore, the frequently argued trajectory is towards greater flexibility and performance in labour markets and remuneration.

A range of anecdotal, quantitative and qualitative evidence (Rowley and

Table 11.4   Key characteristics of traditional and newer management in Korea

Area	Traditional characteristics	Newer characteristics
Core ideology	Organization first Collective equality Community oriented	Individual respected Individual equity Market principle adopted
Human resource flow	Mass recruitment of new graduates Job security (lifetime job) Generalist oriented	Recruitment on demand Job mobility (lifetime career) Development of professional
Work system	Tall structure Line and staff; function based Position based	Flat structure Team systems Qualification based
Evaluation and reward system	Seniority (age and tenure) Pay equality For advancement in job grade/job No appraisal feedback Single-rater appraisal	Ability, performance (annual) Merit pay For pay increases Appraisal feedback 360° appraisal
Employee influence	Less involvement Less information sharing	Involvement of workers Information sharing

Bae 2002) indicates management changes here. That management behaviour changes were attempted and practised could give strong signals that others might follow this route. However, there were also counter-examples of management behaviour continuity. As well as the exact coverage in terms of spread (between and within companies), we can also question the depth and acceptance of changes. The rhetoric may well be different from the reality of positions. Interestingly, differential changes to lifetime employment can also be compared and contrasted with Japan, with its 'reluctant restructuring', and Vietnam, where it is being 'phased out' (see relevant chapters in this volume). Institutional theory (Meyer and Rowan 1977) and isomorphism (DiMaggio and Powell 1983) play a role (see Bae and Rowley 2001). Then there are also particular cultural (obligations, loss of face) and institutional (unions, limited unemployment support) constraints (Bae and Rowley 2001; Rowley and Benson 2002).

Labour–management conflict resolution

The management of labour has been critical to Korea. This has occurred in a variety of contexts, from authoritarian and military governments and corporatism to lifetime employment. Also, the labour movement played an integral role against occupation and supported democratization. In terms of one dimension of conflict, labour disputes varied from just 4 in 1970 to 322 in 1990, with peaks of 3,749 in 1987 and 1,873 in 1988. Partly in response to the Asian crisis, strikes increased by 65 per cent, from 78 (44,000 workers) to 129 (146,000 workers) in 1997–8.

Trade union developments

From the early twentieth century, low wages, hazardous conditions and anti-Japanese sentiments contributed to union formation (Kwon and O'Donnell 2001). From the 1920s, unions increased, reaching 488 and 67,220 members in 1928. The 1930s witnessed a decline with repression for Japanese war production and internal splits. Union numbers fell to 207 and 28,211 members by 1935 (Kwon and O'Donnell 2001). The post-war radical union movement, the *Chun Pyung*, was declared illegal by the US military government, which restricted political and industrial activities to encourage US 'business unions'. The subsequent strikes and General Strike resulted in 25 dead, 11,000 imprisoned and another 25,000 dismissed. A more conservative, government-sponsored, industry-based movement was decreed, signalling labour's incorporation by the state, conflict repression and an 'authoritarian corporatist approach' (Kwon and O'Donnell 2001: 29). Thus, the government officially recognized the Federation of Korean Trade Unions and became increasingly interventionist, enacting a battery of laws regulating hours, holidays, pay and multiple and independent unions, establishing the Labour Management Council (LMC) system, promoting more 'cooperative' forms of trade unionism, even prohibiting conflicts in foreign businesses (Kwon and O'Donnell 2001).

The *chaebols*' diversity of approaches towards labour management was partly influenced by their growth strategies (Kwon and O'Donnell 2001). For instance, economic growth and focus on minimizing labour costs resulted in the expansion and concentration of workforces in large-scale industrial estates with authoritarian and militaristic controls. The pressure and nature of the labour process was indicated in the volume of industrial accidents, some 4,570 in 1987 compared with smaller numbers in larger workforces (although with sectoral impacts, of course), such as 513 in the USA and 658 in the UK (Kang and Wilkinson 2000). Labour resistance was generated, the catalyst for conflict and re-emergence of independent unions from the 1970s. Employers responded by disrupting union activities, sponsoring company unions and replacing labour-intensive processes by automating, subcontracting or transplanting overseas. From the late 1980s, companies also softened their emphasis on strict supervision and work intensification by widening access to paternalistic labour management practices and welfare schemes, subsidized school fees and housing benefits (Kang and Wilkinson 2000). Nevertheless, trade unionization grew from 12.6 per cent in 1970, peaking at 18.6 per cent in 1989.[5]

During the 1990s independent trade unions established their own national organization, with federations of *chaebol*-based and regional associations. An alternative national federation, the Korean Confederation of Trade Unions (*minjunochong*), emerged in 1995. It organized the 1996 General Strike (Bae *et al.* 1997), enhancing its legitimacy. However, the economic whirlwind of the Asian crisis then hit. Trade union density fell back to 11.5 per cent by 1998.

Obviously, labour strength and influence also depends on environment and contexts, such as the location, legal constraints and opportunities operating and the nature and character of the disputes themselves. In Korea, unions are strategically well located in ship and automobile manufacture as well as in the power, transportation and telecommunications industries. As we have seen above, conflicts can be high profile, large scale and confrontational. This nature has remained. For example, the 1992 week-long occupation of Hyundai Motor was ended by 15,000 riot police storming the factory (Kim 2000). In 2002 there was the imprisonment of unionists, refusal to recognize public sector unions and ending of the power workers' strike after several weeks of public threats and intimidation and surrounding their camp at the Myong-dong Cathedral with riot and secret police.

This is the context for the more recent ideas of increased employee involvement, participation and partnership that have emerged at dual levels. Examples at the macro level include the neo-corporatist type Presidential Commission on Industrial Relations Reform (1996) and the tripartite Labour–Management–Government Committees (*nosajung wiwonhoe*) on Industrial Relations (1998) (Yang and Lim 2000). At the micro level there is the example of LG Electronics which looked at practices in plants in the USA (Saturn, Motorola) and Japan. We noted earlier the possible cultural constraints on this.

In sum, from the late 1980s the institutions, framework and policies of labour management all shifted under pressures from political liberalization and civilian governments, joining the ILO (1991) and OECD (1996), trade union pressure and the Asian crisis. Nevertheless, the frames of reference and perspectives for management remain strongly unitary. In contrast, this is less so for labour, with stronger pluralist, and even radical, perspectives evident. This dichotomy often continues, as indicated by the recent arrests of unionists, with strikes damned as 'obstacles to business', and public threats to prevent the power workers' dispute escalating into a general strike.

Implications for managers

Implications can be seen in terms of not just indigeneous, but also other Asian and Western, managers. One implication concerns the need to recognize paradoxes between concepts and management behaviour and managerial characteristics noted earlier in the chapter.

Ghoshal and Bartlett (1997) suggested transformation and management roles and tasks in eras of high uncertainty. The change is for: (1) operating-level managers from 'Operational Implementers' to 'Aggressive

Entrepreneurs'; (2) senior-level managers from 'Administrative Controllers' to 'Supportive Coaches'; (3) top-level managers from 'Resource Allocators' to 'Institutional Leaders'. These can be applied to some Korean corporations. One issue is that traditional culture facilitated top-down, paternalistic and authoritarian styles of leadership, similar to the former roles of management suggested by Ghoshal and Bartlett (1979). Yet, given a highly uncertain global environment and knowledge-based economies, some transition is necessary. This cultural conflict is another task to be resolved.

Third, the influence of the internationalization of Korean companies and influx of foreign capital produces tension between 'traditional' and 'professional' managers, in particular those with experience of education or work in the West. For example, there may be increased expectations and requirements in corporate governance, such as for transparency and more rigorous recruitment and selection. Also, in terms of the lengthy strained negotiations with Western companies, managements on both sides of the table need to recognize the reasons, which are not just process or tactically based, but have cultural dimensions.

Fourth, there is a need for greater understanding of the applicability of Western management concepts (Rowley 1997a; 1997b; Rowley and Benson 2000a; 2000b). The shifts from more traditional organizational systems, with strong internal labour markets, towards external labour markets are not 'cost free'. Yet, managers are often unaware of these potential downsides. There is the problem of trying to maintain commitment, loyalty and teamwork in an era of easier dismissal and greater focus on individual, sometimes short-term, performance. Nor are managers aware of possible alternatives, such as a social market (European) model. This may partly be due to the dominance of the USA in Korea in its business and educational spheres (and some unquestioning of views). For instance, perceived 'inflexibilities', such as seniority and long-term employment, can generate flexibilities such as willingness to change and stimulate innovation and long-term development. In contrast, some 'flexibilities' produce problems and inflexibilities, as when companies look to solve problems is a short-term fashion by cutting labour and training at the cost of alternatives and long-term and dynamic growth. If this latter route were more constrained with obstacles, management would be encouraged to consider alternatives to compete (Rowley 1997a; 1997b). There is also a practical implication in terms of the critical mass, and who is first to try such numerically flexible external labour markets and forgo the security and certainties of the internal labour market. What happens if this does not work or the company fails? There is no going back for employees as previous recruitment was based on limited ports of entry and careers and pay on seniority. They must seek more of the same insecure employment.

There are also many underplayed problems in 'measuring' performance. These concern performance appraisals in general, when linked to rewards, and in Asian contexts. For instance, there are well known tendencies in human nature that lead towards subjective aspects in appraisals. Furthermore, it is very common in the prescriptive and practitioner types of literature to recommend that appraisals should not be linked to remuneration. Finally, there are cultural biases. For example, *inhwa* and the requirements to care for the well-being of subordinates hamper appraisals, encouraging tolerance and appreciation of efforts and not being excessively harsh in assessing sincere efforts[6] (Chen 2000). These should warn against naive prescription and acceptance of the usefulness of 'best practices'.

Fifth, there is the problem of demographics. Korea is facing an aging population and workforce. Yet, the traditionally homogeneous and inclusive society, population, workforce and management make required changes and responses in terms of a multicultural workforce problematic. The areas of managing diversity, and the requisite training for it, have key roles in this.

Finally, there is an implication for management in terms of a greater need to recognize the perspectives that abound in management. A ubiquitous unitary outlook was always partial, but this is increasingly so in a globalized world with greater exposure to businesses, such as from Europe, often with stronger pluralist perspectives. That in such frameworks disagreements and conflicts are not seen as aberrations, but normal, and even useful, needs to be recognized by management. Alternative mechanisms for dealing with labour management can then be explored. There would then be less highly confrontational and entrenched approaches, with greater use of processes such as collective bargaining, negotiation and even conciliation, mediation and arbitration, despite the cultural problems mentioned above.

Conclusions

We have outlined the key broad dimensions and developments of management and culture in Korea. This clearly shows that the context is important. While institutional perspectives remain important, culture also retains its salience for management and understanding its behaviour and practices. The roller-coaster of Korea's development indicates the need for careful analysis of the roles of management and culture as they have been both canonized then vilified. Both these labels may be too deterministic, stark and naive. However, what usefully emerges from this is a greater balance as to the role of management and culture in economies, which ultimately rest on an amalgam of foundations. Also, there may be less hagiography of management and pointless search for some magic 'one best way' elixir to manage, which, as we should not forget, remains complex and often specific as the power of particular management and culture is pertinent and persists.

Notes

1   Korea was one of the original little 'Tigers', sometimes referred to as little 'Dragons'.
2   This strategy may be contrasted with that of India or Pakistan.

3 The decline in demand of the US economy in 2002 may in time undermine the recovery in Korean exports.
4 See the chapter on Japan in this volume for similarities.
5 Korea has one of the most active labour movements in Asia in terms of unionization, apart from Japan.
6 This trait may well be apparent in most Confucian-influenced Asian societies.

References

Bae, J. and Rowley, C. (2001) 'The impact of globalization on HRM: the case of South Korea', *Journal of World Business* 36(4): 402–28.

Bae, J., Rowley, C., Kim, D. H. and Lawler, J. (1997) 'Korean industrial relations at the crossroads: the recent labour troubles', *Asia Pacific Business Review* 3(3): 148–60.

Cameron, K. S. (1978) 'Measuring organizational effectiveness in institutions of higher education', *Administrative Science Quarterly* 23: 604–32.

Carroll, H. L. (1993) 'A sociological view on why firms differ', *Strategic Management Journal* 14: 237–49.

Chen, M. (2000) 'Management in South Korea', in M. Warner (ed.), *Management in Asia Pacific*, London: Thomson, pp. 300–11.

Child, J. (1972) 'Organizational structure, environment and performance: the role of strategic choice', *Sociology* 6: 1–22.

Cho, Y. H. and Yoon, J. (2002) 'The origin and function of dynamic collectivism: an analysis of Korean corporate culture', in C. Rowley, T. W. Sohn and J. Bae (eds), *Managing Korean Businesses: Organization, Culture, Human Resources and Change*, London: Cass, pp. 70–88.

Chung, K. H. and Lee, H. C. (1989) 'National differences in managerial practices', in K. H. Chung and H. C. Lee (eds), *Korean Managerial Dynamics*, New York: Praeger, pp. 163–88.

Chung, K. H., Lee, H. C. and Jung, K. H. (1997) *Korean Management: Global Strategy and Cultural Transformation*, Berlin: de Gruyter.

DiMaggio, P. and Powell, W. (1983) 'The iron cage revisited: institutional isomorphism and collective rationality in the organizational field', *American Sociological Review* 48: 147–60.

Ghoshal, S. and Bartlett, C. A. (1997) *The Individualized Corporation: A Fundamentally New Approach to Management*, New York: HarperCollins.

Hambrick, D. C. and Mason, P. A. (1984) 'Upper echelons: the organization as a reflection of its top managers', *Academy of Management Review* 9(2): 193–206.

Hofstede, G. (1991) *Cultures and Organizations*, London: McGraw-Hill.

Kang, Y. and Wilkinson, R. (2000) 'Workplace industrial relations in Korea for the 21st century', in R. Wilkinson, J. Maltby and J. Lee (eds), *Responding to Change: Some Key Lessons for the Future of Korea*, Sheffield: University of Sheffield Management School, pp. 125–45.

Kim, J. and Rowley, C. (2001) 'Managerial problems in Korea: evidence from the nationalised industries', *International Journal of Public Sector Management* 14(2): 129–48.

Kim, K. D. (1994) 'Confucianism and capitalist development in East Asia', in L. Sklair (ed.), *Capitalism and Development*, London: Routledge, pp. 87–106.

Kim, L. (1998) 'Crisis construction and organizational learning: capability building in catching-up at Hyundai Motor', *Organization Science* 9: 506–21.

Kim, S. and Briscoe, D. (1997) 'Globalization and a new human resource policy in Korea: transformation to a performance-based HRM', *Employee Relations* 19(4): 298–308.

Kim, Y. (2000) 'Employment relations at a large South Korean firm: the LG Group', in G. Bamber, F. Park, C. Lee, P. Ross and K. Broadbent (eds), *Employment Relations in the Asia-Pacific*, London: Thomson, pp. 175–93.

Kwon, S.-H. and O'Donnell, M. (2001) *The Chaebol and Labour in Korea: The Development of Management Strategy in Hyundai*, London: Routledge.

Lee, C. (2000) 'Challenges facing unions in South Korea', in G. Bamber, F. Park, C. Lee, P. Ross and K. Broadbent (eds), *Employment Relations in the Asia-Pacific*, London: Thomson, pp. 145–58.

Lee, H. (2002) 'The relationship between features of business groups and founders' characteristics: evidence from the comparison of Samsung and Hyundai group', *Korean Journal of Management* 10(1): 55–94 (in Korean).

Lee, H.-C. (1997) *Cultural Characteristics of Korean Firms and New Culture Development*, Seoul: Bakyungsa (in Korean).

Meyer J. and Rowan, B. (1977) 'Institutionalized organizations: formal structure as myth and ceremony', *American Journal of Sociology* 83(2): 340–63.

Miller, D. and Dröge, C. (1986) 'Psychological and traditional determinants of structure', *Administrative Science Quarterly* 31: 539–60.

Morden, T. and Bowles, D. (1998) 'Management in South Korea: a review', *Management Decision* 36(5): 316–30.

Oh, I. and Park, H. J. (2002) 'Shooting at a moving target: four theoretical problems in exploring the dynamics of the *chaebol*', in C. Rowley, T. W. Sohn and J. Bae (eds), *Managing Korean Businesses: Organization, Culture, Human Resources and Change*, London: Cass, pp. 44–69.

Park, W. W. (2002) 'Corporate culture change campaigns in Korea: lessons from their failure', in C. Rowley, T. W. Sohn and J. Bae (eds), *Managing Korean Businesses: Organization, Culture, Human Resources and Change*, London: Cass, pp. 89–110.

Pucik, V. and Lim, J. C. (2002) 'Transforming HRM in a Korean *chaebol*: a case study of Samsung', in C. Rowley, T. W. Sohn and J. Bae (eds), *Managing Korean Businesses: Organization, Culture, Human Resources and Change*, London: Cass, pp. 137–60.

Quinn, R. E. (1988) *Beyond Rational Management*, San Francisco: Jossey-Bass.

Rowley, C. (1997a) 'Comparisons & perspectives on HRM in the Asia Pacific', *Asia-Pacific Business Review* 3(4): 1–18.

Rowley, C. (1997b) 'Reassessing HRM's convergence', *Asia Pacific Business Review* 3(4): 198–211.

Rowley, C. (2002) 'South Korean management in transition', in M. Warner (ed.), *Managing Across Cultures*, London: Thomson, pp. 178–92.

Rowley, C. and Bae, J. (1998a) 'The Icarus paradox in Korean business and management', *Asia Pacific Business Review* 4(2): 1–17.

Rowley, C. and Bae, J. (1998b) 'Korean business and management: the end of the model', *Asia Pacific Business Review* 4(2): 130–9.

Rowley, C. and Bae, J. (1998c) (eds) *Korean Businesses: Internal and External Industrialization*, London: Cass.

Rowley, C. and Bae, J. (2002) 'Globalization and transformation of HRM in South Korea', *International Journal of Human Resource Management* 13(3): 522–49.

Rowley, C. and Benson, J. (2000a) 'Global labour: issues and themes', *Asia Pacific Business Review* 6(3/4): 1–14.

Rowley, C. and Benson, J. (2000b) 'Globalization, labour and prospects', *Asia Pacific Business Review* 6(3/4): 300–8.

Rowley, C. and Benson, J. (2002) 'Convergence and divergence in Asian HRM', *California Management Review* 44(2): 90–109.

Rowley, C., Sohn, T. W. and Bae, J. (2002) (eds) *Managing Korean Businesses: Organization, Culture, Human Resources and Change*, London: Cass.

Song, B.-N. (1997) *The Rise of the Korea Economy*, Oxford: Oxford University Press.

The Economist (2002) 'Dead deals walking', 9 February: 61–2.

Ward, A. (2002a) 'Seoul music strives for a global audience', *Financial Times* 8 February: 12.

Ward, A. (2002b) 'The glory days of Hyundai sit firmly in the past', *Financial Times* 29 February: 26.

Whitely, R. (1991) 'The social construction of business systems in East Asia', *Organization Studies* 12(1): 1–28.

Yang, S. and Lim, S. (2000) 'The role of government in industrial relations in South Korea: the case of the Tripartite (Labour-Management-Government) Committee', in R. Wilkinson, J. Maltby and J. Lee (eds), *Responding to Change: Some Key Lessons for the Future of Korea*, Sheffield: University of Sheffield Management School, pp. 113–23.

12 Culture and management in Taiwan

Wen-Chi Grace Chou

Introduction

The rapid development of technology spread, greater international migration and the expanding global economy have combined to make us rethink the international interplay between national, social and corporate culture. Robertson (1992; 1995) suggested the terms 'Relativitation' and 'Glocalization' to denote the connectedness between globalization and localization. In Hall's view (1996), globalization implies a kind of Western domination and local cultural identity will possibly be strengthened but will also be relativized by the impact of globalization. It seems that two trends have coexisted and developed together. In daily life, advertisements on TV transmit a similar message, e.g. HSBC's 'Global Finance, Local Wisdom'. Indeed, the better we understand embedded culture through life experiences and historical records, the better we will be able to grasp international and often multicultural trade, business and management.

In recent decades, Hofstede (1991) and Trompenaars and Hampden-Turner (1998, Chinese version) have used a comparative approach towards cultural diversity and management. Fukuyama (1995) noted how social trust originating from different cultures plays a critical role in shaping economic prosperity and patterns of organization. Since culture is a very complicated, dynamic and long-term cultivated process with a number of unwritten rules or under the table/habitual practices, it is not easy to deconstruct. In the past, several studies have attempted to explain Taiwanese economic development using cultural, state-centred, market, dependence and world system approaches. In this chapter, I make no attempt to provide a causal analysis with culture and economic development, but rather delineates how culture and management have been intertwined in the Taiwan context. More importantly, the chapter will discuss how this relation has been impacted and changed by the new economy, without, however, falling into economic determination.

In his classic work *The Protestant Ethic and the Spirit of Capitalism*, Max Weber opened the horizon of economic and culture relations and argued that Confucianism impeded Chinese economic development. However, economic growth in East Asia has repudiated Weber's proposition. As a result, Confucianism has commonly been regarded in the Western world as being representative of Chinese culture (see Chapter 2 in this volume). Some scholars used 'Vulgar Confucianism' to differentiate, including self-discipline, familialism, hard work, thrift, high emphasis on education and relationship orientation (Zhai 1999: 62). However, as indigenous sociologists in Taiwan (Ku 1999) pointed out, current Chinese culture has been 'over-Confucianized' and is no different from Chinese personalities or characteristics. Further, Taiwan has specific historical and cultural expressions, so as Lee (1991) and Ku (1999: 42) suggested, we should not equate Chinese culture and Taiwan culture.[1]

Besides the 'blurring' of the term Confucianism, under the current massive economic restructuring or transformation we must also note how changes in economic structures and management methods have impacted culture. Changes to other social structures and social relations and their impact on culture changes are as important as economic changes. The above factors have interacted with and reshaped the relationship between management and culture in Taiwan.

First, I shall briefly discuss Taiwan's historical and economic background. Then, I shall describe the characteristics of Taiwan's social culture. After providing this general background, I will delineate and analyze corporate culture, management behaviour, management methods and conflict resolution. Finally, the chapter will address implications for managers.

Historical setting

Like many other countries, Taiwan is multicultural and multi-ethnic. Through occupation and colonization by different countries, Taiwan has absorbed different cultural elements from different sources and now hopes to find or shape its unique culture (Lee 1991). The following will provide a brief historical account.

After Portuguese navigators named the Island *Ilha Formosa*, or 'beautiful island', the Spanish and the Dutch were the next group of Europeans to come to Taiwan. In 1622, the Dutch East India Company was established. Taiwan became a trading and transshipment centre for goods moving between a number of areas, and ever since then, Taiwan has been involved in the global economy. After thirty-eight years, Cheng Cheng-Kung forced the Dutch out in 1662 and restored the Ming Dynasty. Cheng Cheng-Kung set up schools for the young, introduced Chinese laws and customs, and built the first Confucian temple in Taiwan. The Ching Dynasty established a province in Taiwan in 1886. However, in 1895, the Ching Dynasty was forced to cede Taiwan to Japan after losing the Sino-Japanese War. In 1912, the Republic of China (ROC) was established when Dr Sun Yat-Sen led revolutionary action to overthrow the Ching Dynasty. The last colonial phase in Taiwan was the period of Japanese rule from 1895 to 1945. Unlike the Dutch, who in the seventeenth century colonized Taiwan more for immediate commercial gain, the Japanese gave priority to establishing political control over the island. With strict police control, compulsory Japanese education and cultural assimilation were emphasized. Japanese colonization had extensive effects in areas such as infrastructure, agricultural development, education and business. When the Japanese surrendered to Allied forces in 1945 following their defeat in the Second World War, they returned Taiwan. However, by 1949, the communists had occupied most of the Chinese mainland, and the Nationalist (*Kuomintang* KMT/*Guomindang*) Party retreated from China to Taiwan.

To facilitate state projects, the Nationalist Party enforced the 'Temporary Provisions Effective during the Period of Communist Rebellion' in Taiwan in 1948. On 19 May 1949, the Taiwanese Garrison Command proclaimed an Emergency Decree throughout Taiwan. These two 'Empire Decrees' became the legal basis for the exercise of martial law in Taiwan for over three decades. Two years before, in February 1947, the massacre of thousands in the '228 Incident' made people question their pursuit of democracy and freedom. This kind of historical trauma and political terror (often called 'White Terror' in Taiwan) continued for a long time. The prohibition of the right to strike under the two 'Empire Decrees' was not annulled until 15 July 1987, when the two laws were lifted. Since that time, Taiwan has embarked on the process of democracy in many different ways. When talking about the participation issue at the enterprise level, apart from one traditional custom, the saying that 'Silence is golden', given past repressive political experiences, cannot be ignored by the Taiwanese people.

With the outbreak of the Korean War in 1950, US President Harry S. Truman ordered the US Seventh Fleet to protect Taiwan against Chinese communist attack. The USA also provided Taiwan with economic aid during this period. Land reform and a series of economic development plans undertaken during the 1950s and 1960s drastically reduced the inflation of wartime years and rapidly increased the island's productivity. In 1971, the United Nations gave China's seat to communist-ruled Beijing. In the following decade, numerous countries transferred their diplomatic ties from Taipei to Beijing. President Chiang Ching-Kuo and his successor Lee Teng-Hui countered these moves with a programme of pragmatic diplomacy, economic development and democratic reform, thereby re-enhancing Taiwan's status in the international community. On 18 March 2000, the new democratically elected president Chen Shui-Bian, from the opposition party, came to power and ended fifty years of governance by the Nationalist Party.

In terms of ethnic diversity, apart from some 402,000 indigenous peoples (less than 2 per cent of the total population), the Hakkas and Fujianese comprise about 85 per cent of the population, with Fujianese outnumbering Hakkas by about three to one. This latter group is generally referred to as 'mainlanders' and comprises less than 15 per cent of the population. These different groups each have a distinct dialect and culture, and more often than not their political ideologies differ. Their attitudes towards wage and saving patterns are also different. Beginning in 1989, Taiwan began to allow the importation of foreign workers and foreign maids from Thailand, the Philippines, Malaysia, Indonesia and Vietnam. The increasing number of foreign brides has also enriched the diversity of Taiwan's culture and posed a new demand for multicultural training programmes on the part of government and non-profit organizations.

Economic background

The following discussion attempts to summarize Taiwan's economic development since 1949. For convenience and simplicity, the history of Taiwan's economic development can be divided into four periods. The first period, from 1949 to 1960, is the import-substitution stage; the second, from 1961 to 1973, is the export-oriented stage; the third, from 1974 to 1986, was the second import-substitution and export-led stage; and the last, from 1987 to the present, is the liberal and international stage.

1949–60: import-substitution stage

Like other developing countries, Taiwan's initial industrial development strategy was mainly based on import substitution. Between 1952 and 1957, consumer goods as a share of total imports fell from 19.8 to 6.6 per cent. After a period of time, the domestic market for consumer goods became increasingly saturated. The Nineteen-Point Program of Economic and Financial Reform in 1960 pushed the Taiwanese government to liberalize controls on trade and industry, promote exports and create a climate to stimulate private local and foreign investment.

1960–73: export-oriented stage

The decade of the 1960s was characterized by extremely high and rapid economic growth. The annual growth rate for per capita income more than doubled, from 2.7 per cent in the 1950s to 5.8 per cent in the 1960s. The major reason for this growth was the expanded role of the industrial sector, which grew from 10 per cent annually in the 1950s to 20 per cent in the 1960s. As a result, the industrial sector displaced the agricultural sector in terms of relative importance in economic development (Ranis 1979: 221). In addition, between 1962 and 1972, exports of goods and services rose from 13 per cent to nearly 43 per cent of GDP, and the share of industrial products in these exports increased from 51 per cent to 83 per cent.

How did this meteoric development come about? There were many factors contributing to this phenomenon. First of all, the relaxation of Cold War tensions facilitated the expansion of world trade (Gold 1986). Second, during this time, low-priced Japanese textiles, plastics and electronic products had flooded the US market, forcing American capitalists to find other production sites with low costs so that they could compete with the Japanese in the US market. Taiwan possessed a cheap, abundant, disciplined and educated labour force. Following the commencement of investment by American firms in Taiwan, large Japanese corporations also started to invest in Taiwan to retain their market share in the USA. Taiwan thus became a vital site for global production.

To attract more foreign capital, beginning in 1965 the government established three export processing zones (EPZs). The first one was in the harbour at Kaohsiung, a port city in the south of Taiwan. The second and third such zones were established at nearby Nantze and in Taichung in 1969. Nantze is very near Kaohsiung, while Taichung is in the middle of the island of Taiwan. All investors in these EPZs, both foreign and local, enjoyed tax incentives and avoided import duties on equipment and parts as long as they exported all that they manufactured or assembled. In the EPZs and elsewhere, foreign capital was concentrated in a few sectors, mostly in electronics and to a lesser extent in plastics and garments (Investment Commission 1997: 6).

1974–86: the import-substitution and export-led stage

Just before the profound effect of the shock of the oil crisis of the early 1970s, Taiwan was diplomatically frustrated by Mainland China. Moreover, the period 1972–5 was one of a series of drastic shocks to the world economy. These shocks were felt strongly in Taiwan, a small trade-oriented economy, and reversed the previous steady growth in per capita income, industrial production, exports and imports that had continued more or less uninterrupted since 1952, causing the highest inflation rates since the early 1950s. These inflationary shocks were worsened by growing labour shortages that caused sustained wage increases in manufacturing (Ranis 1979).

At this time, the state devised a flexible, multi-faceted strategy to reduce Taiwan's vulnerability to the instability of the global economy and global politics, primarily by vertically integrating and deepening industry and, to compensate for its diplomatic isolation, by substituting economic ties for political ones. In 1978, like Singapore, Taiwan's government restructured the economy by upgrading the capital and technology components of industry. In 1977, the Council for Economic Planning and Development (the CEPD) was established and began to shift the emphasis towards industrial restructuring, stressing technology-intensive, non-polluting, non-energy-guzzling industries, instead of heavy or capital-intensive ones.

1987 to the present : the liberal and international stage

Heavily based on export-led industrialization, Taiwan's economy grew at an annual rate of 9.32 per cent from 1965 to 1986 and at an annual rate of 7.49

per cent from 1987 to 1995. However, it slowed to 5.7 per cent from 1996 to 2000 and −1.9 per cent in 2001. The production value of the industrial sector amounted to 46.7 per cent of GDP in 1987 but had decreased to 32.4 per cent by 2000. The manufacturing sector, which was formerly the largest part of the industrial sector, also showed a decline to 26.4 per cent in 2000. In contrast, the production value of the service sector increased from 48.0 per cent in 1987 to 65.5 per cent in 2000 (Statistics Department 2002). Regarding international trade, in 1999 Taiwan's trade is the world's fifteenth largest, amounting to 232.3 billion dollars. Among this, the export value is around 121.6 billion and ranked fourteenth in the world.

The government is not only trying to diversify its market destinations, but has also joined international organizations such as APEC (Asian Pacific Economic Consortium, which it joined in 1991) and the WTO (World Trade Organization) in 2002. The government has therefore begun to take measures gradually to liberalize its economy. Furthermore, in 1993, the government announced 'Proposals to Promote the Economy' consisting of two major policy goals: facilitating industrial upgrade and establishing the Asia Pacific Regional Operations Centres (the APROC plan). Currently, building up a 'Green Silicon Island' is the paramount goal for the new government.

Societal culture

In this section, the lessening importance of Confucianism will be discussed. Moreover, I will briefly explore other important dimensions – religion, education, social relations – to show how these have impacted on Taiwan's culture and also on management and business operation.

Confucianism is now perhaps only one type of philosophy seen in Taiwan.[2] Its discourse mainly focuses on ethical behaviour in society with the aim of establishing harmonious relationships between individuals. In Taiwan's current educational system, Confucianism is only part of the content of the Chinese literature course. People regard Confucian temples more as halls to honour Confucius rather than places of worship. Every year, on his birthday, 28 September, a ceremony is held to memorialize Confucius as the model teacher since he taught all who wished to learn and also taught according to his pupils' talents. Therefore, his birthday is also designated as Teachers' Day in Taiwan. But, in one sense, it is difficult to categorize Confucianism as a core value system. Also, as stated before, the question of whether views of Chinese culture have been 'over-Confucianized' is worthy of attention. Further, Confucianism may have different implementations and implications in different Chinese societies (see Chapters 2, 3 and 10). Therefore, we need to look at other social milieux in Taiwan.

First of all, let us look at religion. The latest figures released by the Ministry of the Interior in December 1999 indicate that about 10.8 million people in Taiwan – almost half of the population – are religious believers. Of these, 42.1 per cent are Taoists and 34.0 per cent are Buddhist. Protestants and Catholics account for 5.5 per cent and 2.8 per cent respectively. Another folk religion called I-Kuan Tao attracted 7.8 per cent of people. The three major religions all emphasize the worship of ancestors and prayers to avoid risk and obtain good fortune for their pursuits, including jobs or business operations.

Other Chinese folk religions have been significantly influenced by Buddhism and Taoism; however, they are neither Buddhist nor Taoist. The difficult pioneer environment of seventeenth- and eighteenth-century Taiwan created a strong need for religion. Folk religion was thus transplanted from the mainland to Taiwan and new gods and rituals were created to meet the needs of security and survival, i.e. the Earth God and Matsu. Traditional magical calculations such as geomancy (*Feng-Shui*) and physiognomy (*Kan-San*) are still available. For example, when a company wants to move, it may see a Feng-Shui consultant first, or stock market speculators may consult fortune tellers to make decisions.

Some customs related to management and work at a general level are worth mentioning here. In many companies and shops, on the second and sixteenth days of the lunar month, a table is set up and an offering of fruit, food and incense is made to the Earth God. On the first auspicious day following the Chinese New Year break, often on the fifth when businesses reopen, another offering is made to the Earth God. For employees, at the end of every lunar year, employers pay their respects to the Earth God and provide a banquet for their employees (called *Wei-Ya* in Chinese). The arrangement of a meal by employers is a traditional custom held in the Taiwanese workplace, regardless of the size of the plant. The aim of this activity is to allow employers to express their gratitude to staff. In the past, this repast was spiced by the knowledge that the chicken's head on the table reputedly pointed to the person the employer expects to leave the plant. Now, it no longer carries this double meaning, but the banquet is still held to show employers' gratitude for their employees' hard work throughout the year.

Education is the agent of socialization and cultural transmission to the next generation. Throughout the decades of Taiwan's economic growth, the government has placed particular emphasis on education. However, it is worthwhile pointing out here that there is a mass of educational reforms underway to meet contemporary needs, and this has deep implications for cultural change. In the past, students were required to take the Joint College Entrance Examination to gain admission to a university. However, this highly competitive system places tremendous stress on young people and may kill opportunities to develop their own creativity and independent thinking. Nowadays, variety, creativity and independent thinking are strongly emphasized and students may enter college by application or selection by recommendation. Bilingual education has also been started at elementary schools. Also, the young people of today have easy access to the Internet and pop culture from other countries.

In social relations, *quanxi*[4] (i.e. 'relationships') still plays an important part in social interaction. There is a popular saying in Chinese: 'If you have good relationships, things will be OK, but if you have no relationships, things will not go well.' Chinese 'personal orientation' differs from the 'issue orientation' found in some Western countries. Having meals together provides a chance not only to eat but also to do business in an informal or implicit way, and forms a part of local business culture. After the meal, some companies may even provide a further opportunity to have drinks (so called 'second round') or even provide erotic services (so called 'third round') to please their customers or business partners. The 'Red Envelope' (*Hong-Bao* in Chinese) culture sometimes may involve a kind of bribe to achieve a goal in an unethical way. However, in politics and in business, the government has attempted to ease this bad image. One of the major issues for the current government was the fight against 'black gold politics' and it won the election in the end.

In gender relations, the patriarchal ideology is still hard to eradicate.[5] However, generally speaking, gender attitudes have become more equal than in the past. Women's employment is accepted and encouraged. However, because of insufficient child care and other reasons, the female participation rate has stayed more or less the same, around 45 per cent, during the last decade. Gender segregation is still alive. However, through the efforts of women's organizations and lesbian groups, Taiwan's gender boundaries have become more flexible. The Gender Equality at Work Act has also just been passed after twelve years of effort. How this new legislation will impact gender equality in the workplace culture is worthy of further observation.

Corporate culture

Social culture impacts corporate culture. In addition, the impact of corporate culture on management style and corporate performance is an important issue in management studies (Buller *et al.* 2000). The structure of ownership, technology, markets and founders' value preferences all influence corporate culture. Owing to space constraints, this chapter will mainly focus on the difference in the ownership structure and the size of enterprises and discuss what their corporate culture is like at a general level.

The majority of enterprises in Taiwan are privately owned. However, state-owned enterprises (SOEs) have been an important part of Taiwan's development and are now undergoing privatization. Workers in SOEs enjoy employment for life and their bonuses and welfare provisions are also better than those of private workers. Therefore, they are sometimes called the 'labour aristocracy'. There are thus two types of corporate culture. In one type workers concentrate on flattering their superiors or using bribery to be promoted. The other is the typical civil servant style. These workers do not like to be promoted in an unethical way. Instead, they choose to do as little work as they can and still keep their privileged status (Taiwan Labour Front 2001). Now, because of strict government budgeting, several SOEs have been forced to privatize and have lost their perquisite of lifetime employment at the same time (cf. the Chinese case, Chapter 2). Moreover, the government itself has also set a goal of gradually reducing the number of civil servants. A great deal of modernization of employment in government has taken place.

There has been more research on the issue of corporate culture in private enterprises. Wu (1994) used the random strata selection method to compare 189 Taiwanese, Japanese and American enterprises. Principal component factor analysis identified four types of corporate culture: innovation, organizational identity, risk avoidance and societal feedback. Results showed that American enterprises favour the innovation style, and their level of organizational formalization and integrity are higher than Taiwanese and Japanese enterprises. Japanese firms place more emphasis on teamwork and team leadership, while Taiwanese firms emphasize an authority-oriented style (see Chapter 6). Wu and Chen (1999) did further analysis on 600 managers and obtained similar results. The differences between Japanese and American enterprises in Taiwan were also described in Lee (1996) who emphasized more the impact of national cultures.

The above studies, regardless of the research method used, are cross-sectional. The longitudinal approach is lacking. It is important to know the differences among different enterprises, but it is also important to recognize changes with time. Chou's research (2000) on textiles companies and an ongoing project on the consumer electronics industry can fill this gap. Taking a historical view to see how the corporate culture has changed, research has shown that a paternalistic style of corporate culture is hard to sustain because of the challenge from economic restructuring (i.e. capital relocation, intensified competition, bleak profits), from organizational restructuring (welfare cuts, downsizing, performance orientation), from the awareness of workers' consciousness (individual, labour unions) and also from governmental labour legislation (non-transferable retirement payments to transferable ones). Even in Japanese joint ventures, Chou has found that the seniority principle has lost its prominence. In terms of wages and promotions, performance will be the most important concern for managers. However, to prevent opposition from workers, the changes have been brought in gradually. In high-tech industries, tremendously high bonuses are used to provide incentives to workers in Taiwan. The knowledge base and innovation have been highly encouraged.

One of the factors explaining Taiwan's economic success is its large number of small and medium-sized enterprises (SMEs, companies with fewer than 200 workers in manufacturing or less than NT$8 million of sales value in the service industry). SMEs comprised 98.1 per cent of all enterprises and 80.6 per cent of workers. Before 1987, SMEs accounted for more than 60 per cent of total exports but this number has now declined to one-third (*Yearbook of SMEs* 1997). SMEs in Taiwan have developed the advantage of 'flexible production' to the maximum and are characterized by less formalization and less worker protection. However, with its flexibility and lower labour costs, Taiwan has been in global production since the 1960s. But why does Taiwan have more SMEs and how is this possible? Shieh (1992) used an analysis of outsourcing factories to show that the Taiwanese have the inclination to become bosses; and indeed, his book called Taiwan the 'Boss Island'. There is also a popular local folk saying which holds: 'better a big fish in a small pond than a small fish in a big pond' (Zhai 1999).

Family enterprise is another point. In Taiwan, research has shown that, besides the family ethic, two other major pillars or functions for family enterprises are tax avoidance and reducing labour disputes (Wang 2001). In small enterprises, unpaid family workers are one of the major sources of labour. The boss's wife is frequently called '*Lao-Ban-Niang*' and is often in charge of some important business tasks (Lui and Chiu 1999). In larger enterprises, recruitment of family members can help businesses avoid tax without being detected, and can transform the labour–management relationship into a personal relationship. However, as Chou (2000) and Wang (2001) found, when there are conflicts of interest, familial relations are hard to sustain. Likewise, Chung (2001) accepted that the market and culture have played a part in shaping large business groups in Taiwan; however, the author emphasized that institutional incentives are even more important.

Managerial behaviour

In response to economic challenges, there have been changes not only to corporate culture but also to managerial behaviour. This section aims to provide a brief description of how management behaviour differs according to the type of enterprise.

The first case we will consider is that of SOEs experiencing privatization. As an example, it took eight years to complete the privatization of one firm, starting in 1986 (Taiwan Labour Front 2001). Lifetime employment has been disappearing. Through active campaigns by labour unions, workers received some compensation without satisfaction. In terms of new management behaviour, total personnel cost has been kept fixed. The more workers employed, the less average wages each will receive. Second, the level of workers' basic wages has been lowered, and bonuses or benefits based on their work performance have been added. Third, there has been intensified gender segregation, and the largest cuts to monthly wages have been to the salaries of female personnel. Fourth, there has been increased labour utilization. Since the downsizing of the labour force has increased average profits, the division and competition of labour has also increased at the same time.

For other SOEs or government services, with a strong call for restructuring, downsizing is still speeding up, and this puts great pressure on today's civil servants.

For private enterprises, the current economic restructuring has produced great pressure to improve competitiveness. Several measures have been taken to combat the challenges from the external economy. Taking one Japanese joint venture electronics company as an example,[6] the company continues to restructure itself to reduce costs, increase full participation and enhance efficiency. Teamwork and suggestion boxes have been used for a long time to increase participation. However, owing to increased competition after entry to the WTO, the company will continue to downsize its labour force and increase early retirements. The current workers feel uncertain as to whether they can safely keep their jobs. In another large electronics company, Chou's fieldwork (2002) has also shown that less priority is given to seniority wages; performance plays a more important role in promotions and wage increases.

As for the family enterprises, the lack of separation between ownership and management is a serious problem, as there can be some unethical barriers to organizational efficiency. This dual system (familialism and professionalism) sets up a potential conflict within the organization. However, according to Yen (1996), there are two ways to resolve this conflict. One is to professionalize family members; the other is to invite professionals to become family members. However, during the course of transition, the middle level of managers may be lost since they lack the personal relationships to be promoted to the smaller number of high-level positions. Family enterprises do have the advantage of flexibility and efficiency due to the lower degree of formalization, and these benefits will be lost if factionalism and cliques are too strong and irrational communication prevails.

Managerial values

Owing to differences in prospects for profit, market structures and technical levels, there are some differences in managerial values. One of the approaches that has been adopted to maintain a harmonious working environment is paternalistic management. However, the paternalistic style of factory management was created and has been transformed in recent decades. Clearly, there are many factors in Taiwanese history that have been conducive to the rise of paternalism. Hsiung (1996) studied satellite factories with less than thirty workers in Taiwan, and suggested that ethnicity and kinship were the two primary sources of paternalism. The fact that recruitment was based on personal connections affected employment relations. These circumstances led to 'communal paternalism' in the workplace, as termed by Deyo (1989: 159), and were seen as a means of employer control in Taiwan.

As regards the factory, the paternalistic style of management has the effect of channelling the conflict between labour and management in a more implicit way and putting production relations on a personalized footing, at least to some extent. Apart from this, many firms attempt to provide more welfare services for their employees as an alternative to large increases in monetary wages (Galenson 1979: 421). By providing these fringe benefits, labour turnover was held at around 2 per cent between 1972 and 1975 (Galenson 1979: 409). Work itself therefore not only is perceived as a cash relationship, but also engenders a sense of obligation and gratitude to the employer. However, employers were able to exert control, either explicitly or implicitly, through welfare provisions. The authority relationship thus pivoted on a base of non-wage welfare provisions as well as monthly wages and bonuses. In addition, personal bonds arising from recruitment and daily working relations complicated or obscured formal labour–management relations. Furthermore, even when labour legislation existed, many employers ignored it. Factory life was often subject to the whim of employers, dictated in informal terms as they alone saw fit.

Chou's case studies (2000) demonstrate a shift from a deferential relationship based on paternalistic provisions, as seen in the 1970s and 1980s, to the impersonal relationship of the 1990s, when several paternalistic mechanisms changed (e.g. kinship, employee referral, recruitment/ introduction fees, child care centres and dormitories for indigenous workers) and redundancies occurred on a wide scale. In the former period, capitalists had provided non-cash welfare provisions as a result of economic prosperity and a high demand for rural labour. Also, in the face of the oil crisis in the 1970s, capitalists had provided such welfare provisions instead of wage increases to reduce high labour turnover. This is the background for the origin of paternalistic capitalism in Taiwan. However, in the latter period, capitalists removed non-cash welfare provisions and non-wage benefits when faced with economic downturns and intense global competition. Workers' potential obedience is now based on formal state labour legislation rather than on the traditional personal ties or clientism. This heralds a new era and the demise of paternalistic capitalism in Taiwan.

In the case of high-tech industries, state support and a high amount of capital investment, research and development and cooperation with the USA have created high productivity and value with a lower number of employees and thus developed different styles of management values. In high-tech companies, the greatest concern is to stabilize the core workers and to stimulate their potential. Therefore, these companies often provide large amounts of job training and very high bonuses (Chang and You 2002). However, one point worth making is that these firms have not encouraged the establishment of labour unions, as such unions have implications for labour conflicts which are not welcome in high-tech companies. Though some labour organizations have pushed for a labour union, the government and the companies themselves are still not very keen to set one up.

Labour–management conflict resolution

There are different levels at which labour–management conflict may be resolved, i.e. the enterprise, administrative and judicial levels. At the enterprise level, available means include labour unions, labour management councils, and personnel or HRM departments. For some factories that use foreign labour, a new position called foreign labour coordinator may be available. Apart from these formal mechanisms, informal mechanisms are also very important at present. Quite often, formal mechanisms are only resorted to after the informal channels have failed.

As Deyo (1989: 161) states:

> Conflict among these workers can be structurally and subjectively organized less around categories of class than around those of patrimony, kinship, and paternalism. The conflict need not manifest itself in class mobilization and strikes. Rather, it can assume non-collective forms and occur in private rather than public places.

Therefore, managers may try to sort out conflicts through personal links, if available. If informal mechanisms do not work, then the managers turn to formal ways.

As of the end of 2000 labour unions in Taiwan totalled 3,836 units with 2,868,330 members. Union density was 38.5 per cent as a whole. Basically, there are two main types of labour unions in Taiwan: industrial unions (20.9 per cent) and occupational unions (49.2 per cent) (*Yearbook of Labour Statistics* 2001). The declining trend in industrial union membership appears to be ongoing. According to union law, workers should organize labour unions if they are in an enterprise with thirty workers or more. The new revision proposed for union law will change compulsory unions to free-entry unions.

In contrast to the history of labour unions in Western countries, most of Taiwan's unions have not come into being as a result of an awakening of workers to their rights. Instead, unions have been promoted by government objectives due to fear of political insecurity since such fear was used by the communists to overthrow the nationalist government on Mainland China. When the nationalists retreated to Taiwan, all types of labour union were initially prohibited. Later, for the purpose of political security and economic stabilization, the government actively established labour unions in public enterprises and large-sized private businesses by nominating or appointing union leaders who would follow the orders of the ruling party. The right to strike was abolished until 15 July 1987. After that date, more and more autonomous labour unions were established. In the workplace, there are not only labour unions but sometimes labour management councils.

The Labour Standards Law requires that the enterprise set up a labour management council to promote cooperation and increase work efficiency if the factory employs more than thirty persons. In principle, meetings of the council must be held once every month. If the number of employees is over 100, there must be at least five representatives from each side. Basically, labour and management hold the same number of seats. Union cadres can be elected, but they must number less than one-third of the total representatives.

Generally speaking, labour unions in Taiwan are like company unions. The current global trend also makes unionization harder to achieve than ever before, since job security is the most serious concern in the worker's mind. Without a job, what is the use of a labour union? But, on the other hand, without further efforts to promote solidarity among workers, individual labour rights and interests will be in danger.

Compared with the past, workers have become more autonomous. They have experienced a kind of 'ideological break' after the breakdown of company welfare and company relocation and redundancy (Chou 2002). The current international economic competition and changes in corporate culture on the other hand curtail bargaining power. It is impossible to ask a company not to relocate, but it is possible to ask the company to make information more open. Once there are changes to be made, the union wants the company to communicate better. Therefore, it is indeed a hard time for workers when global capitalism makes it hard for their employers to resist the need to restructure. This is especially true for production workers with few qualifications. It is also true for a shrinking and more differentiated labour force containing foreign workers.

Implications for managers

Culture can shape economic activity and has been called 'the Spirit of Chinese Capitalism' (Redding 1990). However, at the same time, culture will be changed through economic restructuring. Both sides of the story are equally important and relate to each other. To respond to economic challenges, massive educational reform has taken place, including the abolition of a unitary route of entry to college through the Joint College Entrance Exam, an increasing variety of educational materials, an emphasis on Taiwan's culture and customs, and an emphasis on English or second foreign language training. In enterprises, there have been transformations in lifetime employment, seniority-based prominence, working hours and so on. Currently, atypical employment, flexible working hours, performance orientation, early retirement and downsizing of the labour force have appeared in increasing amounts.

Besides economic restructuring, changes in state legislation are another force that influences corporate culture. To respond to the needs of or requests from enterprises, the new government has approved flexible working hours and proposed to change non-transferable retirements into transferable ones. At the same time, the government has also reduced the working week from 48 hours to 84 working hours every two weeks. The

Gender Equality at Work Act and Occupational Injury Workers' Protection Act were passed in 2002. How these new laws will impact the current corporate culture, including gender equality and safe working environment, is worthy of continued observation.

Moreover, the introduction of foreign workers and foreign professionals has added new elements to the current multi-ethnic society. Some people have called these foreign workers and professionals Taiwan's fifth ethnic group. Apparently, different nations, ethnicities, genders, ages, physical situations and work positions have required current managers in Taiwan to bear these factors in mind. Therefore, diversity training for management is also very important, as well as multicultural training.

Conclusions

Culture is inevitably an integral part of economic operations. How economics has been integrated with society and culture is one of the major themes examined by economic sociologists, and how corporate culture has impacted management performance is likewise a popular theme in management studies. This chapter has aimed to point out briefly the need to re-examine the current status of Confucianism in Taiwan's economic activities: to what extent we can say it is still a core and dominant ideology remains a question today. Here I would like to emphasize that the formation of culture has a long and specific history and institutions. Having been occupied by different nations and with different ethnic groups, Taiwan has gradually developed its own culture. As are other countries experiencing global competition, Taiwan is finding its way out. We can see that globalization has impacted Taiwan's current culture but also pushed Taiwan to pursue or rediscover its own culture.

Will economic globalization develop a kind of homogeneous global culture? I have some reservations. Challenges from globalization have pushed Taiwan to find and develop its local culture, and the government is making efforts to preserve local characteristics. Therefore, we can see that globalization and localization have been interpenetrative and will be synthesized together. For management domains, it seems that several values have been adopted by different enterprises, i.e. increasing competitive advantage, efficiency and flexibility. Thus, some incompatible or impeding measures have changed, including lifetime employment and the seniority principle. Also, in education, the topic of how to strengthen students' international competitiveness and help them to understand and cherish local culture and dialects has gained momentum.

Nevertheless, the new trend in management culture can be said to be a response to the new economy. When the corporate world asked the government to deregulate the labour market, the government also had its own political and social concerns in terms of re-regulating the labour market. Therefore, in Taiwan, we have seen not only changes in corporate culture and management, but also government maintenance of the minimum wage, enhancement of employment services as well as the new laws on gender equality at work and occupational industry compensation. These laws will impact the future corporate culture to a greater or lesser extent. Therefore, owing to different historical contingencies, changes in different countries may not be necessarily homogeneous. Culture and management in Taiwan are thus not constantly unchanged and based only on Confucianism.

Notes

1 Sociologists in Taiwan have aimed to identify themselves in world academia by rethinking Chinese culture and its relations with Taiwan. However, partly due to the renaissance of Taiwanese identity, since the late 1980s, local sociologists have started to discover the subjectivity and particularity of Taiwan society in many different ways.

2 The current status of Confucianism in Taiwan is really a big and serious question. One social psychologist, Dr K. K. Huang, has made theoretical efforts in the internal structure of Confucian thought and its impact on East Asia's modernization. Further, Dr D. Lin, as a judicial sociologist, has provided a dialectical analysis of Confucianism and the law and even pointed out that the impact of Confucianism on Taiwan's centrally legal framework is minimized owing to Westernization. Here, I want only to emphasize that the influence of Confucianism on management is shaking and decreasing because of, among other reasons, the emergence of modern managers who receive their training from the Western world. Therefore, more detailed research on this field is required.

3 The tradition of the banquet, '*Wei-Ya*', has been kept for a long time regardless of the size of the enterprise. However, during the period of economic downturns, some enterprises have abolished it because of bleak profits.

4 *Quanxi* has become a popular term in Western academia to interpret the practice of social relations in East Asia. In Taiwan, those relevant researches include how social network, social trust and social capital have an impact on the establishment of new enterprises, the daily transaction of business, employee recruitment, etc.

5 Though traditional gender ideology is still available for older people, gender boundaries set up by patriarchy and Confucianism are becoming hard to hold to truly. With the advocacy and awareness raised by women's organizations, gender equality rights have gained support and momentum, especially among the younger generation.

6 This research is part of my ongoing research project entitled 'Changing employment relations in the global economy: case studies of consumer electronics industries in Taiwan'. This research, funded by the National Science Council (NSC), is an empirical study to document and analyse these changing processes and experiences, with special reference to management methods and employment relations. Moreover, this research is affiliated with one international white goods study conducted by Professors Theo Nichols, Peter Fairbrother and Hwe Beynon at Cardiff University.

References

Buller, P. F., Kohls, J. J. and Anderson, K. S. (2000) 'When ethics collide: managing conflicts across cultures', *Organizational Dynamics* 28(4): 52–66.

Chang, C. Y. and You, B. L. (2002) *Made by Taiwan: Booming in Information Technology Era*, Taipei: Times (Next Series).

Chou, W. C. G (2000) 'Changing employment relations in the global economy: case studies of Taiwan textile industries', Unpublished PhD thesis, Bristol University.

Chou, W. C. G. (2002) 'Transformation of industrial authority and paternalistic capitalism in the global economy: case studies of Taiwan's textiles industries', *International Journal of Human Resource Management* 13(3): 550–568.

Chung, C. N. (2001) 'Markets, culture and institutions: the emergence of large business groups in Taiwan, 1950s-1970s',*Journal of Management Studies* 38(5): 719–45.

Deyo, F. (1989) *Beneath the Miracle: Labour Subordination in the New Asian Industrialism*, Berkeley, CA: University of California Press.

Fukuyama, F. (1995) *Trust: The Social Virtues and the Creation of Prosperity*, New York: Free Press.

Galenson, W. (1979) 'The labour force, wages and living standards', in W. Galenson (ed.), *Economic Growth and Structural Change in Taiwan*, Ithaca, NY: Cornell University Press.

Gold, T. B. (1986) *State and Society in the Taiwan Miracle*, New York: Sharpe.

Hall, S. (1996) 'The global, the local, and the return of ethnicity', in Charles Lemert (ed.), *Social Theory: The Multicultural and Classical Readings*, Oxford: Westview Press, pp. 626–33.

Hofstede, G. (1991) *Culture and Organizations: Software of the Mind*, London: McGraw-Hill.

Hsiung, P. C. (1996) *Living Rooms as Factories: Class, Gender and the Satellite Factory System in Taiwan*, Philadelphia: Temple University Press.

Investment Commission (1997) *Statistics on Overseas Chinese & Foreign Investment, Technical Cooperation, Outward Technical Cooperation, Indirect Mainland Investment, Guide of Mainland Industry Technology*, Taipei: Ministry of Economics.

Ku, C. H. (1999) 'Confucian culture and economic ethnic', in *Social Theory and Practice*, Taipei: Yun-Chen (in Chinese).

Lee, C. (1991) *The Ugly Face of Taiwanese People – Self Reflectivity*, Taipei: Qian-Wei.

Lee, C. R. (1996) 'Impacts of organizational culture on management performance – a comparative analysis of Chinese, Japanese, and American management',*Chinese Journal of Administration* 59: 63–100.

Lui, T. L. and Chiu, T. M. Y. (1999) 'Global restructuring and non-standard work in newly industrial economies: the organization of flexible production in Hong Kong and Taiwan', in A. Felstead and N. Jewson (eds), *Global Trends in Flexible Labour*, London: Macmillan, pp. 166–80.

Ranis, G. (1979) 'Industrial development', in W. Galenson (ed.), *Economic Growth and Structural Change in Taiwan*, Ithaca: Cornell University Press.

Redding, G. (1990) *The Spirit of Chinese Capitalism*, Berlin: Walter de Gruyter.

Robertson, R. (1992) *Globalization: Social Theory and Global Culture*, London: Sage.

Robertson, R. (1995) 'Glocalization: time–space and homogeneity–heterogeneity', in M. Featherstone *et al.* (eds), *Global Modernities*, London: Sage.

Shieh, G. S. (1992) *"Boss" Island: The Subcontracting Network and Micro-Entrepreneurship in Taiwan's Development*, New York: Peter Lang.

Statistics Department (2002) *Economic Indicators*, Taipei: Ministry of Economic Affairs. Available online at: <http:////www.moea.gov.tw//~meco//stat//four//english//english4.htm> (accessed 15 May 2002).

Taiwan Labour Front (2001) *New State-Owned Policy – A Critique of Taiwan's Privatization*, Taipei: Business Week Publishers.

Trompenaars, F. and Hampden-Turner, C. (1998) *Riding the Waves of Culture: Understanding Cultural Diversity in Global Business*, Taiwan: McGraw-Hill International Enterprises (trans. into Chinese by S. P. Yuan).

Wang, H. R. (2001) 'Familialism or enterprise? The conflict between social value and market principle', in W. N. Chang (ed.), *The Enterprise Structure in Taiwan and Competitiveness*, Taipei: Lian-Jing, pp. 297–312 (in Chinese).

Wu, W. Y. (1994) 'Corporate culture in Taiwanese, American and Japanese companies and their management style', *Journal of National Cheng Kung University* 29(Hum. & Soc. Section): 63–90.

Wu, W. Y. and Chen, S. H. (1999) 'Corporate culture, organizational structures, and management styles for Taiwanese, American, and Japanese firms: an empirical investigation in Taiwan',*Journal of Industrial Management* 1(1): 135–64.

Yearbook of Labour Statistics (2001) Taipei: Council of Labour Affairs.

Yearbook of SMEs (1997) Taipei: Department of SMEs, Ministry of Economics.

Yen, C. F. (1996) 'Culture and structure in Taiwanese family enterprise – dual system approach', *Chung Yuan Journal* 24(4): 1–9.

Zhai, B. R. (1999) *Social Theory and Comparative Culture*, Taipei: Hong-Ye (in Chinese).

13 Culture and management in Thailand

Vinita Atmiyanandana and John J. Lawler

Introduction

The Thai economy has, over the past two decades, ridden the proverbial roller-coaster. Driven by a huge influx of foreign direct investment, economic growth reached double-digit levels in the first part of the 1990s, achieving for a time what was purportedly the highest growth rate in the world. A string of bad business decisions and excessive foreign indebtedness brought about the collapse of the economy in 1997, with Thailand being the first 'domino' to fall in the Asian financial crisis. Economic stagnation in the aftermath of 1997 had, by mid-2002, given rise to a more robust recovery and signs of optimism in the business community. Though many factors combined to move the Thai economy in these many directions, managerial practices have played a leading role, both for better and worse.

Contemporary management in Thailand has its roots in several places. As with most of the rest of South-East Asia, the entrepreneurial community is largely Chinese and thus the conventional approaches of traditional Chinese family enterprises are widespread.[1] In addition, Thailand has a large number of state-owned enterprises (SOEs), which have operated in a more bureaucratic manner. And foreign multinational corporations (MNCs) have played a major role in shaping managerial practices in Thailand, particularly in more recent times.

It is important to recognize that in Thailand business is interconnected with other important social institutions in ways that are much closer and more difficult to disentangle than what we like to think is normally the case in industrialized Western societies. Business, government, the judiciary, the military and many aspects of social life are all linked through a complex network of social connections and relations, a process virtually identical to what the Chinese term *guanxi*. Of course, this is the case in much of the rest of the region, where the rule of man typically trumps the rule of law. Much of the current debate in Thailand regarding both managerial and political reform involves a clash between forces favouring what is in effect the Westernization of the political and economic systems (including corporate governance and business management) and those favouring retaining essential 'Asian values'. Thus culture and cultural change, also major themes of this volume, are significant in understanding management practices in Thailand.

Historical setting

History and politics

Thailand, which had been called Siam until 1939, literally means 'the land of the free', reflecting in part that it was the only South-East Asian country to have escaped colonization by a European power. The Thai people had their original home in the south-eastern provinces of China. Their kingdom, Nan Chao, was founded in the early seventh century AD. Continually invaded by their Chinese neighbours, the Thais moved southwards and established the kingdom of Sukhothai in the thirteenth century AD (SarDesai 1997). The capital eventually moved closer to the coast, to Ayuthaya (near modern-day Bangkok), where control of the diverse Thai principalities was consolidated and a unified country emerged. Ayuthaya was sacked and destroyed by archrival Burma in the late eighteenth century, leading ultimately to the establishment of a new (Chakri) dynasty and capital in Bangkok.

Thai kings seem to be most revered for their benevolence and duty to the country, rather than as conquerors or autocrats, which perhaps has influenced contemporary Thai managers. The most beloved of Thai kings have generally been depicted as strong, but paternalistic, leaders. Thus it is said that King Ramkamhaeng of the Sukhothai period, who developed the Thai alphabet and is viewed as one of the greatest of all kings, was readily available to people of all ranks, even to the extent of having a bell at the entrance to his palace that any subject could use to summon the king for urgent consultations at any time (Jumsai 2000), truly an 'open-door' policy.

The 1932 revolution ended the absolute monarchy and resulted in the establishment of a constitutional monarchy. The post-revolutionary period saw a number of military coups and dictatorships for the next forty years. However, the rapid growth in the economy, which began in the 1980s, generated a large middle class that has been a strong force for democracy. Thailand has evolved into a vital, if not always perfect, democracy during the 1990s (Phongpaichit and Baker 1995). Although political corruption is an ongoing problem, two governments led by Prime Minister Chuan Leekpai have been given high marks for efforts at economic and political reform, especially in the aftermath of the 1997 Asian financial crisis (El Kahal 2001). Prime Minister Chuan was succeeded by Thaksin Shinawat in 2001, who, while more successful in addressing economic problems, is widely seen as autocratic and not an enthusiastic supporter of democracy.

Creating an open, transparent and accountable governmental system remains a great challenge. The mechanisms of democracy are in place, though the system has often been subverted to promote the personal enrichment of political leaders. There is an important connection between politicians and the business community that has fuelled corruption. The economic collapse in 1997 was certainly promoted by these relationships. Huge amounts of money totally disappeared from banks and financial institutions after the collapse, much of it apparently ushered out of the country to secure bank accounts. Yet the new middle class in Thailand, largely a product of the more successful and legitimate side of Thai business, has been increasingly impatient with corrupt practices and represent a force for change. Of course, an unknown quantity in all of this is the military. There is a history of varied ideologies and competing factions within the military (Phongpaichit and Baker 1995). Fundamentally nationalist, the military sees as its duty the protection of the common good. Thus excessive corruption on the part of civilian politicians has often served as a basis (or pretext) for coups. But a popular uprising against the last coup in 1992 has had a sobering effect on the military, which has so far shied away from political involvement since then.

Population and demographics

Thailand, located at the centre of South-East Asia and with a land area about the size of the American state of Texas, had an estimated population of about 62 million in 2001. Its ethnic composition is somewhat diverse, though at least 75 per cent of the population is ethnically Thai.[2] About 95 per cent of the Thai population is Buddhist, with the Theravada school being dominant. About 4 per cent of the population is Moslem and most of these people, who are mainly ethnic Malays, live in the southern provinces bordering Malaysia. The Moslem population generally feels marginalized and there has been a long-standing insurgent movement in these provinces. There are also many mountain tribe groups, but most live fairly primitively in remote areas of the famous 'Golden Triangle' in northern Thailand. They are semi-nomadic and not well integrated into Thai society. Thailand is a central player in the Association of South-East Asian Nations (ASEAN) and maintains generally good relations with its neighbours, apart from occasional border clashes with Myanmar (Burma).

Ethnic Chinese constitute the most significant minority group in Thailand, making up about 15 per cent of the population. The Chinese play a critical role in the Thai economy, one that far exceeds their numbers. Most private sector companies were started by Chinese families and continue to be controlled by these families, even those companies that are now publicly traded. There was large-scale Chinese immigration during the nineteenth century. Generally drawn to urban areas initially as skilled artisans and workers, the Chinese soon began establishing businesses and largely created the Thai private sector economy (Phongpaichit and Baker 1995).

Over time, the Chinese have become highly assimilated in Thailand and relations between the two communities are generally absent the hostility common in Malaysia and Indonesia. In fact, Bangkok is sometimes said to be a 'Chinese city in disguise'. Once excluded from government and the military, Thai–Chinese now occupy important positions in these sectors. Yet the Thai–Chinese are also very much linked to the *Nanyang* globally and leading Thai–Chinese families are a part of the 'bamboo network' that connects entrepreneurial overseas Chinese throughout the region (see Chapters 3, 10 and 12). The Thai–Chinese also often maintain links to China (see Chapter 2), through family and other relationships that facilitate business activities.

Economic background

Thailand's economic success has been largely driven by an export-oriented economic development policy. The economy has moved away from a fairly heavily agrarian orientation in the 1970s to its current industrial base. However, around 70 per cent of the population still lives in rural areas, although the distribution of income heavily favours the urban population. In general, Thailand was able to achieve high rates of economic growth and low rates of inflation, at least up until the Asian economic crisis of 1997. A major triumph of Thai policy has been in the area of population control, with the annual population growth rate declining from over 4 per cent in the early 1970s to only about 1 per cent by the late 1990s (*Thailand in Figures* 1997). However, Thailand has also had to deal with a major health problems in the form of the AIDS epidemic. It is estimated that about 2 per cent of the population are infected with HIV, giving it one of the highest infection rates outside of sub-Saharan Africa. The spread of AIDS was once seen as a major threat to the country's continued economic progress. However, aggressive governmental and private initiatives have been highly successful in containing the spread of the disease and Thai anti-AIDS policies are considered a model for other heavily afflicted developing countries.

During Thailand's period of rapid growth prior to 1997, its relatively low wages afforded it considerable competitive advantage, especially in labour-intensive industries with low skill requirements. Despite a fairly strong higher education system, Thailand has unfortunately not invested as heavily in primary and secondary education as it should and it lags behind many other countries in the region in this respect. Until quite recently, mandatory education ended at the seventh grade. Thus, although the country has a high literacy rate (around 95 per cent), the general population has relatively low levels of educational attainment, with perhaps less than one-third of all Thais finishing high school. This has hurt Thailand in its efforts to move beyond an economy based on labour-intensive, low-value-added industries. There are chronic shortages not only of managers and professionals, but also of skilled workers capable of operating complex machinery and holding front-line supervisory positions.

The Asian financial crisis of 1997 brought about massive unemployment and economic decline, necessitating that Thailand secure billions of dollars in loans from the IMF. Thailand's real growth rate plummeted between 1996 and 1998. In the mid-1990s, the unemployment rate was around 2.8 per cent (*Thailand in Figures* 1997), but after the 1997 crisis, the rate increased to around 7 per cent (this probably understates the true impact, as large numbers of unemployed people withdrew from the labour force and returned to their villages). The effects of the crisis had begun to abate by early 2000 and the economy began to grow at a modest rate.[3] The government of Prime Minister Chuan Leekpai was generally applauded for successes in several areas, including pursuing prudent fiscal and monetary policies, managing the balance of trade and balance of payments, initiating reforms in the financial sector, privatizing state enterprises, and expanding the social safety net (El Kahal 2001). However, unemployment remained high as companies restructured and 'downsized'. This led to a decline in Prime Minister Chuan's popularity and the defeat of his party in the 2001 elections.

More recently, the global recession that started in 2001 and was exacerbated by the September 11 bombings in the USA clearly hampered economic recovery, though Thailand experienced at least positive economic growth (though well beyond the stellar levels of a decade earlier). As noted, by the early part of 2002, there was generally greater optimism among investors and the index for the long-dormant Stock Exchange of Thailand (SET) grew nearly 40 per cent in the first half of 2002. Yet Thailand confronts continuing competitive challenges – especially in the emergence of China as a dominant economic force in the region – that will undoubtedly hamper efforts to regain pre-1997 levels of growth. Much of the foreign direct investment that once poured into Thailand has moved to China, with its generally lower production costs, huge market and often superior human resource base. Thailand's major concern will need to be improving its over-taxed infrastructure and upgrading the skills and competencies of its workforce. Thailand can no longer expect to compete on the basis of favourable labour costs, as Thai wages significantly exceed those of China and emerging economies such as Vietnam and India. Long-term competitiveness will require movement towards higher value-added and more capital-intensive production technologies. But that will require significantly increasing the education level of its workers, which is low by regional standards. Companies will also need to devote greater resources to training and development, something that indigenous companies have not always been willing to do.

Societal culture

Understanding Thai culture is critical to understanding Thai management. Apropos of a country located in Indochina, its culture is strongly influenced by both those of China and India (see Chapters 2 and 4). The Thai language is tonal and grammatically similar to Chinese. However, much of its vocabulary is drawn from Sanskrit. Buddhism is a central feature of Thai life, though some Thais still pay homage to certain Hindu deities. Buddhism spread to Thailand through Sri Lanka directly from India, and thus is different in fundamental ways from the Mahayana Buddhism of China, Korea, Japan and even nearby Vietnam.

Within Hofstede's (1980) well-known system for classifying national cultures, Thailand, as with the rest of the region, scores high on the collectivist and power distance dimensions, what Triandis (1995) would term 'vertical-collectivist' culture: one that is characterized by deference to authority and a strong sense of group cohesiveness. Yet in truth, Thai culture is much more nuanced–there may be a strong tendency towards collectivism and hierarchy, but the extent to which such values are exhibited depends much on context. As with the Japanese (see Chapter 6), there would seem to be a strong sense of national identity, of 'Thai-ness', that binds people together.

The role of religion

In understanding Thai culture, we need to look first at the central role that Theravada Buddhism plays in Thai society. Almost all major life events in Thailand are somehow connected to Buddhism and many of the country's national holidays are Buddhist holy days. Indeed, the highest authority in Thai society is the sangha (Buddhist clergy and hierarchy) and even the king must pay homage to the lowliest monk. Most Thai males spend at least a short period in the monkhood. Theravada Buddhism is the religion not only of ethnic Thais, but also of most of the assimilated Chinese, who play a dominant role in business. The Theravada school differs in several important ways from the Mahayana school common to Chinese communities outside South-East Asia. In addition, neither Confucianism nor Taoism are so important in the Thai–Chinese community, especially among the most highly assimilated Chinese.

Theravada and Mahayana Buddhism share a common belief in the 'Four Noble Truths' of Buddha and certain other basic tenets. However, there are some important outward differences between the two schools, as well as fundamental philosophical differences. Theravada Buddhism traces its origins to the original teachings of Buddhism, whereas Mahayana Buddhism, which also developed in India, emerged from a reform movement several hundred years after Buddha's death. Theravada Buddhism stresses spiritual enlightenment through largely individual meditation and reflection (Trainor 2001). Consequently, Thais (along with Burmese, Laotians and Cambodians) generally believe that the only path to enlightenment and nirvana is detachment from worldly affairs and an ascetic lifestyle. Thus, it would be difficult, though perhaps not impossible, for anyone besides a monk to achieve enlightenment (though many Thais in old age will pursue more detached and even ascetic lives). Even so, Buddhists believe that karma (the sum of both good and bad deeds one achieves during life) helps determine one's next life and most Thais seem concerned mainly with achieving a good 'next life' rather than the blissful state of nirvana. The sangha is the dominant force in the Theravada school, interpreting and preserving dogma. Theravada Buddhists believe that people can achieve a state of enlightenment *arahant*, but not Buddhahood. In contrast, Mahayana Buddhism places more emphasis on good works in daily life, not just meditation and asceticism, as a means of achieving enlightenment. In addition, the Mahayana believe that everyone, not just monks or ascetics, has the potential to reach spiritual enlightenment and indeed a state of Buddhahood (Blum 2001). The Mahayana see asceticism, especially among monks, as self-centred and ignoring the needs of the larger community.

The predominance of Theravada Buddhism seemingly impacts important aspects of Thai culture. Enlightenment is not viewed as achievable through secular pursuits; it may lessen materialism. Indeed, those who have been especially successful are often depicted in their later years as contemplative and more detached from worldly affairs. The centrality of Buddhism means that values associated with acquiring positive karma (merit), such as kindness towards others, particularly the less fortunate, has a strong influence on managerial behaviour: the ideal Thai leader is seen as more of a benevolent father than an autocrat. However, the strong belief in karma also affects the social order. A class system is quite evident in Thai society and is rooted to a considerable extent in religious belief. However, the notion of class and hierarchy is different than was traditionally so in Europe, where class lines were often immutable. And though karma plays a role in Thai class differences, this system bears no relationship to the rigidities of the Hindu caste system, which is similarly based on karma (see Chapter 4).

Collectivism and hierarchy

There are plenty of examples of both collectivist and hierarchical cultural practices in Thai society (Komin 1990; Holmes and Tangtongtavy 1995). As a predominantly collectivist culture, social connections and networks are a central feature of Thai life. Networks and connections function in a manner quite similar to the Chinese notion of *guanxi*[4] (Tsui *et al.* 2000). Thus success in business and employment often depends on *mee sen* (literally 'to have strings'). Family is central in Thai society and the members of one's extended family define the most significant social network. Connections also evolve in ways similar to Chinese and other East Asian cultures as in *guanxi* (see Chapter 2): one's bloodline, attending the same school or university, coming from the same geographic area or village, being part of the same political movement, interacting at work, or just being friends. Ritualistic behaviour, such as entertaining others and gift giving, serves to reinforce personal connections. Behaviour within social networks tends to be quite particularistic. Thus one has special obligations to those to whom one is most closely connected and it would be considered unethical to ignore such obligations. Consequently, favouritism and nepotism are not traditionally viewed negatively, though this may be changing among younger and more Westernized Thais.

An emphasis on the maintenance of harmonious relationships is another typically Asian aspect of Thai culture. One is expected to maintain calmness and a 'cool heart' (*jai yen*). One can express feelings, but not in a strongly emotional manner, at least in public. Loss of face is an important social sanction and means of maintaining social control. Thais are also very concerned about causing loss of face to others and will avoid exchanges that create the potential for loss of face. Thus direct confrontations, criticisms of others and explicitly denying requests are generally avoided. Telling someone 'no' is an art form that requires considerable use of non-verbal communication and careful inflections of the voice while avoiding literally saying 'no' (e.g. one may convey denial of request by saying 'yes' with little enthusiasm).

Thais tend to be quite fatalistic and rely on a panoply of techniques and methods to foretell the future, suggesting more of a sense of external than internal control. Fortune telling and related techniques are widely used. These methods can influence managerial decision making. For example, many of the high-rise buildings constructed during in recent years were designed in accordance with feng-shui principles and thus oriented at particular angles with respect to Bangkok's Chao Praya River. The collapse of the Bangkok real estate market at the time of the Asian financial crisis was blamed by some on a change in the course of the river, which was assumed to have disrupted 'energy flows' relative to these buildings. The use of 'face reading' techniques by managers to select employees or carry out business negotiations is apparently not uncommon.

Hierarchy and deference to authority are expressed symbolically and reinforced in many ways in Thai society. Traditions and practices associated with the royal family help to reinforce class distinctions. In addition, belief in karma as a determinant of one's social standing means Thais tend to believe that one's current status is related to the way one led one's prior lives. High status is a reward for a good prior existence, just as low status is a sanction for poorly led prior lives. Thus high status is seen as earned and deserving of respect; low-status individuals can hope to enhance their good karma and move on to a better next life through enduring their position in this life and leading good lives (including respecting their superiors). The Thai language contains numerous honorifics used to communicate status differentials in conversations. Ritualistic greetings, involving folded hands (known as a *wai*) and various degrees of bowing, symbolize relative status.

Although class and social background are important determinants of social position, many other factors can enter the picture. As with most Asian cultures, status increases with age and is also affected by gender (but not to nearly the same extent as in Japan and Korea, see Chapters 6 and 11).

Educational attainment is another important determinant of status. Being a graduate of a leading university, and the social networks opened to one as a consequence of this, provides considerable opportunity for mobility. The military is another means of social advancement, particularly if one attends one of the country's elite military academies. The social networks that develop within academy cohorts are extremely strong and can provide advantage throughout one's life, including a post-military business career.

In traditional Thai society, wealth per se did not play a central role in determining status and rank. High-status commoners of Thai ethnicity normally acquired status by serving the monarchy, either in the civil service or the military. The establishment of SOEs led to a managerial elite among ethnic Thais. Private enterprise, however, was traditionally the province of the ethnic Chinese and though many of these families grew wealthy, there were social barriers between the entrepreneurial Chinese and higher status ethnic Thais. The increasing assimilation of the Chinese community in Thailand and the opportunities for financial success with rapid economic growth broadened the appeal of working in the business sector. Thus success in business, and the wealth and power that can come from it, are now also important contributors to social standing.

There are a number of distinctive Thai cultural practices that need to be understood within the context of the collectivist and hierarchical nature of Thai society (Holmes and Tangtongtavy 1995; Siengthai and Vadhanasindhu 1991), some of which we have already mentioned (e.g. *mee sen, jai yen*). *Bunkhun* is the practice of reciprocity in social relationships. This can be seen as a factor that holds together the social hierarchy. It is not just the case that subordinates must be deferential and obedient to superiors. It is also the case that superiors must be kindly to and supportive of their subordinates. Thus an exchange relationship exists, in which the superior offers protection and support to the subordinate who, out of gratitude, engages in the actions and behaviours desired by the superior. So there is a flow of favours in both directions. Many of the cultural values of Thai society centre on kindliness and benevolence. Certainly the ideal leader is strong, but also beneficent and caring. And relationships between those of equal rank (or even different ranks) may involve acts of kindness and consideration for which nothing is expected in return. *Nam jai* refers to acts of spontaneous kindness (without the expectation of reciprocity) and *hen jai* (seeing and understanding the true nature of another). Another such value is *kreng jai*, which is difficult to translate and can have many manifestations, including consideration for others, humility, avoiding imposing on or troubling others, not embarrassing others, and avoiding going over the heads of others. An attitude of *krieng jai* can operate between equals and between superiors and subordinates and is dominant influence on Thai behaviour.

Though hierarchical, Thai society is not rigid. Thailand has often been characterized as a 'loose' rather than a 'tight' society, one in which social rules are not rigidly followed nor expected to be (in contrast to, say, Japan, see Chapter 6) (Triandis 1995). Indeed Phillips (1966), in one of the leading ethnographic studies of Thai culture, asserts that Thais are much more individualistic than is widely assumed – they engage in the rituals of a vertically collectivist society, but do so as matter of choice and are quite capable of pursuing a more independent life.[5]

Two other important Thai values suggest this trait. One is *sanuk* (literally 'fun'). Thai culture endorses the view that life is to incorporate copious amounts of fun and joy and not to be taken too seriously, even in the context of work. Another is captured by the expression *mai pen rai*, which is opposite to the expression *pen rai* (which literally means something matters). Thus, the term means something does not matter or is, in fact, all right. Again, this expression has complex nuances. It suggests that adverse outcomes will get better, so one should not worry about them. It is related to the fatalistic tendencies of Thai culture mentioned above, but is not to suggest an unwavering fatalism that gives rise to a lack of initiative and unwillingness to take action in the face of adversity. A better interpretation is that Thais accept adversity as a normal aspect of life and are not easily ruffled by it, a reflection of the concept of 'resignation' rooted in Buddhist thought, as well as proclivity to live in harmony with nature.

With economic development, Thailand has been subject to extensive external cultural influences, both from Asia (particularly Japan) and the West. Yet there is a strong force supporting the retention of core cultural values. Hoecklin and Payne (1995: 5) quotes one leading Thai executive, who, when queried as to the possibility of Thai values being displaced by an emerging global culture, responded:

> We are born with *kreng jai* and *bunkhun*. They are inside our heart. But inevitably in the future the cultures from the USA and Europe will come in and mix. But we are not afraid that we will lose our values. The majority of Thai managers – more than 95 per cent – are (and will remain) typically Thai.

Corporate culture

Although there are many corporate and organizational cultures and styles of management encountered in Thailand, there are some distinct forms that are quite frequently encountered. Lawler *et al.* (1989) proposed a typology of strategic types that differentiated firms based on ownership: family-owned enterprises, publicly traded corporations, subsidiaries of Western multinationals, and subsidiaries of Japanese multinationals (see Chapter 6). In the case of joint venture companies involving Thai and foreign partners, the management system typically reflected the style of the majority or dominant partner.

Foreign-controlled companies

Lawler *et al.* (1989) found Western subsidiaries placed great emphasis, as might be expected, on rational control as the dominant management philosophy, giving rise to standardization of procedures and managerial practices and a reliance on corps of professional managers. Most had relatively few expatriate managers, but the Thai managers normally had either studied in Europe, North America or Australia or had work experience in other Western multinationals. European subsidiaries relied more on localization of employment practices, with perhaps only one European working in the company (normally the managing director), someone who had often been in Thailand for many years and was often fluent in Thai. The American companies were more ethnocentric, endeavouring to utilize American-style management practices. Expatriates typically worked on shorter assignment cycles (usually around three years).

Japanese subsidiaries also tended to utilize HRM systems based on home-country practices (see Chapter 6). The dominant strategic focus in Japanese subsidiaries was acculturation: employees were hired mainly into entry-level positions, socialized into corporate values from the start, and promoted from within. So ideological identification with organizational values and organizational commitment were the principal means of securing and maintaining worker commitment. Japanese companies also tended to use large numbers of expatriates in management positions. As a consequence, opportunities for Thais to advance into higher level positions were quite limited (unless, perhaps, they spoke Japanese), a sore point with some workers. Lawler *et al.* (1989) observed that Japanese managers were often surprised that Thai workers would not be as committed to their jobs as Japanese workers. Thus values such as *sanuk* and *mai pen rai* were difficult for Japanese managers to understand or accept. Despite these problems, there were characteristics of Japanese companies that appealed to Thai workers. In contrast to the more systematic and rationalized management systems in subsidiaries of Western MNCs, Japanese subsidiaries relied much more on social networks and personal relationships for attracting and keeping employees. Thai workers were seen to be more familiar and comfortable with the collectivist orientation of Japanese managers. And Thai workers felt that their jobs were more secure in Japanese companies, despite generally lower pay than in subsidiaries of Western MNCs.

More recent research indicates that there may be some changes in the managerial approaches taken by foreign subsidiaries, at least those associated with American multinationals. Bae *et al.* (2002) stated that Thai subsidiaries of US-based multinationals are increasingly prone to utilize 'high involvement work system' techniques, involving greater employee discretion and less formalized control systems. Such changes are not observed in the case of subsidiaries of European-based multinationals, though have always been present to some extent in the Japanese subsidiaries.

Thai-controlled companies

As we have noted, Chinese immigrants to Thailand have been the country's entrepreneurial core and many companies in Thailand follow managerial approaches commonly encountered in Chinese family-owned enterprises throughout Asia. Defining characteristics of traditional Chinese enterprises include relatively small size, short life cycle, centralized control exercised by a family patriarch (or sometimes matriarch), paternalistic management, heavy reliance on family members in key management positions, limited use of formal and standardized management techniques (such as job evaluation, PERT analysis), the significance of personal relationships (i.e. *guanxi*) in both the internal and external aspects of management, and relatively short organizational life cycles (Chen 1995; R. Chan 2000).

Although rooted in Chinese traditions, the assimilation of Chinese entrepreneurial families into Thai society has meant that the leadership style is also strongly influenced by Thai values. Farh and Cheng (2000) observed that the paternalistic management style of Chinese-owned enterprises could be categorized into three distinct, but interrelated, forms: authoritarian leadership, benevolent leadership and moral (i.e. charismatic) leadership. The quintessential leader in Thai society would be one who is primarily benevolent, though utilizes authoritarian approaches as needed. Thais would generally not expect business owners, or even leaders in other types of institutions (except perhaps members of *sangha*), to be moralistic and self-sacrificing. The hierarchical nature of the society means that there are status differences and leaders are expected to be strong and also highly knowledgeable. Thai managers generally do not expect to be questioned by subordinates and owners are at the apex of the company and do not expect to be questioned by lower level managers. Thai values emphasize that subordinates should be diffident and reserved in the presence of superiors, much more than in Chinese society (Holmes and Tangtongtavy 1995). A leader who appeared to waiver by not acting as if he (or she) knew the answer to a problem (even if he did not) would be seen to be weak and lose face.

Thais' general deference to authority means that the actual exercise of control through sanctions and other authoritarian methods is generally not needed, so long as the leader acts in accordance with Thai values and expectations. We have already noted many of the central cultural values that are related to leader behaviour, such as reciprocity in hierarchical relationships (*bunkhun*), kindliness and empathy (*nam jai* and *hen jai*), and general consideration for others regardless of rank (*kreng jai*). All of these notions link well to the notion of the benevolent leader, a model we have noted is reflected in the popular image of Thailand's most beloved monarchs. The Thai penchant for fun and a relaxed lifestyle (*sanuk*) and taking life as it comes (*mai pen rai*) are other desirable leader qualities. Thus, a company head, especially in Thai-owned enterprises, is most effective when he (or she) acts as a loving parent, but one prepared to exercise authority at least in extreme circumstances.

Lawler *et al.* (1989) argued that the dominant controlling theme in family-owned enterprises was not really strategic action but rather a reliance on extant national culture as a means of keeping such organizations together and functioning. As we have noted, there is a general sense of 'Thai-ness', so that the *kohn Thai* (Thai people) as a whole are a relevant social group and workers, managers and owners all see themselves as part of this larger community. The organizational culture of the conventional family enterprise in Thailand is really Thai national culture adapted to the organizational setting.[6]

Not all family-owned enterprises remain small or medium-sized companies. Many have grown quite large and some are MNCs in their own right. Most larger scale Thai companies, however, started as smaller scale family-owned enterprises and are still controlled by the founding families (there are also many SOEs in Thailand and these are generally being privatized, so this is another way in which larger scale companies are established). As these organizations grow, they often spawn new companies, so that many of the larger Thai companies are really very much like conglomerates (Phongpaichit and Baker 1998). Different companies in the group may be headed by different family members, giving rise to a structure similar to the pre-war Japanese *zaibatsu* or Korean *chaebol* (see Chapters 6 and 11). With growth, there are limits to the number of family members available to hold key management positions. These companies may also need to raise capital externally, producing accountability demands. Thus what has been characterized as 'management by entourage' (Isarangkhun na Ayuthaya and Taira 1977) becomes less feasible. Managers from outside the family must be hired. Consequently, management in Thailand has become increasingly sophisticated in larger scale companies as the demand for professional managers has grown.

Managerial professionalization has been facilitated by the numerous MBA and other management programmes that have been established over the past decade. Most of these programmes are modelled after business programs in the USA and Europe. Several North American, European and Australian institutions have established residential programmes in Bangkok and many Thais travel abroad to earn business degrees. Traditionally, young ethnic Thais from upper and middle-class families pursued degrees in law, political science or public administration, with the intention of working for the government or an SOE. Now they are more inclined to pursue much more lucrative business careers. Thus there is a growing cadre of professional managers in Thailand. This includes not only ethnic Thais pursuing business degrees, but also the younger members of entrepreneurial Thai–Chinese families. Traditionally, Chinese business owners might have had their children pursue technical degrees (e.g. engineering) on the assumption that managing a firm was largely intuitive and a matter of having the right personal connections. Today they are more apt to see the value of professional management education (e.g. an MBA on top of a technical degree) for their children destined to enter the family business (particularly the larger and more globally active of these companies). These trends have generated the introduction of management techniques common to Western companies in larger scale indigenous Thai companies. However, this does not mean a wholesale abandonment of the more traditional style of leadership and management described above. It would seem that the social aspects of management in these companies – the reliance on networks, paternalistic leadership, a strong role for family members in the upper levels of management – still dominate. Professionalization of management has led to more changes in the technical aspects of middle and lower level management. In the longer term, as this new cadre of professional managers moves up organizational hierarchies, we may see greater changes reflected at the strategic level as well.

Lawler *et al.* (1989) characterized the strategic theme of larger scale and publicly traded Thai companies as one that integrates both rational control (via contemporary management techniques) and social control (through reliance on networks and Thai culture). Their view of a distinction between the fundamental characteristics of closely held family enterprises and larger scale firms is supported in research by Pyatt *et al.* (2001). They found three distinct 'architectures' in Chinese family-owned enterprises in both Hong Kong (see Chapter 3) and Thailand. The first of these is similar to the traditional family enterprise described above: smaller scale operations, extensive use of networking, extensive use of family members, etc. Two other forms, labelled 'international' and 'transnational' architectures, bear similarities to publicly traded companies. Both international and transnational family-owned or controlled enterprises rely on trust and interpersonal networks, but also utilize more sophisticated management techniques and, at least in the case of the transnational type, professional managers from outside the controlling family.

Managerial behaviour

As we have noted, networking and using personal connections are fundamental aspects of doing business in Thailand. Apart from the collectivist nature of Thai culture, this is promoted in Thailand, as in much of the rest of Asia, by a general absence of strong and reliable commercial law and publicly available business information. Business relationships are thus typically supported by the interpersonal trust fundamental to social networks, as opposed to the legalistic foundations of business practices in the USA and much of Western Europe. However, business transactions conducted through informal networks lack transparency and accountability to investors and other organizational stakeholders. Asian business networks, including those functioning in Thailand, are notoriously particularistic (Hamilton 1996) and often seen by Westerners as promoting 'crony capitalism'. Business transactions are often carried out because of the personal obligations that might exist between the individuals involved rather than the rational assessment of the merits of a project (Phongpaichit and Baker 1998). Many of the banks in Thailand and most of its principal investment houses had significant financial problems (or simply went under) after 1997 because huge loans and investment funds went to projects of dubious merit, but where the entrepreneurs seeking funds had connections. As Sheridan (1999: 180) observed:

> When a man applies for a loan, the first thing the proverbial Thai banker asks is: Do I know this person ... what connections do I have with him, what connections can I build with him? The first question is not: What is the creditworthiness of this load application, does it satisfy objective rules and criteria, is the business plan convincing?

Another important area is managerial decision making. As we have observed, Thai firms are strongly hierarchical. Leaders may be benevolent, but, in the main, tend to reserve most important decisions to themselves or, perhaps, a limited circle of senior managers and significant family members. Even the children of company owners sometimes complain about the auto-cratic nature of strategic decision making in family-owned or controlled enterprises. Hierarchy and patronage within Thai firms means that team-work is not easily accomplished (Holmes and Tangtongtavy 1995).

When the Thai economy blossomed in the late 1980s and early 1990s, such an approach to management was not especially problematic; Thailand was able to compete on low labour costs and enjoyed a huge influx of foreign investment. But today Thailand confronts a much different environ-ment. Globalization means that there are newer emerging economies, especially China (see Chapter 2), but also Vietnam (see Chapter 14) and other South-East Asian countries, that present great competitive challenges to Thailand. Thai companies can no longer prosper by competing simply on low labour costs, as the newer emerging economies can often undercut Thai producers. Top-level managers in Thai companies will need to depend more extensively on knowledge developed and acquired at lower levels within the firm – that is, to transform their firms into flexible and high-performance work systems. The hierarchical nature of Thai culture poses a significant impediment to this sort of organizational transformation.

Networks are important within Thai companies as well as in the external Thai business relationships (Lawler *et al.* 1989). Hiring, promotion and financial rewards are often linked to an individual's personal connections. This occurs not only at the higher echelons, but also in the case of lower level jobs. Factory workers use their connections to secure employment within a company for friends, relatives or those who come from their home villages. The house servants of a factory owner might use their influence to obtain jobs in the factory for friends or relatives. SOEs in Thailand often reserve jobs for the children of current employees. Western companies have difficulties with such explicit favouritism and nepotism. They may implement rules prohibiting such practices, but it is not clear how effective these are. When it comes to serving the needs of those to whom they have obligations, Thais can be very creative.

There are reports of Asian-owned companies being extremely abusive of their workers, whether the companies are indigenous or foreign. Chan (2000) observed this in the case of China, where working conditions in such companies can often be exploitive and even abusive (in both Chinese-owned companies and those owned by other Asian-based companies). There are certainly instances of abusive management in Thailand, but these are more infrequent and often involve smaller firms at the margins of an industry. There are reports in the Thai press periodically of the police raiding establishments where workers (often young people who have recently migrated to the Bangkok) have been kept as virtual slaves. Several years ago, it was discovered, after many workers fell ill, that their employer was spiking their drinking water with amphetamines (i.e. 'speed') in the failed hope of improving productivity. In the main, however, Thai workers tend to be relatively independent when it comes to work relationships. Collectivism expresses itself in loyalty to family or friends, but not particularly extensive commitment to a single company. Indeed, companies often experience high turnover rates, so a major problem has often been to attract and retain industrial workers, many of whom are quite happy to return to their villages if they confront oppressive or uncomfortable working conditions (though voluntary turnover has seemingly declined in the post-1997 period). It is difficult to recruit Thai workers for the least attractive jobs, so large numbers of often-illegal foreign workers (most often from neighbouring Burma) typically fill these positions. While labour inspectors might be paid off in some circumstances, widespread abuse would certainly attract the attention of Thailand's fiercely independent press. Finally, as we have discussed at length, the conventional leadership style of Thai and Thai–Chinese managers favours a marriage of authority and benevolence, rather than just strictly authoritarian leadership. A Thai employer or manager who did not act in this manner would soon lose the respect and loyalty of his (or her) employees (who would likely seek employment elsewhere).

A very significant exception to this general rule would have to be the Kader Toy Company fire in 1983, which killed 188 of the company's workers (Phongphaichit and Baker 1998). Many of the workers were killed because fire exits had been locked to prevent workers from leaving the plant during work hours, so escape routes were blocked. Thais would note that Kader was a Hong-Kong-based company, but dangerous working conditions are not uncommon in Thai-owned companies as well. Phongphaichit and Baker (1998) observe that industrial accident rates jumped significantly throughout the 1990s. This was likely due in large part to high growth rates and the inability of regulatory agencies to keep pace with economic expansion. Of course, there are frequent instances of bribery of labour inspectors. Moreover, the fatalistic nature of Thais perhaps limits appropriate concern with health and safety matters – if it is one's time to go, then there is little that can be done.

Labour–management conflict resolution

Employment practices in Thai-owned firms range from the rather ad hoc to the very systematic and sophisticated (Lawler *et al.* 1998). The former situation is common in more traditional family-owned enterprises, where pay and employment opportunities may be linked largely to ascriptive factors, such as gender and age. Isarangkhun na Ayuthaya and Taira (1977) observed the predominance of such practices in an early study of employment practices in Thailand and these seemingly continue in many Thai-owned companies (Lawler *et al.* 1989). Training is often quite limited, particularly for lower level workers. Also formal performance evaluations are not so common, in part because this presents the opportunity for loss of face and disharmony. Since hiring often takes place through social networks, there is little screening and evaluation of employees according to established and validated criteria. More sophisticated policies tend to be found in larger companies, though HRM approaches are quite mixed. While Chainuvati and Granrose (2001) found that Thai firms often lacked sophisticated career planning systems, Dubey-Villinger (2001) found that service sector companies (particularly in the hotel and tourism sector) were placing increasing emphasis on training and development, in large part because the government was attaching much more importance to such activities.

An important issue confronting Thai firms in the post-1997 era is how they will respond to globalization. Various types of high-performance work systems (HPWSs), in which firms create more flexible and responsive organizations through greater worker discretion and autonomy, have seemingly been quite successful in Western cultures. Asian cultures tend to be viewed as too hierarchical to allow for the successful implementation of these techniques. Yet Bae and Lawler (2000) found that firms in Korea that utilized HPWS practices had higher performance levels than firms that utilized more conventional Korean management techniques. A case study by Lawler and Atmiyanandana (2001) in Thailand found that an American company in the agribusiness sector was, in fact, quite successful in implementing certain features of HPWSs, even with relatively low- level and poorly educated workers.

Conflict resolution in Thailand is generally quite informal. There is a labour movement, but it is very weak in the private sector (the only appreciable concentration of union members is in the SOEs) (Lawler and Suttawet 2000). Even when formal mechanisms exist for a worker to bring a grievance (either through a union contract or a company procedure), the tendency of Thai workers is to avoid direct conflict and the potential for loss of face (both to the employee and the supervisor). Informal channels of communication are much more suited to the Thai style. Thus intermediaries often act as a means of expressing dissatisfaction to a superior. However, the intermediary must be trusted and respected, perhaps someone who has been in the organization for a long time (an 'old hand'). Such a person can informally convey an employee's concerns to a supervisor in a non-threatening manner and without the potential for either party to experience loss of face. If superiors do not act on such informal requests, then Thai workers might resort to other means of making their point. One such stratagem might be a 'gossiping' campaign. Again, this is non-confrontational, but can be embarrassing to a supervisor, so represents an escalation in the level of conflict (since the supervisor might lose face through such an action). At the extreme, should widespread grievances not be addressed, Thai workers are perfectly capable of some form of more formal concerted action, including forming unions and conducting strikes. Such actions seem, however, to be more common in foreign companies where more informal mechanisms are not so likely to work. One example of this is the protracted strike against American-based Seagate Technologies relating to health and safety issues. The plant of one Japanese company was burned by its workers when it cancelled payment of an annual bonus. Industrial conflict is quite possible, it is just that the threshold necessary to trigger worker action is much greater than in most Western cultures.

Implications for managers

We have explored significant aspects of management in Thailand, observing the many ways in which it is rooted in Thai culture and religious practice. Although these forces are often similar to those in other parts of Asia, there are clearly unique features that serve to differentiate Thailand from its neighbours. Thais share in common with most other East and South-East Asian societies strong collectivist and hierarchical tendencies. However, the Thai focus would most often be on the family or community, not the business organization. Thus Thais are not likely to exhibit the sort of commitment to their employers traditionally seen in Japan or Korea and are more like the Chinese in this respect. But in contrast to East Asian cultures, Thais often note there is a 'softness' to their culture that mandates benevolence and caring on the part of employers towards their subordinates. Thus the harsh side of management that can be observed in Asian companies (i.e. R. Chan 2000) is much less apt to be seen in Thailand. Effective management in Thailand must also recognize a more relaxed attitude towards work, and perhaps life in general, that is a part of Thai culture (i.e. *sanuk*).

Thailand shares much in common with other more traditional societies, including those of South-East Asia and many outside Asia. The important question here is how will increasing modernity impact Thailand and the manner in which its organizations are managed? As with many developing countries, there is a major split between urban and rural areas, with urban dwellers, particularly in Bangkok, exhibiting values and work orientations more like those found in highly advanced economies. However, at least from anecdotal evidence, the degree of urban cultural transition is much less than in places such as Taiwan, Singapore, Hong Kong and the most rapidly growing parts of China. As with other parts of South-East Asia, there is a concern with preserving traditional values in the face of immense economic and social change.

Conclusions

We should not, then, expect Thais to be rapid adopters of the core values that drive Western culture and business. This may be good for the Thai psyche, but could have important and possibly deleterious consequences in the case of Thai management. The issue of corporate governance comes most immediately to mind, particularly in light of the 1997 Asian financial crisis. The heavy use of personal connections, particularism in decision making and lack of transparency in business transactions mean that Thai organizations are likely to have continuing difficulty in functioning well in the global economy. Despite the adoption on the surface of many Western business practices, Thai managers will likely place greater weight on the implications of business decisions for the maintenance of social relationships than economic efficiency. This will make post-1997 international investors wary of committing funds to Thailand and generate difficulties in dealing with foreign, particularly Western, companies. Moreover, although Thai companies may do well in times of global economic expansion, they may well be apt to confront difficulty in responding to the next 1997 crisis because of the manner in which information is often distorted or ignored as a consequence of conventional management practices.

Notes

1   See Chapters 2, 3, 10 and 12 for comparisons.
2   This is somewhat less than the Han ethnic hegemony in China as a percentage.
3   Thai GDP growth was up about 4 per cent in 2002 over 2001.
4   *Guanxi* can mean 'relationships' where it has a positive connotation or 'back-door' entrée where less so.
5   Hofstede (1980: 222) scored Thais as low in individualism.
6   This may be analogous to the reference in the PRC to 'with Chinese characteristics'.

References

Bae, J. and Lawler, J. J. (2000) 'Organizational and HRM strategies in Korea: impact on firm performance in an emerging economy', *Academy of Management Journal* 43(3): 502–517.

Bae, J., Chen, S. J., Wan, D., Lawler, J. J. and Walumbwa, F. (2002) 'Human resource strategy and firm performance in Pacific Rim countries', Working Paper, Institute of Labor and Industrial Relations, University of Illinois.

Blum, M. L. (2001) 'Mahayana Buddhism', in K. Trainor (ed.), *Buddhism*, Oxford: Oxford University Press.

Chainuvati, V. and Granrose, C. S. (2001) 'Career planning and development of managers in Thailand', in J. B. Kidd, X. Li and F. J. Richter (eds), *Advances in human resource management in Asia*, London: Palgrave.

Chan, A. (2000) 'Chinese trade unions and workplace relations: state-owned and joint-venture enterprises', in M. Warner (ed.), *Changing workplace relations in the Chinese economy*, London: Macmillan.

Chan, R. (2000) 'Overseas Chinese management styles', in J. T. Li, A. S. Tsui and E. Weldon (eds), *Management and organizations in the Chinese context*, London: Macmillan.

Chen, M. (1995) *Asian management systems: Chinese, Japanese, and Korean styles of business*, London: International Thomson Business Press.

Dubey-Villinger, N. (2001) 'Thai business culture: hierarchy and groups, initiative and motivation', in J. B. Kidd, X. Li and F. J. Richter (eds), *Advances in human resource management in Asia*, London: Palgrave.

El Kahal, S. (2001) *Business in Asia-Pacific*, Oxford: Oxford University Press.

Farh, J. L. and Cheng, B. S. (2000) 'A cultural analysis of paternalistic leadership in Chinese organizations', in J. T. Li, A. S. Tsui and E. Weldon (eds), *Management and organizations in the Chinese context*, London: Macmillan.

Hamilton, G. (1996) *Asian business networks*, Berlin and New York: Walter de Gruyter.

Hoecklin, L. A. and Payne, M. (eds) (1995) *Managing cultural differences: strategies for competitive advantage*, New York: Addison Wesley.

Hofstede, G. (1980) *Culture's consequences: international differences in work-related values*, Beverly Hills, CA: Sage.

Holmes, H. and Tangtongtavy, S. (with Tomizawa, R.) (1995) *Working with the Thais: a guide to managing in Thailand*, Bangkok: White Lotus.

Isarangkhun na Ayuthaya, C. and Taira, K. (1977) 'The organization and behaviour of the factory work force in Thailand', *The Developing Economies* 13(1): 16–36.

Jumsai, M. (2000) *Popular history of Thailand*, Bangkok: Chalermnit.

Komin, S. (1990) *Psychology of the Thai people: values and behavioral patterns*, Bangkok: National Institute of Development Administration (NIDA).

Lawler, J. J. and Atmiyanandana, V. (2001) *Case study: Cargill Sun Valley (Thailand)*, Champaign, IL: Gender in Agribusiness Project, University of Illinois.

Lawler, J. J. and Suttawet, C. (2000) 'Globalization, and deregulation in Thailand', in C. Rowley and J. Benson (eds), *Globalization and labour in the Asia-Pacific region*, London: Frank Cass.

Lawler, J. J., Zaidi, M. and Atmiyanandana, V. (1989) 'Human resource strategies in Southeast Asia: the case of Thailand', in K. Rowland and G. Ferris (eds), *International human resource management*, Greenwich, CT: JAI Press.

Lawler, J. J., Siengthai, S. and Atmiyanandana, V. (1998) 'HRM in Thailand: eroding traditions', in C. Rowley (ed.), *Human resource management in the Asia-Pacific region* London: Frank Cass.

Phillips, H. (1966) *The Thai peasant personality*, Berkeley, CA: University of California Press.

Phongpaichit, P. and Baker, C. (1995) *Thailand: economy and politics*, Oxford: Oxford University Press.

Phongpaichit, P. and Baker, C. (1998) *Thailand's boom and bust*, Bangkok: Silkworm Books.

Pyat, R., Ashkanasy, N., Tamaschke, R. and Grigg, T. (2001) 'Transitions and traditions in Chinese family businesses: evidence from Hong Kong and Thailand', in J. B. Kidd, X. Li and F. J. Richter (eds), *Advances in human resource management in Asia*, New York: Palgrave.

SarDesai, D. R. (1997) *Southeast Asia: Past and present*, 4th edition. Boulder, CO: Westview Press.

Sheridan, G. (1999) *Asian values, Western dreams: understanding the new Asia*, Crows Nest, NSW: Allen & Unwin.

Siengthai, S. and Vadhanasindhu, P. (1991) 'Management in a Buddhist society', in J. M. Putti (ed.), *Management: Asian context*, Singapore, McGraw-Hill.

Thailand in Figures (Fourth Edition) (1997) Bangkok: Alpha Research.

Trainor, Kevin (2001) 'Theravada Buddhism', in K. Trainor (ed.), *Buddhism*, Oxford: Oxford University Press.

Triandis, H. (1995) *Individualism and collectivism*, Boulder, CO: Westview Press.

Tsui, A. S., Farh, J. L. and Xin, K. R. (2000) 'Guanxi in the Chinese context', in J. T. Li, A. S. Tsui and E. Weldon (eds), *Management and organizations in the Chinese context*, London: Macmillan.

14 Culture and management in Vietnam

Ying Zhu

Introduction

Management and culture are inseparable elements regarding business operation and production at enterprise level and economic development at societal level. Cultural foundations have a profound influence on the formation of certain types of management strategies and practices. Without a better understanding of the cultural roots of a particular society, management would exist in an artificial abstract pattern which cannot be implemented and studied effectively because management is dealing with people who are cultural carriers.

East Asian development has been explained in culturalist terms which argue that cultural factors determined the successful outcome of economic development in this region (Redding 1995). However, we believe that three interrelated issues may work here: (1) cultural factors are influential on the formation of a certain management pattern and related mind-set, e.g. Confucianism is crucial for many elements in East Asian management concepts and practices, and Vietnam is part of that; (2) culture is not isolated and unchangeable, but constantly involved in exchange, modification, and transformation; and (3) social norms including political, economic, and historical factors also influence managerial thinking and reshape the outcome of managerial approaches and practices.

This chapter tackles these issues by using the example of Vietnam, a hybrid economy in the stage of transition. In this chapter, social, political, economic, and historical backgrounds are reviewed before the illustration of management and culture in Vietnamese enterprises. The chapter is concluded by highlighting the unique characteristics of a hybrid and transitional paradigm of management in Vietnam and the implications for business operation from an empirical point of view as well as management thinking from a theoretical point of view.

Historical setting

Vietnam was divided into North and South after World War II until unification in 1975. For many years, Vietnam has been the focal point of the struggle for and against colonialism, of the ideological war between capitalism and socialism, and, more recently, of the conflict between different approaches to economic reforms (Beresford 1989).

In Vietnam certain cultural and socio-economic differences between North and South pre-dated the formal separation of the two regions in 1954 (Beresford 1989). However, a socialist central planning system based on the neo-Stalinist doctrine dominated the country from 1954 in the North and since 1975 in the South. The development of heavy industry was the state's first economic priority. State-owned enterprises (SOEs) and collective-owned enterprises (COEs) were the only sectors permitted to operate in this economic system. Their activities were heavily subsidized and all prices were fixed by the state.

SOEs were a crucial element of the socialist economy because it was these enterprises which manufactured the bulk of Vietnam's products and controlled most of its important industries. They also employed a large number of semi-skilled and skilled workers and capital investment as well as making an important contribution to the state's revenue and sharing in a large proportion of its expenditure.

Vietnam started taking its first steps towards economic reform in 1986, marked by the Sixth National Congress of the Vietnamese Communist Party resolution of *doi moi*, namely economic renovation (Perkins 1993; Ljunggren 1993). Under the *doi moi* policy, the government wanted to promote economic development by introducing a market-oriented economic system with enterprise autonomy and opening the economy for international trade and investment (Chan and Norlund 1999; Zhu and Fahey 2000).

Economic background

Economic development in Vietnam can be divided into several phases: pre-1975, 1975–86, and 1986 to the present. During the pre-1975 period, the country was divided and two different economic systems were operating along ideological lines. Then a period of adjustment after unification was characterized as unifying the national economic system under the socialist planning system. While economic reform was implemented by the government in 1986, more changes have occurred in Vietnam since then.

Pre-1975 economy

In North Vietnam, like China, the primary task of economic development was socialist industrialization, of which the key issue was the development of state-owned heavy industry. In the process of implementing the objective of developing heavy industry, the North Vietnamese government had to make some adjustments to its macro-economic strategy (Beresford 1989). North Vietnam suffered heavily from the US bombing campaign during the early 1960s. As a result, the government had to transfer some of the factories to the countryside and was forced to delegate some of the administrative responsibility for industrial and agricultural production to local governments. It was due to the aid from China and the Soviet Union that the North Vietnamese economy was able to survive (Fforde and Paine 1987).

In South Vietnam, the government worked under the sponsorship of the USA and the economic policies were based on private ownership and a free-market system (Nguyen 1987). One of the guiding principles of economic development in the South was to raise the standard of living in rural areas to a level closer to that in urban areas. It placed importance on agricultural development and planned to create the conditions for private enterprise to flourish. However, many years of war forced South Vietnam to depend completely on American aid for survival. Inflation was rampant and investment was extremely limited in agriculture and manufacturing industry, while the demand for consumer goods rose due to the rapid increase in population (Nguyen 1987).

Economy between 1975 and 1986

The victory of the liberation movement in 1975 led to a new policy on socialist transition in the South and the aim was to complete such transition by the end of the Second Five-Year Plan in 1980 (Beresford 1989). The plan stated that 'Vietnam would move from small scale production to large scale socialist production in about twenty years. Priority was given to rational development of heavy industry on the basis of developing agriculture and light industry' (Vo 1988: 59).

Although the government was enthusiastic to push such an ambitious plan, it failed miserably to meet any of the plan's targets and about 10,000 out of 13,246 rural communes established in the South collapsed by the early 1980. In addition, total food production stood at 14.4 million tons compared to the target of 21 million tons in 1980 (Vo 1988).

The government admitted that the previous policies had failed to create economic development at the Fifth National Congress in March 1981 (Fforde and Vylder 1996). There was an adjustment in the Third Five-Year Plan (1981–5) which gave high priority to solving problems in food production and emphasizing the development of light industry in the short term, while the long-term goal still remained an industrialized economy (Vo 1988). At the end of the Third Five-Year Plan, however, agricultural targets were not achieved and large-scale manufacturing industries still encountered serious difficulties.

A gradualist reform since 1986

The economic reform program (*doi moi*) officially started with regulations passed at the Sixth National Congress in December 1986 (Zhu and Fahey 1999). The new set of policies aimed to rectify the inefficiencies of the state industrial sector, streamline the development of the non-state agricultural sector and allow economic autonomy at the enterprise level in responding to market competition. It sought to reduce intervention from the state and remove many of the constraints on the operation of the private sector. The eventual goal was to gradually transform Vietnam from a centrally planned economy into a 'socialist market economy' through step-by-step reform (Woo *et al.* 1997; Zhu and Fahey 2000).

The major reform initiatives include reforming and restructuring SOEs, encouraging foreign investment and establishment of foreign-owned enterprises (FOEs), allowing the domestic private sector to develop, opening up market competition and reducing government control over price, liberalizing the banking and financial sectors, and providing enterprise autonomy on labour recruitment and dismissal and eventually the establishment of a labour market (Fahey 1997).

Since the beginning of *doi moi*, Vietnam has experienced economic growth unlike that of the past (Fforde and Vylder 1996). Real GDP growth rates peaked in 1992 and 1995 according to official statistics. However, economic difficulties still existed, especially during the Asian financial crisis which adversely affected the Vietnamese economy. Most economic sectors and regions in Vietnam reported declines in the rate of GDP growth, foreign direct investment (FDI), and international trade (Moreno *et al.* 1999).

For instance, GDP growth was only 4.8 per cent in 1999 compared to 9.3 per cent and 8.1 per cent in 1996 and 1997 respectively (World Bank 1998; CIEM 1999; SDV 2000). FDI inflows to Vietnam in 1998 continued the downward trend experienced in 1997, with US$2 billion of implemented investment about 70 per cent of the total implemented investment capital in 1997 (Freeman 1998; CIEM 1999). The Asian financial crisis was the main cause of the sharply reduced FDI inflow (Freeman 1998; Riedel and Tran 1998; Le 2000). In recent years, FDI from Asian countries accounted for 70 per cent of total FDI inflow to Vietnam. In 1998, however, FDI from those countries decreased to only 45 per cent of total FDI (CIEM 1999; Athukorala 1999).

International trade was also gloomy under the influence of the Asian crisis. In 1998, for instance, the growth in the value of exports was only 2.4 per cent, the lowest rate since 1991 (CIEM 1999). Under this pressure, the government imposed administrative measures to control imports in order to reduce trade deficits. As a result, imports declined by 1 per cent in 1998 (CIEM 1999). Although the current account deficit was reduced, in the long term this will have negative effects on domestic consumption and economic growth due to the increase of the prices of imported goods for production (Ariff and Khalid 2000).

The liquidation of SOEs and other so-called 'production units' and less foreign investment have led to an increase in unemployment (Leung 1999; Nguyen 2000). In 1998, for instance, the official rate of unemployment in the urban areas was 6.9 per cent, compared to 5.9 per cent and 6 per cent in

1996 and 1997 respectively (CIEM 1999). There is a tendency towards higher unemployment in large cities and industrial centres. In addition, underemployment in the rural areas is serious. The internal migration from the rural areas to the urban industrial areas also increases the pressure on the labour market.

The recent effort of reform is focusing on the restructuring of existing SOEs. Since 1998 the government has been pushing for further mergers of SOEs. At the end of 1998, there were ninety-one large-size, so-called General Corporations being formed with 1,400 enterprise members, which hold 66 per cent of total capital, 47 per cent of turnover, and 70 per cent of contributions of all SOEs to the government budget (CIEM 1999). In addition, there were 116 SOEs being transformed into joint stock companies (JSCs) (Doanh and Tran 1998; CIEM 1999; Frydman *et al.* 1999).[1]

However, both internal and external difficulties force the existing companies, no matter if they are public sector companies such as SOEs and JSCs, or private sector companies such as domestic private enterprises (DPEs) and FOEs (including both joint ventures (JVs) and wholly owned foreign enterprises (WOFEs)), to speed up organizational reform (World Bank 1994). In fact, transforming the old management system into a new hybrid management system combining both Vietnamese and foreign management strategies and practices is one of the central reform priorities among those enterprises in order for them to survive in market competition. Hence, we will illustrate in the following sections the influence of Vietnamese societal culture and the corporate culture of Vietnamese enterprises on the formation of the current hybrid and transitional paradigm of management in Vietnam.

Societal culture

Vietnamese society has experienced many changes, from the early years of Chinese political and cultural influence (111 BC to AD 939), French colonization, Japanese invasion, and American occupation, to later communist rule and independence, and more recently economic reform and engaging the global economy. All of these historical events have left their mark on Vietnamese society.

Fundamentally, traditional thinking in Vietnam was influenced by ancient Chinese philosophies, predominantly by Confucianism (cf. Chapter 2 on China). Confucius (Kongzi, 551–479 BC) developed a set of teachings based on absolute respect for tradition (early Zhou Dynasty) and on a carefully ranked hierarchy founded on primary relationships between members of families and between the people and their rulers (De Mente 1994). It has been seen as a philosophy guiding people's daily life. The major ideas of Confucius were three basic guides (i.e. ruler guides subject, father guides son, and husband guides wife), five constant virtues (i.e. benevolence, righteousness, propriety, wisdom, and fidelity), and the doctrine of the mean (i.e. harmony). Confucius believed that *Ren* or human heartedness/benevolence is the highest virtue an individual can attain and this is the ultimate goal of education (McGreal 1995). *Ren* is a strictly natural and humanistic love, based upon spontaneous feelings cultivated through education.

The path to the attainment of *Ren* is the practice of *Li*, which represents social norms. *Li* can be interpreted as rituals, rites, or proprieties. In its broadest sense, the term includes all moral codes and social institutions. In its fundamental but narrow sense, it means socially acceptable forms of behaviour (McGreal 1995). In addition, *Li* involves the deliberate devices used by the sages to educate people and maintain social order.

Since *Li* is a term for moral codes and social institutions, people are tempted to think that the practice of *Li* is to enforce conformity with social norms at the cost of individuality (McGreal 1995). However, in Confucianism, an individual is not an isolated entity. Confucius said: 'In order to establish oneself, one has to establish others. This is the way of a person of *Ren*' (McGreal 1995: 5). Therefore, individualization and socialization are but two aspects of the same process.

The principle governing the adoption of *Li* is *Yi*, which means righteousness or proper character and is a principle of rationality. *Yi* is the habitual practice of expressing one's cultivated feeling at the right times and in the right places. Confucius said: '*Junzi* (a perfect person or superior) is conscious of, and receptive to, *Yi*, but *Xiaoren* (a petty person) is conscious of, and receptive to, gains' (McGreal 1995: 6).

According to Confucius, the right method of governing is not by legislation and law enforcement, but by supervising the moral education of the people (McGreal 1995: 6). The ideal government for him is a government of *Wuwei* (non-action) through the solid groundwork of moral education. The reason given by Confucius is:

> If you lead the people with political force and restrict them with law and punishment, they can just avoid law violation, but will have no sense of honour and shame. If you lead them with morality and guide them with *Li*, they will develop a sense of honour and shame, and will do good of their own accord.
>
> (McGreal 1995: 7)

This is the doctrine of appealing to the human heart: self-realization towards world peace (harmony) and a peaceful world and orderly society are the ultimate goals of Confucianism.

Confucianism came to Vietnam after 111 BC when the Chinese emperor colonized Vietnam and brought important technology, including water buffaloes, ploughs, pig rearing, market gardening, printing, minting of coins, silkworm breeding, porcelain manufacture, and international trade. In addition, a Chinese model of bureaucracy, the judicial system, and the education system was implemented in Vietnamese society. Even the written language was based on Chinese characters. This fundamental influence still exists in the current Vietnamese society.

However, another most profound influence in the modern history of Vietnam is communism. Several key issues are related to such influence. Politically, it emphasized Leninist democratic centralism and proletarian dictatorship, which legitimize Communist Party control (see Chapter 2 on China). Economically, it implemented a centrally planned economic system for many years until recent reform. The state controlled planning, material allocation, production, labour, and distribution systems. In social relations, it believed in egalitarian principles and mutual respect. Women's position was improved under communist rule compared to the 'old society'. Wage differentials were limited and collectivism was extremely important.

On the other hand, private ownership and entrepreneurship did exist in the South before unification in 1975. A large overseas Chinese business community (see Chapters 3, 10, and 12) was very active in Saigon (the current Ho Chi Minh City) until 1978 when the communist government wanted to take over the private sector in the South.

These phenomena show that a mixed and diverse cultural element rooted in Vietnamese society and a generalization of the homogeneous cultural paradigm can be problematic. This is also the case for corporate culture due to the diversity of ownership in Vietnam today.

Corporate culture

Since economic reform started, a diversity of ownership of enterprises has emerged. Not only have the traditional SOEs been transformed into new ventures, such as group companies or JSCs, but also other private ownership enterprises have been developed, such as DPEs and FOEs. Certainly, the corporation is the basic economic unit in a society and it carries certain cultural elements which were determined by organizational history, the political, economic, and social environment, and the cultural tradition and roots of the particular enterprise (e.g. Vietnamese vs. foreign enterprise). In this section, a more Vietnamese-oriented approach is illustrated by using the example of SOEs in the pre- and post-reform eras, though it may have some implications for foreign enterprises operating in Vietnam.

Under the pre-reform system, SOEs were integrated into a system of mandatory state planning. Enterprise inputs, including labour, were assigned by government plan. In this sense, the corporate culture was based on socialist principles which emphasize the following key elements: (1) party leadership at the enterprise level; (2) state ownership; (3) planning system; (4) egalitarianism and harmony; (5) company as family and same interests between managers and workers; (6) workers as masters of the society and company; (7) trade unions as the transmission belt between the party and masses and the dual roles of trade unions.

The fact is that during the pre-reform period, enterprises did not necessarily acquire labour with the right set of skills and were invariably overstaffed because the labour administration arranged employees for individual firms (Doanh and Tran 1998). In addition, enterprises had few ways to motivate or discipline employees. The reward system had only an indirect relation to enterprise efficiency and individual labour effort. It was based on a narrowly defined egalitarianism as well as the tendency to reward labour on the grounds of seniority and contribution to the party as well as to the war effort in the past.

The area of personnel management had a rigid function in allocating jobs and managing personnel files. Due to the absence of the labour market, pre-reform personnel management was inward looking with a focus on issues such as the distribution of wages, provision of welfare, and routine promotion of workers and cadres from lower ranks to higher ranks according to regulations.

However, in the early stages of *doi moi* (1988–91), reform of the SOEs was intensified (Zhu and Fahey 1999). In order to create a more flexible labour market and employment relations system, the government relinquished its control over the recruitment and employment of workers. Therefore, individual firms gained autonomy in deciding on the number of workers hired, the terms of employment, and the discharge of employees.

The corporate culture has been gradually modified under the influence of government policy and new economic and employment environments. Some old concepts have gradually been phased out, such as party leadership at the enterprise level, state ownership, and the planning system. However, other old concepts still play crucial roles without very much change. New concepts have been added to the existing paradigm, such as flexibility, competition, quality, and human resources (capital). The changes of government policy, macro-economic environment, and corporate culture influenced management practices at the enterprise level.

Managerial behaviour

Since enterprise management obtained greater autonomy, the quality of managers has become more important for the survival of the enterprise in market competition. In fact, the criteria for managerial selection have been more restrictive with an emphasis on educational background and experiences. In addition, the age of managers has become much younger than that during the pre-reform period, and nowadays most of them are in their 40s (see Zhu 2002).

A recent survey by the author shows that the realization of flexibility and competitiveness of enterprises depends on the type of employment relations established and practised by the management (Zhu 2002), namely adherence to rules, common values, and norms, 'transformational' managerial roles, importance of line managers, freedom in personnel selection, harmonization of work conditions, and in-house training.

There is a mixture of control and nurturing in the majority of the firms sampled by Zhu (2002). Most senior managements did demonstrate a more transformational leadership, and both middle management and the HR manager demonstrated the more transactional approach. In addition, in all respondent firms the emphasis was placed on respect for rules. All of them emphasized personnel procedures and rules as the basis of good managerial practice. This indicates that compliance with rules is more important in the sample firms than the flexibility model, suggesting that the aim is employee commitment (Zhu 2002).

However, there were some variations in variables such as individual performance pay and strategic roles for HR managers. Due to the corporate cultural emphasis on harmony, it was difficult for these enterprises to fully implement individual performance pay. Otherwise, jealousy would disturb the harmony. In addition, the variation concerning the strategic role of HR managers is also problematic. Generally speaking, the position of HR manager was not a specialized one and in most of the firms was filled by line managers (Zhu 2002). HR managers had little involvement in their firm's strategic planning. Among the majority of the firms sampled, the HR task was more operational (wage, social welfare calculations) than strategic. This is clearly the traditional role of the so-called 'personnel manager'.

Managerial values

One of the outstanding values among the Vietnamese enterprises was maintaining harmonious relationships within the enterprise even though they operated in a market environment. A paternalist management pattern where employers are related to employees as 'parents' and the company is seen as a 'family' still has a certain influence. From the culturalist point of view, the Vietnamese characteristics of managerial values are rooted in their tradition. It is obvious that the cultural background of a society plays a significant role in the formation of a company culture. As for the traditional Vietnamese management style, people were important and enterprise costs were not thought about all that much. This was the vision that dominated Vietnamese organizational culture with its focus on people. In return, a highly committed workforce strengthened the unity of the organization. The outcome here could reasonably be expected to be lower turnover and absenteeism.

However, in the post-reform era, this attitude has gradually changed, especially among younger employees. The fixed-term contract employment system has largely contributed to this change. Except for people who have worked for SOEs for a long time and have attained a high position in the enterprise, most workers have no problem in changing their place of work for purely economic reasons.

The philosophy of collectivism is also found in the Vietnamese organization in terms of the group-oriented approach. Group-based activities including teamwork and decision making, quality control, and incentives are common managerial practices. In the Vietnamese organization, leadership and decisions are team based (Zhu 2002). Another group-based activity relates to the payment of bonuses. A bonus is considered as a specific individual incentive. However, in Vietnam, the bonus computation does not reflect a large degree of influence by personnel evaluation, but via organizational performance. In fact, this shows that even in the incentive scheme in Vietnam, a collective orientation is still fundamental (Zhu 2002).

Employee involvement is an integral part of the flexibility approach. In the recent survey by Zhu (2002), the degree of involvement was uneven from firm to firm. In addition, the level of involvement varied substantially between various schemes and also between various groups of employees. In some firms only executive teams are included in the committees that meet regularly to give feedback to management or to inform participants about the firm's strategy. In other firms, workers at all levels are involved in these consultative committees.

Information-sharing schemes were widely adopted as well. In fact, not only was general information on production plans and schedules provided, but also this information was accompanied with strategies to improve production and employee performance. Individual grievance mechanisms also existed in a majority of the firms. In most cases, parallel grievance channels through HR and the union do exist. These indicate that the participation of Vietnamese workers has improved in recent years and that puts a positive light on the development of industrial democracy in the future.

Labour–management conflict resolution

In fact, there is no homogeneous labour–management conflict resolution in Vietnamese enterprises. In some enterprises, workers prefer to rely on their union for a resolution, while in other firms, they go to the management board. The new initiatives on conflict resolution include mediation between union and management within the enterprise and mediation and arbitration at the regional labour administration level (Zhu and Fahey 2000).

Certainly, the industrial relations system in Vietnam does not conform to the conventional Western view of labour–management interactions. The role of trade unions, as propagated under the Communist Party state and re-enforced under the Trade Union Law and Labour Code, is to assist management in achieving a productive enterprise (Zhu and Fahey 2000). Therefore, placing the nature of the Vietnamese trade unions in the political and economic context raises an alternative system of worker control. The question is whether unions constrain or assist management in their attempts to introduce more flexibility into labour management (Zhu 2002).

The Trade Union Law was established in 1989 as part of the institutionalization of the industrial relations system. Since the law was established, every SOE in Vietnam has had to have a union secretary board. All of the SOEs studied in the survey (Zhu 2002) had a union and the percentage of union members was more than 90 per cent. Some of them have part-time officials and others have full-time officials. Unions in these firms met frequently and most of them have grievance procedures. In addition, they all have a collective agreement negotiated between management and union (Zhu 2002). Clearly, the structural conditions for active unionism existed in a majority of the sample firms.

However, there is an uneven role of unions among these firms. The range of the union's function can be from minimum to active. Some unions have a moderate involvement, such as organizing training, political study and campaign, and productivity competitions, looking after workers' welfare, signing the collective agreement, maintaining the harmonious relationship between management and workers, and helping the management to achieve the company's target, etc. Other firms' unions not only have these moderations, but also have a more active role in terms of participating in decision making as a member of the company board, negotiating on lay-offs, wages, and working conditions, forming a Workers' Conference to supervise and monitor management performance, etc. Hence, the dual role of trade unions in Vietnamese enterprises is very obvious: on the one hand, unions protect workers' interests; on the other hand, it is union's responsibility to assist the company in maintaining harmony and achieving higher productivity (Zhu 2002).

The challenges facing trade unions is particularly obvious in issues concerning labour flexibility and enterprise productivity (Zhu 2002). Workers and their representatives are also concerned about the need to improve the firm's performance. Union officials at the enterprise level expressed a clear message that they would support strategies adopted by the management that seek to improve the firm's efficiency. Nevertheless, workers can become the victims of reform, in particular those employees working for SOEs which are being restructured (Benson *et al.* 2000: 193). At the national and regional levels, a large number of SOEs' employees have been laid off (Zhu and Fahey 2000). However, in the sample SOEs, both management and union tried hard to keep their employees' jobs within the company. During the interviews with these managers and union leaders, a sense of obligation and caring for their fellow workers was quite apparent (Zhu 2002). In that sense, both Confucianist and socialist principles still have a profound influence on management–labour relations.

In the current economic and political climate in Vietnam, the diversity of ownership systems challenges the trade unions not only to provide services and protection to their traditional SOE members, but also to play a more active role in defending the interests of workers in the private sector, including FOEs and DPEs. So far, this has not been very successful. Even after implementation of the Labour Code in 1995, most private companies did not follow the law to encourage the formation of unions, and the lack of enforcement of law in Vietnam also enables those companies to avoid this (Walsh 1995; Nguyen 1997).

Implications for managers

The economic reform (*doi moi*) in Vietnam created dramatic changes in both market and firms and consequently led to the adaptation of different organizational strategies. For instance, SOEs are engaging in restructuring to become JSCs and obtaining more management autonomy. The range of business operations is wider and more export oriented compared to that several years ago. FOEs (including JVs and WOFEs) establish their organizations based more on international standards, such as adopting a company board to supervise management, less middle-level management, and decentralization of control. They normally use more advanced technology in their production systems compared to local firms and develop business areas with which local firms have difficulties in competing (Zhu 2002).

Globalization, a market-oriented economy, and a multi-ownership system intensify the pressure on companies and individual people to become more competitive and flexible. One of the important strategies for companies to survive is to develop new ways of maximizing the potential of their human capital. Nowadays, most managers and employees are eager for change and willing to adopt new ways. However, historical and ideological barriers sometimes discourage the adoption of new systems. For instance, traditional personnel management still plays a crucial role among the majority of enterprises in which control is more important than empowerment of human resources.

These issues have implications for the way management is likely to develop in Vietnam. Certainly, there is no dominant paradigm existing in Vietnam today. The author's research, however, has demonstrated that the current hybrid management practices are probably in a transitional stage, one that depends as much on the level of government, trade unions, and foreign capital involvement as it does on any attempt for the enterprise to become more competitive. It is also hard to predict that the future outcome of the management model would be a convergent one given the situation of unpredictable economic climate in the Asian region and government policy in Vietnam.

Conclusions

It is obvious that cultural background has undoubtedly played a significant role in the process of formation of the management approach. In Vietnam, there is a core value system based on the combined characteristics of Confucianism, Western colonization, and communism which still have a strong hold on the mind-set of the players in this drama, although there can be caveats placed on its role as the main independent variable.

We have also seen that management in Vietnam has only recently emerged from the strait-jacket of the 'command economy'. In today's Vietnam, there is a greater labour market flexibility than in the pre-reform system. The lifetime employment system is being phased out entirely as the country enters an era of greater openness in its product and factor markets. Social security has also been diluted and is now dependent on an individual worker's contributions supplemented by the employer's.

While we cannot posit a full degree of convergence of Vietnamese management towards the Western management paradigm, a certain degree of 'relative convergence' (see Warner 2002) may be the outcome. The trends towards globalization can only strengthen these tendencies, although we can see that Vietnamese management is currently in a distinctive hybrid and transitional paradigm.

Notes

1   The stock market was not established in Vietnam until October 2000. The joint stock companies are in fact 'equitized' companies which only share stocks internally or through existing business networks among enterprises, especially SOEs, and not joint stock companies in the normal sense (CIEM 1999; Zhu 2000).

References

Ariff, M. and Khalid, A. M. (2000) *Liberalisation, Growth and the Asian Financial Crisis: Lessons for Developing and Transitional Economies in Asia*, Cheltenham: Edward Elgar.

Athukorala, P. (1999) 'Developing with foreign investment', in S. Leung (ed.), *Vietnam and the East Asian Crisis*, Cheltenham: Edward Elgar, pp. 146–64.

Benson, J., Debroux, P., Yuasa, M. and Zhu, Y. (2000) 'Flexibility and labour management: Chinese manufacturing enterprises in the 1990s', *International Journal of Human Resource Management* 11(2): 183–96.

Beresford, M. (1989) *National Unification and Economic Development in Vietnam*, London: Macmillan.

Chan, A. and Norlund, I. (1999) 'Vietnamese and Chinese labour regimes: on the road to divergence', in A. Chan, B. Kerkvliet and J. Unger (eds), *Transforming Asian Socialism China and Vietnam Compared*, Sydney: Allen & Unwin, pp. 204–28.

CIEM (1999) *Vietnam Economy in 1998*, Central Institute for Economic Management, Hanoi: Education Publishing House.

De Mente, B. (1994) *Chinese Etiquette and Ethics in Business*, Lincolnwood: NTC Business Books.

Doanh, L. D. and Tran, T. C. (1998) 'The SOE reform policies in Vietnam and their implementation performance', in *Study on Economic Development Policy in the Transition Toward a Market-Oriented Economy in Vietnam, Phase 2*, Hanoi: Ministry of Planning and Investment and Japan International Cooperation Agency, Vol. 4: 19–49.

Fahey, S. (1997) 'Vietnam and the 'Third Way': the nature of socio-economic transition', *Journal of Economic and Social Geography* 88(5): 469–80.

Fforde, A. and Paine, S. (1987) *The Limit of National Liberation: Problems of Economic Management in the Democratic Republic of Vietnam*, London: Croom Helm.

Fforde, A. and Vylder, S. (1996) *From Plan to Market: The Economic Transition in Vietnam*, Boulder, CO: Westview Press.

Freeman, N. J. (1998) 'Bust or boom?', *Vietnam Business Journal* June: 58–9.

Frydman, R., Hessel, M. P. and Rapaczynski, A. (1999) 'When does privatization work? The impact of private ownership on corporate performance in the transition economies', *Quarterly Journal of Economics* 114(4): 1153–91.

Le, T. (2000) 'Top three investor headaches listed', *Vietnam Investment Review* No. 449.

Leung, S. (1999) 'Crisis in Asia and Vietnam's economic policy response', in S. Leung (ed.), *Vietnam and the East Asian Crisis*, Cheltenham: Edward Elgar, pp. 3–8.

Ljunggren, B. (1993) 'Concluding remarks: key issues in the reform process', in B. Ljunggren (ed.), *The Challenge of Reform in Indochina*, Cambridge, MA: Harvard University Press, pp. 349–83.

McGreal, I. (1995) *Great Thinkers of the Eastern World: The Major Thinkers and the Philosophical and religious Classics of China, India, Japan, Korea and the World of Islam*, New York: HarperCollins.

Moreno, R., Pasadilla, G. and Remolona, E. (1999) 'Asia's financial crisis: lessons and implications for Vietnam', in S. Leung (ed.), *Vietnam and the East Asian Crisis*, Cheltenham: Edward Elgar, pp. 31–54.

Nguyen, A. T. (1987) *South Vietnam Trial and Experience: A Challenge for Development*, Athens, OH: Ohio University Press.

Nguyen, M. D. (2000) 'Some issues on ownership in Vietnam', *Journal of Economics and Development*19(4): 4, Hanoi: National Economics University.

Nguyen, T. A. (1997) 'Labour laws relating to foreign enterprises in Vietnam', *Asian Commercial Law Review* 2(6): 215–21.

Perkins, D. H. (1993) 'Reforming the economic systems of Vietnam and Laos', in B. Ljunggren (ed.), *The Challenge of Reform in Indochina*, Cambridge, MA: Harvard University Press, pp. 1–19.

Redding, G. (1995) *The Spirit of Chinese Capitalism*, Berlin: de Gruyter.

Riedel, J. and Tran, C. S. (1998) 'The emerging private sector and the industrialization of Vietnam', *Report on the Project: Vietnam's Emerging Private Sector and Promising Private Companies*, Hanoi: James Riedel and Associates.

SDV (2000) *Vietnam Statistical Yearbook 2000*, Hanoi: Statistics Department of Vietnam.

Vo, N. T. (1988) 'Party policies and economic reforms: the Second and Third Five Year Plans examined', in D. G. Marr and C. P. White (eds), *Postwar Vietnam: Dilemmas in Socialist Development*, Ithaca, NY: Cornell University Press, pp. 77–90.

Walsh, P. B. (1995) 'Vietnamese labour law: can labour peacefully coexist with foreign investment, economic development, and structural reform?', *Transnational Lawyer* Spring(8): 125–57.

Warner, M. (2002) 'Globalization, labour markets and human resources', *International Journal of Human Resource Management* 13(3): 1–15.

Woo, T., Parker, S. and Sachs, J. (1997) *Economies in Transition: Comparing Asia and Eastern Europe*, Cambridge, MA: MIT Press.

World Bank (1994) 'Vietnam: public sector management and private sector incentives', *World Bank Economic Report*, Hanoi: The World Bank Office.

World Bank (1998) *Vietnam Rising to the Challenge*, Washington, DC: World Bank Economic Report.

Zhu, Y (2002) 'Economic reform and human resource management in Vietnamese enterprises', *Asia-Pacific Business Review* 8(3): 115–34.

Zhu, Y. and Fahey, S. (1999) 'The Impact of economic reform on industrial labour relations in China and Vietnam', *Post-Communist Economies* 11(2): 173–92.

Zhu, Y. and Fahey, S. (2000) 'The challenges and opportunities for the trade union movement in the transition era: two socialist market economies – China and Vietnam', *Asia-Pacific Business Review*, Special issue on *Globalization and Labour Market Deregulation: Trade Unions in the Asia Pacific Region*, 6(3&4): 282–99.

Index